INTERROGATING **POSTFEMINISM**

Console-ing Passions

Television and Cultural Power

Edited by Lynn Spigel

INTERROGATING POSTFEMINISM

Gender and the Politics of Popular Culture

Edited by Yvonne Tasker and Diane Negra

Duke University Press   Durham and London   2007

© 2007 Duke University Press

All rights reserved

Printed in the United States of America on acid-free paper ∞

Designed by Heather Hensley

Typeset in Monotype Garamond by Tseng Information Systems, Inc.

Library of Congress Cataloging-in-Publication Data appear on the
last printed page of this book.

CONTENTS

ACKNOWLEDGMENTS

The editors would like to express their appreciation to the contributors for their work in developing these essays, to Hannah Hamad for the considerable help she provided as project assistant, to Desi Van Til and Sarah Churchwell for assistance in obtaining illustrations, to Rachel Hall for her assistance in preparing the bibliography, to Lindsay Steenberg for compiling the index, and to the School of Film and Television Studies at the University of East Anglia and the Department of Modern Culture and Media and the Cogut Center for the Humanities at Brown University, both of which generously provided material assistance during the completion of this book.

We also wish to acknowledge the numerous colleagues and graduate students who helped to facilitate the April 2004 conference Interrogating Postfeminism: Gender and the Politics of Popular Culture at the University of East Anglia from which this volume grew. As the conference administrator, Heather Laing made a considerable contribution to the generation of this project.

Finally, we thank Ken Wissoker (the definition of a kind, thoughtful, and supportive editor) and the staff at Duke University Press, as well as the press's readers, who furnished the best kind of reports, those that blend challenge and encouragement in equal measure.

Angela McRobbie's essay appears with the permission of the author and *Feminist Media Studies*.

Yvonne Tasker and Diane Negra

Introduction

FEMINIST POLITICS AND POSTFEMINIST CULTURE

P ostfeminism broadly encompasses a set of assumptions, widely disseminated within popular media forms, having to do with the "pastness" of feminism, whether that supposed pastness is merely noted, mourned, or celebrated. Crucially for us, postfeminism suggests a more complex relationship between culture, politics, and feminism than the more familiar framing concept of "backlash" allows. Feminist activism has long met with strategies of resistance, negotiation, and containment, processes that a model of backlash—with its implication of achievements won and then subsequently lost—cannot effectively incorporate within the linear chronology of social change on which it seems to be premised. What appears distinctive about contemporary postfeminist culture is precisely the extent to which a selectively defined feminism has been so overtly "taken into account," as Angela McRobbie has noted, albeit in order "to emphasize that it is no longer needed."[1]

The limits of the kind of gender equality enacted within contemporary popular media culture are profound: they are marked by the valorization of female achievement within traditionally male working environments and the celebration of surgical and other disciplinary techniques that "enable" (i.e., require) women to maintain a youthful appearance and attitude in later life.[2] As the essays in this collection demonstrate, such a limited vision of gender equality as both achieved and yet still unsatisfactory underlines the class, age, and racial exclusions that define postfeminism and its characteristic assumption that the themes, pleasures, values, and lifestyles with which it is associated are somehow universally shared and, perhaps more significant, universally accessible. If, as bell hooks writes, "feminism is for everybody," postfeminism is in many ways antithetical to the notion of an open society in which all members are valued in accordance with their distinct identities.[3] Postfeminist culture's centralization of an affluent elite certainly entails an emphatic individualism, but this formulation tends to confuse self-interest with individuality and elevates consumption as a strategy for healing those dissatisfactions that might alternatively be understood in terms of social ills and discontents. Indeed, as hooks and others note, the limited inclusion of certain women within privileged educational, professional, and other work contexts results as much from the demands of a consumer-led capitalism (for both new forms of labor and new forms of consumption) as from a thoroughgoing response to the demands of feminist activism.[4]

Postfeminist culture works in part to incorporate, assume, or naturalize aspects of feminism; crucially, it also works to commodify feminism via the figure of woman as empowered consumer. Thus, postfeminist culture emphasizes educational and professional opportunities for women and girls; freedom of choice with respect to work, domesticity, and parenting; and physical and particularly sexual empowerment. Assuming full economic freedom for women, postfeminist culture also (even insistently) enacts the possibility that women might *choose* to retreat from the public world of work. Postfeminist fictions frequently set aside both evident economic disparities and the fact that the majority of women approach paid labor as an economic necessity rather than a "choice." As this suggests, postfeminism is white and middle class by default, anchored in consumption as a strategy (and leisure as a site) for the production of the self. It is thus also a strategy by which other kinds of social difference are glossed over. The limits of this construction and the challenges it poses for feminist scholarship are questions we return to below.

Postfeminism does not always offer a logically coherent account of gender and power, but through structures of forceful articulation and synergistic reiteration across media forms it has emerged as a dominating discursive system. It generates and draws strength, for instance, from a rhetorical field that produces buzzwords and slogans to express visions of energetic personal empowerment (the borrowed African American idiom "You go, girl!" the phrase "girl power," etc.). Meanwhile postfeminism draws on and sustains an invented social memory of feminist language as inevitably shrill, bellicose, and parsimonious. Thus, while feminism is constituted as an unwelcome, implicitly censorious presence, it is precisely *feminist* concerns that are silenced within postfeminist culture. Reference to "the F word" underscores the status of feminism as unspeakable within contemporary popular culture.[5]

The demand for content to fulfill diverse delivery systems continues to drive contemporary popular media, drawing in the process, as McRobbie suggests, on the talents of young women (and men) conversant with feminist critiques of representation. Recent books such as those by Kim Akass and Janet McCabe (2004) and Ariel Levy (2005) exemplify the emergence of popularized feminist scholarship. While Levy, a journalist, explores the formulaic female sexualities of a culture in which (most often young) women enthusiastically perform patriarchal stereotypes of sexual servility in the name of empowerment, Akass and McCabe, who are both academics, have produced an anthology that mixes fan-style appreciations of *Sex and the City* with feminist critique. Publications of this kind mark a new space of convergence between journalism, popular fiction, and academic analysis.[6] Despite the emergence of accessible accounts such as these, postfeminism nevertheless works to invalidate systemic critique. As McRobbie writes in her influential essay, reprinted here, "The new female subject is, despite her freedom, called upon to be silent, to withhold critique, to count as a modern sophisticated girl, or indeed this withholding of critique is a condition of her freedom."[7]

In line with this peculiarly silent visibility, postfeminism also perpetuates woman as pinup, the enduring linchpin of commercial beauty culture. In fact, it has offered new rationales for guilt-free consumerism, substantially reenergizing beauty culture (primarily for women but sometimes also for men through new archetypes such as the seemingly ubiquitous "metrosexual") and presiding over an aggressive mainstreaming of elaborate and expensive beauty treatments to the middle class. Nicely evocative of the positive embrace of consumer-led beauty culture and the new freedom to disassociate from the "burdens" of feminism is B. Ruby Rich's anecdote about body hair: "Passing by a shop that did waxing one day with my then-girlfriend, we whimsically decided to go in and put an end, for no apparent reason, to a decade of ideological attachment."[8] Here is feminism "taken into account" in a somewhat different, though related, fashion to that identified by McRobbie; for Rich, this anecdote points to the complex intersection of feminist politics, appearance, and consumption and to the ways in which living with feminism and living as a feminist have changed over the last few decades.

If postfeminist popular culture celebrates female agency and women's powers of consumption, it also anxiously raises the possible consequences of female independence, crudely: emotional isolation for women (a preoccupation that neatly sidesteps questions of women's economic instability); and loss of power for men (again, a formulation premised on the somewhat tenuous assumption that all men previously occupied equally elevated positions of social and economic power). For us, postfeminism signals more than a simple evolutionary process whereby aspects of feminism have been incorporated into popular culture—and thereby naturalized as popular feminism. It also simultaneously involves an "othering" of feminism (even as women are more centralized), its construction as extreme, difficult, and unpleasurable. Kathleen Karlyn has shrewdly observed that one of the biggest challenges for feminism in the academy involves coming to grips with generational impasses at a time when "feminism itself seems most evident as a 'structuring absence' for middle class young women."[9] As teachers and researchers committed to producing feminist work in an antifeminist context (whether that of academic institutions, themselves increasingly led by a student-consumer model, or the wider political culture), we find postfeminist culture to be provocative in all the senses of that term: it is troubling and yet at the same time compelling.

It also seems important that we assert the material consequences of postfeminism in the academy. While McRobbie suggests that feminist work is now canonized within university curricula, we are more cautious in our optimism.[10] Indeed, we suggest that the very dynamics that McRobbie identifies in relation to popular culture, whereby feminism is knowable and can thus be set aside, have consequences within the academy too. In this context we might frame the 2005 scandal related to then Harvard University president Larry Summers's comments about female academics' facility for science.[11] The all too familiar misogyny of elite academic institutions can be contextualized by the gender inequities of the largest corporation in the United States, Wal-Mart; gendered inequities of pay, benefits, and basic respect for female employees have been played out in the ongoing class action suit *Dukes v. Wal-Mart.* At the same time, the low-cost superstore draws on the rhetoric of family values in its advertisements, presenting consumption as an option for women with low incomes, not just the affluent woman we have identified as the most visible emblem of postfeminist culture. With Wal-Mart and other low-cost chains, we see the triangulation of invisible (and often offshore) female workers, highly visible female consumers, and female celebrities for whom such chains offer opportunities for ancillary profit via clothing lines, housewares, and other product streams. As Liza Featherstone writes in *The Nation*: "Through shoppers and 'associates' [i.e., employees] alike, Wal-Mart is making billions from female poverty."[12] Such dynamics, which extend gender inequities (often in the guise of opportunity and freedom), underline the necessity of a feminist critique that is cognizant of the economic context in which contemporary working lives and popular culture are experienced.

The distinction between feminist *politics* and a postfeminist *culture* that is broadly taken for granted serves as one starting point for this anthology, providing the title for this introduction. It should go without saying that feminism as a political force has certainly been expressed culturally and that there is clearly a politics at stake in postfeminism. Indeed, as we have suggested, postfeminist discourses rarely express the explicit view that feminist politics should be rejected; rather it is by virtue of feminism's success that it is seen to have been superseded. In this context, we argue that the transition to a postfeminist culture involves an evident erasure of feminist politics from the popular, even as aspects of feminism seem to be incorporated within that culture (and how feminism itself is understood within such formulations is not, of course, insignificant). As a result, postfeminist culture poses particular challenges to feminist media studies, a discipline often characterized by an interest in reading popular culture against the grain, seeking out those traces of feminism that might be available to female viewers and readers. This work is rendered more complex when we consider that contemporary popular culture is produced, in part at least, in response to feminism. That is, feminism forms an important part of contemporary culture, as Anna Feigenbaum shows here with respect to independent and industry-produced popular music. As such, it is no surprise to find evidence of feminism's presence within popular culture. To some extent, postfeminist culture throws into crisis our clear sense of what feminist media studies does when feminism is acknowledged and academic approaches are mainstreamed. Our task, then, is to break through both the token approaches to feminism and the anti-intellectualism adopted by popular culture. We believe that postfeminism has become so installed as an epistemological framework that in many ways our culture has stopped asking the kinds of questions that it appears to "settle." This book attempts to (re)open those questions.

Postfeminism and the Ambivalence of "Post"-ing

Our contention is that postfeminism as a concept and a cultural phenomenon repays close interrogation; in the process, we wish to situate it alongside other "posts," including postmodernism and post-civil-rights discourse. All three posts involve an implicit understanding of history and historical change. Yet, as Bill Readings and Bennet Schaber suggest with respect to postmodernism, the posting of feminism means that feminism itself remains in the frame. They write: "We all have heard the word postmodernism. It is in the news. And yet it cannot be just the news, what is new, what is modern. It must be in some sense after the new, post, and yet must at the same time not yet have arrived, must have got caught in the post."[13] Readings and Schaber are specifically concerned with avoiding a modernist construction of history in which postmodernism emerges as simply "the most recent modernism"; for us the question of chronology, and of change, is pressing in a somewhat different manner since postfeminist culture speaks both to and against the very feminism within which we situate our scholarship.

Within this anthology, both Lisa Coulthard and Martin Roberts note a relationship between postfeminism and postmodernism, although they do not treat this relationship as the central theme of their essays. The preemptive irony that McRobbie pinpoints as a defining characteristic of postfeminist culture evidently chimes with the parodic play associated with postmodern aesthetics.[14] Like postmodernism, postfeminism involves a particular relationship to late capitalist culture and the forms of work, leisure, and, crucially, consumption that thrive within that culture. Indeed, much postfeminist rhetoric is of a piece with the exhortations of the 1990s "New Economy" and the displacement of democratic imperatives by free market ones identified by Thomas Frank as "market populism." As Frank observes, in this period the concept of the market itself was invoked as proof of social egalitarianism and opportunity: "Markets were serving all tastes; they were humiliating the pretentious; they were permitting good art to triumph over bad; they were extinguishing discrimination; they were making everyone rich."[15] This "market populism that identif[ies] the will of the people with the deeds of the market" both supports and is supported by the individualist, acquisitive, and transformative values of postfeminism.

Postfeminism is also highly compatible with the hyperaestheticization of everyday life that Virginia Postrel sees as characteristic of early-twenty-first century culture. According to Postrel, "Today's aesthetic imperative represents not the return of a single standard of beauty, but the increased claims of pleasure and self-expression."[16] Such "aesthetic pluralism," as she calls it, "represents a major ideological shift," and it is important to consider postfeminism's taxonomizing functions in such demographically catalogued cultures.[17] With its frequent emphasis on luxury lifestyling and retail pleasures, postfeminism is thoroughly integrated with the economic discourses of aspirational, niche-market Western societies. The broad imposition of a politics of lifestyle, as Imelda Whelehan has noted, "leaves many victims in its wake — those who don't conform to its preferred images and those who are too poor to exercise 'control' over their lives through the 'liberation' of consumerism."[18] Postfeminism dovetails closely with a heightened social and economic emphasis on showplace domesticity, virtuoso parenting, and technologies mobilized in the name of family cohesion. It may very well be one of the ideological connectors between a contemporary sense of unfettered material entitlement and a moral discourse of virtuous familialism.

Post-civil-rights discourse similarly provides an important context for the anthology as it seeks to draw out the racialized marking of postfeminist culture. Kimberly Springer's essay explores the articulation of black women, in terms both new and familiar, within postfeminist media culture. Such analysis of gendered and racial types is staged within a developing media context, one in which, as Herman Gray writes, commodified "representations of American blackness circulate widely via mass media and popular culture, achieving in the process some measure of global visibility, influence, admiration, imitation, or scorn."[19] One of postfeminism's signature discursive formulations couches the celebration of female achievement (whether on the playing field, in the concert arena, or in the boardroom) within traditionalist ideological rubrics. For instance as Tara McPherson has observed in the context of the Women's National Basketball Association (WNBA), the promotion of black female stars as role models depends on a linkage between their physical prowess and their safe embodiment of acceptable images of blackness and femininity (images that, as McPherson shows, often highlight a contrast between the propriety of the "black lady" and a demonized "black street culture").[20] The commodification of ethnicity and a racially marked "urban" culture is also explored in this volume by Sarah Banet-Weiser in her analysis of girls, diversity, and the commercial strategies adopted by Nickelodeon, the children's cable television channel. Once again difference is commodified rather than politicized within mainstream culture; such cultural processes are predicated on an implicit chronology that firmly "posts" activisms centered on the consequences of racial inequities. Such political and cultural work is produced in this chronology as a phenomenon of the past whose traces shape the present.

While it has been argued that aspects of postfeminism appeared in popular media as far back as the early 1980s, it was during the 1990s that the term became concretized, both as a discursive phenomenon and as a buzzword of U.S. and U.K. journalism. Since the 1990s, popular culture in those countries has also been characterized by a dramatically heightened address to women consumers. The construction of women as both subjects and consumers, or perhaps as subjects only to the extent that we are able and willing to consume, is one of the contradictions at the core of postfeminist culture. Postfeminism is, we contend, inherently contradictory, characterized by a double discourse that works to construct feminism as a phenomenon of the past, traces of which can be found (and sometimes even valued) in the present; postfeminism suggests that it is the very success of feminism that produces its irrelevance for contemporary culture. In fact, the question is more complex than this since, as Sarah Projansky makes clear, postfeminist discourse deploys a variety of positions with respect to feminism, at times celebratory and at times laying blame for contemporary anxieties at the door of a past politics now felt to be misconceived.[21] What the many discursive postfeminisms identified by Projansky share is their relationship to the pastness of feminism, a feature commented on earlier; herein lies a suggestion that social change with respect to gender norms has been experienced, concretized even, through the passage of time.

Indeed, one of postfeminism's key functions is to negotiate the failure of contemporary institutions and the prospect of social death. Postfeminism fre-

13 Going on 30 structures an operative contrast between Jenna's (Jennifer Garner) girlish enthusiasm and her rival's calculation.

quently imagines femininity as a state of vitality in opposition to the symbolically deathly social and economic fields of contemporary Western cultures, and the highest-profile forms of postfeminist femininity are empowered to recharge a culture defined by exhaustion, uncertainty, and moral ambiguity. Thus, the postfeminist heroine is vital, youthful, and playful while her opposite number, the "bad" female professional, is repressive, deceptive, and deadly. In the romantic comedy *13 Going on 30* (2004), the distinctions drawn between Jenna and Lucy, who have known each other since childhood and are now editors at the same women's magazine, starkly illustrate this dynamic. When the magazine is challenged to reconceptualize itself (to undergo, in effect, a makeover), Jenna's youthful enthusiasm takes center stage. Making her presentation of a high school graduation concept for the magazine while wearing a bright pink ensemble and holding a pink balloon, she declares that she "wants to put life back into the magazine," underscoring the importance of remembering "what's good." By contrast, while her colleagues shudder and cringe, the manipulative and scheming Lucy envisions a "deadly serious" redesign concept she deems "fashion suicide," featuring gaunt, unhappy-looking women in dark clothing. Jenna's proposal narratively inverts but ideologically extends the film's broader focus on the retention of youth. Her concept showcases the ritual of high school graduation, symbolically de-aging the magazine's female subjects and reinforcing the film's plot, for Jenna has, in fact, magically time traveled to the physical age of thirty though her psychology remains that of an adolescent. Near the close of the film, she will gratefully return to adolescence after having endured romantic, creative, and professional disappointment as an adult woman.

As this example suggests, many postfeminist texts combine a deep uncertainty about existing options for women with an idealized, essentialized femininity that symbolically evades or transcends institutional and social problem spots. In concert with this, as many of the essays in the volume show, postfeminism evidences a distinct preoccupation with the temporal. Women's lives are regularly conceived of as time starved; women themselves are overworked, rushed, harassed, subject to their "biological clocks," and so on to such a degree that female adulthood is defined as a state of chronic temporal crisis. *13 Going on 30* is only one of a number of media texts that specialize in time-shifting fantasies that conflate youthfulness and the past. In this context of beset contemporary femininity, it is perhaps unsurprising that so many of the contributors to this anthology draw examples from the broad categories of lifestyle programming and reality television, with several essays focusing on the significance of the makeover as a recurrent trope of postfeminist media.[22] With its particular capacity to articulate the ordinary, reality TV provides a rich nexus of the desire for transformation, the yearning to achieve perfection in one's physical self and/or domestic environment, and the need to avoid at all costs a politicized understanding of these dynamics.[23]

Moreover, the makeover, whether of body or lived environment, enacts, as Sadie Wearing demonstrates in this volume, a particular form of temporality in which youth is fetishized and change accelerated or even presented as instantaneous. This accelerated temporality is characteristic of postmodern culture more broadly, as is the presentation of consumption itself as both therapeutic and transformative. Like daytime talk shows, makeovers trade in the vulnerability and resilience of their participants, functioning as simultaneously exploitative, sentimental, and compelling. Thus, the makeover mobilizes familiar tropes. As Brenda R. Weber writes of ABC's *Extreme Makeover*, "The story it tells—one of suffering and transformation, of desperation and joy—is as old as narrative itself."[24] But it does so in a contemporary context that aligns female consumption with freedom in a fashion that is (perversely perhaps) informed by feminism, even as that feminism is firmly "posted." Similarly, as Kimberly Springer notes in this volume, while reality TV is more than willing to make use of the "angry black woman" as a type, the question of why she might be angry remains unspoken. And, as Paul Gilroy writes with respect to the domestic makeover so central to British television schedules, "By exploring the process of changing private space and refining the ability to act there, these shows offer an implicit justification of the refusal to act elsewhere." In articulating rapid transformations, the makeover format works to suggest that "taste and lifestyle preference are much more important elements of identity than ethnicity, class, or regional ties could ever be."[25]

Postfeminism in all its guises posits the contemporary as surpassing feminism, leaving it behind. In doing so, it implicitly draws strength from the anxiety of aging at work in so many of its texts. Postfeminist representational culture is, of course, acutely age conscious; a variety of "chick" fictions from *Bridget Jones's Diary* (2001) and *How Stella Got Her Groove Back* (1998) to *Sex and the City* (1998–2004) and *13 Going on 30* have shown themselves to be exceedingly precise about the ages of their female protagonists. Meanwhile, the cult of youth is being technologically facilitated on a variety of fronts; myriad forms of reality TV, for example, dedicate themselves to staging rejuvenating transformations and the fantasy that aging can be managed away. The ambivalence about aging that strongly characterizes such fictions is also extended to feminism itself. As postfeminism has raised the premium on youthfulness, it has installed an image of feminism as "old" (and by extension moribund).

Interrogating Postfeminism speaks to an emerging body of work that names and analyzes postfeminism but remains unsure about its material, limits, and theoretical territory. The essays here engage with postfeminism as a concept and a political and cultural phenomenon, as well as offering specific analyses exploring postfeminism through a range of media and cultural practices. It is our contention that part of the significance of postfeminist culture lies in its pervasive presence not just in film, television, and popular literature but in advertising, magazines, music, and political discourse. We recognize that a comprehensive analysis of current postfeminist culture is beyond the scope of one volume. It would entail, for instance, an examination of a range of social behaviors and trends, including (among others) the explosive growth of the bridal industry, the emergence of "chick lit" as a staple form on best-seller lists,[26] the heightened importance of the day spa and the nail salon within service economies, the changing cultural status of cosmetic surgery, the dissolving line between sex worker and service worker when it comes to women in the workplace, and the aggressive mainstreaming of pornography. Our goal is not to produce a sociology of postfeminism but to analyze as many of these media and cultural contexts—and the intersections between them—as possible.[27]

Throughout, the anthology is shaped in and by an awareness of the potential reach of postfeminism as a concept. We are also guided by a sense of the continuing importance of a strongly articulated feminist critique of popular culture and a reluctance to recertify the postfeminist canon simultaneously produced by journalism and (increasingly) academia, even as the essays presented here inevitably engage with that canon. The necessity of feminist critique, at a time when women face significant challenges to their economic well-being, hard-won reproductive rights, and even authority to speak, while popular culture blithely assumes that gender equality is a given, seems to us self-evident. Postfeminist assumptions concerning gender—which, as we have seen, broadly revolve around the cultural and economic freedom of Western women—are promulgated in a context in which women's actual social health is extremely problematic. If liberation is linked to consumption and aspiration, what of the pressing economic and social issues that have to do with the long-term poverty that results from women's lower pay, limited job opportunities, and child-care responsibilities?[28] We believe that postfeminism participates in the ideological and economic normalization of new patterns of exclusion and demographic propriety in the United States and the United Kingdom. Moreover, globalization is producing complicated new networks of exchange and reliance among women. Phenomena such as the "feminization of migration" present a vital opportunity to treat issues of class, nationality, and ethnicity.[29] In her work on fantasies of "downshifting" to idealized domesticity, Joanne Hollows indicates the importance of these issues in the British context.[30] Writing on retreatism within American popular culture, Diane Negra notes that similar fantasy work is undertaken by a set of romantic comedies and television dramas that centralize the protagonist's "unlearning" of feminism and her decision to leave an urban professional environment and/or return to an idealized hometown.[31] In this anthology, Suzanne Leonard explores the ramifications of class on gendered representation in the United States, taking up the figure of the "bored woman worker" in such films as *The Good Girl* (2002).

In the increasingly privatized context of the United States and the United

Kingdom, access to education, health care, and a living income during retirement are all linked to full-time employment. And, while few conservatives would openly argue that women should be denied the vote, many women may nonetheless feel disenfranchised by political discourse.[32] In this context, we argue that postfeminism increasingly operates as a rationale for the brutalities of the emergent "New Economies" of both the United States and the United Kingdom. Marita Sturken and other critics have observed how a post-9/11 climate has shifted the American image repertoire to emphasize "traditional working-class masculinity and wives holding down the home front."[33] In the new climate of fear and vulnerability that is ushering in a rollback of civil rights, both the state and exalted popular culture franchises offer fantasies of patriarchal protection. As Kathleen Karlyn has observed, neither "the one" of the *Matrix* cycle (1999, 2003) nor "the king" of the *Lord of the Rings* trilogy (2001, 2002, 2003) are presented with a trace of irony despite their overblown imagery of white male authority. Instead this is the terrain of a pervasive new humanism that "evades its own politics."[34] These blockbuster franchises are postfeminist in the most conservative sense. Of course, feminist activism continues in important areas of contemporary social policy that have to do with self-determination in relation to reproduction and women's physical health, just as feminist issues, including sexual and domestic violence, remain urgent sites of gender politics. Yet in arguing that barriers to equality are as much cultural as legislative we seek here to address the distinct issues posed by a postfeminist culture in which women are assumed to have achieved equality.

Postfeminist Predilections, Postfeminist Blind Spots

One of the goals of this anthology is to extend an intellectual "conversation" within Anglo-American feminist scholarship. Postfeminism is a pervasive phenomenon of both British and American popular culture, often marked by a high degree of discursive harmony evidenced in such "transit" texts as *Bridget Jones's Diary*, *Sex and the City*, *I Don't Know How She Does It*, *Bergdorf Blondes*, and (as Martin Roberts analyzes in this volume) *What Not to Wear*. Indeed, many of the most prominent texts in female-centered genres (including the *Bridget Jones* print and film franchise, *Ally McBeal* [1997–2003], and the aforementioned *Sex and the City*) have been decidedly transatlantic, either originating in the United States and becoming hits in the United Kingdom or the reverse. The regularity of cross-cultural traffic of this sort is such that it suggests an interesting slant on the vaunted Anglo-American "special relationship" trumpeted by political conservatives in recent years.[35] While the emergence of a postfeminist canon (one alluded to in the examples cited above) has become increasingly evident, it is nonetheless the case that postfeminism means different things in these national and cultural contexts.[36] One of the goals of the collection is to explore the intersections between British and American configurations of popular feminism as postfeminism. In this way, we hope to address questions of cultural dissonance when an American "we" is presumed to be general—in other words, the inward-looking features of American cultural criticism (but also the assumption that the United States is itself a unified and undifferentiated cultural space). The international exportation of American popular culture requires broader understandings, and the temptation to generalize is not coincidental, as we will see. Yet there are national specificities to postfeminism, addressed here through the essays by Martin Roberts and Hannah Sanders in particular.

The essays presented here draw examples from a range of media—television, film, music, and print journalism—locating these texts within different critical and cultural contexts. We have been guided by what we regard as the necessity of looking beyond journalistic canons of postfeminist culture (which are reliant on high-profile television series such as *Sex and the City* or *Desperate Housewives* [2004–], for instance). There are at least two dimensions to this expanded perspective. On one hand, there is an awareness that postfeminism represents a cultural turn impacting a diversity of media products, including those targeted at male consumers, as Steven Cohan's analysis of the 2003 American cable hit *Queer Eye for the Straight Guy* makes clear. Some of the most male-identified genres are highly readable in postfeminist terms, and some of the essays in this volume undertake the work of beginning to theorize postfeminist masculinity. Indeed, the shift from women's studies to gender studies and the proliferation of academic (and journalistic) analyses of masculinity are a characteristic trend of the 1990s and 2000s.[37] In June 2004, the cover of a supplement to the London *Times* asked, with little trace of irony, "Are Men the New Women?" (a claim founded, it seems, on increased levels of body and fashion awareness and—of course—consumption among men). Whether in *Queer Eye for the Straight Guy*, British dramas such as *Life Begins* (2004), British reality shows such as *Wife Swap* (Channel 4, 2002–; ABC, 2004), or "specials" such as *Britain's Worst Husbands* (ITV, 2004), straight white men are presented as in need of change. Straight masculinity is thus rendered comic—albeit temporarily and under certain circumstances—and straight women can be included in the joke, even as they are discussed in traditional sexist evaluative terms as "hot" by the queer guys or painted as just plain foolish for choosing such unattractive or inattentive male partners. Meanwhile, as Douglas Battema and Philip Sewell have argued in a discussion of the trend toward "masculinist" television programming, late 1990s and early 2000s popular culture frequently deployed ironic humor to allow "regressive, recidivist masculinity to emerge unscathed from ongoing cultural struggles."[38]

A second reason to resist an emergent postfeminist canon is the potential complicity of that canon with postfeminism's limited race and class vision; in this context, it is crucially important to test how postfeminism's emerging narrative protocols and tropes are and are not ascribed to women of color and working-class women. In this volume, Sadie Wearing and Martin Roberts demonstrate the sharply drawn class parameters of the fashion makeovers enacted in the British shows *10 Years Younger* (2004–5) and *What Not to Wear* (2002), while Suzanne Leonard highlights the sense of aimlessness and inertia several recent films link to women's participation in the service economy. Tracking the presence and absence of race discourses in both postfeminist representation and the scholarship on postfeminism remains a vital task.[39] Once again the emerging postfeminist canon alluded to in popular commentaries, and which forms the examples discussed in much scholarly writing, is exclusionary. In this volume, Kimberly Springer draws attention to the specificity of the "black chick flick," for instance, a cycle of romantic comedies focusing on African American women (*Waiting to Exhale* [1995], *Down in the Delta* [1998], *Diary of a Mad Black Woman* [2005]) that adopt distinct strategies in comparison to those retreatist rom-coms that have thus far attracted critical attention within feminist media studies (*Kate and Leopold* [2001], *French Kiss* [1994], *Someone Like You* [2001]).[40] Both the critical exclusion of texts directed specifically at African American women and the ways in which these films might work to nuance feminist accounts of contemporary popular culture are relevant here.

To this extent, our aim is that this anthology will point to the significance of postfeminism for those working in a range of other areas, particularly in relation to questions of race, sexuality, class, and age. While these concerns *are* present in current thinking, this anthology insists on the potential of a diverse feminist politics (one that addresses class and race as emphatically as it does gender and generation) in response to a postfeminist culture exemplified by the figure of the white, middle-class, heterosexual woman. In short, we wish to ask: is it possible to bring into being a postfeminist critical practice that expands feminism as much as it critiques it? Accordingly, some of the essays in this volume point to the ways in which the feminist project has stalled but then abundantly demonstrate the continuing productivity of feminist scholarship through energetic engagements with new texts. In this volume, Anna Feigenbaum shows the importance of female music performance to feminist media studies while Sadie Wearing opens up the complexities that questions of age and aging pose for feminist scholarship on popular media culture. Elsewhere Charlotte Brunsdon's analysis of the 8:00 to 9:00 pm slot and lifestyle programming on British television demonstrates the importance of recognizing the pleasures of being addressed by mainstream culture and the necessity of understanding these processes within the context of power.[41] Feminist critique fundamentally emphasizes the operations of power, whether economic, social, ideological, or representational. Postfeminist culture, with its enhanced but particularized female visibility, in no way invalidates this task.

Conceptualizing and Contending with Postfeminism

This volume responds to and significantly extends a range of existing publications in the field of media and gender studies. Since the primary aim is to map and interrogate postfeminism and its impact on, and relationship to, contemporary popular culture, the volume updates and widens the definitions and debates forged in landmark publications such as Tania Modleski's *Feminism without Women: Culture and Criticism in a "Post-feminist" Era* and Sarah Projansky's *Watching Rape: Film and Television in a Post-feminist Culture*.[42] Yet to date surprisingly few publications have explored the subject in detail, and postfeminism's increasing ubiquity and political and cultural ambiguity mean that a good deal more concerted scholarly work in the field needs to be undertaken. At present, much of this work exists in the form of articles rather than books, a good deal of it published in journals such as *Feminist Media Studies* and *Genders*.[43] As we have noted, postfeminism can be situated in relation to other aspects of consumer capitalist culture. Thus, perspectives on it are importantly shaped by scholarly work that is conceptually pertinent while not necessarily centralizing postfeminism per se. In particular, we would draw attention to scholarship that seeks to theorize questions of culture and power such as Naomi Klein's *No Logo*, Paul Gilroy's *Postcolonial Melancholia*, Thomas Frank's *One Market under God: Extreme Capitalism, Market Populism, and the End of Economic Democracy*, and Herman Gray's *Cultural Moves: African Americans and the Politics of Representation*.[44] In this volume, the essays by Angela McRobbie, Martin Roberts, and Sadie Wearing underline the value of interdisciplinary research in making sense of the disciplinary forces through which bodies are produced as gendered, classed, and aged.

As an edited collection, *Interrogating Postfeminism* is able to provide a more pluralistic account of postfeminism than a single-authored volume would be able to do. Many of the contributors explore the relationship between feminism and postfeminism (in terms of both the historical and political dimensions of this relationship). Thus, the volume expands the field of publications that have sought to map a trajectory of feminism and postfeminism and offer feminist critiques of contemporary gender politics, for example, Imelda Whelehan's *Modern Feminist Thought: From the Second Wave to "Post-feminism"* and *Overloaded: Popular Culture and the Future of Feminism*, Joanne Hollows's *Feminism, Femininity, and Popular Culture*, and more popularized accounts such as Christina Hoff Sommers's *Who Stole Feminism? How Women Have Betrayed Women* and Natasha Walters's *The New Feminism*.

Besides engaging with broader feminist debates, the essays in this volume also discuss specific film, television, and popular music texts. As such, the volume engages with, and may be situated within, the rich body of feminist film and television studies publications that focus on popular culture and the politics of representation. In recent years, a number of significant books have provided a context for this volume: Yvonne Tasker's *Working Girls: Gender and Sexuality in Popular Cinema*; Sharon Willis's *High Contrast: Race and Gender in Contemporary Hollywood Films*; Jacinda Read's *The New Avengers: Feminism, Femininity, and the Rape-Revenge Cycle*; Bonnie J. Dow's *Prime-Time Feminism: Television, Media Culture, and the Woman's Movement since 1970*; Charlotte Brunsdon's *The Feminist, the Housewife, and the Soap Opera*; and most recently Susan Douglas's and Meredith Michaels's *The Mommy Myth: The Idealization of Motherhood and How It Has Undermined Women*. Moreover, in this volume the essays by Sarah Banet-Weiser, Anna Feigenbaum, Sarah Projansky, and Hannah E. Sanders all discuss the figure of the "girl" and "girl power" in relation to postfeminism, updating and reinflecting works such as Angela McRobbie's *Feminism and Youth Culture* and Valerie Walkerdine's *Daddy's Girl: Young Girls and Popular Culture*, which have identified female youth culture as an important site for feminist scholarship. As evidenced by Anita Harris's recent edited volume *All about the Girl: Culture, Power, and Identity* and Mary Celeste Kearney's *Girls Make Media*, scholarly interest in girls and culture continues to generate important interventions.

Within popular media culture itself, some of the highest-profile postfeminist franchises have centralized girls and girlhood, fusing empowerment rhetoric with traditionalist identity paradigms (in cinema, *The Princess Diaries*, *What a Girl Wants*, and *Mean Girls*; in television, *Ally McBeal* and *Joan of Arcadia*; in music, Britney Spears and Avril Lavigne). Moreover the "girling" of femininity itself is evident in both the celebration of the young woman as a marker of postfeminist liberation and the continuing tendency to either explicitly term or simply treat women of a variety of ages as girls. To some extent, girlhood is imagined within postfeminist culture as being for everyone; that is, girlhood offers a fantasy of transcendence and evasion, a respite from other areas of experience. The fantasy character of girlhood in so many postfeminist fictions is suggested by its recurrent association with magic, including the enchantments of consumption.[45] In analyzing such representations, we need to take care, as Sarah Projansky reminds us, to distinguish actual girls and their culture from the use of the term to refer to young women. Thus, her essay in this volume seeks to map the different ways in which the girl is used as a representational sign within print journalism. In part, this process involves an acknowledgment of the difficulty of portraying adult women within postfeminist culture, a problem that clearly relates to the construction of feminism as unspeakable noted by various scholars, including Angela McRobbie and Charlotte Brunsdon. Further, it is important to avoid, or at least analyze, the simultaneous denigration and appropriation of girls' culture.

To some extent, a focus on the girl results not only from the pervasive representations of girlhood and girlishness but from the extent to which generational metaphors are so central to postfeminism. Both helpful and limiting, the generational construction of girls and young women as enjoying the freedoms secured by the activism of their mothers and grandmothers is a repeated trope of postfeminist culture. As this suggests, one of the central issues with which we are dealing here is the relationship between postfeminism (as a popular idiom) and third-wave feminism as a more scholarly category. Both share a dissatisfaction with the feminism they seek to supplant or supplement. They also inscribe a chronology characterized by elision, the former of the continuing vitality of feminist activism, the latter, as Kimberly Springer notes elsewhere, of the history of black feminist movements.[46] While the academy has admitted some forms of difference in a pro forma way, other forms of difference seem more excluded than ever. A familiar tension within academic feminism—its tendency to be defined in narrow social terms—is, as we have seen, solidified in postfeminist culture's imagining of women's success as particularized in class and race terms. By contrast, queerness, which can be constituted in terms of both whiteness and consumerism, has served a mediated function within postfeminist culture (and, we might add, feminist scholarship).[47] Stripped of its original confrontational political agenda, queerness can be effectively co-opted through a rhetoric of choice such that sexual identity is primarily expressed through consumption practices. In this way, popular media (particularly television) tend to construct queerness as a lifestyle choice associated with affluent urban modes of consumption. Class, however, which raises the perilous specter of immobility and a (relative) inability to consume, remains a problem area associated with ill-disciplined bodies.

It is clear that postfeminism is deployed and understood diversely within scholarly work; terms such as *new sexism* and *retrosexism* have been used to describe postfeminism, which in turn needs to be carefully differentiated from third-wave feminism (the latter a self-identification rather than a tag provided by popular media). Definitive conceptualizations of postfeminism are as elusive as references to postfeminism are pervasive. Thus, in part the contradictory aspects of postfeminist discourse relate to its resolutely popular character; that is, the term has been generated and primarily deployed outside the academy, lacking the rigor we expect of scholarly work. To this extent, the questions facing feminist scholars have less to do with the usefulness of postfeminism as a concept (its incoherence might be seen as a limiting factor in this context) than with the strategies we might adopt in relation to its pervasive insistence on the bleakness and redundancy of feminism. As we might expect of a popular mode, postfeminism also constructs feminism as other, as extreme. It is the supposed difficulty of feminism, its rigidity and propensity to take things "too far," that a middle of the road, middle-class postfeminism rejects.[48]

In this context, it is also appropriate to consider the figure of the active or action heroine, an emblematic and problematic icon of female empowerment within postfeminist culture. As much as feminist criticism has had an ambivalent relationship with the figure of the active heroine, she continues to fascinate, as evidenced in such recent publications as Linda Mizejewski's *Hardboiled and High Heeled: The Woman Detective in Popular Culture*, Cynthia Lucia's *Framing Female Lawyers: Women on Trial in Film*, and Linda Ruth Williams's *The Erotic Thriller in Contemporary Cinema*. The ubiquity of the action heroine more specifically (Lara Croft, Buffy the Vampire Slayer) as a reference point in various publications provides evidence that academics, critics, and students want to discuss this figure, in some instances in an attempt to reconcile politics and pleasure, which are perceived as in some way contradictory.[49] It is important to point to the potential for female spectatorial pleasure in relation to popular culture, as scholars in feminist media studies have done, and to engage with actual audiences, as Hannah E. Sanders does in this volume in her exploration of British teens as an audience for the American series *Charmed*. All the same, as writers such as Christine Holmlund, Sarah Projansky, and others make clear, there is much more to feminist analysis than the celebration of pleasure or consumption, however transgressive we may feel it to be.[50] In this volume, Lisa Coulthard's discussion of violence, action, and feminism through Tarantino's high-profile *Kill Bill* movies addresses these concerns. For Coulthard, the proliferation of feminist writing in relation to the action heroine or kick-ass girl is problematic to the extent that it evades an exploration of the meaning of violence, the feature that is for her most striking about these film texts. We might also note the tendency to explore action heroines with little reference to questions of race and ethnicity.[51] Just as black chick flicks are typically sidelined in writing on romantic comedy and the contemporary woman's picture, so it is rarely the action films that centralize women of color that have preoccupied feminist commentaries on the genre.[52] To some extent, it is the circular logic of the "mainstream" that is at issue here; those examples most often cited in critical and journalistic writing are selected as significant on the basis of factors such as widespread commercial appeal, top box-office performances, and so on. While this is both understandable and productive, we (also) live in a culture defined by niche markets, a postnetwork era in which film and television studies can ill afford to restrict its focus to canonical, high-profile texts.

We recognize that this collection cannot do justice to the full range of representational trends and forms associated with postfeminism, and the question of "postfeminist masculinities" lies largely outside of our purview. It is worth observing, however, that postfeminist representation typically celebrates women's strength while lightly critiquing or gently ridiculing straight masculinity. It makes regular use of gay male identities, as Steven Cohan's discussion of authoritative queerness in lifestyle television in this volume establishes. Indeed, some of the most quintessentially postfeminist genres, such as the wedding film, rely on out (yet nonconfrontational) gay men. As Elizabeth Freeman points out, for instance, "representations of 'straight' weddings often focus on a gay participant whose presence in the ceremony and exclusion from its results seem to guarantee heterosexual marriage."[53] Yet it is important to note that postfeminism absolutely rejects lesbianism in all but its most guy-friendly forms, that is, divested of potentially feminist associations and invested with sexualized glamour. The simultaneous indulgence in and critique of voyeurism in the Showtime television series *The L Word* is perhaps indicative; lesbian lives are simultaneously fetishized and celebrated, mediated through a curious heterosexual gaze that is marked as both male and female.

We are not in the business of simply celebrating icons of postfeminist culture: the self as a project; kick-ass, working-out women as expressions of agency; or freedom as the freedom to shop or have cosmetic surgery. Our responsibility as feminist critics is to approach the popular with a skeptical eye, questioning whether identity politics inevitably generates a politics of the self, culminating in the "self as project" so characteristic of postfeminism. Equally, however, we are not engaged in interrogating or understanding postfeminist culture simply as a forerunner to rejecting it. The images and icons of postfeminism *are* compelling; the women and girls who (literally) buy into this visual and narrational repertoire are not simply dupes. As an idiom, postfeminism popularizes (as much as it caricatures) a feminism it simultaneously evokes and rejects. Thus, many of the essays in this collection aim to explore the address postfeminist culture makes to female spectators while acknowledging its limitations.

Within the broad field of media studies, critical commentary continues to pose questions about the meaning of popular texts in either-or terms. Thus, texts from *Buffy* to Britney are either progressive or regressive, liberating or containing. Underpinning this anthology is a reservation as to how far such a model can take us. Can it ever, we ask, reflect the complexity and ambivalence of popular culture or postfeminism? Postfeminist culture is evidently postmodern in character, its self-reflexivity mobilizing the terms of its own critique. Postfeminist culture does not allow us to make straightforward distinctions between progressive and regressive texts. Nevertheless, it urgently requires us to develop new reading strategies to counteract the popularized feminism, figurations of female agency, and canny neutralization of traditional feminist critiques in its texts.

Feminism challenges us to critique relations of power, to imagine the world as other than it is, to conceive of different patterns of work, life, and leisure. Postfeminist culture enacts fantasies of regeneration and transformation that also speak to a desire for change. Clearly, however, it is unhelpful to mistake one for the other. The challenges facing feminist media critics of an earlier era centered on the need to make women visible, to denaturalize the construction of women's culture as inherently trivial or banal. The contemporary challenges that postfeminist culture poses for feminist media studies are rather different. Postfeminism displaces older forms of trivialization, generating a sense of newness, yet it also refreshes long familiar themes of gendered representation, demonstrating the ongoing urgency of speaking feminist critique.

Notes

1. McRobbie, "Post-feminism and Popular Culture," 254. McRobbie's seminal essay is reprinted in this volume.
2. In the United Kingdom, supermodel Claudia Schiffer ends a current television advertisement for an antiaging product with the telling phrase, uttered straight to camera in a blandly reassuring tone, "Let surgery wait." Cosmetic surgery is here invoked, in a quite taken for granted manner, as compulsory rather than optional, although consumers can postpone the inevitable, perhaps suggesting the unpalatable aspects of such invasive procedures. For a discussion of the plastic surgery industry and contemporary body politics, see Blum, *Flesh Wounds*.
3. hooks, *Feminism Is for Everybody*.
4. Ibid., 50.
5. Ironic references to feminism as "the F word" are a familiar feature of popular media culture in the United Kingdom.
6. Levy, *Female Chauvinist Pigs: Women and the Rise of Raunch Culture*; McCabe and Akass, *Reading "Sex and the City."* In the British context, it is also relevant to note the visibility of feminist scholars as public intellectuals with commentators such as Germaine Greer disseminating their ideas through print journalism and other media forms in addition to traditional publication techniques.

7. McRobbie, "Post-feminism and Popular Culture," 260.

8. Rich, *Chick Flicks*, 24.

9. Karlyn, "*Scream*, Popular Culture, and Feminism's Third Wave."

10. McRobbie, "Notes on Postfeminism and Popular Culture," 5.

11. An article by James Wolcott in *Vanity Fair* goes so far as to predict a looming new "battle of the sexes" in light of persistent gender inequities. He reads the Summers scandal as the explosion of "a protracted build up of exasperation over the persistent under-representation of women in positions of prominence and authority, and the mulish inability of powerful men to recognize the scope of the problem, or their tendency to rationalize it with voodoo genetics and Victorian-parlor sociology" ("Caution," 67).

12. Featherstone, "Wal-Mart Values."

13. Readings and Schaber, "Introduction," 6.

14. McRobbie, "Post-feminism and Popular Culture," 259.

15. Frank, *One Market under God*, 68.

16. Postrel, *The Substance of Style*, 10.

17. Ibid., 11.

18. Whelehan, *Overloaded*.

19. Gray, *Cultural Moves*, 4.

20. McPherson, "Who's Got Next?"

21. Projansky, *Watching Rape*, 67.

22. This is also in line with the amount of scholarly work relating to reality TV. Two recent collections stand out in this regard: Oullette and Murray, *Reality TV*; and Holmes and Jermyn, *Understanding Reality Television*.

23. For analyses of another category of postfeminist Anglo-American transit text, the nanny series (in which British child-raising experts train American families to deal with their recalcitrant children), see Kim, "Elevating Servants, Elevating American Families"; and Ouellette, "Nanny TV."

24. Weber, "Beauty, Desire, and Anxiety."

25. Gilroy, *Postcolonial Melancholia*, 119. Although Gilroy refers to British shows such as *Changing Rooms* and *Ground Force*, the evacuation of the potential for social change is also dramatically (even excessively) foregrounded in the ABC series *Extreme Makeover: Home Edition*, which mobilizes commerce and communities in the service of consumption.

26. On the emergence of chick lit, see Ferriss and Young, *Chick Lit*.

27. We also recognize that trends toward media conglomeration within global capitalism are generating new ancillary markets through a synergistic heightening of the relationship between film and television texts and related forms of consumer behavior. For a case study of one such synergy, see Levine, "Fractured Fairy Tales and Fragmented Markets."

28. In 2002, American women with full-time, year-round employment earned 76 percent of male income. On gender and aging, see the special issue of *Feminist Economics* 11:2 (July 2005).

29. For a discussion of the complex interdependencies between first-world women employers and their third-world women employees see Ehrenreich and Hochschild, *Global Woman*.

30. Joanne Hollows's discussion of the downshifting narrative in recent British popular culture addresses the compartmentalization of domesticity in feminist scholarship and feminist lives and asks probing questions about the fantasy of reclaimed (often rural) domesticity that has proved so saleable in print fiction, reality television, and the celebrity personae of domestic sensualists such as Nigella Lawson. See Hollows's "Can I Go Home Yet?"

31. Negra, "Girls Who Go Home."

32. One sign of the political estrangement of American women is to be found in the fact that 22 of the 45 million single women in the United States in 2000 did not cast a vote in the 2000 presidential election. See Loth, "Women Who Vote, and Those That Don't." The particular terms within which women can achieve political success are evident with respect to Condoleezza Rice in Kimberly Springer's essay in this volume. In a somewhat earlier British context, several of the representational tropes identified by Springer with respect to Rice featured in responses to Margaret Thatcher, who was styled as sexless on the one hand (the "iron lady") and as caught in illicit passion with then U.S. president Ronald Reagan on the other. Jacqueline Rose discusses Thatcher as an icon of fearful femininity in "Margaret Thatcher and Ruth Ellis."

33. Sturkin, "Masculinity, Courage and Sacrifice," 444.

34. Karlyn, "Feminism and Its Discontents."

35. Of course, some of these texts may present themselves as globally generic and be culturally protective at the same time. For instance, in the *Bridget Jones* novel and its sequel the British hero rescues Bridget after she has been victimized by the actions of a foreign male. In addition, culturally specific postfeminist franchises still flourish. One example is the series of novels *Five Go Mad in . . .* , which relies on British traditions of same-sex groups taking vacations together that would probably not be as clear and resonant to a reader without this cultural frame of reference.

36. The extent to which regional differences are also at issue is an aspect that we acknowledge but do not have the space to address here.

37. Tania Modleski's pathbreaking study *Feminism without Women: Culture and Criticism in a "Postfeminist" Era* confronts directly the ways in which the centrality of "new" men and "new" masculinities in American culture are achieved at the expense of women.

38. Battema and Sewell, "Trading in Masculinity," 261.

39. Some of the scholarship on the celebrity talk show host and postfeminist icon Oprah Winfrey has begun to move in this direction. See in particular Illouz, *Oprah Winfrey and the Glamour of Misery*. Illouz offers a commentary on Winfrey's selective engagement with the problematics of race, noting, for instance, that she "consistently twists political categories and transforms them into ethical and spiritual ones" (24).

40. For a discussion of the retreatist strategies of a set of post-9/11 romantic come-

dies, see Negra, "Structural Integrity, Historical Reversion, and the Post-9/11 Chick Flick."

41. Brunsdon, "Lifestyling Britain."

42. For an exploratory discussion of the specifics of British postfeminism, see Ashby, "Postfeminism in the British Frame."

43. Lotz, "Postfeminist Television Criticism"; Brunsdon, "Post-Feminism and Shopping Films"; Kim, "Sex and the Single Girl"; Moseley and Read, "Having It Ally"; Negra "Quality Postfeminism?"

44. Klein, *No Logo.*

45. See Moseley, "Glamorous Witchcraft."

46. Springer, "Third Wave Black Feminism?" Springer writes, "In sum, as we learn more about women of color's feminist activism, the wave analogy becomes untenable" (1062).

47. On the mediating function of queerness and the figure of the gay best friend, see Dreisinger, "The Queen in Shining Armor."

48. Joanne Hollows has noted, for instance, the prohibitive connotations of feminism with respect to the construct of a luxurious domesticity as a guilty pleasure ("Can I Go Home Yet?").

49. See, for example, the edited volumes McCaughey and King, *Reel Knockouts*, and Inness, *Action Chicks.*

50. Holmlund, *Impossible Bodies*; Projansky, *Watching Rape.*

51. For an analysis that does foreground these questions, see Beltrán, "Mas Macha."

52. Although Pam Grier's 1970s films are widely referred to, for instance, little feminist scholarship engages these films in detail. For a recent analysis that takes on this task see Holmlund, "Wham! Bam! Pam!" See also DeVere Brody, "The Returns of Cleopatra Jones." In contemporary terms, while African-American performers such as Vivica A. Fox regularly star and support in action roles, these films are rarely centered within a feminist scholarship that devotes considerable energy to high-profile white action heroines such as those in the *Alien* and *Terminator* cycles or *Buffy the Vampire Slayer.*

53. Freeman, *The Wedding Complex*, 2.

Angela McRobbie

1 Postfeminism and Popular Culture
BRIDGET JONES AND THE NEW GENDER REGIME

Complexification of Backlash?

This article presents a series of possible conceptual frames for engaging with what has come to be known as postfeminism. It understands postfeminism to refer to an active process by which feminist gains of the 1970s and 1980s come to be undermined. It proposes that, through an array of machinations, elements of contemporary popular culture are perniciously effective in regard to this undoing of feminism while simultaneously appearing to be engaging in a well-informed and even well-intended response to "feminism." It then proposes that this "undoing," which can be perceived in the broad cultural field, is compounded by some dynamics in sociological theory (including the work of Anthony Giddens and Ulrich Beck) that appear to be most relevant to aspects of gender and social change. Finally, it suggests that by means of the tropes of freedom and choice that are now inextricably connected with the category of "young women," feminism is decisively "aged" and made to seem redundant. Feminism is cast into the shadows, where at best it can expect to have some afterlife, where it might be regarded ambivalently by those young women who must in more public venues stake a distance from it, for the sake of social and sexual recognition. I propose a complexification, then, of the backlash thesis that gained currency within forms of journalism associated with popular feminism.[1]

The backlash for Susan Faludi was a concerted, conservative response to the achievements of feminism. My argument is that postfeminism positively draws on and invokes feminism as that which can be taken into account, to suggest that equality is achieved, in order to install a whole repertoire of new meanings, which emphasize that it is no longer needed, that it is a spent force. In Britain this was most vividly seen in a newspaper column, "Bridget Jones's Diary," and in the enormously successful book and films that followed.[2] For my purposes here, postfeminism permits the close examination of a number of intersecting but also conflicting currents. It allows us to examine shifts of direction in the feminist academy while also taking into account the seeming repudiation of feminism within this same academic context by those young women who are its unruly (student) subjects. Broadly, I am arguing that for feminism to be "taken into account" it has to be understood as having already passed away. This is a movement detectable across popular culture, a site where "power . . . is remade at various junctures within everyday life, [constituting] our tenuous sense of common sense."[3] Some fleeting comments by Judith Butler suggest to me that postfeminism can be explored through what I would describe as a "double entanglement."[4] This comprises the coexistence of neoconservative values in relation to gender, sexuality, and family life (e.g., George W. Bush supporting the campaign to encourage chastity among young people and in March 2004 declaring that civilization itself depends on traditional marriage) with processes of liberalization in regard to choice and diversity in domestic, sexual, and kinship relations (e.g., gay couples now able to adopt, foster, or have their own children by whatever means and, in the United Kingdom at least, full rights to "civil partnerships"). It also encompasses the existence of feminism as at some level transformed into a form of Gramscian common sense, while also fiercely repudiated, indeed almost hated.[5] The "taken into accountness" permits an all the more thorough dismantling of feminist politics and the discrediting of the occasionally voiced need for its renewal.

Feminism Dismantling Itself

The impact of this "double entanglement," which is manifest in popular and political culture, coincides, however, with feminism in the academy finding it necessary to dismantle itself. For the sake of periodization, we could say that 1990 (or thereabouts) marks a turning point, the moment of definitive self-critique in feminist theory. At this time, the representational claims of second-wave feminism come to be fully interrogated by postcolonialist feminists such as Gayatri Chakravorty Spivak, Trinh Thi Minh-ha, and Chandra Talpade Mohanty, among others, and feminist theorists such as Judith Butler and Donna Haraway, who inaugurated the radical denaturalizing of the postfeminist body.[6] Under the prevailing influence of Michel Foucault, there is a shift away from feminist interest in centralized power blocs (e.g., the state, patriarchy, and law) to more dispersed sites, events, and instances of power conceptualized as flows and specific convergences and consolidations of talk, discourse, attentions. The body and also the subject come to represent a focal point for feminist interest, nowhere more so than in the work of Butler. The concept of subjectivity and the means by which cultural forms and interpellations (or dominant social processes) call women into being, produce them as subjects while ostensibly merely describing them as such, inevitably means that it is a problematic "she," rather than an unproblematic "we," that is indicative of a turn to what we might describe as the emerging politics of postfeminist inquiry.[7]

In feminist cultural studies, the early 1990s also marks a moment of feminist reflexivity. In "Pedagogies of the Feminine" Charlotte Brunsdon queried the (hitherto assumed) use value to feminist media scholarship of the binary opposition between femininity and feminism, or as she put it the extent to which the "housewife" or "ordinary woman" was conceived of as the assumed subject of attention for feminism.[8] Looking back we can see how heavily utilized this dualism was and also how particular it was to gender arrangements for largely white and relatively affluent (i.e., housewifely) women. The year 1990 also marked the moment at which the concept of popular feminism found expression. Andrea Stuart considered the wider circulation of feminist values across the landscape of popular culture, in particular magazines in which quite suddenly issues that had been central to the formation of the women's movement, such as domestic violence, equal pay, and workplace harassment, were now addressed to a vast readership.[9] The wider dissemination of feminist issues was also a key concern in my own writing at this time, in particular the intersection of these new representations with the daily lives of young women who, as subjects ("called into being") of popular feminism, might then be expected to embody more emboldened (though also of course "failed") identities. This gave rise to the idea of feminist success. Of course, no sooner is the word *success* written than it is queried. How could this be gauged? What might be the criteria for judging degrees of feminist success?

Female Success

Admittedly there is some extravagance in my claim for feminist success. It might be more accurate to remark on the keen interest across the quality and popular media (themselves wishing to increase their female readers and audiences) in ideas of female success. As feminist values are indeed taken on board within a range of institutions, including law, education, to an extent medicine, and likewise employment and the media, high-profile or newsworthy achievements of women and girls in these sectors show the institutions to be modern and abreast with social change. This is the context, then, within which feminism is acknowledged, and this is what I mean by feminism taken into account. Feminist success has, so far, only been described sporadically.[10] Within media and cultural studies, both Brunsdon and myself have each considered how with feminism as part of the academic curriculum (i.e., "canonized"), then it is not surprising that it might also be countered; that is, feminism must face up to the consequences of its own claims to representation and power and not be so surprised when young women students decline the invitation to identify as a "we" with their feminist teachers and scholars.[11] This interface between the feminist academy and the student body has also been discussed in American feminist journals, particularly in regard to the decline of women's studies.[12] Back in the early 1990s (and following Judith Butler), I saw this sense of contestation on the part of young women, and what I would call their "distance from feminism," as one of potential where a lively dialogue about how feminism might develop would commence.[13] Indeed, it seemed in the very nature of feminism that it gave rise to disidentification as a kind of requirement for its existence. But, still, it seems now, over a decade later, that this space of "distance from feminism" and those utterances of forceful non-identity with feminism have consolidated into something closer to repudiation than ambivalence, and it is this vehemently denunciatory stance that is manifest across the field of popular gender debate. This is the cultural space of postfeminism.

In this context, it requires both imagination and hopefulness to argue that the active, sustained, and repetitive repudiation or repression of "feminism" also marks its (still fearful) presence or even longevity (as afterlife). What I mean by this is that there are different kinds of repudiation and different investments in such a stance. The more gentle denunciations of feminism (as in the film *Bridget Jones's Diary*) coexist, however, with the shrill championing of young women as a "metaphor for social change" on the pages of the right-wing press in the United Kingdom, in particular the *Daily Mail*. This anti-feminist endorsement of female individualization is embodied in the figure of the ambitious "TV blonde."[14] These so-called "A1" girls are glamorous high achievers destined for Oxford or Cambridge and are usually pictured clutching A-level examination certificates. We might say these are ideal girls, subjects par excellence, and also subjects of excellence. Nor are these notions of female success exclusive to the changing representations of young women in the countries of the affluent West. As Spivak has argued, in the impoverished zones of the world, governments and nongovernmental organizations (NGOS) also look to the minds and bodies of young women, for whom education comes to promise enormous economic and demographic rewards.[15] Young women are a good investment, they can be trusted with microcredit, they are the privileged subjects of social change. But the terms of these great expectations on the part of governments are that young women must do without more autonomous feminist politics. What is consistent is the displacement of feminism as a political movement. It is this displacement that is reflected in Judith Butler's sorrowful account of Antigone's life after death. Her shadowy, lonely existence suggests a modality of feminist effectivity as spectral; she has to be cast out, indeed entombed, for social organization to once again become intelligible.

Unpopular Feminism

The media have become the key site for defining codes of sexual conduct. They cast judgment and establish the rules of play. Across these many channels of communication, feminism is routinely disparaged. Why is feminism so hated? Why do young women recoil in horror at the very idea of the feminist? To count as a girl today appears to require this kind of ritualistic denunciation, which in turn suggests that one strategy in the disempowering of feminism includes it being historicized and generationalized and thus easily rendered out of date. It would be far too simplistic to trace a pattern in media from popular feminism (or "prime-time feminism," including that found in such TV programs as *LA Law*) in the early 1990s to niche feminism (BBC Radio 4's *Woman's Hour* and the Women's Page of the *Guardian* newspaper) in the mid-1990s and then to overtly unpopular feminism (in the new century), as though these charted a chronological "great moving right show," as Stuart Hall once put it in another context.[16] We would need a more developed conceptual schema to account for the simultaneous feminization of popular media with this accumulation of ambivalent, fearful responses. We would certainly need to signal the full enfranchisement of women in the West, of all ages, as audiences, active consumers of media and the many products they promote, and, by virtue of education, earning power and consumer identity a sizable block of target market. We would also need to be able to theorize female achievement predicated not on feminism but on "female individualism," on success that seems to be based on the invitation to young women by various governments that they might now consider themselves free to compete in education and work as privileged subjects of the "new meritocracy." Is this, then, the New Deal for New Labour's "modern" young women: female individualization and the new meritocracy at the expense of feminist politics?

There are various sites within popular culture where this work of undoing feminism with some subtlety becomes visible.[17] An advertisement showing the model Eva Herzigova looking down admiringly at her substantial cleavage enhanced by the lacy pyrotechnics of the Wonderbra was throughout the mid-1990s positioned in major high-street locations in the United Kingdom on full-size billboards. The composition of the image had such a textbook "sexist ad" dimension that one could be forgiven for supposing some ironic familiarity both with cultural studies and with feminist critiques of advertising.[18] It was, in a sense, taking feminism into account by showing it to be a thing of the past, by provocatively "enacting sexism" while at the same time playing with those debates in film theory about women as the object of the gaze and even with female desire.[19] The picture is in noirish black and white and refers explicitly through its captions (from "Hello Boys" to "Or

Are You Just Pleased to See Me?") to Hollywood and the famous lines of the actress Mae West. Here is an advertisement that plays back to its viewers well-known aspects of feminist media studies, film theory, and semiotics. Indeed, it almost offers (albeit crudely) the viewer or passing driver Laura Mulvey's theory of women as objects of the gaze projected as cityscape within the frame of the billboard. Also mobilized in this ad is the familiarity of the term *political correctness*, the efficacy of which resides in its warranting and unleashing such energetic reactions against the seemingly tyrannical regime of feminist puritanism. Everyone, and especially young people, can give a sigh of relief. Thank goodness, the ad seems to suggest, it is permissible, once again, to enjoy looking at the bodies of beautiful women. At the same time, the advertisement also hopes to provoke feminist condemnation as a means of generating publicity. Thus, generational differences are also produced; the younger female viewer, along with her male counterparts, educated in irony and visually literate, is not made angry by such a repertoire. She appreciates its layers of meaning; she "gets the joke."

When in a TV advertisement (1998–99) another supermodel, Claudia Schiffer, takes off her clothes as she descends a flight of stairs in a luxury mansion on her way out of the door toward her new Citroën car, a similar rhetoric is at work. This ad appears to suggest that, yes, this is a self-consciously "sexist ad." Feminist critiques of it are deliberately evoked. Feminism is "taken into account" but only to be shown to be no longer necessary. Why? Because it now seems that there is no exploitation here; there is nothing remotely naive about this striptease. She seems to be doing it out of choice and for her own enjoyment. The ad works on the basis of its audience knowing Claudia to be one of the world's most famous and highly paid supermodels. Once again the shadow of disapproval is evoked (the striptease as a site of female exploitation) only instantly to be dismissed as belonging to the past, to a time when feminists used to object to such imagery. To make such an objection nowadays would run the risk of ridicule. Objection is preempted with irony. In each of these cases, a specter of feminism is invoked so that it might be undone. For male viewers, tradition is restored, or, as Beck puts it, there is "constructed certitude," while for the girls what is proposed is a movement beyond feminism to a more comfortable zone where women are now free to choose for themselves.[20]

Feminism Undone?

If we turn attention to some of the participatory dynamics in leisure and everyday life that see young women endorse (or else refuse to condemn) the ironic normalization of pornography, where they indicate their approval of and desire to be "pinup girls" for the centerfolds of the soft-porn "lad mags," where it is not at all unusual to pass young women in the street wearing T-shirts bearing phrases such as "Porn Queen" or "Pay to Touch" across the breasts, and where, in the United Kingdom at least, young women quite happily attend lap-dancing clubs (perhaps as a test of their sophistication and "cool"), we are witness to a hyperculture of commercial sexuality, one aspect of which is the repudiation of a feminism invoked only to be summarily dismissed.[21] As a mark of a postfeminist identity, young women journalists refuse to condemn the enormous growth of lap-dancing clubs. They know of the existence of the feminist critiques and debates (or at least this is my claim) through their education; as Shelley Budgeon has described the girls in her study, they are gender aware.[22] Thus, the new female subject is, despite her freedom, called upon to be silent, to withhold critique in order to count as a modern, sophisticated girl. Indeed, this withholding of critique is a condition of her freedom. There is quietude and complicity in the manners of generationally specific notions of cool and, more precisely, an uncritical relation to dominant, commercially produced, sexual representations that actively invoke hostility to assumed feminist positions from the past in order to endorse a new regime of sexual meanings based on female consent, equality, participation, and pleasure, free of politics.[23]

Female Individualization

By using the term *female individualization* I am explicitly drawing on the concept of individualization that is discussed at length by sociologists, including Anthony Giddens, Ulrich Beck, Elisabeth Beck-Gernsheim, as well as Zygmunt Bauman.[24] This work is to be distinguished from the more directly Foucauldian version found in the work of Nikolas Rose.[25] Although there is some shared ground between these authors, insofar as they all reflect on the expectations that individuals now avidly "self-monitor" and that there appears to be greater capacity on the part of individuals to plan "a life of one's own," there are also divergences. Beck and Giddens are less concerned with the effectivity of power in this new friendly guise as "personal adviser" and instead emphasize the enlargement of freedom and choice, while in contrast Rose sees these modes of self-government as marking out "the shaping of being" and thus the "inculcation of a form of life." Bauman bewails the sheer unviability of naked individualization as the resources of sociality (and welfare) are stripped away, leaving the individual to self-blame when success eludes him or her. (It is also possible to draw a political line between these authors, with Bauman and Rose to the left and Giddens and Beck "beyond left and right.")[26] My emphasis here is on the work of Giddens and Beck, for the very reason that it appears to speak directly to the postfeminist generation. In their writing, there are only distant echoes (if that) of the feminist struggles that were required to produce the newfound freedoms of young women in the West. There is little trace of the battles fought, of the power struggles embarked upon, or of the enduring inequities that still mark out the relations between men and women. All of this is airbrushed out of existence on the basis that, as they claim, "emancipatory politics" has given way instead to life politics (or, in Beck's terms, the subpolitics of single-interest groups). Both of these authors provide a sociological account of the dynamics of social change understood as "reflexive modernization." The earlier period of modernization ("first modernity") created a welfare state and a set of institutions (e.g., education) that allowed people in the "second modernity" to become more independent and able, for example, to earn their own livings. Young women are as a result now "disembedded" from communities where gender roles were fixed. And, as the old structures of social class fade away and lose their grip in the context of "late" or second modernity, individuals are increasingly called upon to invent their own structures. They must do this internally and individualistically, so that self-monitoring practices (the diary, the life plan, the career pathway) replace reliance on set ways and structured pathways. Self-help guides, personal advisers, lifestyle coaches and gurus, and all sorts of self-improvement TV programs provide the cultural means by which individualization operates as a social process. As the overwhelming force of structure fades, so also, it is claimed, does the capacity for agency increase.

Individuals must now choose the kind of life they want to live. Girls must have a life plan. They must become more reflexive in regard to every aspect of their lives, from making the right choice in marriage to taking responsibility for their own working lives and not being dependent on a job for life or on the stable and reliable operations of a large-scale bureaucracy, which in the past would have allocated its employees specific, and possibly unchanging, roles. Beck and Giddens each place a different inflection on their accounts of reflexive modernization, and these arguments appear to fit very directly with the kinds of scenarios and dilemmas facing the young women characters in the narratives of contemporary popular culture (especially so-called chick lit). There is also a real evasion in this writing of the ongoing existence of deep and pernicious gender inequities (most manifest for older women of all social backgrounds but also for young black or Asian women and also for young working-class women). Beck and Giddens are quite inattentive to the regulative dimensions of the popular discourses of personal choice and self-improvement. Choice is surely, within lifestyle culture, a modality of constraint. The individual is compelled to be the kind of subject who can make the right choices. By these means, new lines and demarcations are drawn between those subjects who are judged responsive to the regime of personal responsibility and those who fail miserably. Neither Giddens nor Beck mount a substantial critique of these power relations, which work so effectively at the level of embodiment. They have no grasp that these are productive of new realms of injury and injustice.

Bridget Jones

The film *Bridget Jones's Diary* (an international box office success) draws together so many of these sociological themes it could almost have been scripted by Anthony Giddens himself. Aged thirty, living and working in London, Bridget (played by Renée Zellweger) is a free agent, single and childless and able to enjoy herself in pubs, bars, and restaurants. She is the product of modernity in that she has benefited from those institutions (education) that have loosened the ties of tradition and community for women, making it possible for them to be "disembedded" and to relocate to the city to earn an independent living without shame or danger. However, this also gives rise to new anxieties. There is the fear of loneliness for example, the stigma of remaining single, and the risks and uncertainties of not finding the right partner to be a father to children as well as a husband. In the film, the opening sequence shows Bridget in her pajamas worrying about being alone and on the shelf. The soundtrack is "All by Myself" by Jamie O'Neal, and the audience laughs along with her in this moment of self-doubt. We

In *Bridget Jones's Diary*, Bridget (Renee Zellweger) embodies an enthusiastic embrace of her own sexual commodification. Here her costume suggests a knowing, even ironic, consent to a contemporary culture of commercial sexuality.

immediately know that what she is thinking is, "What will it be like if I never find the right man, if I never get married?" Bridget portrays the whole spectrum of attributes associated with the self-monitoring subject: she confides in her friends; she keeps a diary; she endlessly reflects on her fluctuating weight, noting her calorie intake; she plans, plots, and has projects. She is also deeply uncertain as to what the future holds for her. Despite the choices she has, there are also any number of risks, of which she is regularly reminded, the risk that she might let the right man slip from under her nose (hence she must always be on the lookout), the risk that not catching a man at the right time might mean she misses the chance of having children (her biological clock is ticking); there is also the risk that, partnerless, she will be isolated, marginalized from the world of happy couples. Now there is only the self to blame if the right partner is not found.

With the burden of self-management so apparent, Bridget fantasizes about very traditional forms of happiness and fulfilment. After a flirtatious encounter with her boss (played by Hugh Grant), she imagines herself in a white wedding dress surrounded by bridesmaids, and the audience laughs loudly because they, like Bridget, know that this is not how young women these days are meant to think. Feminism has intervened to constrain these kinds of conventional desires. It is, then, a relief to escape this censorious politics and freely enjoy that which has been disapproved of. Thus, feminism is only invoked in order to be relegated to the past. But this is not simply a return to the past; there are, of course, quite dramatic differences between the various female characters of current popular culture from Bridget Jones to the "girls" in *Sex and the City* and to Ally McBeal, and those found in girls' and women's magazines from a prefeminist era. The new young women are confident enough to declare their anxieties about possible failure in regard to finding a husband, they avoid any aggressive or overtly traditional men, and they brazenly enjoy their sexuality without fear of the sexual double standard. In addition, they are more than capable of earning their own living, and the degree of suffering or shame they anticipate in the absence of finding a husband is countered by sexual self-confidence. Being without a husband does not mean they will go without men.

With such light entertainment as this, suffused with irony and dedicated to reinventing highly successful women's genres of film and TV, an argument about feminism being so repudiated might seem heavy-handed. These are hardly rabid antifeminist tracts. But relations of power are indeed made and remade within texts of enjoyment and rituals of relaxation and abandonment. These young women's genres are vital to the construction of a new "gender regime" based on the double entanglement that I have described. They endorse wholeheartedly what Nicholas Rose calls "this ethic of freedom," and young women have come to the fore as the preeminent subjects of this new ethic. These popular texts normalize postfeminist gender anxieties so as to re-regulate young women by means of the language of personal choice. But even "well-regulated liberty" can backfire (the source of comic effect), and this in turn gives rise to demarcated pathologies (leaving it too late to have a baby, failing to find a good catch, etc.) that carefully define the parameters of what constitutes livable lives for young women without the occasion of reinvented feminism.

Notes

This essay was originally published as "Post-feminism and Popular Culture" in *Feminist Media Studies*.

1. Faludi, *Backlash*.
2. "Bridget Jones's Diary" appeared first as a weekly column in the *Independent* in 1996; its author, Helen Fielding, then published the diaries in book form. The film *Bridget Jones's Diary*, directed by Sharon McGuire, opened in 2001. The sequel, *Bridget Jones: The Edge of Reason*, directed by Beeban Kidron, opened in November 2004.
3. Butler, Laclau, and Žižek, *Contingency, Hegemony, and Universality*, 14.
4. Butler, *Antigone's Claim*.
5. McRobbie, "Mothers and Fathers, Who Needs Them?"

6. Spivak, *A Critique of Postcolonial Reason*; Trinh, *Women Native Other*; Mohanty, "Under Western Eyes"; Butler, *Gender Trouble*; Haraway, *Simians, Cyborgs, and Women*.

7. Butler, *Gender Trouble*; *Bodies That Matter*.

8. Brunsdon, "Pedagogies of the Feminine."

9. Stuart, "Feminism."

10. For accounts of girls' achievement in education, see Arnot, David, and Weiner, *Closing the Gender Gap*; and Harris, *Future Girl*.

11. Brunsdon, *Screen Tastes*; McRobbie, *In the Culture Society*.

12. Brown "The Impossibility of Women's Studies."

13. Butler, "Contingent Foundations"; McRobbie, *Postmodernism and Popular Culture*.

14. McRobbie, "Feminism v. the TV Blondes." The *Daily Mail* has the highest volume of female readers of all daily newspapers in the United Kingdom. Its most frequent efforts in regard to promoting a postfeminist sensibility involve commissioning well-known former feminists to recant and blame feminism for contemporary ills among women. For example, the issue of 23 August 2003 featured Fay Weldon in "Look What We've Done." A caption reads, "For years feminists campaigned for sexual liberation. But here, one of their leaders admits all they have created is a new generation of women for whom sex is utterly joyless and hollow."

15. Spivak, *A Critique of Postcolonial Reason*.

16. Hall, *The Hard Road to Renewal*.

17. Brunsdon, "Feminism, Postfeminism."

18. Williamson, *Decoding Advertisements*.

19. Mulvey, "Visual Pleasure and Narrative Cinema"; de Lauretis, *Technologies of Gender*.

20. Beck, *Risk Society*.

21. See Gill, "From Sexual Objectification to Sexual Subjectification."

22. Budgeon, "Emergent Feminist Identities."

23. By the normalization of porn, or "ironic pornography," I am referring to the new popular mainstreaming of what in the past would have been soft-core pornography out of reach of the young on the "top shelf." In a post-AIDS era, with sexual frankness an imperative for prevention, the commercial British youth media now produce vast quantities of explicit sexual material for the teenage audience; in recent years, and as a strategy for being ahead of the competition, this has been incorporated into the language of "cool." With irony as a trademark of knowingness, sexual cool entails "being up for it" without revealing any misgivings, never mind criticism, on the basis of the distance entailed in the ironic experience.

24. Giddens, *Modernity and Self-Identity*; Beck and Beck-Gernsheim, *Individualisation*; Bauman, *Liquid Modernity*; Bauman, *The Individualised Society*.

25. Rose, *Powers of Freedom*.

26. Giddens, *The Third Way*. Anthony Giddens is the architect of the Third Way politics that was embraced by New Labour in its first term of office, and this writing drew on an earlier work, *Beyond Left and Right*. Likewise, Ulrich Beck was connected with the Neue Mitte in Germany, though the German "Third Way" had rather less success than its British counterpart.

Sarah Projansky

2 Mass Magazine Cover Girls

SOME REFLECTIONS ON POSTFEMINIST GIRLS AND
POSTFEMINISM'S DAUGHTERS

Commodified pro-girl rhetoric has taken the feminist out of feminism.
—ELLEN RIORDAN

Becoming aware of what it is to be a young woman today almost inevitably
means being touched by elements of feminist discourse.
—ANGELA MCROBBIE

In American popular culture throughout the twentieth century, girls appeared as important figures, and at particular historical moments (prior to the emergence of postfeminism in early 1980s popular culture) they were even the topic
of temporarily incessant public discussion (e.g., white slavery
anxiety in the 1910s, Shirley Temple in the 1930s, sexual delinquency in the 1950s, and sexual exhibitionism in the 1970s).[1]
Catherine Driscoll, for example, argues, that "in the first half
of the twentieth century girls were repeatedly, and even *obsessively*, associated with the rise of mass culture and accompanying cultural changes."[2] In my review of *Time* magazine since its
initial publication in 1923, I found that girls have appeared on
the cover almost every year after 1945 and even periodically be-

fore that. As a supposedly "national" newsmagazine aimed at a nondifferentiated audience (which therefore means aimed at white, heterosexual, middle-class men), for girls to appear on the cover suggests that they (or the social issues they represent) hold the status of "serious" news important to the population at large.

Specifically, between 1945 and 1979 girls appeared on the cover of *Time* in three loosely defined categories. First, they appeared in relation to film, media, and entertainment as stars (e.g., Shirley Temple [1/8/45], Elizabeth Taylor [8/22/49], Diane Lane [8/13/79], and Nadia Comaneci [8/2/76]) and as unnamed figures representative of rock and roll (5/21/65) and sports (6/26/78). Second, they appeared in relation to political and social issues, for example, of school reform (2/20/50, 10/19/53, 9/14/59, 11/14/77), "today's teenagers" (1/29/65), antiwar protest (5/18/70), busing (11/15/71), and feminism (11/28/77). They also appeared as political daughters (5/30/55, 7/28/75, 7/26/76, 2/7/77) and political symbols (e.g., in Lyndon Johnson's infamous political ad on nuclear destruction [9/25/64]). Third, they appeared (generally in the context of a two-parent, two-child [girl-boy] family) as symbols of particular kinds of family citizenship: a peaceful Christmas (12/27/48), suburban life (3/15/71), "What It Means to Be Jewish" (4/10/72), and middle-class African Americans (6/17/74).

Despite this substantial attention, American popular culture has produced a seemingly ever increasing focus on girls since the late 1980s, arguably marking the present and recent past as a particularly intense and sustained moment of cultural obsession with them. For example, looking to *Time* and *Newsweek*, girls have been featured on the covers of each of these magazines multiple times a year almost every year since 1983, appearing as many as five times on *Time* in 1993 and on *Newsweek* in 2002. Looking at television in particular, Sarah Banet-Weiser points to the early and mid-1990s as a significant moment when "the rhetoric of girl power . . . found currency in almost every realm of . . . children's popular culture." Citing the Spice Girls, Riot Grrrls, T-shirts declaring "Girls Kick Ass!" and "Girls Rule!" Nike's "Play Like a Girl" advertising campaign, the 1999 Women's World Cup Soccer tournament, the creation of the Women's National Basketball Association (wnba), and the publication of best-selling books such as Mary Pipher's *Reviving Ophelia: Saving the Selves of Adolescent Girls* (1994) and Rosalind Wiseman's *Queen Bees and Wannabes: Helping Your Daughter Survive Cliques, Gossips, Boyfriends, and Other Realities of Adoles-*

cence (2002), Banet-Weiser sets up the context in which Nickelodeon's ground-breaking series *Clarissa Explains It All* (1991–94) emerged and "initiated a new trend in [television] programming that actively rejected the conventional industry wisdom that children's shows with girl leads could not be successful."[3] Janie Victoria Ward and Beth Cooper Benjamin also point to the early 1990s as a key moment in the cultural representation of girls. They argue that at this time both scholarly and popular discourses, particularly in the areas of psychology and education, identified a "crisis" around girls in texts such as *Reviving Ophelia* and a 1992 report by the American Association of University Women (AAUW) titled *How Schools Shortchange Girls*.[4] Focusing particularly on girls and sports in the post-cold-war 1990s, C. L. Cole analyzes the televisual flow between an episode of *Buffy the Vampire Slayer* and a McDonald's advertisement depicting sponsorship of "the first girls' All American High School (AAHS) Basketball Game" through a little girl who "tosses her doll aside" to follow in the footsteps of her older sister's basketball prowess. For Cole, this construction of the sports girls is specific to the post-cold-war context of the early to mid-1990s. She writes: "Both figures of revolution—the new extreme sport figure, Buffy, and the girl basketball player—are inextricably linked to narratives of progress: Title IX, girl power, and American democracy. The powerful girl figure is an American post-cold war icon."[5]

In thinking about representations of girls in American popular culture, then, I would argue that the current moment—defined as approximately 1990 to the present—draws on a long-standing tradition of focusing cultural attention on girls as problems, as victims of social ills, as symbols of ideal citizenship, and as all-around fascinating figures. But it also intensifies and sustains these representations to the point where—as the scholars I have discussed and my review of *Time* and *Newsweek* covers suggest—something new is happening.

Discourses of Girls and Postfeminism

Many scholars place this "newness"—as Meenakshi Gigi Durham puts it, these "new girl icons," "new 'kick-ass' girl heroines," and "neogirlhood"—either explicitly or implicitly in the context of postfeminism.[6] Most generally and obviously, the current proliferation of discourse about girls literally coincides chronologically with the proliferation of discourse about postfeminism, with the heightened cultural profile of girls perhaps lagging behind postfeminism by only five or ten years. While this historical congruence is important to recognize in and of itself, scholars have also looked at the ways girl discourses activate, draw on, and contribute to popular discourse about feminism and postfeminism. Read together, three scholars in particular lay out this coconstitutive dynamic. On the one hand, in "Good Girls, Bad Girls: Anglocentrism and Diversity in the Constitution of Contemporary Girlhood," Christine Griffin argues that in the 1990s "girl power . . . constituted the world as inherently 'postfeminist.'"[7] Here girl power depends on postfeminism for its existence. On the other hand, addressing the representation of adult women as opposed to girls, Yvonne Tasker and Diane Negra argue that "in postfeminist representational culture, age is only acknowledged to the extent that its effects can be erased by cosmetic surgery. The 'girling' of femininity more generally—the competent professional adult woman who is made safe by being represented as fundamentally still a girl—is itself characteristic of postfeminist representations."[8] Here postfeminism depends on girlness, is defined by it in fact. Thus, together Griffin and Tasker and Negra illustrate how discourses of postfeminism and girlness produce these terms in such a way that they depend on each other for their very definitions and existence.

Many other scholars have looked at more specific aspects of the contemporary link between postfeminist and girl discourses. For example, Angela McRobbie argues that the aspect of postfeminism that defines feminism as "out of date" depends on girlness and youth. She writes: "To count as a girl today appears to require [a] ritualistic denunciation [of feminism], which in turn suggests that one strategy in the disempowering of feminism includes it being historicised and generationalised and thus easily rendered out of date. . . . Thus the new female subject is, despite her freedom, called upon to be silent, to withhold [a potential feminist] critique, [in order] to count as a modern sophisticated girl."[9] Elsewhere McRobbie argues that magazines for girls have "shifted decisively away from . . . [an earlier] docile sensibility, replacing it instead with a much more assertive and 'fun-seeking' female subjectivity. . . . The magazines even seemed to have absorbed a sprinkling of feminist ideas, especially on the problem pages. At this point then there is a loosening up of the opposition between feminism and femininity," another way in which postfeminism might be defined.[10] Looking at film, Mary Celeste Kearney argues that "the representation of female adolescence in U.S. cinema changed dramatically during the last decade of the twentieth century," such that many contemporary films about girls "incorporate contemporary feminist themes" such as "confidence, assertiveness, and self-respect apart from boys and through same-sex relationships."[11] When, drawing on McRobbie, Kearney argues that these changes occurred because "of the popularization of feminist ideas," she implies that these films about girls offer a specifically postfeminist version of feminism.[12] Looking at television more than film and what Kearney would no doubt define as more problematic texts, Rachel Moseley argues that "teen witch texts" (e.g., *Sabrina the Teenage Witch* or *Charmed*) articulate postfeminism through the representation of sparkle (literalized through costume, soundtracks using a xylophone or celesta, and special effects of "magical sparkling dust in the air") and glamour.[13] In these texts, glamour comes to mean "the conjunction of ideal femininities and (sexual) power," a concise potential definition of postfeminism as well.[14] Also looking at television, Banet-Weiser, drawing on Bonnie Dow's arguments, contends that, "the cultural dynamics that produced girl power within the constant flux of media representations of gender in the 1990s not only produced a hip new slogan, but were also part of a more general shift toward mainstreaming feminism into popular and dominant culture."[15] Finally, emphasizing the issue of commodification, Durham suggests that following early 1990s feminist scholarship, which defined "girls' adolescence as a time of crisis, . . . popular culture recognized the potential of a new girl audience and created for it the new girl hero."[16] Implicitly the "new girl hero" could function as a solution to the presumed crisis of girls' adolescence but still function as a commodified figure marketed to the commodified girl audience and in turn marketed to advertisers.

What I am suggesting, then, is that the work of these (and other) scholars suggests that, whether it is in the form of out-of-date feminism, the linking of feminism and femininity, popularized feminism, glamour, mainstreamed feminism, or the commodified girl hero, since the 1990s postfeminist discourse has produced the conditions for the emergence of girl discourse and *girl discourse contributes to and sustains postfeminism.*[17] Furthermore, this exchange takes place across many areas of popular culture, including magazines, film, television, advertising, T-shirts, sports, popular psychology and education, and music.

Why did the discourses of postfeminism and the heightened cultural profile of girls emerge and intensify almost simultaneously and why have they come to depend on each other? I think there are many answers to these questions, of which I would like to mention five. First, both postfeminism and girlness can be seen as part of a focus on youthful femininity in contemporary popular culture. Thus, examining these two sets of discourses together, as well as paying attention to their areas of overlap, can help produce a larger picture of the contemporary definition of femininity more generally. Second, one could read the cultural obsession with girlhood as a response to postfeminism, a kind of "backlash" against the particular 1980s postfeminist woman who is unhappy with how career has displaced family or who has returned to a rather boring neotraditionalism. Thus, by displacing adult women and focusing on girls, by defining as irrelevant many aspects of postfeminism, this backlash does not have to reject postfeminism entirely. From this perspective, postfeminist girls are too young to have discovered that they "can't have it all" and therefore are much more fun.

Following Tasker and Negra, a third explanation could be that girlness — particularly adolescent girlness — epitomizes postfeminism. If the postfeminist woman is always in process, always using the freedom and equality handed to her by feminism in pursuit of having it all (including discovering her sexuality) but never quite managing to reach full adulthood, to fully have it all, one could say that the postfeminist woman is quintessentially adolescent (e.g., as Driscoll defines adolescence as always in process) no matter what her age.[18] It would be in this context that popular phrases and slogans such as "girls rule," "girls kick ass," "girlie," "girlfriends," "you go girl," and the ubiquitous "girl power" are marketed and applied to grown women as easily as to young girls and teens. A fourth explanation, which follows from the previous two readings, could be that turning toward girls is a way to keep postfeminism fresh in the context of corporate commodity culture. From this perspective, whether the obsession with girls marginalizes or privileges grown women is irrelevant as long as postfeminism continues to sell — ideally to both women and girls.

Finally, emphasizing the lag of five to ten years between the critical mass of postfeminist discourse in American popular culture of the early to mid-1980s and the critical mass of girl discourse in the late 1980s to early 1990s, I would argue that contemporary representations can be understood to cast girls as the daughters of postfeminism and postfeminist women, produced by and raised in a postfeminist milieu. From this perspective, these girls are the products of postfeminism, and any anxieties about or celebrations of them are implicitly also anxieties about and celebrations of postfeminism. In other words, I am suggesting that many of the ways in which contemporary popular culture represents girls can be understood to be working through questions about the effects of postfeminism—on mothers, daughters, and the gendered organization of the present and future society—just as representations of postfeminist women can be understood to be working through questions about the effects of feminism.

Accessing the Contemporary Field of Girlhood

Who are these discursive postfeminist daughters? How are they defined? How similar or different are they from postfeminist women? How might they solidify and/or revise the meanings of postfeminism as the twenty-first century progresses? Recent scholarship at the intersection of cultural and girls studies has begun to describe popular culture representations of girls across a variety of media. In this essay, I offer a modest contribution to this discussion by focusing on *Time* and *Newsweek* magazine cover representations of girls since 1990, particularly in relation to discourses of postfeminism.

I should be clear that throughout this essay when I use the terms *girl*, *girlhood*, and *girlness* I am referring to the discursive construction of these concepts in popular culture. This is not a study of actual girls but of how girls are figured in one particular area of popular culture: mass magazine covers. Certainly, there are complex relationships to be drawn between these representations and both the actual girls who stand as models for those representations (particularly when those models represent "themselves," as in the examples of the magazine covers that feature dead and kidnapped girls or girl sports stars, both of which I discuss later in this essay) and the actual girls who might encounter these magazine covers in their daily lives. Just as surely, those relationships are not "one-to-one"; thus, in no way do I mean to suggest that the girl discourses I discuss in this essay stand in for actual girls. In other words, this essay explores how contemporary U.S. popular culture conceives of girls and what the implications are for how this discourse produces an understanding of what girlhood and girlness mean, but it is not about how actual girls interact with those representations.[19]

I chose *Time* and *Newsweek* covers for this study of discursive girls for a number of reasons. First, magazine covers are an area of popular culture to which girls studies scholars often refer, but—other than some work on girls' magazines emphasizing primarily internal text and advertising—to my knowledge they have not yet been examined in detail.[20] Second, because *Time* and *Newsweek* are marketed as newsmagazines for the general reading public, theoretically girls (who are neither central to mainstream news nor definitive of the general reading public) may be less likely to appear on their covers than on, for example, the covers of *People*, *Seventeen*, or *Good Housekeeping* (to mention just a few magazines with more specific niche markets). Thus, arguably, when girls *do* appear on *Time* and *Newsweek* covers the topic they represent may take on resonance or significance beyond just another weekly news story. Since *Time* and *Newsweek* are not marketed to women specifically or defined by popular or scholarly critics as key postfeminist texts, when intersecting discourses of postfeminism and girlhood do make it onto their covers that occurrence arguably marks a substantial cultural pervasiveness of postfeminist girls.

Admittedly, the covers of two magazines form a rather limited (or—more charitably—focused) area of study.[21] In this essay, I do not analyze the articles associated with the covers themselves, I do not analyze the relationship between advertising and text within the pages of the magazines, and, although I do refer to some well-known popular culture examples beyond the magazines, I do not provide a thorough analysis of the wider field of cultural representations of girls. Instead, I focus on the *Time* and *Newsweek* covers in order to try to capture fleeting images, those one might see while standing in line at the grocery store, buying gum at a magazine stand, or passing by the magazine section in one's local bookstore on the way to some other part of the store. Who are the girls who look out at us in these moments? What do these "cover girls" represent? If the cover representations of these girls are all we know about these particular issues of *Time* and *Newsweek*, what version of girlhood is being offered to us as part of the cultural landscape?

The Contemporary Field of Girlhood
on *Time* and *Newsweek* Covers

Much like postfeminist discourses, *Time* and *Newsweek* cover girls can be organized into two large and contradictory but also intersecting categories. Specifically, girls in contemporary American popular culture tend to be either what Anita Harris calls, in *Future Girl: Young Women in the Twenty-first Century*, "at-risk" or "can-do." Either they are endangered by the world around them (including the proliferation of choices in part provided by feminism

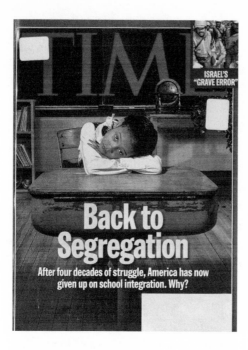

On mass market magazine covers the figure of the vulnerable girl frequently stands in for complex social issues, in this case the persistence of racial inequities in America. (*Time* 29 April 1996.)

and postfeminism) and their personal choices within this context or they are able to take control of this new and rapidly changing environment and eschew unhealthy desires and impulses in order to become idealized citizen subjects. The can-do girl is the "future girl" of Harris's book title, the "kind of young woman celebrated for her 'desire, determination and confidence' to take charge of her life, seize chances, and achieve her goals."[22] Importantly, however, many girls in popular culture are simultaneously at-risk *and* can-do. In other words, some girl figures emerge through both sets of discourses, setting up an uneasiness, ambiguousness, and ambivalence around girlhood, much like the ambivalence many scholars have identified in postfeminist discourses. In what follows, I develop a discussion of these three sets of girls — at-risk, can-do, and at-risk/can-do — through an analysis of *Time* and *Newsweek* covers since 1990 while also drawing on a few examples from the larger popular culture context.

AT-RISK GIRLS

Popular representations often present girls as symbols for various non-gender-specific social ills. Here the girls could presumably be at-risk themselves, but they primarily stand in for risks to society as a whole. In chronological order, since 1990 *Time* and *Newsweek* have featured girls on their covers in order to foster worry about life for the Kurds after the American invasion of Iraq (N 4/15/91), the threat of lead to children (N 7/15/91), children growing up scared (N 1/10/94), the failure of school integration (T 4/29/96), the question of "who speaks for kids" in a "more perilous . . . America" (T 6/3/96), children's learning disabilities (N 10/27/97), the New China (N 6/29/98), testing in schools (N 9/6/99), divorce (T 9/25/00), the decrease in teachers available to teach children (N 10/2/00), the controversy over the term *God* in the Pledge of Allegiance (N 7/8/02), depression (N 10/7/02), the increase in adult-onset diabetes (T 12/8/03), the aftermath of the 2004 tsunami (N 1/10/05), and babies and autism (N 2/28/05).

In each of these examples, the girls are anonymous.[23] They do not appear as characters in the stories inside the magazine. In fact, many of the articles begin with stories about *boys* who are at risk for these various issues. Thus, the cover girls set up anxiety and work to encourage the consumer to buy the magazine, but the magazine's specific concern for girls stops there. While theoretically images of boys (and in some cases adults) might work equally well to illustrate these social concerns (and they do sometimes appear), more often girls symbolize the vulnerability and difficulties associated with each of these issues. In the examples I have listed, even when girls appear with boys (as on the growing up scared, New China, and Pledge of Allegiance covers), the structures of the covers foreground the girls in some way. In short, the cover girls offer a gendered representation of generally nongendered issues. Their youthful femininity marks a heightened vulnerability, but that vulnerability is dissociated from girlhood and stands in for something else.

I call this type of cover the "girl as X" representation. Many scholars have identified the girl as X phenomenon in other contexts. For example, Lauren Berlant argues that "it is in [the little girl's] name as future citizen that state and federal governments have long policed morality around sex and other transgressive representations."[24] She argues further, "We should understand that these disturbing figures [of little girls] are fetishes, effigies that condense, displace, and stand in for arguments about who 'the people' are."[25] McRobbie makes a similar argument in *Feminism and Youth Culture*. She writes, "Young women in Britain today have replaced youth as a metaphor for social change. They have become a touchstone, and sometimes a problem for the whole society."[26] And in the introduction to *Girls: Feminine Adolescence in Popular Culture and Cultural Theory*, Driscoll describes her book as "a map of how girls function as a set of statements about late modern culture."[27] Working specifically on film, in her essay on the representation of girls' anger in *Freeway* (1996), Kimberley Roberts argues that "even though [*Freeway*] is not exclusively targeted at teenage girls as the ideal audience, it does use the teenage girl as a means to convey certain messages about power, authority, and the status of contemporary feminism."[28] Thus, in this instance the film uses girls as figures to deliver a critique of contemporary gender relations but not in relation to youth per se.[29]

I do not want to argue that reading representations of girls as stand-ins for "other" social issues is problematic in and of itself. Indeed, the use of stand-ins, or figures, that indexically take the discursive space of a topic that is not by any logical means related to it—and thus merely has, at best, associational relations to the figure—is a frequently used representational process in popular culture. And it is of the utmost importance to note, as all these authors do, that girls in late-twentieth-century popular culture, *in particular*, are central to this representational process. While each of these authors also addresses the specific construction of girlhood in the texts examined, I am somewhat uncomfortable with this common critical argument because it displaces questions about how girlness itself is defined in these contexts. In other words, while I argue that since 1990 girls have functioned as stand-ins for various topics on *Time* and *Newsweek* covers, this observation says little about how girlhood is defined in this context.

To get beyond describing how the girl as X phenomenon on *Time* and *Newsweek* covers uses girlish vulnerability to focus attention elsewhere (on boys, the threat of lead, anxieties about school integration, etc.), I ask what this girlish vulnerability looks like. Or, to put it another way, what version of girlness figures as the most vulnerable? Based on these *Time* and *Newsweek* covers, the most vulnerable girl is young and white, with blue, green, or hazel eyes and blond (or occasionally light brown) hair.[30] She has an impassive face and stares directly into the camera. Her face is central to the frame, usually featured in close-up. Exceptions to this description are predictable. For issues outside the United States (the Kurds, New China, the tsunami), the girl is racialized, matching the expected racial category for the location under discussion. For issues within the United States, only two covers feature girls who clearly are of color, and both appear to be African American: the *Time* cover about school integration features an African American girl, while the *Newsweek* cover about the Pledge of Allegiance features an African American girl, a blond white girl, and an Asian American boy.[31] The only girls who appear to be above the age of twelve are on the covers about depression, growing up scared, and educational testing. The only girls who are looking away from the camera are on the covers about the Pledge of Allegiance (all three children are looking up, as though at a flag), the tsunami (the girl is looking down), learning disabilities (the girl is looking at a multicolored cube she holds in her hand), and divorce (the girl is looking directly ahead, slightly to the left of the frame). Even the eight-month-old baby (named as Lauren Lanning) on the cover about babies and autism looks directly into the camera.

The predominant youthfulness of the cover girl makes her vulnerability uncontested. She is young enough that she could not possibly be at fault for the woes she symbolizes. She is thus a passive figure in need of protection. While she most often gazes directly at the camera (and thus the viewer), in the context of her innocent youthfulness that gaze seems to challenge the viewer to take her predicament seriously rather than suggesting any kind of agency of her own to address the problem at hand. The fact that she appears most often in close-up fixes her in a passive position, disembodied and reduced to her figurative face. Additionally, her whiteness makes her generic in the context of a popular culture, in which whiteness remains dominant and unspoken.[32] When she is not white, she is no longer generic and represents international issues (which are specifically "there" not "here") or an issue specifically about race in the United States such as school integration. The only cover to attempt any kind of "multicultural" representation of American youth is the one about the Pledge of Allegiance. On this cover, however, the two children of color flank the white girl, who stands in the center of the frame.

Overall, then, on *Time* and *Newsweek* covers the youth, disembodiment, and whiteness of the girl as X define girlness as vulnerable, passive, and generic. This is perhaps the version of girlhood on the covers of these magazines least connected to postfeminism. The issues this girl stands in for are not about feminism or postfeminism, let alone gender. She is not engaged in negotiating a path between femininity and independence, between sexuality and work or education. She simply is an image that leads the viewer elsewhere. Nevertheless, from the perspective of my earlier suggestion that, given their historical congruence, girl discourses work through a cultural response to postfeminist discourses, this passive and vulnerable girl can be understood to be a version of neotraditionalism, a reinscription of an *unquestionable* feminine vulnerability, available for cultural signification. If postfeminism questions feminine vulnerability, this youthful and passive girl reaffirms it. That this girl as X is overwhelmingly racialized as white marks yet another link between her and postfeminist discourses.

In addition, contemporary popular culture often figures girls as particularly vulnerable because they are girls. Here the girl can still be understood to be functioning as a stand-in for some social problem, but that social problem is directly linked to her identity as a girl. Thus, these examples more directly define girlhood itself. In 1994, Mary Pipher named this vulnerable girl Ophelia in her best-selling self-help book *Reviving Ophelia: Saving the Selves of Adolescent Girls*. Pipher describes how the self-confident and independent young girl is transformed into a self-doubting and troubled teenage girl in large part because of the influence of the media and peers. This vulnerable Ophelia is ubiquitous. For example, not too long ago, as I was driving around town half listening to National Public Radio, I heard a Stanford law professor being interviewed about his work in and on children's media. He used an image that was supposed to speak for itself to emphasize why we need to "change" the media. He said (and I paraphrase): "When I saw my five-year-old daughter dancing like Britney Spears in front of a mirror, I realized that something was wrong." While he avoided mentioning exactly what was wrong (was it his daughter's act of dancing, the emulation of a female pop star, the implication of sexuality [although he did not use the word *sexual*]?), his example activated a girl as vulnerable, girl as innocent, girl as endangered, girl in need of protection trope that is quite common. Thus, this girl is in danger (from "the media") *because she is a girl*, and thus she is in need of protection (by parents and other adults).

On *Time* and *Newsweek* covers since 1990, the issues of concern for vulnerable girls have been kids and sex (T 5/24/93), the genetic basis of breast cancer (N 12/6/93), girls entering puberty early (T 10/30/00), sexual exploitation and the Internet (N 3/19/01), and the possibility of selecting the sex of one's baby (N 1/26/04). Other covers feature models who appear just old enough to be interpreted as women but young enough to still figure as girls. The topics of these covers are abortion debates (T 7/9/90), date rape (T 6/3/91), global prostitution (T 6/21/93), and rape in Bosnia (N 1/4/93).

On these covers, the at-risk girls again appear to be white, except for the girl-woman who represents global prostitution—she is identified as working in Bangkok and appears to be Thai. Interestingly, however, the generic white girls-women on these covers are almost all dark haired (only the girl at risk from sex is blond), as opposed to the primarily fair-haired X girls. Thus, when the represented threat is more directly linked to girlness, her whiteness becomes attenuated. Furthermore, many of these covers are in black and white, and the abortion cover is in the style of a painting rather than a photograph. These more stylized representations potentially produce a distance between viewer and image, such that the responsibility for protecting the girl is arguably decreased or perhaps more difficult to carry out. Just under half of these girls look away from the camera, adding to the distance between the viewer and the image.

These "vulnerable because they are girls" covers invite the viewer to gaze at the girls' failures, but, unlike the girl as X covers, they do not hold the viewer as responsible for solving the problems. And, importantly, our gaze is directed at issues specifically linked to postfeminism: access to feminine sexuality (kids and sex, early puberty, abortion), potential dangers of feminine sexuality (prostitution, rape), concern for women's health (breast cancer, rape), work (prostitution), and the very existence of gender difference (selecting the sex of one's baby). While all of these issues are also central to feminism, the kind of anxiety produced figures more often as postfeminist than feminist, at least for me. For example, the breast cancer cover text reads: "The hunt for the breast cancer gene. Jo Cunningham, 59, had breast cancer. Her daughter Julie, 29, had a preventive mastectomy. Will Alexandra, 5, be spared?" What I am calling the postfeminist anxiety is for little Alexandra's future rather than a more feminist anxiety about why the medical establishment normalizes surgery as a form of prevention for women's health, for example. And the postfeminist investment is in the truth the female body can reveal (the "breast cancer gene") rather than a more feminist investment in asking why science is focusing on genetics rather than, say, the environment, women's lack of access to good health care, or the historical lack of medical research that takes gender differences into account.[33] My point is not that this *Newsweek* cover should be asking what I am calling (admittedly quite subjectively) more feminist questions. Rather, my point is that the structure of this cover offers a particularly individualized and "truth in the stable female body"—that is, postfeminist—version of breast cancer. And, while breast cancer is the "problem" here, arguably postfeminist attention to this issue is now required. Thus, overall, as postfeminist issues are more prevalent in the *Time* and *Newsweek* cover girl representations and the viewer is more distanced from these issues, arguably postfeminism is beginning to take a place alongside the viewer as a responsible party in relation to these social problems.

A third type of girls at-risk cover focuses on individual girls who are not only vulnerable but are in fact violated, primarily through kidnapping or death. These are actual, everyday girls who make the cover of these national newsmagazines as a result of their violation rather than as stand-ins or models, as are the girls in the previous two categories. Thus, these girls serve as extreme examples of the danger all girls are in simply by existing. Since 1990, *Time* and *Newsweek* have featured covers about murder (Elisa Izquierdo [T 12/11/95], who died from child abuse; JonBenet Ramsey, a child beauty pageant star who was killed by a still unidentified attacker in her home [N 1/20/97]; and Kayla Rolland, a six-year-old girl who was killed by a six-year-old boy in a school shooting [T 3/13/00 and N 3/13/00]), two covers about kidnapping (the Shah girls, who were kidnapped by their mother [T 5/11/98]; and Elizabeth Smart, who was kidnapped and presumed dead but found alive [T 3/24/03]), one cover about parental rights and adoption (Jessica DeBoer [T 7/19/93]), and one cover about parental rights and surrogacy (Anna Schmidt, formerly "Baby Jessica" [3/21/94]).

The violated girls who make the covers of these magazines are primarily white, and they are primarily very young, well under the age of ten.[34] JonBenet Ramsey and Kayla Rolland—the blond, white girls—are openly smiling in these photos, while Elisa Izquierdo, whose name and appearance both signify Latinaness, not only is not smiling but appears in an out of focus black and white photo. Thus, the girl of color is distanced from the viewer, implying either less responsibility or more difficulty in fulfilling the responsibility for protecting her, while the white girls are openly available to the viewer, smiling in their pretragedy lives and thereby heightening the pathos of their death.

In the previous three at-risk categories—girls as symbols of the effects of social problems unrelated to gender, girls in danger because they are girls, and particular violated girls as illustrative victims—girls are without agency or subjectivity. Even though most of them look directly into the camera, as though challenging the viewer to take them seriously, take action, or reflect on his or her own responsibility for them or the social issues they represent, the girls are caught primarily in close-ups, positioned as stationary symbols unable to act on their own behalf. As a result, these girls are in need of protection, and the viewer is called on, as an adult, to respond as a protector, sometimes implicitly through a postfeminist perspective. The girls thus function as a form of titillation, drawing the viewer in while simultaneously interpolating that viewer as a responsible social citizen. Some covers even address the viewer directly as a parent who is responsible for a child, offering advice, alerting the parent to potential dangers, and posing ethical dilemmas. The *Time* cover on Jessica DeBoer refers to "common sense," while other covers address the viewer as a member of the "American public," thus calling on a nation unified in its concern for the girl. One cover, however, positions the viewer not so much as responsible for the girl but as also at risk. Here the girl serves as the symbol of dangers to adults: the *Time* cover that uses an eleven-year-old girl to represent adult-onset diabetes asks "Are you at risk?"

Overwhelmingly, then, the at-risk covers depend on a vulnerable, passive girl to produce concern in viewers, sometimes for the girl herself but more often over a larger social issue or even for oneself and one's family. Yet, in a few examples at-risk girls have more agency. In this fourth category, girls are still affected by society at large, they are still at risk, but they make unwise choices within this context, becoming, for example, sick, addicted, violent, sexual, or pregnant. Thus, part of their risk is their own fault. This personal responsibility, in fact, is an important aspect of the at-risk girl identified by Harris. Specifically, she argues that in the cultural construction of the at-risk girl "failure is deemed to be the consequence of an individual limitation."[35] Similarly, McRobbie, discussing "young, single mothers" in particular, argues that they have been "demonized by governments on both sides of the Atlantic. Their reckless behavior (often blamed on feminism) is seen as signaling the decline of family life and even as encouraging the criminalization of young men who no longer have a role as responsible father figures."[36] The emphasis on female individualism, which is such a marked feature of postfeminist discourse, thus works to shift responsibility for girls' at-risk status to the girls themselves.

Just as *Reviving Ophelia* became a best seller epitomizing the vulnerable girl in need of protection, a handful of books on "mean girls" represent this unwise decision-making at-risk girl. For example, *Odd Girl Out: The Hidden Culture of Aggression in Girls* (2002); its sequel, *Odd Girl Speaks Out: Girls Write about Bullies, Cliques, Popularity, and Jealousy* (2004); and *Queen Bees and Wannabes: Helping Your Daughter Survive Cliques, Gossip, Boyfriends, and Other Realities of Adolescence* all construct the concept of an active mean girl who contributes to the daily trauma of other vulnerable girls. The recent film *Mean Girls* (2004) draws explicitly on these books, epitomizing this at-risk girl with agency.

While *Time* and *Newsweek* have not directly represented the mean girl, each magazine has had at least one cover that relates to this character in that the girls are at risk at least in part because of their own bad choices. Specifically, *Newsweek* featured Krista Blake, who was infected with AIDS at the age of sixteen, and *Time* featured an unnamed teenage model representing "what ecstasy does to your brain." In both cases, these girls made bad choices (unprotected sex, drug use). The article on AIDS, in fact, is listed in the table of contents under the magazine's lifestyle section, even though it is also the cover story. Both girls sport the characteristic impassive gaze into the camera, but both also have their faces obscured in some way. Thus, both simultaneously "address" the viewer with their gaze and are distanced from the viewer, arguably by means of their "wrong" choices. In neither case, then, is the viewer quite so responsible for the girls or the social issues they represent, nor is the viewer really in danger from these social issues as long as he or she avoids making the poor choices—such as having sex, using recreational drugs, and choosing to be mean—that are, at least in part, made possible by postfeminism. As Harris puts it when discussing popular culture constructions of girls' delinquency and the attribution of "disordered patterns of consumption," such as eating disorders or the use of drugs, alcohol, and tobacco, "Girlpower is about being confident and assertive, [but] it should not be taken too far. . . . [These girls] have misunderstood girlpower."[37]

CAN-DO GIRLS

The flip side of the at-risk girl is Harris's can-do girl, the girl who is able to manage her surroundings and avoid the pitfalls that plague the at-risk girl and in fact stands in for the ideal "future citizen." This is the girl who has successfully taken hold of the opportunities that feminism, postfeminism, commodity consumption, deregulation in the workplace, and democracy afford her. She is healthy and well adjusted. From one perspective, the can-

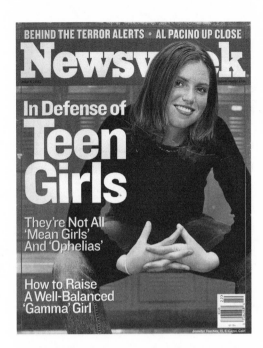

Can-do images of girlhood abound in contemporary popular journalism, although they are often counterbalanced by the suggestion that empowered girls are also at risk. On display here is a characteristic mixture of visual directness and rhetorical threat. (*Newsweek*, 3 June 2002.)

do girl is a "boot-strapping" figure, suggesting that at-risk girls just need to make better choices. On the other hand, the existence and (at least on *Time* and *Newsweek* covers) dominance of the at-risk girl suggest that the can-do girl, despite her success, is always in a tenuous position, always in danger of falling into the at-risk category. As Harris puts it, the image of the at-risk girl is a "warning to all young women that failure is an ever-lurking possibility that must be staved off through sustained application."[38]

While can-do girls appear less often on *Time* and *Newsweek* covers than do at-risk girls, when they do appear the girl as X category is dominant such that the girl stands in for social issues that are not gender specific but does so in a gendered way. Again in chronological order, the covers have featured can-do girls standing in for the issues of teaching science to kids (N 4/9/90), the joys of fatherhood (T 6/28/93), and home schooling (N 10/5/98). They also appear on the covers of two *Newsweek* issues on the one hundred best high schools in the United States (N 6/2/03, N 5/16/05). While any of these topics could be presented in an anxious way, on these covers they are not. Instead, each cover declares the positives of these topics and features a girl to illustrate them. For example, the girl on the "teaching science" cover wears a half smile and looks up, as though at the various symbols of science circling her head: a beaker, a space shuttle, a microscope, the Earth, and the formula E = MC². Above those symbols appear the words "Not just for nerds: How to teach science to our kids." Rather than asking, for instance, "Are we teaching science right?" *Newsweek* simply promises to tell its readers the best way to teach it. Similarly, on the *Time* fatherhood cover, although there is a little bit of anxiety, pleasure is dominant. The text reads: "Fatherhood: The guilt, the joy, the fear, the fun that come with a changing role." The potential guilt and fear, however, are absent from the image, which features a father holding his young daughter in his arms. They are smiling at each other (not at the camera), and she is gently touching his face. The image is in such soft focus that the pixels are visible, giving a fantasy, dream, or fairy-tale quality to the scene.

The girls on four of these five covers again appear to be white, although two of them have dark hair. The home-schooling cover girl, however, appears to be of color, perhaps African American, Latina, or multiracial. She has long, kinky, black hair, light brown skin, and hazel eyes. Thus, among all the girl as X covers, both at-risk and can-do, only two feature girls of color as symbols of issues unrelated to race: the Pledge of Allegiance cover (though even there she is featured with a white girl and an Asian American boy) and this home-schooling cover.[39] All the girls on these can-do girl as X covers are smiling, and all of them except the two described above are looking at the viewer. The look at the viewer, however, is not challenging or vulnerable; it does not seem to ask anything of the viewer. Instead, it can be read to function as a promise that everything is going well in these girls' lives. Except for the fatherhood infant, these girls are older than the at-risk girls as X. Here, youth is not needed to signify vulnerability.

While these covers do not represent postfeminism in any direct way, the girls as X can be understood to exist in relation to postfeminism. Specifically, the topics at issue—education and fatherhood—are both related to postfeminist discourses about women's (and men's) access and relationship to education and parenting. These can-do cover girls seem to suggest that women's changing relationship to education and parenting is working out just fine, that fathers are there to step in, and that girls are happy to engage with science and alternatives such as home schooling and are well prepared to attend the very best high schools.

Another set of covers activates the same can-do girl but links her directly to activities and issues related to girls' lives. The topics are everyday heroes

(N 5/29/95), a cover specifically "in defense of teen girls" (N 6/3/03), virginity (N 12/9/02), and reading Harry Potter (T 6/23/03). Interestingly, only the "in defense of teen girls" cover features a girl alone; the other three feature girls and boys. These girls are engaging in age-appropriate activities (reading Harry Potter books, virginity, being a hero), and they do so in comfortable partnership with equally healthy boys. Again they are predominantly white. The everyday heroes cover does feature two dark-skinned African American teens (one girl and one boy), but arguably this cover is also about issues of race because it is about "making a difference," presumably in racialized, underprivileged environments, and the students are specifically identified as coming from "L.A.'s Food from the 'Hood" organization. The only other cover in this category that features girls of color is the Harry Potter cover: of the fourteen children visible, one has dark brown skin (although most of his or her face is cut off), and two of the girls have light brown skin. All of these girls are older, and the broad smiles of every one communicate not just a can-do attitude but also the deep pleasure they take in their activities. Thus, even though the Harry Potter cover refers to the "secret life of kids" (which could be worrisome for the reader), the children seem so happy and playful (they are all wearing the distinctive black-rimmed Harry Potter glasses) that their secret lives could easily be imagined to be filled with only fun and pleasure. And, even though the virginity cover could be understood also to refer to anxiety about the possibility that teens are having sex at "too young" an age, the pairing of the girl with a boy in a playful rather than sexualized way (he is holding her on his back, giving her a piggyback ride, and they are both wearing simple, nonrevealing clothing) and the cover's statement that the article inside will tell the reader "why more teens are choosing not to have sex" suggest a nonanxious approach to the topic. All is well in these girls' worlds, including their relationships with boys. Implicitly, then, these covers assuage anxiety about the effect on girls of postfeminism's insistence on gender equality and a female identity defined through sexual performance.

Time and *Newsweek* represent the can-do girl not only through these "everyday girls" but also through high-profile famous girls, particularly athletes. Since 1990, several famous girl athletes have appeared on the covers of these magazines: Jennifer Capriati (tennis player, N 5/14/90), Kim Zmeskal (Olympic gymnast, T 7/27/92 and N 8/10/92), Kerri Strug (Olympic gymnast, T 8/5/96), Michelle Kwan (Olympic figure skater, N 2/16/98), Tara Lipinski (Olympic figure skater, T 3/2/98), Sarah Hughes (Olympic figure skater, T 2/11/02), and Carly Patterson (Olympic gymnast, N 8/16/04). Additionally, several covers have featured athletes who are no longer girls but became famous as girl athletes and thus arguably still signify girlness: Kristi Yamaguchi (Olympic figure skater, twenty years old when featured, N 2/10/92), Serena and Venus Williams (nineteen and twenty-one years old, respectively, when featured, T 9/3/01), and Michelle Kwan (twenty-one years old when featured for the second time, N 2/18/02).[40] The only nonathlete famous girl featured on a *Time* or *Newsweek* cover since 1990 was Chelsea Clinton, who appeared with her parents on *Time*'s cover of 8 August 1998. She was eighteen years old at the time.

Except for the *Newsweek* cover featuring Zmeskal and the one featuring Clinton, all of these covers represent these girls as unquestionably can-do, celebrating their physical achievements in a context framed by the "freedoms" of postfeminism.[41] Most appear in action, smiling for the camera, with headlines such as "Tara! Tara! Tara!" (Lipinski), "Gym Dandy" (Zmeskal, T 7/27/92), "The Sisters vs. The World" (Venus and Serena Williams), "The 8th Grade Wonder" (Capriati), "Jewel on Ice" (Yamaguchi), "Soul on Ice" (Kwan, N 2/16/98), and "Can Kwan Kick Ice?" (Kwan, N 2/18/02). Kerri Strug is particularly can-do as she is featured with both ankles bandaged, carried by her coach, wearing her team gold medal, and holding a bouquet of flowers aloft. The headline reads "Courage"; emphasizing her can-do-ness in the face of adversity, Strug's picture is paired with an image from the bombing at the 1996 Olympics, identified by the headline "Cowardice."

All of these athletes participate in "feminine sports"—figure skating, gymnastics, and tennis—but sports nonetheless, marking the postfeminist post–Title IX moment to which I briefly refer in this essay's introduction.[42] Furthermore, most stand in as symbols of "America," Olympic athletes who compete for the nation rather than themselves (some are, in fact, identified as "belonging" to "America"). These athletes thus function perfectly as Harris's ideal citizen future girl. Although the majority of these athletes are white, fitting both postfeminism's and the *Time* and *Newsweek* cover girl profiles, some are not. In particular, this is the one category in which obviously Asian American girls appear (at least on the cover of *Newsweek*) in the form of figure skaters Kwan and Yamaguchi. Serena and Venus Williams are the only obviously African American girl or young women athletes, and their images are somewhat different from those of the others to the extent that they are pictured actually participating in their sport, showing concentration and effort. The headline sets them up in tension with "the world," and the small print refers to "Taunts! Tantrums! Talent! Why the women, led by Venus and Serena Williams, are pushing the men off center court." Thus, there is a dis-ease that goes along with their success—dis-ease within the women's tennis world (taunts and tantrums), between women's and men's tennis (the men are being pushed off center court), and—perhaps more patriotically—between the United States (represented by Venus and Serena Williams) and the world. Collectively, then, it is the white can-do girls whose postfeminist participation in sports is most palatable. Finally, it is also worth noting that these athletes are typically older than the at-risk girls, with Capriati the youngest, identified as being in the eighth grade. Thus, these girls, on the threshold of adulthood, are presumably old enough to hold their own and fulfill their can-do promise.

THE DOUBLE MODEL: AT-RISK/CAN-DO GIRLS

Thus far I have attempted to illustrate two contradictory (but related) aspects of contemporary representations of girls: the vulnerable and/or violated girl who sometimes makes poor choices, contributing to her own vulnerability and violation; and the healthy and/or spectacular girl who is able to harness the plethora of opportunities available to her in order to make good on her potential. While I would argue that, at least numerically, the at-risk girl is more prevalent on the covers of *Time* and *Newsweek*, these magazines are fully committed to representing the can-do girl as well. On the one hand, these two versions of girlhood can be seen as contradictory. I would argue, however, that in fact these girl types simply manifest two different ways in which print journalism discourse addresses ambivalence about girls. Focusing specifically on postfeminism, these two versions of girlhood help to express ambivalence about the potential effects of feminism and postfeminism. They are concerned with the consequences of growing up in a postfeminist era. Given that popular discourse in the United States has never wholly embraced postfeminism as a positive event, it is not surprising that the girls' postfeminism can be understood to have produced ambivalence as well.

To return to *Time* and *Newsweek* for a moment, while most of the girls as X on the covers of these magazines are *either* at-risk *or* can-do, a number of them articulate both vulnerability and health. These examples most clearly illustrate a cultural ambivalence about what I am terming postfeminism's daughters. Covers on child brain development (т 2/2/97), hunting (т 11/30/98), the border with Mexico (т 6/11/01), home schooling (т 8/27/01), and "what teachers hate about parents" (т 2/21/05) use girls to illustrate presumably genderless topics through girls in particular. Each cover uses the girl in a particularly ambivalent way. For example, on the child brain development cover, the girl is featured with several genderless babies. She appears to be approximately four years old and is the only child old enough to be identified as gendered. She is smiling for the camera while playing a violin, looking particularly can-do. Yet the text addresses specifically the way a child's brain develops in relation to the issues of "child care" and "welfare reform." While as a violin-playing four-year-old this child signifies class privilege and therefore most likely would not be associated with welfare reform, child care may be an issue for her and, by extension, for the nation. What will happen to this child prodigy if she is put into child care, by implication because her mother, who is working in order to maintain the class privilege that provides violin lessons to four-year-olds, chooses to leave her there rather than staying at home? The hunting cover features a girl with a man, perhaps her father, in a small area in the top right portion of the page. The father is holding the young girl from behind as she takes aim with a rifle in the foreground of the small picture. Here ambivalence emerges around this girl-child participating in a typically masculine activity—hunting. The print reads: "Should kids hunt?" This corner image appears on a cover about Ritalin featuring a young boy as the model. The main text asks: "How do you know it's right for your kids?" While each question posed by the magazine is gender neutral, both images can be read as gendered, given that hunting is generally considered a masculine activity and given that attention deficit disorder (which Ritalin is used to treat) is diagnosed much more often in boys. Anxiety relating to the girl's participation in this masculine activity is thus framed by more general concerns surrounding boys, men, and masculinity in a postfeminist era: fears of boys being outstripped in school, of white male redundancy, and so on.

The Mexican border cover is particularly ambivalent. The girl, who appears to be Mexican (or Mexican American), is in the extreme right foreground of the frame, and her body seems to be almost coming off the page toward the viewer. She is wearing sunglasses, which obscure her eyes, and she has her mouth open as though she is talking or laughing. She wears a purple dress and is holding a pink parasol. Her teeth are visible; some are adult teeth, some are still baby teeth, suggesting that she is relatively young. Behind her, slightly out of focus, a younger boy sits in a stroller, also wearing sunglasses. The text reads: "What's happening on the border is amazing. Come see how it's changing your world. Welcome to Amexica." *Amexica* is printed in red, white, blue, and green colors, mixing the colors of the American and Mexican flags. While none of the words on the cover expresses direct anxiety, the cover nevertheless can be read as anxious. The girl is jumping out of the frame, almost imposing herself on the viewer. The word *America* is transformed into *Amexica* and the color green invades the more expected red, white, and blue. Additionally, viewers are told that the border is changing "your world," implying that we do not already occupy the literal or figurative border. Interestingly, the girl is not just coded as Mexican (or Mexican American) but also arguably as postfeminist through her assertive stance and daring fashion sense (mixing pink and purple with identity-hiding sunglasses). Thus, this girl figures as troubling not only because of her unclear national status but also because of her somewhat aggressive femininity; here an assertive female attenuates a traditionally constituted (white, patriarchal) image of the nation.

The home-schooling cover that I include in this category is different from the wholly can-do home-schooling cover mentioned above. Here the girl again appears to be particularly can-do—she is seated at a bright red desk with a book open in front of her, smiling at the camera and surrounded by her mother and three brothers (no father figure is in sight)—but the text asks: "Is home schooling good for America?" Thus, while she seems to be embracing the opportunity afforded by the choice her mother has made, the text is anxious about the choice. Finally, the "what teachers hate about parents" cover features a very small image of a girl, captured within a picture frame within the center of the cover photo, standing in for the "child" over whom parents and teachers debate. One father is holding this picture while he asks a question of a teacher, who is seated at a desk and looking at the camera in exasperation, hand to the side of her face. Another father gestures menacingly at the teacher, as does a mother. The text reads: "Pushy dads. Hovering moms. Parents who don't show up at all. Are kids paying the price?" While the girl in the picture frame is smiling broadly, suggesting a well-adjusted and happy life, the parent figures and the teacher's frustration suggest that she is vulnerable nevertheless, arguably in part because of a postfeminist concern with girls' education (think of the AAUW report *How Schools Shortchange Girls*).

Except for the Mexican border cover, then, on which the girl does not appear to be vulnerable herself, the potential vulnerability of these girl characters is further produced by their blond whiteness (only one girl has dark hair, and she still appears to be white) and their youth (all appear to be under ten years old). Thus, they mirror the vulnerable figure who appears repeatedly on the anxious at-risk girl covers. In short, they are can-do girls who are accessing the benefits of postfeminist choices (primarily made by their parents), but their hold on that status is tenuous.

Covers that address issues related to girls' lives more directly also sometimes bring out the ambivalence I am discussing here. Both *Newsweek* and *Time* had covers on gender difference in the early 1990s (N 5/28/90 and T 1/20/92) in which the girls can be read as both vulnerable and healthy because of their gender. A cover on Jessica Dubroff, a girl of seven who attempted to pilot a plane across the country (accompanied by her father and flight instructor), who died when her plane crashed, activates a can-do image of a young girl who pursued a masculine activity while simultaneously defining that independence as dangerous (T 4/22/96). The cover image pictures her in close-up, wearing a leather jacket and a pink cap that reads "Women Fly."[43] A cover on life in high school after the Columbine shooting presents smiling, seemingly healthy girls and one (unsmiling) boy but refers directly to the stress and danger that the word *Columbine* now signifies. Finally, a cover on gender and autism (N 9/8/03) addresses the fact that autism is diagnosed in boys much more often than in girls and features a young nonautistic girl with her autistic twin brother to illustrate this idea.

The two gender-difference covers are quite similar in how they depict the relationship between the girl and the boy. On the *Newsweek* cover, the girl is closer to the center of the frame, wearing a traditional dress with bows in her hair. She is looking, however, at the silver toy gun the boy holds in his hand as he gestures toward it, perhaps explaining something to her. Although she holds a naked baby doll in her arms, she is paying no attention to it. Thus, while each child is engaging in traditional gender behavior, the girl can be read as uninterested in it, intrigued instead with the masculine gun. The cover manages to suggest both that children do engage in traditional gendered behavior and that girls (but not boys) also may reject that behavior. The text reads "Guns and dolls. Scientists explore the differences between girls and boys," but the image of both the girl and the boy engaged with the toy gun suggests that perhaps there are fewer differences than scientists may be looking for. The text of the *Time* cover on gender difference again assumes that such differences do exist: "Why are men and women different? It isn't just upbringing. New studies show they are born that way." Once again, however, the image can be read to imply otherwise. The boy is centered, and he is holding up his arm, displaying his bicep muscle. He wears a red T-shirt and blue shorts. The girl, who stands next to him, is wearing a blue and white striped outfit that is somewhat feminine. She has her arms folded across her chest and looks toward the boy and his muscle, smiling. Perhaps the dominant reading of the image is of gender difference—he makes a muscle and she admires it, and they both wear typically gendered clothes. Yet her stance, with arms crossed, and her interest in muscularity can both be read as a departure from typical femininity. Perhaps as she looks toward him and his muscles she is looking not toward her future love interest but toward her future (postfeminist) persona? Certainly, reading across these two images, there is an evident anxiety about femininity, a not quite sufficient quality about the femininity that both girls enact.

Once again, the cover girls in this category are white and, except for the life after Columbine cover, below the age of ten. Thus, despite their seeming independence and interest in masculine things, they simultaneously signify as vulnerable in that context. These images do not offer an easy relationship between women and independence, agency, and masculinity. Comparing the two covers of Kim Zmeskal fits here as well. While *Time* seems to have no qualms about Zmeskal competing in the Olympics at the age of sixteen, using the headline "Gym Dandy," *Newsweek* is concerned, using the headline "It hurts. Do we push teen athletes too hard?" *Newsweek*'s image of Zmeskal shows her possibly in pain, with her arm up to her face, as she looks to the side of the frame. This is not the smiling Zmeskal of the *Time* cover but rather a troubled, hardworking, embattled girl. Together these two covers capture the ambivalence about the appropriateness of girls' independence, their can-do attitude, and their embodiment of girl power.

Newsweek's "in defense of teen girls" cover is also relevant here. The text on this cover states, "They're not all 'mean girls' and 'Ophelias.' How to raise a well-balanced 'gamma' girl." This cover, while defending the normality of teen girls, nevertheless evokes the twin specters of the mean girl (at risk as a result of her choices) and Ophelia (vulnerable simply because she is a girl), against which it defends teen girls in general. In other words, the cover acknowledges the existence of these other discursive girl types even while suggesting that they are not of much concern. In the manner of what I would call the anti-Ophelia books published soon after *Reviving Ophelia*, this cover insists on the normality of girls in the face of the overwhelming discursive construction of girls' vulnerability and even cultural threat.[44] Thus, even though on the surface it is entirely optimistic about girls, this cover carries the specters of the at-risk girl and the can-do girl who no longer does or simply doesn't. Changing Harris's context slightly, I would argue that "what is constructed here is the never-good-enough girl who must perpetually observe and remake herself."[45] While the smiling girl on the cover of this *Newsweek* issue may not be directly involved in observing and remaking herself (at least at the moment), perhaps—the text of the cover seems to suggest—the viewer or the viewer's daughter should be.

Collectively, and setting aside some variation, these cover girls are vulnerable and passive when they are young but responsible for the paths their lives take (whether they are turning out well or badly) when they are older. These girls are overwhelmingly white, and when they are not they are distanced in one way or another from the protective attitude encouraged in the viewer or from the simple pleasures of success expressed by the white cover girls. Regardless of age and race, these girls activate postfeminist discourses, sometimes implicitly and sometimes explicitly. Their relationship to this postfeminism is ambivalent; they both succeed and fail because of the cultural and social changes postfeminism is understood to have wrought, and they illustrate both the promise and the disaster of postfeminism. Or, to approach this from the other direction, discourses of postfeminism enable both the promise and the disaster of discursive girls' lives.

Disruption and Containment?

One way to make sense of this tension between the can-do girls and the at-risk girls is through a "disruption-containment" model of criticism. In other words, the ambivalence I am identifying in and across these collective mass magazine covers can be understood to illustrate the ways in which girls can be disruptive in popular culture (whether the disruption comes, for example, from can-do activities such as winning gold medals or displacing men on the tennis courts or at-risk activities such as using recreational drugs or trying to fly a plane across the country at the age of seven) while simultaneously being contained by popular culture (whether the containment comes, for example, from the passive, paralyzing vulnerability of the at-risk X girls or from the overwhelming cheerfulness of the can-do girls, who are satisfied with reading Harry Potter books or remaining virgins).

Many scholars writing about contemporary depictions of girls, in fact, engage this disruption-containment argument. Specifically, they build an argument about hegemony, acknowledging the way in which girls' anger about, resistance to, and transformation of social ideologies of gender, sexuality, and race appear in some popular culture texts but also acknowledging that that anger, resistance, and transformation is usually "contained" in one way or another. This is the opposite, I think, of the Ur-article Charlotte Brunsdon discusses in a recent essay on postfeminism. Brunsdon sees some scholars disidentifying with (a certain kind of constructed and thereby crystallized) feminism in order to claim popular culture for another kind of (better, more hip?) feminism. She admits she has written this essay herself but is concerned that it creates "censorious feminists" very similar to the feminists popular culture constructs.[46] For Brunsdon, the repetition of disidentification "enacts a paralysis" within feminist criticism.[47] While I do not doubt the existence of this Ur-article, within girls studies in particular I see the opposite argument being repeated. Specifically, I see another set of scholars identifying the feminist *potential* in various girl texts but claiming that the potential is ultimately *contained*.

For example, Rachel Moseley frames her discussion of teen witch texts with the following argument: "While at times these texts engage with [a deconstruction of hegemonic feminine ideals] directly, I nevertheless suggest that the ideological project of the teen witch text in relation to femininity and power—glamour—is *ultimately superficial*, and that the particular ways in which this project is textually articulated are revealing of the pleasures and paradoxes at the heart of the postfeminist project."[48] And, in her analysis of the television show *My So-Called Life* (1994–1995), Michelle Byers argues that "the intersecting identity categories of difference [in this show, gender, sexuality, race, and class] are mobilized by this text only to be shut down again and

again. Although initially embraced, the other is, *in the end*, always pathologized."[49]

Again, I would emphasize that my concern is not with individual articles
but rather with the *repetition* of the disruption-containment argument across
numerous scholarly articles.[50] One of the strengths of Moseley's and Byers's
essays is that the authors examine *how* the texts appear to depict difference,
feminism, and/or girls' political viability but then, as Byers puts it, "position
the reader in a place where [those differences] can be ignored."[51] In short, I
would argue that it is crucial to describe the disruption-containment model,
as does all this scholarship, wherever we find ourselves positioned on this
intellectual continuum. I would suggest that these arguments emerge in the
process of coming to terms with postfeminism both in popular culture *and*
as a historical moment in which we all have to negotiate our positions as
"feminist media critics" in the context of the contemporary state of feminist
scholarship located in the spaces of the contemporary academy. These differing perspectives are all logical and necessary developments in our thinking.
Yet from the perspective of girls studies the problem with these approaches,
for me, is that they pretty much define all postfeminist media representations.
In other words, postfeminism is by definition contradictory, simultaneously
feminist and antifeminist, liberating and repressive, productive and obstructive of progressive social change. Whether critics see feminism or antifeminism as more dominant in the end is a matter of interpretation and degree.
Thus, the disruption-containment model does not get us much farther along
in understanding the complexity of popular culture's girlhood in particular.

One way beyond this impasse might be to avoid claiming either disruption
or containment, emphasizing the both/and nature of postfeminist representations of girls. For example, Banet-Weiser sees "girl power shows on Nickelodeon as . . . representing a kind of feminism, one that is fundamentally
about tension and contradiction . . . about the individual pleasures of consumption and the social responsibility of solidarity." Refusing to argue that
these shows are either ultimately feminist or ultimately co-opted, she argues
instead that a feminist media studies project must "attempt to understand"
third wave and girl power discourses "on their own terms."[52] Similarly, in her
work on girls' magazines McRobbie sees a "productive tension . . . a dependence on feminism and a disavowal of it" in evidence.[53] She looks carefully at
feminist discourses in the magazines, her pedagogical practices with young
women who hope to work at the magazines, and the work of women editors

and journalists at the magazines who are explicit about their commitment to aspects of feminism. She writes of her goal of avoiding a feminism that is "a narrow and restricted political entity" in its response to these magazines.[54] Importantly, this narrow feminism could either embrace the feminism in the texts or reject the texts due to the constraints they place on that feminism. McRobbie's goal is to avoid making either argument while acknowledging the tension between what I am here calling disruption and containment.

Building on the both/and approach I identify in Banet-Weiser's and McRobbie's work, I would argue that the challenge for girls studies of popular culture is to focus attention on the inextricable combination of disruption and containment, and of at-risk and can-do, in the contemporary popular discursive construction of girlhood. In other words, I would argue that rather than "taking sides" feminist media criticism might point out that the collective representation of girls in popular culture repetitively, even obsessively, *asks* us to take sides (e.g., to defend teen girls, reject mean girls, or protect Ophelias). And I would argue that a further challenge for girls studies is to emphasize the way girl discourse mobilizes age, race, and agency—alongside postfeminist discourse—to delimit the kinds of sides available for us (hypothetically) to take. In this essay, then, I have tried to identify (but not to follow) the popular culture path that insists that feminism and postfeminism must be opposed and that girlness is defined by tensions among meanness, vulnerability, and personal responsibility. This is not so much a both/and argument as an argument about the way the both/and structure of postfeminist girl discourse produces a particular kind of (complex, contradictory, and ambivalent) girlness.

Notes

1. The quotations that open this essay are from Riordan, "Commodified Agents and Empowered Girls," 80; and McRobbie "Sweet Smell of Success?" 211. On white slavery, see, for example, Grieveson, "Policing the Cinema." On Shirley Temple, see Vered, "White and Black in Black and White." On sexual delinquency, see Schaefer, *"Bold! Daring! Shocking! True!"* On sexual exhibitionism, see Hatch, "Fille Fatale."
2. Driscoll, *Girls*, 11, emphasis added.
3. Banet-Weiser "Girls Rule!" 120.
4. Ward and Benjamin, "Women, Girls, and the Unfinished Work of Connections."
5. Cole "Suburban Icons/Communist Pasts," 231. For related discussions of the 1990s as a "new" moment for girls, see Riordan, "Commodified Agents and Empowered Girls"; and Taft, "Girl Power Politics."
6. Durham, "The Girling of America," 25, 26–28.

7. Griffin, "Good Girls, Bad Girls," 33.

8. Tasker and Negra, "In Focus," 109.

9. McRobbie, "Post-feminism and Popular Culture," 258, 260.

10. McRobbie, "*More!*" 195.

11. Kearney, "Girlfriends and Girl Power," 125.

12. Ibid., 130.

13. Moseley "Glamorous Witchcraft," 408.

14. Ibid., 405.

15. Banet-Weiser, "Girls Rule!" 125. See also Dow, *Prime-Time Feminism*.

16. Durham, "The Girling of America," 25. As examples of that scholarship, she lists Brown and Carol, *Meeting at the Crossroads*; Orenstein, *Schoolgirls*; and Pipher, *Reviving Ophelia*.

17. See Budgeon and Currie, "From Feminism to Postfeminism." Scholars who make a specific distinction between 1980s texts that feature girls, but not yet in a post-feminist way, and 1990s texts that feature girls in specifically postfeminist ways include Moseley (in "Glamorous Witchcraft" she compares *The Breakfast Club* [1985] to *Charmed* [1998–]) and Banet-Weiser (in "Girls Rule!" she compares *My Little Pony (and Friends)* [1986] to *Clarissa Explains It All* [1991–94]).

18. In *Girls*, Driscoll writes: "Despite how obviously puberty seems to define a boundary between girlhood and womanhood and a field for female adolescence, adolescence is not a clear denotation of any age, body, behavior, or identity, because it has always meant the process of developing a self (though that has meant very different things in different sociohistorical contexts) rather than any definition of that self" (5–6).

19. Working from a number of different perspectives, various scholars have looked at the relationship between popular culture representations of girls and girls themselves. For examples of some of the best of this work, see Carney, "Body Work on Ice"; Chin, *Purchasing Power*; Gaunt, "Dancin' in the Street to a Black Girls' Beat"; Kenny, *Daughters of Suburbia*; Ruiz, "The Flapper and the Chaperone"; and Valdivia and Bettivia, "A Guided Tour through One Adolescent Girl's Culture."

20. For example, see Budgeon and Currie, "From Feminism to Postfeminism"; Currie, *Girl Talk*; Kruckemeyer, "Making Room for Teen Voices"; McRobbie, "*More!*"; and Schurm, "Teena Means Business."

21. Focusing only on magazine covers is not without precedent. For example, see Lehnus, *Who's on Time?*; and Kitch, *The Girl on the Magazine Cover*.

22. Harris, *Future Girl*, 1.

23. Occasionally, small print provides names, but the articles are not specifically about the particular girls named on the cover. Hence, I would still consider them to be primarily anonymous.

24. Berlant, *The Queen of America Goes to Washington City*, 58.

25. Ibid., 66–67.

26. McRobbie, *Feminism and Youth Culture*, 201.

27. Driscoll, *Girls*, 12.

28. Roberts, "Pleasures and Problems of the 'Angry Girl,'" 221.

29. See Forman-Brunell, "Truculent and Tractable."

30. Only three of the girls on these covers have brown eyes.

31. One other cover features a girl who could be read as a girl of color: the one on the *Newsweek* cover about depression could be interpreted as either white or Latina. Of course, all my comments about the racial identity of these models are based on my own subjective reading of bodily clues. My point is not to argue that these figures are or are not "actually" of a particular race but to point to the ways in which socially constructed visual codes of race and racialization function on these covers.

32. There is a large body of scholarship on this, much of which addresses the "everything and nothing" quality of whiteness. See Dyer, "White." For fuller discussions of this scholarship, see Negra, *Off-White Hollywood*; and Projansky and Ono, "Strategic Whiteness as Cinematic Racial Politics."

33. For a discussion of representations of breast cancer in popular culture, as well as the relationship between neoliberalism, corporate capitalism, and the "fight" against breast cancer, see Samantha King, *Pink Ribbons, Inc.*

34. Only Elizabeth Smart is clearly a teenager. The *Time* cover does not provide either the ages or names of the Shah girls, but they appear to be at least preteens.

35. Harris, *Future Girl*, 16.

36. McRobbie, "Sweet Smell of Success?" 207.

37. Harris, *Future Girl*, 29.

38. Ibid., 27.

39. As mentioned above, the breast cancer cover features a family that can be read as perhaps Latina, and the school integration cover, which is specifically about race, features an African American girl.

40. *Newsweek* ran a series of covers on the Nancy Kerrigan and Tonya Harding scandal (1/17/94, 1/24/94, and 2/21/94), but both skaters were in their twenties at the time. Thus, I am not including these covers as examples of girls.

41. I return to the Zmeskal covers later in this essay. The Clinton cover directly refers to the family's request for privacy in relation to the Monica Lewinsky and impeachment events. Nevertheless, all three Clintons are smiling, implying their can-do attitude.

42. See Banet-Weiser, "Girls Rule!"; and Cole, "Suburban Icons/Communist Pasts."

43. For more on Jessica Dubroff, her "Women Fly" cap, and her masculine-feminine persona, see my "Girls Who Act Like Women Who Fly."

44. Such books include Shandler, *Ophelia Speaks*; Gray, *In Your Face*; Sonnie, *Revolutionary Voices*; Nam, *Yell-Oh Girls!*; Hernandez and Rehman, *Colonize This!*; and Jacob, *My Sisters' Voices*.

45. Harris, *Future Girl*, 25.

46. Brunsdon, "Feminism, Postfeminism, Martha, Martha, and Nigella," 113.

47. Ibid., 114.

48. Moseley, "Glamorous Witchcraft," 407, emphasis added.

49. Byers, "Gender/Sexuality/Desire," 727, emphasis added.

50. Just to make the point that, although I am uncomfortable with *emphasizing* this approach I nevertheless see the importance of *making* the argument, I will mention an article I wrote with a colleague, Leah R. Vande Berg, on the television series *Sabrina, the Teenage Witch* (1996–2003). In the conclusion to that essay, we write: "We do want to acknowledge the possibility that *Sabrina* is providing young women and girls with ways of understanding themselves as independent and powerful, with images of play and pleasure that cross and destabilize gender binaries. . . . [But] our analysis suggests that the series' more powerful ideological work is the revelation of the role that popularized feminism plays in *maintaining* [emphasis in the original] rather than undermining gender, race, and class hierarchies. *Ultimately* [emphasis added], we read Sabrina's escapes from containment as co-opted multiculturalism and seductive consumerism, and therefore as antifeminist" (Projansky and Vande Berg, "Sabrina, the Teenage . . . ?" 36. For related disruption-containment arguments, see Gateward, "Bubblegum and Heavy Metal"; Owen, "Vampires, Postmodernity, and Postfeminism"; Roberts, "Pleasures and Problems of the 'Angry Girl'"; and Taft, "Girl Power Politics." For related disruption-containment arguments specifically focused on the commodification of girls, see Durham, "The Girling of America"; Kruckemeyer, "Making Room for Teen Voices"; and Riordan, "Commodified Agents and Empowered Girls."
51. Byers, "Gender/Sexuality/Desire," 720.
52. Banet-Weiser, "Girls Rule!" 136, 137.
53. McRobbie, "*More!*" 200.
54. Ibid., 207.

Hannah E. Sanders

3 Living a *Charmed* Life
THE MAGIC OF POSTFEMINIST SISTERHOOD

I LOVE this program i think that provides a fantasy for everyone who
watches but with realistic aspects, e.g. the potions and working in the
kitchen the haloween episodes, things like that. V good i think the only
thing i'd like to have introduced is a coven, in which they are apart ofor
to see them do more circles to prepare themselves or something!!! holly xx
—HOLLYIVY, 1 JANUARY 2003, 1:53 P.M.

Teen television is one of the most prolific subgenres to
emerge from the American media culture of the mid-
1990s.[1] Combining the generic traits of sit-com, teen soap
dramas, soap opera, and fantasy television, *Charmed* entered
British television (and it is with the British reception of the
show that I am primarily concerned) at a time when shows such
as *Buffy the Vampire Slayer* (BBC 2, 1998–2004), *Sabrina, the Teenage
Witch* (ITV, 1997 ongoing), and *Roswell High* (Channel 4, 2002–
2004) were establishing themselves. *Charmed* comfortably sits
alongside these aforementioned texts for, despite its (arguably)
rather more "adult" characterizations and narratives, it positions itself as a generically hybrid drama accessible to a female
teen audience. In this essay, I argue that the modalities of empowered femininity described in *Charmed* demarcate a space

for a healthy postfeminist discourse that does not reject the emancipatory politics of second-wave feminism.

As Glyn Davis and Kay Dickinson argue, to fully understand the emergence and significance of "Teen TV," one must consider the representational conventions employed in specific texts *and* the modes of consumption and social practices that operate around and identify them as teen television.[2] I claim this approach to discuss a text that does not posit adolescents as central characters but focuses instead on young women who, in a fashion akin to that experienced by the characters in *Dawson's Creek, Buffy the Vampire Slayer*, and *Roswell High*, are anxiously negotiating the transition into an adult identity. *Charmed* follows the lives of the four Halliwell sisters who, discovering their magical heritage as "chosen ones," take up the baton of their foremothers in order to fight evil, protect "innocents," and further the powers of good. As such, they gain magical powers and knowledge that mark them as different. Each sister has a specific power: the middle sister, Piper (Holly Marie Combs), can freeze time and explode matter; Phoebe (Alyssa Milano), the youngest, can levitate and has premonitions; Prue (Shannen Doherty), the eldest, can perform telekinesis; and later Paige (Rose McGowan), the long-lost sister, can orb through time and space, mystically heal, and move objects, as Prue could before her demise. In addition to these special powers, the sisters make potions, write spells, consult the magic book, and together hold the "power of three," the ability to destroy evil through collective will. Alongside this "witch-work," the sisters have the task of trying to lead "normal" lives; as the seasons progress, their roles shift in this respect. Piper tries to run P3, a nightclub, and chooses to have a baby. Phoebe attends college and becomes a successful journalist. Prue pursues a career as a photographer before her untimely death, and later Paige trains to become a social worker, eventually resigning in order to stay at home and "retrain" as a witch.

The Halliwells' duty to be magical, successful, worldly women epitomizes the postfeminist dialectic of "having it all," the assumption that feminism's goals have been achieved and all that modern women have to do is choose a lifestyle from the endless range of options now available to them. To the teen audience of this show, the heady mixture of magic, action, and emotion likely offers an action-driven vision of adult female empowerment. In addition, the series' investment in magic offers the teen audience a secondary viewing pleasure.

The *Charmed* sisters and the book of magic that binds them to each other, the manor, and their foremothers.

In this essay, I draw on my Internet reception study of British girls who identify as teenage witches through spiritual lifestyle choices partially formed through identification with the models of female witches found in mainstream media texts such as *Charmed*. Between 2001 and 2004, I researched female British teens age eleven to eighteen who were self-fashioning themselves as witches. Through a specifically designed research Web site, www.witchwords .net, participating teenagers demonstrated how they engaged in a complex configuration of viewing, consuming, identification with visual icons, and self-construction. These engagements drew on a myriad of historical and gendered discourses of feminine identity constitution and regimes of power, reinvigorating an old feminist icon of unruly femininity. This research demonstrated that the incorporation of the witch figure into mainstream female youth culture presented a resistive prospect for certain teen girls at the beginning of the 2000s. The affiliations of these girls clearly reflect concepts of embodied power, whether put into practice through stylistic changes, linguistic deviations, or media consumption. Moreover, their activities licensed feminine agency and an engagement with feminism at a time when feminism had largely become proscribed and/or redundant for many young women.

The teen witch craze in Britain can be understood as a particular articulation of post–Spice Girls girl power, a form of postfeminism located around notions of female Britishness in the 1990s. With the emergence of laddette culture and girl power, discourses of female empowerment focused on young women's and teenage girls' engagement with popular culture and reformulations of feminist discourses regarding social behavior and consumerism. For contemporary British teen witches, the engagement with girl power, the mainstreaming of alternative and New Age spiritualities, and the increasing visibility of adult witchcraft and pagan cultures operate alongside the accessibility of information through the Internet and interactive television and images of teenage witchcraft presented within mainstream media. This cohesion has created a particular matrix of discourses regarding self-identification, relationships with place and community, and notions of power available to British teen girls. The representations of young women as witches offer a vision of empowered "girldom," one that reflects the tenets of feminism within a culturally acceptable framework.

The impact of mainstream texts, such as *Charmed*, on the constitution of a teen witch's identity is complex. At times, the images in such texts are refuted by the teen witches in my online research as a source of victimization and misunderstanding, but they are similarly celebrated as key descriptors for the possibilities of magic and feminist empowerment. The privileging and politicizing of the domestic space and female essentialism and the use of feminine linguistic idioms that establish community, validating a shared sense of sublimation yet challenging those who seek to oppress, consuming the self as a magical being, are as apparent in the online dialogues of British teen witches as they are in the narrative structures of *Charmed*.

Series such as *Charmed*, *Buffy the Vampire Slayer*, and *Sabrina* interpolate a female audience through the provision of girls' and women's supernatural powers; teen girl audiences are invited to find new sources of spiritual identification, where spiritual identity and girl power are finally reconciled. Power is not simply won for *Charmed*'s witch sisters, however. The postfeminist sentiment of having and doing it all is demonstrated in *Charmed*'s depiction of the continual demands placed on the trio by others and their heritage while trying to fulfill personal and professional desires and ambitions. Rachel Moseley states that the privileging of the domestic realm and roles and the refusal to represent the unruly witch icon of second-wave feminist politics expel the power inherent in these characterizations to feminism's backlash;

for Moseley, these new witches reinforce women's glamorous respectability rather than questioning the status quo.[3] As this essay discusses, the power of these saccharine witches may indeed be an "articulation of postfeminist difficulties."[4] but this does not negate the potential for a politicized reading or empowering viewing pleasure. The display of sisterhood is central to the reclamation of feminist politics in this show and is a central pleasure for a young female audience seeking new icons of female power.

Charmed draws on discourses of the contemporary working woman alongside traditional, conservative discourses of femininity (and witchcraft) to demonstrate the evolving nature of women's effective, if mysticized problem solving. The series routinely explores the problems and pleasures of contemporary femininity through the sisters' identities as witches. From decisions regarding marriage, family, choosing appropriate (or inappropriate) partners, and juggling careers to the demands of their unusual destiny as witches, these female characters struggle with their identities as witches while trying to succeed in the workplace. Although the series posits a female voice and contemporary women's concerns as primary story arcs, the politics of *Charmed* can be understood as neither exclusively feminist nor postfeminist. Instead *Charmed* is positioned between these two discourses of political and personal liberation, enabling a dialogue between the two. To what extent the series' makers have consciously repackaged feminist politics in a postfeminist series in order to reach a certain audience demographic is hard to ascertain.[5] However, *Charmed*'s ability to investigate positions of feminine empowerment is certainly one of the pleasures of viewing the series for the teen audience; it offers a heady mixture of girl power, delighting in the traditional arenas of feminine identity performance. As L., a sixteen-year-old respondent, says when asked why she enjoys the series, "I'd rather be the characters in *Charmed* than in *Buffy*, they're more attractive, more intelligent—unlike Willow, who's a geek and has a kind of dumbness about her . . . and I want their house, it's San Francisco!"[6] Although L. identifies herself as a feminist interested in witchcraft, her statement certainly supports Tanya Krzywinska's argument that, "Individual access to power (through witchcraft) has perhaps a greater attraction for a young 'postfeminist' audience. . . . The model that is more likely to influence this group is the recent kick-arse and looking-good woman warriors of television and film, who single-handedly take on the ills of the world."[7]

The teen witch respondents in my reception research state that they regularly enjoy watching *Charmed*. For them, it is the second most popular television series after *Buffy*, receiving 51 percent of respondents' votes; girls of thirteen and fifteen are the age groups that most enjoy the series. Girls identifying as witches are clearly engaged in its pleasures irrespective of its lack of cultural status.[8] The series privileges a feminine voice and female power while describing the traumas of contemporary femininity with both a serious attitude and parodic flair. Moreover, unlike the witches in *Buffy*, the Halliwell sisters exist within an imaginable, tangible vision of the world.

Referencing the conventions of the "monster family" sitcom,[9] *Charmed* continues the tradition in which the "modern suburban family [is] shadowed by darker and mostly 'unspoken' others from pre-modern and irrational tradition."[10] The series can be also be understood as a "female friendship" text that centralizes the bonds between women as primary in its narratives.[11] It is to questions of whether such female-focused texts are "progressive or recuperative" in terms of their construction of political discourses which I now turn.[12] The respondent observation cited earlier identifies the central themes: the representation of plausible relationships between women, which posits a female-centered audience and discourses of women-centered power; and the series' construction of work and affluence. *Charmed*'s construction of sisterhood, in both a familial and feminist reading of the term, encodes the strength of connection between women. The "power of three," the witches' ultimate weapon against evil, only exists when all three sisters are united emotionally and geographically. The series presents an image of femininity primarily focused on the liberation and empowerment of the sisters and the other women in their community. Bonded through magic, the power of sisterhood is represented as the primary relationship, strong enough to overcome all obstacles, however demonic. I acknowledge that this line of analysis is not without problems, for none of the Halliwell sisters are self-identified feminists. Nor does the trio display any political or personal allegiance to feminist movements. However, if, as bell hooks suggests, "feminism is a struggle to end sexist oppression,"[13] then the Halliwell sisters can be read as feminist icons, fighting demons that threaten to limit their potential as women and sever their familial ties.

For the teen witch audience, this embodiment of contemporary womanhood is simultaneously glamorous, fraught, and aspirational, offering adolescent females a vision of adult femininity that articulates both feminist and postfeminist discourses of female identity. In understanding *Charmed* as an inspiration for the British teen witch community, I examine the sisters' struggle with identity as symbolic of the entrance into adult femininity, educating the teen decoder by describing the possibilities and pitfalls of an empowered adult identity. Furthermore, through fighting evil, the sisters constantly negotiate their relationships with each other. Demon fighting metaphorically displays their struggles with each other and the personal struggle of each sister with concepts of autonomy, communal effort, and connections. Thus, it is important to investigate the description of the source of the sisters' power, asking whether it corroborates a discourse of essentialized female corporeality and genealogy as "special."

The Strength of Blood: Discourses of Sisterhood in *Charmed*

Witchcraft in literature and art has frequently been aligned with groups of women and particularly women in a family unit. As Diane Purkiss states in her analysis of witches in history, "Given the centrality of maternity and of the maternal body to understandings of the witch, we might be tempted to analyse the idea that witchcraft runs in families in bodily terms."[14] The image of the three crones from Shakespeare's *Macbeth* cackling and stirring a cauldron of poison exists in the contemporary imagination as a fearful reminder of the power invoked by unruly women gossiping, laughing, and plotting together. Thus, although the image of the lone witch as liminal and uncanny is central to the historical iconography of weird women, there is a considerable weight of cultural connotation behind the depiction of female witches together, defined as sisters through a shared biological heritage and a shared status as "other."

Similarly, second-wave feminism's encouragement of female consciousness-raising through group activity, activism, study, and endeavor was one of the key ways in which feminist debate was conducted. As Linda C. Badley states, "Feminists have claimed solidarity and identity with the persecuted witches of the early modern period."[15] Grassroots networks of women engaged in questioning and communicating feminist politics and practices evolved from 1950s "coffee morning" forums to established organizations of feminist consciousness-raising groups in the 1970s. Women's centers and advice services proliferated, frequently subdividing into forums for the discussion of women's position in the workplace and issues of sexual health and preference.[16] In this context, *sisterhood* emerged as a political term that encapsulated the collective struggle of women (problematically denying difference until it was claimed specifically for and by women of color) in all realms of public and private life.

The focus on domesticity and consciousness-raising discussions in *Charmed*, evoked in the Halliwell sisters' problem solving, continually echoes the institutional organization and political focus of second-wave feminism. The centrality of women's networks helped define the shape of sisterhood during the modern battle against patriarchy and is reflected in the resolution of the sisters' problems encountered in every episode of *Charmed*. Yet, the use of sisterhood as a political motif isn't the only historical arena in which such politically driven consciousness-raising groups occurred, and others are drawn on in the series.

Equally significant is the women's spirituality movement, also known as the goddess spirituality movement, which emerged in the 1970s and gained visibility in the 1980s with the work of Carol Christ, Barbara Walker, and Merlin Stone.[17] The connection between feminist politics and the historical, often mythicized imaginings of witchcraft practices was made explicit in the literature and art of this burgeoning "theological" field. Erica Jong, for example, clearly expresses the correlations between feminist politics and witchcraft in her introduction to *Witches*: "I imagine a coven of proto-feminist witches who attempt to compensate for the female's lack of power by making spells and riding through the air."[18] By appropriating the witch as a motivating political image and the practices of neopagan witchcraft, while heralding the divine feminine as a theological model, the women's spirituality movement articulated a politics of feminist sisterhood intended to bond women politically and spiritually. As Mary Daly decrees in her seminal study *Beyond God the Father*, "Sisterhood, then, by being the unique bonding of women against our reduction to low caste is Antichurch. . . . The development of sisterhood is a unique threat, for it is directed against the basic social and psychic model of hierarchy and domination upon which authoritarian religion as authoritarian depends for survival. This conflict arises directly from the fact that women are beginning to overcome the divided self and divisions from each other."[19]

Some contemporary feminists reclaimed the witch once more, as such figures gained visibility in mainstream depictions of female solidarity, as seen in the films *The Craft* (Andrew Flemming, 1996) and *Practical Magic* (Griffin

Dunne, 1999) and television series such as *Buffy*. Marcia Gillespie, the editor of *Ms*, highlighted the currency of the witch as contemporary postfeminist icon in the magazine's October 1999 issue, discussing the witch's legacy of sexual deviance, communal disruption, and potential emasculation congruent with the feminisms of our time.[20]

The modalities of sisterhood found in each of these cultural moments and forms is brought to bear on the structuring of sisterhood in *Charmed*. Yet, unlike Moseley's assertion that the new feminist witch of the 1990s restrains the rebellious potential of female sisterhoods found in earlier representations of witch communities, the depiction of magical bonding between women displayed in *Charmed* acts as a politicized point of identification for contemporary teen girl audiences. The explicit feminist politics within each of these earlier cultural movements is renegotiated in the narrative and representations of this mainstream show, repackaging and reformulating the legacies of sisterhood for an audience familiar with populist postfeminist debate. Yet for a youthful audience assuming the pleasures and pitfalls of second-wave feminism such revisionings reinvigorate the debates of female empowerment with new force. The combination of entering into a magical identity and adult femininity (a symbiotic process in *Charmed*'s narrative) articulates a position of self-determination, a perception of autonomous subjectivity that enables the characters to make different choices, tackle personal rather than social difficulties, and struggle with a sense of power. In this way, it can be argued that the feminism constructed in the show and consumed by this audience is, as Bonnie Dow states "lifestyle" or "individualist" feminism of a kind critiqued elsewhere in this volume.[21] Yet the element of sisterhood, articulating this self-determination within a community of women, suggests a less didactic conception of postfeminism's articulation of feminist rhetoric.

In *Charmed*, the three female protagonists share a common history and biological connection from which their magical heritage stems and through which they have to negotiate sibling relationships and resolve familial tensions. The main characters of *Charmed* are women who led successful, "normal" lives until the revelation of their chosen destiny in their early twenties. This destiny precedes them as individuals, stemming from the maternal line; they must adapt to the power that emanates through their corporeality. The correlation between the powers of witchcraft and familial inheritance are well established in historical witchcraft discourses.[22] In *Charmed*, the connection between bodies incorporates the corporeal and the incorporeal, power in life and beyond death, for example, when Prue dies or in the sisters' constant petitions to their mother Patti (Finola Hughes) and Grams (Jennifer Rhodes). This description of female power can be understood in terms of the legacy of second-wave feminism. The Halliwell sisters frequently call upon Grams, the ghostly elder of the Halliwell family, in order to help them resolve a threatening situation. Grams, arguably a remnant of prefeminist culture, is constructed as the ultimate "good witch" of fairy tale narratives. Popular feminism's lack of visibly older women is potentially countered here, although Grams's constitution as a nurturing figure focused on the safety and desires of others is symptomatic. It is Grams who confirms the sisters' romantic involvements, marrying Piper to Leo (Brian Krause) and frequently offering sage advice to the sisters about their thwarted romantic lives. In a fashion akin to the generational assembly displayed in *Practical Magic*, these older witches are the instigators of female community and yet are positioned in the narrative as politically impotent and meddling, attempting to alleviate the younger generation's suffering under the pressures of "having it all" by interfering with their romantic lives.

It is the sisters' mother, Patti Halliwell, who offers the most feminist potential in the show. Divorced and dead, and remarkably absent from the series' narratives, she predominantly appears in flashback episodes set in the 1970s. Patti is represented as dismissive of men, focused on her career and her magic but ultimately thwarted by male demons within the narrative of 'That 70s Episode' (1:17). The show's marginalization of her character is interesting for my purposes for, although the show emphasizes the solidarity of the female family line irrespective of personal differences, the omission of Patti's voice implies a political alliance between Grams and the modern Halliwells, suggesting a mutuality between the prefeminist, feminine cultures of the 1950s and contemporary postfeminism. In the process, Patti is discredited as the "bad mother," unruly because she is divorced and rather footloose yet autonomous within the show, a trope well traversed in the iconography of popular witches.[23] Despite these generational machinations, and the problematizing of the only woman historically and stylistically located in relation to second-wave feminism, *Charmed* repeatedly encodes the centrality of genealogical continuity in the display of female power, a biological connectivity that exists irrespective of personal or political differences.

This essentialist vision of female empowerment, alongside the predication of traditional roles within the show, exemplifies the new traditionalism of postfeminist iconography. For Sarah Projansky this new traditionalism of backlash postfeminism construes feminism "as threatening to the family."[24] However, in *Charmed* new traditionalism is coupled with feminist notions of female *collectivism*, which partially recuperates a female family for feminist politics. Further, the focus on blood kinship heightens the dimension of racial exclusion; the postfeminist family here is an exclusively white, affluent version. To an adolescent girl audience familiar with single parenting (which is still primarily practiced by women), this depiction of grandmother-mother-daughter relationships as "essentially" magical could be read as a postfeminist concession; a recognition of women's facility to "care" while acknowledging that this frequently comes not as a choice but in response to circumstances that have social and spiritual "benefits."

The enabling of others through witchcraft is central to current teen witchcraft practices and the shows depicting young women as witches; the focus for these teenagers is frequently on the use of ritualized magic or witchcraft beliefs to empower the self in a difficult situation, thus transforming the situation and the self for the better.[25] In a culture in which family units are constantly changing and teenagers have limited external resources to draw on in times of such difficulty, the practice of magic, inspired by popular texts such as *Charmed*, describes women's empowerment as a consequence of female to female relationships, whether familial or otherwise, where to be female is to be special. Ann and Barry Ulanov describe the role of sisters in portrayals of witchcraft as pointing to "the possibility of connection to the collective elements of the feminine."[26] The depiction of the "collective elements of the feminine" suggests an essentialist reading of the witch sisters' powers in *Charmed*. In all "power of three" spells (the most potent form of magic available to them), the spell can only be said when all three sisters are present and speak in unison, yet, as I will discuss later, this is not at the expense of individuality. The centrality of a collective body and voice to the series' narrative is maintained by means of continual threats from external forces. The Halliwells are born into their identity as witches, a metaphor that works to question the possibility of individual agency, reinforcing discourses of female solidarity and collective identity. As the initial episodes in seasons 1 and 4 (in which Paige arrives) demonstrate, this legacy is both celebrated and resisted, a transition into a new modality of being that the sisters try to avoid and deny. On finding out about her true identity as a witch and a "charmed one" in "Charmed Again, Part One," Paige says that "the most horrible thing is happening to me." Despite Paige's reservations, the episode continues to display the bonds of blood and sisterhood. In the same episode, Piper states, "No matter what we feel or think, she is our sister, and sisters protect each other." This resistance to a new, potentially empowering mode of feminine identity expresses the desire to bypass and revoke the position of adult femininity. Yet it also connotes a temporal celebration of second-wave feminism's claim to female collectivity, which attempts to unite female experience so as to gain political leverage and female emancipation. In a fashion akin to that depicted through the figures of Tara (Amber Benson) in *Buffy* and Sarah (Robin Tunney) in *The Craft*, the correlation between the maternal line and the legacy of witchcraft is substantiated in *Charmed*. The unchangeable nature of the sisters' identity, in which the rules of their existence are predetermined yet continually reestablished, plays a central role in the series. What could be considered a regressive and limiting vision of power relations, however, is negotiated by the use of such powers. The universalized, essentialist magical power the sisters have is used to enable or empower minority groups—women, ethnic minorities, and children—that are vulnerable within the community and under attack from demon entities, frequently in the guise of corporate businessmen. The series continually articulates gender division between men and women, in this way connecting women to environmentalism and community. Frequently the women saved by the Halliwells are local neighbors or colleagues, women who are less powerful in the economic world. Evil women in *Charmed* lack autonomy and are constructed as mythological characters—oracles, seers, and magic users who need men to accomplish their work. Men are constructed as corporate figures; whether it is the corporation of the otherworlds or capitalist corporate structures within this world, the series portrays this as primarily a masculine domain.

The sisters' ability to empower local women is seen in "Magic Hour" (3:2), in which Piper plans her wedding to Leo. The episode cuts between the sisters trying to organize a "normal wedding" and attempting to undo a curse placed on two lovers, Brooke (Elisabeth Harnos) and Christopher (Michael Dietz). Piper's anxiety about not being able to have a mainstream wedding due to the supernatural nature of her work points out the series' central dichotomy—

that the desire for normality is undermined by the sisters' identity and work as witches. In the episode's resolution, Piper decides to save Brooke rather than get married. This moment of self-sacrifice, of placing another woman's well-being above her own desire, encodes two contrasting discourses. Piper's choice between liberating Brooke from the clutches of a lecherous male demon and her own incorporation into the institution of marriage blurs the boundaries of normalized female behavior. This action is abnegating, motivated by the desire to allow the cursed couple to be together, yet through empowering and saving Brooke and listening to her sisters' advice Piper temporarily avoids incorporation into normative heterosexual union.

As this example suggests, in *Charmed* relationships with women and good self-esteem are valued above heterosexual romantic relationships. Marriage is constructed as the ultimate happy ending, yet it is continually undermined; using narrative strategies deployed in traditional sitcoms, this happy ending is always deferred.[27] All of the Halliwell sisters' romantic relationships are unsuccessful yet ongoing, an inevitable consequence of seriality. While in a production context these narrative developments are primarily a result of casting changes, romantic happiness is nonetheless rendered repetitively temporary. This emphasizes the relationship between the sisters as primary but also symbolically articulates how work obstructs relationships. The male characters' allegiance is ultimately to corporate structures and institutions rather than the intimate, domestic structures of the women's lives. Thus, the temporary nature of heterosexual unions and relationships, irrespective of the levels of commitment made, is continually employed, suggesting that all men are potentially untrustworthy or dangerous. *Charmed* displays the distinction between feminine and masculine work, and the relationship between the two, suggesting the incompatibility of these gendered subject positions. In detailing the sisters' inability to maintain romantic relationships, *Charmed* reasserts the endurance and strength of female community.

Although the Halliwells have supernatural powers and are successful career women, they ultimately have to renegotiate their personal desires in order to carry out their duties as witches. Difficulties encountered in negotiating the world of demons, men, work, and domesticity are not passively accepted however, but rigorously negotiated through dialogue between the three sisters. Emotion plays a prominent part in these descriptions. The sisters are portrayed as complex emotional beings, and their domestic life is fraught with problems of communication, self-expression, and truth. This emotional complexity can be seen in "Power Outage" (3:7). The demon Balthazar/Cole approaches another demon, Andras (Jason Carter), to try and create a rift between the three sisters through his ability to amplify hidden emotional resentments to dangerous proportions:

> **Andras:** I can infect anyone. . . . I turn anger into rage. . . . Which sister shall I start with?
> **Cole/Balthazar:** The most vulnerable—the youngest.

As the episode unfolds, each sister has reason to resent the others. Eventually they each use their magical powers to harm another. The camera cuts to their magic book, the Book of Shadows; the cover changes, initiating the witches' loss of power. The only way to restore their powers, as Leo states, is "to try and restore your bond as sisters." Phoebe replies, "For the sake of innocents everywhere I think we should tell each other how we feel." In the outpouring of emotion that follows, the sisters display their solidarity and extol the relationship between feminine corporeality, emotional expression, and magical prowess. Emotional expressions have collective power; they are created and sustained by the relationship the witches have with each other and are often transformed through the power of the therapeutic speech act, which leads to action. These emotions are thus sources of strength, provoking the witches' magical powers into action, and sources of weakness whereby evil influences can divide their collective power. Evil and personal obstacles are treated in the text as similar adversaries—conversation and magical problem solving regarding the two often seamlessly stream from one into another. The powers of emotion, and of fluidity portrayed between the domestic, magical and mundane areas of the sisters' lives, reconfigure traditional structures of power regarding emotionality. In this series, "feelings are social . . . constituted and sustained by group processes . . . irreducible to the bodily organism and to the particular individual who feels them."[28] However, these are not the raw emotions traditionally linked to the body of the unruly witch. The Halliwells' displays of frustration can be understood as a more culturally acceptable form of (female) anger.

Frustration is presented as a powerful emotion throughout the series' story arcs: frustration over not being heard or believed and over the sisters' inability to effectively combine their destinies and personal desires or control their powers. This frustration encodes two political discourses. First, it demonstrates the consequences of postfeminism's assurance that women can "be everything." The sisters express a frustration with which many contemporary women can identify as they endeavor to live up to an overwhelming set of cultural expectations for femininity. The primacy of frustration highlights the impossibility of this task by demonstrating inevitable sacrifices. The sacrifices are those regarding the sisters' romantic and domestic lives; weddings are postponed, dates canceled, and material possessions destroyed. The role of frustration articulates the sisters' desire to be normal individuals, and yet order is restored at every episode's closure, maintaining their focus on each other and consolidating the tension between wanting and having it all. *Charmed* demonstrates that blood ties and the sisters' destiny as witches are paramount, irrespective of the personal sacrifices this demands of them.

Second, frustration is an emotion connoting adolescent identity, immediately recognizable to an adolescent audience frustrated by similar difficulties of self-expression, powerlessness, and traversing emergent adult femininity. For the teen witches on the Witchwords Web site, dialogues regarding individual powerlessness provide the basis for a communal bonding between them. As will be seen below, frustration expressed by teen witches is a consequence of not being understood or legitimized by peers, teachers, and family in relation to their witchcraft practice, a consequence in turn of their lack of cultural status as teenagers. The misrepresentation of their practices in the mainstream images of teen witchcraft also produces frustration.

sarah   7 August 2003, 11:49 a.m.
i knw wot u mean igo 2 a catholic skol we touch on sum religons bt nt even close2 witch craft or pagan wicca its nt fair! if we beliv in sumthng surly its decent anoth 2let ovas learn dats how jesus got knwn wen isay im a witch pepl cal me a satanist!

sara   7 August 2003, 11:53 a.m.
wen i tell pepl im a witch and practise the craft thy think id hav a wart and fly a broomstik on weekdays! alkso do find pepl fink ur a satanist an worship the devil its crazy iknw al chritians go 2 church does anyı get that

The expression of frustration in *Charmed* (and reflected through the witchwords community) creates a forum for female bonding that articulates both feminist and postfeminist discourse. The Halliwell sisters offer innovative possibilities for feminine identity construction to a teen audience from the constructed clash between traditional feminine discourses of essentialist power and feminist politics regarding female communal unity, political emancipation, and the expression of personal emotion. *Charmed*'s representational politics outlines the difficulties demonstrated in feminist thought between the power of women united through a "shared, innate quality" and positionality whereby individual articulation of historical discourses of power relations are considered.[29] The tension between these two forces of feminist resistance is respresentationally figured in the narratives of *Charmed*, highlighting epiphanies in which the recognition of difference and its incorporation into the collective unit enable moments of empowerment.

A Witch's Work Is Never Done:
Domestic Economies of Witch-Work

The appeal of the Halliwell sisters to the contemporary teen audience is not limited to the characters' expression of an action-packed, empathic girl power. These characters can be understood as aspirational images of postfeminism through the sisters' work, consumption, and economic prowess. Work, for the Halliwell sisters, can be defined through two modalities: the work they get paid for and their "witch-work." Witchcraft is displayed as a form of unpaid labor undertaken as each sister holds down some form of career.[30] The witches' day jobs maintain the economic stability of the household, although the Halliwells' finances are given little narrative attention. Throughout the series, however, the women attempt to negotiate between their chosen professions and the demands of their witch-work. Their nonmagical careers are repeatedly disrupted by the needs of their witchcraft and the emotional needs of their sisters. For example, in "Wicca Envy" (1:10), Prue's charismatic male boss, Rex (an evil warlock), tries to frame her for a crime and, as part of a plan to remove the sisters' powers, dates Phoebe, much to Prue's chagrin. A discussion between Piper and Prue during Phoebe's date with Rex demonstrates the witches' desire to separate work from home, an effort that constantly fails.

> **Piper:** She's a big girl, Prue. . . . He's rich, he's stable, he's handsome. You should be happy for her.
> **Prue:** I'm thrilled.

Piper: You're jealous!

Prue: No, no. I'd just like to keep my work world separate from my home world.

Piper: Good luck.

The episode climaxes with the threat of the sisters having to yield their witch powers. The loss of their power, and subsequently their sisterhood, is constructed as a greater threat than the loss of paid employment; in the end, Prue and Phoebe are no longer employed, but the sisters still have their powers. This episode demonstrates the ways in which the sisters' identity as witches continually disrupts their economic stability. Whether they are called away from work to perform urgent duties as witches or their magical abilities are called on in the workplace, the series encodes the career as a space where the witches fail to lead ordinary lives. This is, as Moseley suggests, illustrative of the anxieties inherent in the postfeminist position.[31] Although the series posits as normal and acceptable the need for independent women to work and be economically self-sufficient, their identities as witches preclude stable employment. Their paid work provides opportunities for encountering evil and is frequently the cause of romantic and familial tensions, but it never serves as their primary goal or aspiration. The sisters are never shown discussing their long-term career plans or their desires for a bigger club or a larger paycheck. Although work provides a respite from the chores of witchcraft, when the two realms collide the only certainty is that the sisters' bond with each other will be restored, frequently at the cost of their employment or the development of their careers.

Witch-work takes place in the witches' community, their workplace and in their home. The witch-work enables them to spend time in, and indeed privileges, the domestic space. Through the presence of the Book of Shadows, they are tied to the manor, where most of their problem solving takes place. Similarly, the brewing of potions and writing of spells are primarily shown in the domestic space, the former in the kitchen and the latter in personal bedroom spaces or the attic, which conceals the Halliwell book. The continuous battles with evil forces and the rescue of those under threat frequently result in work being forcefully brought into the home. This can be seen in "Power Outage," in which the sisters' fight leads them to encounter evil within their home; "Sight Unseen" (3:5), in which an intruder threatens Prue; and "Magic Hour," in which the star-crossed lovers are brought into the Halliwell house for healing and safety. Witch-work is continually reinforced as domesticated work, work that needs them or places them in the home.

However, although the house becomes a permeable space where domestic and feminine skills and discourses of healing, hosting, and maintaining order are reinforced, their witch-work also necessitates moves into the community, placing the sisters in physically dangerous situations. Drawing on generic tropes of feminine behavior from horror films, the series frequently depicts the sisters in dark, insalubrious, and potentially threatening environments. In "Magic Hour," they find themselves in a lonely shack in dark scrubland with the threat of demons or trolls to deal with. In "Wrestling with Demons" (3:12), their witch-work takes them into the dark alleyways of San Francisco, a male-dominated corporate office, and a boxing ring. The spaces traversed by the witches while fighting evil are meaningful locations. They contravene connotations of gendered space and are environments beyond the bounds of those where women "should" feel safe. The deliberate use of these spaces demonstrates the Halliwells' physical and metaphysical strength. All potentially threatening encounters are overcome by the witches in these spaces, whether by WWF-style wrestling (flamboyant and rather "stagey"), or, as in "Wicca Envy," where a fight at the corporate office ends in the witches regaining their powers and banishing two evil bosses. Witch-work enables the sisters to enter a variety of social locations and spaces that are connoted as threatening to women. They meet the threat through their cooperation and mystical prowess. Their victory comes either through a physical or supernatural fight or in the form of allegiance and the domestication of the threat (see "Once upon a Time" [3:3], for example).

The nature of witch-work in *Charmed* involves skills that can be similarly understood as articulating a postfeminist position. The sisters draw on their inherited mystical powers, but additionally the series privileges emotional nurturance and domestic skills. Witch-work demands that their skills include those traditionally associated with the "good witch" of fairy tales. It is typically done to help others for the "charmed ones" exist to help innocents. Thus, the theme of witchcraft and witch-work articulates discourses of feminine nurturance. This is not new to witch narratives and can be understood, for instance, in relation to the constructed witch-work of Sabrina Spellman (Melissa Joan Hart) in *Sabrina*. Although the Halliwell sisters are older and a little wiser than Sabrina, through their constantly shifting roles they revisit the negotiation between their witch-work and their personal desires. Their witch-work disrupts their work lives, their romantic lives, and their sister-hood, and their motivation to help others is driven by their desire to liber-ate women from the clutches of evil. The witches accept a raison d'être as nurturers, and their witch-work leads them to encounter female characters who are not believed by others or are trapped or at risk. As the forces of evil usually appear in male form and the evil women in the series are accom-plices or morally neutral, *Charmed* articulates themes of feminism (the desire to emancipate women) and postfeminism (an emphasis on domesticity and women's traditional caring skills).

This can be seen, for example, in both "Coyote Piper" (3:19) and "Once upon a Time." In both, the narrative hinges on listening to women: on hearing Piper as she calls out and believing a little girl who is harassed by fairies. The witch-work involves skills associated with second-wave feminist consciousness-raising, listening to and taking seriously the trials expressed by other women, and seeking modes of emancipation. The ways in which witchcraft is displayed as work are liberating, giving the sisters a source of personal power, even as such work is also driven by altruistic desires. Witch-work is unpaid, a recognizable metaphor of second-wave feminism's argu-ments regarding women's domestic labor going unrewarded and disregarded as work.[32] Witch-work is thus understood as a career, due to the demands and impositions it places on the other areas of the sisters' lives, but it has no form of public recognition outside of the esoteric circle in which they live. Through the activity of magic, witchcraft keeps all the sisters under one roof. Witchcraft is constructed as a labor of love but is displayed without en-tirely tempering the witches' frustration, anger, or resentment. Moreover, the desire and expectation to "do everything" clearly have political implica-tions. Within *Charmed*, the sisters' decisions regarding their different career choices are encoded as naturalized. As such, the series details their ability to "become whatever they want" as long as it doesn't interfere with their witch-work. Ergo, Paige, the newest addition to the Halliwell family, gives up her job in order to stay at home and take care of domestic duties and witch-work full time. This allows Piper to focus on raising her child. While the choices of women's work and the negotiation between staying at home and going out to work convey the postfeminist dialectic between traditional women's roles and contemporary economic expectations, the possibilities made available to the sisters suggest that women are capable of doing everything. Paige's decision to stay at home is promoted as one decision among many and one that benefits the life of the family, whereas Piper's inability to function solely as a "stay-at-home mother" highlights the difficulties of discourses of maternal bliss. Thus, the series highlights the tensions between career choices, suggesting that women should be able to work and have access to a variety of career options. Emotional rather than economic necessity is foregrounded in the show, thus sidestepping the professional and economic challenges currently facing women in the United Kingdom and the United States. However, through the structure of witch-work, *Charmed* challenges the parameters of these choices by suggesting that paid work cannot stand in the way of destiny and duty.

Yet, crucial to my argument, the form of postfeminist "liberation" in the series centers on the dynamic of the sisters unified, denying the postfeminist ethic of individualized feminism. Thus, feminism is not discredited as an outmoded totalizing academic or activist discourse, as would be suggested by critics of postfeminist culture.[33] In "Charmed Again" parts 1 and 2 (4:1 and 4:2, respectively), Piper and Phoebe fight the possessed men around Paige, who attempt to divide the sisterhood. The Source, the ultimate evil (a supernatural male character) tries to turn Paige to the dark side of magic, telling her, "You know where your destiny lies. It lies not with your sisters. It's for no one but you—this is what you've been searching for your whole life, this is why you have the power. . . . Use your power for your own desires, to seek your own revenge." The connection here between separation and evil demonstrates how *Charmed* valorizes the choice for women's solidarity as the ultimate form of empowerment, an empowerment of the self and others. By putting their witch-work first, the series privileges a disregarded version of postfeminism, one that exemplifies the power of collective strength.

Charmed details to the teen audience the range of options available to young women and the means of negotiating these complex areas of expectation through witchcraft, seeing all roles as necessary and equally valued and never singling out any career or lifestyle choice as especially important (even while the availability of choice is taken for granted). The success of each depends on the interdependence of each sister and of being able to negotiate between them the running of their lives.

Signifying the Spectacular: Location, Glamour, and Affluence

By locating *Charmed* on the West Coast of the United States, specifically San Francisco, a connotative relationship is built between the magical landscape and the cultural currency associated with this geographic area.[34] The associative glamour of San Francisco is encapsulated in the Halliwell manor, both its stately exterior and shots of the interior. For the British teen audience, the specific location of the series is perhaps less important as a designated city than as an urban American locale. In *Charmed*, the United States is portrayed as an urban, modern, and dangerous place, a place associated with crime, glamour, and the supernatural. It is also interesting to note that although *Buffy* is set in a fictitious city, Sunnydale, it is clearly described as existing somewhere in California. Both shows are thus located in a region of the United States associated with glamour, affluence, celebrity, and endless summers (despite the realities of San Francisco weather). The appeal of these locations to a British teen witch audience stems from a combination of these exotic, spectacular connotations and the "virtual tourism" this series offers. Furthermore, much of the information on witchcraft available to the British teen originates in the United States, creating a network of consumption and interaction between the two countries. Thus, the localness of *Charmed*, its geographical placement, goes beyond the role of the exotic and instead becomes an extension of an imagined female community with which the British teen witch may already be involved, whether via witchcraft-related Web sites such as The Witches Voice (www.witchvox.com), online covens, or the various witchcraft books written and marketed within the United States.[35]

At the outset of each *Charmed* episode, there is an external shot of the manor in which the sisters live. The house is shot from below so that the structure looms up from the ground, gleaming radiantly in the San Francisco sunshine. The location of the series and the style of house are central signifiers of affluence. The exterior shots of the manor reflect traditional fairy tale descriptions of the witch's house: set apart and surrounded by a "natural" environment, iconic of old money. Reminiscent of the aunts' house in *Practical Magic*, the Halliwell manor encodes discourses of history and tradition around the witches due to its relative age and ornate style. Although the interior of the house is constantly under threat from the forces of evil, it acts as a sanctuary for the victims of evil and the Halliwells. However, the house is continually signified as permeable, as in "Sight Unseen," where an evil force penetrates the house through mirrors described as "portals through which evil can travel." This permeability from unknown and known entities expresses an essential anxiety surrounding the concept of home. The house acts as the stage where evil is fought among the china and antique furniture and thus a place where concepts of domestic, familial bliss are frequently and literally shattered. The artifact-rich interior reflects the sisters' collective and genealogical affluence, a perception reinforced by the size and age of the house. Irrespective of the damage caused by the sisters' battles with evil, there seems to be an endless supply of such items and repairs are only fleetingly discussed. The dichotomy between home as sanctuary and battleground is thus metaphorical; the postfeminist reinvigoration of women's traditional skills is destabilized by the construction of the domestic space. *Charmed* connotes that domestic bliss for contemporary women is essentially fraught and compromised. Home, in *Charmed*, is presented as a space rife with potential dangers, a place where the status quo is always provisional.

Although the Halliwells seem perversely unconcerned about the continuous destruction of their home and the loss of family artifacts, they are not adverse to shopping or consuming at multiple levels. Conspicuous consumption is not only displayed but celebrated throughout the series; the show regularly reminds us of the "powers" of consumption for women, and these discourses are both celebrated and ironically critiqued. This is a central narrative trope in texts that detail postfeminist discourses. As Projansky discusses, postfeminist discourse in advertising and the popular press encourages and valorizes women's ability to consume as a signifier of feminism's success, enabling women to take control of their lives through consumption practices and the "freedom" of choice this implies.[36] In "Magic Hour," in which plans for Piper's wedding are discussed, and "Sight Unseen," in which Prue announces that she has bought the sisters "appropriate footwear for demon hunting," discussions of shopping are frequently injected into the magical narrative. Clothing is the primary commodity that the series uses to display the witches' shopping power. Their ability to partake in consumer culture can be read as an attempt to reclaim feminine "normality" without negating their allegiances to more subversive practices. Consumption of fashion is used to signify the witches' ability to enter mainstream femininity. Shopping is portrayed as a leisure activity for, although the viewer rarely sees the sisters engaged in the act, we are treated to their before and after responses. In this way, the viewer is rewarded with the sisters' consumption; the show assumes that the audience members similarly reward themselves, suggesting an intimacy in the use of clothing as a reward for work achieved and as an emotional surrogate in times of heartache and crisis. This is a point around which the audience is invited to share in the intimacy of the sisters' relationships.

Consumption has another significance, acting as a bond between the sisters through the repeated borrowing, swapping, and exchange of such goods. Operating as currency between the sisters, clothes, shoes, and jewelry serve as signifiers of affluence and intimacy. Although money is rarely discussed, the extensive wardrobes of each sister and the domestic interior connote affluence and glamour, not difference and otherness. For the teen witch audience, this correlation of female power with a celebratory attitude toward consumerism, appearance, and domestic skills articulates the pleasures of female-centered community. *Charmed* represents a community that does not strive to accumulate these fashions; consumption does not motivate the witches' actions but is clearly a payoff and frequently a nexus for sisterly bonding. In the discussion between Piper and Phoebe that follows Prue's death ("Charmed Again, Part Two"), one of the triggers for the outpouring of grief is the story of a dispute and resolution over a piece of borrowed clothing. In *Charmed*, consumption is a vehicle through which to express and celebrate sisterhood. By normalizing the Halliwells' appearance, making them superficially attractive, *Charmed* allows the teenage audience to identify with these powerful women. They become aspirational figures of success, as well as signaling a postfeminist pact between beauty and power.

Conclusion

Charmed's articulation of postfeminist politics and pleasures through the construction of multiple characters and sisterhood demonstrates how the series allows a description of various feminine roles. The types of power the Halliwells hold and their modus operandi do not represent unruly difference but an alternative discourse of female empowerment that settles within mainstream concepts of femininity and feminism. In *Charmed*, witchcraft is the means through which bonds between women are established as primary, where difference has to be understood but a unified community maintained. Although the series does not posit an explicitly feminist stance for its central characters, the engagement and acknowledgment of difference between the women, their relationships with other women, and their ability to sacrifice heteronormative relationships in the pursuit of a "higher good" outline the tensions between the feminist and postfeminist position of these characters. The Halliwells are not granted a position as other in the way Moseley suggests would give them access to countercultural forms of power.[37] Instead the power on offer to these characters is dependent on a concept of the "docile body," a body that is born into a particular destiny and from which no change is possible. Although the essentialism in *Charmed* is central to the understanding of plot development, this is not, I would argue, a universalizing of female corporeal experience. From lifestyle choices to the forms of career undertaken, the Halliwells express different modalities of aspiration and experience. Moreover, they engage with discourses of contemporary femininity—the stress of having it all. The witch sisters articulate a feminism that allows difference, if only white middle-class difference, while displaying the anxieties of modern Western femininity. The pleasures of traditional feminine pursuits such as shopping, dressing up, and gossip are overt, and consumption is not placed in opposition to resistance to dominant modes of expression and self-constitution. These are women who can kick ass when needed, dump men, and banish evil while cooking, looking good, and misunderstanding each other.

Consumption and glamour are figured within the series not as crimes but as pleasures. They do not undermine the power of these women nor succinctly place them in the position of the oppressed. Thus, for the teen witch, these fictional witches epitomize a bricolage of feminine powers from within various discourses of contemporary femininity. The backlash against feminism has successfully created a culture in which it is not cool to be feminist. As Angela McRobbie writes, "Few young women identify themselves as feminist. It is old and weary. . . . On being asked about their image of the feminist, the girls say with one voice "She's a fat, hairy, angry lesbian.""[38] The feminists of current contemporary visual culture are less othered, more glamorous and conventionally visually attractive. The positioning of the Halliwell sisters between discourses of feminism and postfeminism enables the teen witch audience to feel inspired by the bond between women and the problematized relationship between power and style, which is both glamorous and aspirational. Feminist icons must now be beautiful, clever, and willing to run themselves ragged in order to reach a young audience hungry for visions of powerful women that articulate the difficulties of female adult life in order to question and resist the status quo while existing within it.

Notes

1. The epigraph and similar citations in this essay come from teen witch respondents' dialogues on www.witchwords.net, a research Web site that investigated British teenage witchcraft between October 2001 and September 2004. For further information, see my doctoral thesis, "New Generation Witches."
2. Davis and Dickinson, *Teen TV*, 5.
3. Moseley, "Glamorous Witchcraft."
4. Ibid., 421.
5. Constance M. Burge, the series' creator and occasional writer, executive producer, and executive consultant, worked as a writer and consulting producer on shows such as *Ally McBeal* (Fox, 1997) and *Savannah* (WB, 1996). These shows routinely explored the dynamic between traditional gendered expectations and the changing politics of women's lives. Although Burge cannot be held responsible for the character and plot development in these series, her media biography suggests a continuity of interest between *Ally McBeal*, *Savannah*, and *Charmed*.
6. Personal correspondence, 11 June 2003.
7. Kryzywinska, *A Skin for Dancing In*, 119.
8. Television scholarship has avoided much serious discussion of this show, preferring to give attention to complex, groundbreaking texts such as *Buffy*. However, perhaps due to its very lack of moral ambiguity, evident pleasure in consumption practices, and prevalent issues of power corruption, *Charmed* offers a teen girl audience a vision of endurable female collective power despite its formulaic structure.
9. The monster family sitcom actively plays with the conventions of the family sitcom prevalent in American television production throughout the 1960s and 1970s. Thus, shows such as *The Addams Family* (ABC, 1964–67), *The Munsters* (CBS, 1964–66), *Bewitched* (ABC, 1964–72), and *I Dream of Jeannie* (NBC, 1965–70) utilized the otherness of the family's or mother's appearance and lifestyle to license the series' depiction of traditional family values. This is discussed in Hartley, "Situation Comedy—Part One," 66; and in detail in Spigel, "From Domestic Space to Outer Space."
10. Hartley, "Situation Comedy—Part One."
11. See Hollinger, *In the Company of Women*, 7, for a discussion of varieties of female friendship films, a typology that can also be productively employed to discuss television texts such as *Charmed*.
12. Ibid., 4.
13. hooks, "Feminism," 25.
14. Purkiss, *The Witch in History*, 146.
15. Badley, "Spiritual Warfare."
16. See Allen, Sanders, and Wallis, *Conditions of Illusion*.
17. For example, see Christ, *Woman Spirit Rising*; Walker, *Woman's Encyclopaedia of Myths and Secrets*; and Stone, *When God Was a Woman*. It is important to note that the early phase of the women's spirituality movement faced questions regarding the privileging of white middle-class women and the focus on Anglo spiritual traditions. At

the time, few writers and ritualists used these to focus on women's empowerment. For an example, see Teish, *Jambalaya*, which draws on the African Yoruba Lacumi tradition. It can be argued that this initial phase of the women's spirituality movement, with its focus on an exotic white ethnicity, created an impression of "doing diversity" while maintaining discourses of racial disempowerment that were also encountered in early second-wave feminist debates.

18. Jong, *Witches*, 6.

19. Daly, *Beyond God the Father*, 133.

20. Gillespie, cited in Badley, "Spiritual Warfare."

21. Dow, *Prime Time Feminism*, xii–xiii, and chapter 1 in this volume.

22. See, for instance, Davies, *Witchcraft, Magic, and Culture, 1736–1951*.

23. Krzywinska, *A Skin for Dancing In*, 135–44.

24. Projansky, *Watching Rape*, 72.

25. On current teen witchcraft practices, see Sanders, "New Generation Witches."

26. Ulanov and Ulanov, *The Witch and the Clown*, 59.

27. Here I am referring to the circular nature of the narrative structure of the traditional situation comedy, in which the opening situation, usually one of entrapment, is confirmed in the episode's closure. Thus, the status quo is reinstated or reformed at the end of each episode irrespective of the personal or situational transformation the characters have undergone in the narrative's development. In *Charmed*, the characters are trapped within an identity that they cannot escape. Although they continually aspire to be in fulfilling romantic relationships, these are perpetually thwarted by their identity as witches.

28. David D. Franks and E. Doyle McCarthy, *The Sociology of Emotions: Original Essays and Research Papers*, quoted in Bendelow and Williams, *Emotions in Social Life*, 135.

29. Kearney, "Don't Need You," 168.

30. Piper runs P3, a nightclub, while trying to decide whether she should have a child. Phoebe attends college and later is offered work as a journalist, and Prue worked as a photographer. Paige had a blossoming career as a social worker before deciding to stay home and run the "witchy business."

31. Moseley, "Glamorous Witchcraft," 420.

32. Periodically throughout the series, the witches observe that it would be morally unsound to charge for their services, a point that reflects the anticonsumerist discourses of contemporary Wicca and neopagan witchcraft.

33. These are numerous and varied, and much of the current academic writing on postfeminist discourse has been suspicious of or hostile toward current postfeminist trends. See, for example, Modleski's seminal *Feminism without Women*; and more recently Tarrier, "Victoria's Secrets at the OK Corral."

34. For a detailed examination of the cultural significance of San Francisco, see Carolyn Cartier, "San Francisco and the Left Coast," in which she explores the themes of liberalism and leftism alongside the city's "culture of activism," suggesting that this is a city where "lifestyle priorities and their arenas of articulation are arguably more significant than race and ethnicity as leading markers of identity formation" (152).

This is a crucial signification for the show's British audience. Associated from the 1960s with counterculture politics, and from the 1970s with the birth of the American Witchcraft and Goddess Spirituality movements, particularly the activism of the seminal Witch and author Starhawk and the establishment of the Reclaiming Collective in San Francisco (see Starhawk, *The Spiral Dance* and *Truth or Dare*), it is not surprising that the series' creators chose to locate *Charmed* in a region of the United States less associated with magical heritage and folk tradition than with transforming political discourses and the birth of the Age of Aquarius.

35. The majority of teen witch books, including Silver Ravenwolf's best-selling, *Teen Witch: Wicca for a New Generation*, are written by North American authors.

36. Projansky, *Watching Rape*, 80.

37. Moseley, *Glamorous Witchcraft*.

38. Natasha Walters, *The New Feminism*, cited in McRobbie, *Feminism and Youth Culture*, 211.

Suzanne Leonard

 "I Hate My Job, I Hate Everybody Here"
ADULTERY, BOREDOM, AND THE "WORKING GIRL"
IN TWENTY-FIRST-CENTURY AMERICAN CINEMA

The figure of the working woman has been a staple in American feminist discourse for some time. Long before Betty Friedan publicly proclaimed that the solution to female malaise was to be found in employment in the capitalist sphere, Charlotte Perkins Gilman wrote in *Women and Economics* (1898) that women must work outside the home in order to gain economic independence. She argued that because women enter into loveless unions in order to ensure financial security only when they work outside the home can they hope to separate the "sex relation" from the "economic relation." One common mantra in feminist theory, and increasingly in postfeminist culture, is that working women are reminders of the vast economic and cultural gains women have made in the past fifty years thanks mainly to their ability to ensure their own means of financial support.[1] Likewise, in previous eras it was precisely the lack of such economic means that often ensured women's dependence on fathers and husbands. According to this logic, the modern woman is fully capable of supporting herself and free to couple as she chooses; put simply, she may marry for love not money.[2]

As a feminist icon, the modern woman worker is, predictably, white and upper or middle class, as were the women whose discourse fomented the working woman as a feminist model in the 1960s and 1970s.[3] Narrating the story of working women only through the construction of such privileged and educated women is problematic, however, for it ignores the long history that working-class women and women of color have had in the labor force. Not coincidentally, postfeminist media culture has also implicitly accepted the white, middle- to upper-class model of the female worker as exemplary. My objective in this essay is to point out various contemporary representations that challenge these often unexamined celebrations of the woman worker as feminist heroine, a critique they often collapse with an interrogation of the marital institution. Specifically, I argue that, thanks to their employment of the adultery trope as a linking device, narratives such as the film *The Good Girl* (Miguel Arteta, 2002) are able to interrogate the class assumptions made about working women, as well as to trouble still pervasive ideals regarding women's investment in the marital institution. Broadly defined, the focus of this essay is how female adultery, as a cinematic mainstay, can problematize the figure of the twenty-first-century working woman, given its imperative to examine her class-specific relation not only to the public sphere of waged labor but also to the seemingly privatized sphere of marriage.

Work and Marriage: Feminist Legacy and Postfeminist Staple

It is necessary to first offer a suggestive mapping of the relationship between women's work and heterosexual marriage. As I argue, postfeminist culture borrows from a feminist-positive legacy of work but reconfigures the ideological underpinnings of this discussion, in many cases, to reaffirm the centrality of heterosexual marriage. The dialectical relationship between working women and marriage can, on the one hand, be verified by the fact that in many ways feminist affirmations of work have always been referendums on the status of marriage and the family. As both first- and second-wave feminists argued, paid female labor might free marriage of its economic incentives and free women from financial dependence on men. At its most extreme, perhaps, the recognition of women's capacity to earn their own livelihood might even be used to rationalize the dissolution of the marital institution.[4] Yet, despite the record number of female workers now employed in contemporary American culture, the popular conception of marriage as the most vaunted and desirable institution in women's lives has changed little. Indeed, heterosexual marriage remains the sine qua non of most women's lives: relentlessly mythologized as both the greatest achievement and the producer of the greatest happiness. This common perception has been aided, no doubt, by a multi-billion-dollar wedding industry, as well as by the rise in multimedia productions that focus on the wedding ceremony as the site of the achievement of bourgeois aspirations.[5] Similarly, the ongoing popularity of reality shows such as *The Bachelor* and *The Bachelorette* suggests that the nation is still captivated by the courtship narrative that leads to marriage.[6] Such ostensibly "entertaining" shows about women's marital aspirations are often fueled by an implicit pathologization of singlehood and are often offered in concert with more serious reminders of how time pressures are biologically enforced, specifically by declining fertility rates for women over the age of thirty. Collectively, such discourses effectively shame women into believing that if they do not marry and reproduce now it may soon be too late.[7]

This marriage-positive discourse has gained momentum thanks to debates over gay marriage, wherein activists, noting the myriad economic and legal benefits conferred by marriage, have rallied to demand that the same rights be accorded to same-sex couples. Although the divide between gay marriage supporters and detractors is deep, both sides paint the marital institution in highly attractive terms. Similarly, the beneficial economic attributes of marriage are often touted by social and fiscal conservatives who, because they see marriage as a panacea for poverty, advocate the introduction of social programs that encourage stable marriages.[8] For a host of reasons, then, marriage's status as a desirable commitment is a perception that has been left largely unchecked in the early twenty-first century. Likewise, while the denunciation of marriage was once a staple of feminist discourse, since the mid-1980s discussions of the social and political implications of marriage have lost their exigency as a mainstay of the feminist agenda.[9] Affirmative accounts of marriage can even be found in the work of many self-proclaimed third-wave feminists who, in a clear departure from those in the first and second waves, declare that because women's economic situations have altered so dramatically the terms on which they enter into marriage have also changed.[10] In the popular tract, *Manifesta: Young Women, Feminism, and the Future*, for example, Jennifer Baumgardner and Amy Richards remark, "Nowadays, marriage is less likely to be a compromise for our women and more likely to be a choice. . . . Women may keep their last names when they marry, maintain their careers, or have husbands who know how to wield a Dustbuster like a pro—that is, like a woman."[11] The implication of such sentiments is that because paid work has become a cornerstone of female existence, a fact Richards and Baumgartner seem to take for granted, women now enter heterosexual marriage on their own terms rather than as economic dependents or domestic caretakers.

In the postfeminist popular media, these celebratory representations of marriage are even less tempered and often take on an additional valence wherein they emphasize that if push comes to shove a woman's marital status is indeed *more* important than her career. Such portrayals frequently emphasize that female employment, far from being the sort of life necessity that feminists advocated, has the potential to be a hindrance to her "feminine" aspirations. Thus, recent cinematic offerings frequently school twenty- and thirty-something women in the importance of not allowing their careers to overwhelm their marriage or maternal prospects. As Diane Negra argues, films such as *Miss Congeniality* (2000), *The Wedding Planner* (2001), and *Life or Something Like It* (2002) instruct single women on the "need to scale back their professionalism, lest they lose their femininity."[12] To this list I would add *Mona Lisa Smile* (2003), a film that emphasizes the point that Katherine Watson's (Julia Roberts) devotion to her job as an art professor at a small women's college in the 1950s precludes her chance for marital happiness, and also *The Stepford Wives* (2004) and *Spanglish* (2004), wherein women who *are* married find that their professional habits have left them woefully out of touch with the skills necessary to be good wives and mothers.[13] Likewise, films such as *Raising Helen* (2004) and *13 Going on 30* (2004) combine such feminine deficiencies with unconvincing plot machinations, thereby redressing a career woman's inadequacies by fantastical means. In *Raising Helen*, the protagonist, Helen (Kate Hudson), a modeling agency executive, unexpectedly inherits her dead sister's children, a plot device, which, à la the 1980s phenomenon *Baby Boom*, teaches her "how to be a mom," whereas *13 Going on 30* offers a time travel narrative that affords thirteen-year-old Jenna Rink (Jennifer Garner) a glimpse into what will be her unfulfilling future as a conniving and selfish editor of a New York fashion magazine.

Feminist-inflected discussions of the importance of finding suitable, lucrative, and relevant labor have thus receded in a postfeminist culture far more concerned with reminding women of all the personal and romantic goals their laboring might put in jeopardy. This shift in tone is also natural-ized, thanks to the implicit suggestion that the particularities of work are no longer something with which women need concern themselves. Postfeminist culture assumes, in fact, that all women possess the requisite credentials to lay claim to the jobs they desire and that once they do so they will be well com-pensated for their efforts. Existing as a projection of such optimistic general-izations, the postfeminist working girl therefore appears almost inevitably as a white, upper-middle-class woman who is affluent, educated, and urban, as exemplified by paradigmatic figures such as Ally McBeal, Bridget Jones, and *Sex and the City*'s Carrie Bradshaw. Not coincidentally, these women all avoid occupational drudgery, in the sense that they are engaged in high-paying, high-status professions, or are compensated with jobs that grant them a high degree of cultural currency such as working as a newspaper columnist.[14] Such occupations have the added rationale of rendering (somewhat) believable these women's enjoyment of myriad consumer pleasures, for each representa-tion also celebrates the symbolic and material goods to which these women's implied economic freedom ensures them access.[15]

Such models are predicated, then, on the idea that, although the postfemi-nist working girl benefits from a legacy of feminist critique over the issues of marriage and work, for her these debates have little historical specificity or urgent import. Similarly, while professional issues are sometimes rendered in the mediums in which she appears, it is again often with an eye to the dramatic, psychological, romantic, or sensationalized aspects of her labor-ing. Rarely in such representations is her work boring, tedious, or even all that labor intensive. Thus, perhaps because this form of postfeminism in-volves a transition from a feminist emphasis on politics to a postfeminist em-phasis on culture, what we now see in popular culture, I would contend, are representations of working women that are generally quite inattentive to the material conditions and pressures of actual work.[16] Similarly, although there may be an economic rationale for the postfeminist working girl's existence in the workforce, such concerns are not paramount; as Sarah Projansky has argued, postfeminism generally refuses to acknowledge class differences, and thus it dissipates the possible tension between women who *want* to work and those who *have* to work.[17] This ignorance of what is indeed a drastic socioeco-nomic divide between haves and have-nots in American culture, I suspect, directly informs discussions that suggest, as many do, that the greatest dilemma facing working women today is whether or not *to* work. This rhetoric has intensified in recent years, reaching its apex perhaps in the fall of 2003 when the *New York Times* published an article entitled "The Opt-Out Revolution," wherein it elevated to the status of a revolution the trend of affluent, Ivy League–educated, professional women leaving high-earning, high-status careers in droves in order to raise their children. Despite this domestic rationale, the article was somewhat skeptical of what it seemed to suggest was a thinly veiled excuse on the part of these women to devote their time to easier and less time-consuming pursuits; the article opened, for example, on a group of mothers having wine and cheese in a cozy Atlanta living room.[18] There is some sociological evidence to suggest that the opt-out trend is real, though perhaps heavily exaggerated. In March 2005, the *Harvard Business Review* published a study based on a survey of 2,443 female executives, which reported that 37 percent of "highly qualified" women did drop out of the labor force at some point, yet they did so for an average of only 2.2 years. The financial consequences of even these temporary breaks, however, were high—for women working in business who left the workforce for even a short amount of time, earnings dropped an average of 28 percent.[19] It is important to remember, then, that even those who opt out of the paid workforce are likely to see this as a temporary rather than permanent change and likewise enjoy an option open only to the relatively financially privileged. Such supposed trends have nevertheless contributed greatly to shaping the face of contemporary debates over working women, for they exacerbate the already pervasive cultural tendency to frame women's presence in the workplace as merely a "lifestyle choice" and virtually ignore the economic incentives that not only encourage women to work but also often necessitate it.[20]

Indeed, as is borne out by a number of recent economic analyses, millions of women work not to claim a professional identity or at jobs in which they are personally invested but because the financial realities of American life make economic survival otherwise impossible. As Michele Sidler argues in her essay "Living in McJobdom," "For many young women now, the choice whether or not to work is no longer an either/or proposition. Most twentysomething women do not question the possibility of work, and not necessarily because we feel particularly empowered or independent."[21] Contrary to popular reports, the most alarming economic trend in recent years affecting women is perhaps not the fact that they are voluntarily leaving the workplace but rather the far more disheartening reality that the growing economic disparity between the rich and poor in America continues to intensify, in part because, as the economists who authored *Divergent Paths: Economic Mobility in the New American Labor Market* argue, there has been "disproportionate growth of low-wage careers in service industries and nonmanagerial occupations, a pattern that suggests that deindustrialization has left its mark. The frequency of low-wage careers has risen."[22] Such careers, they add, offer few opportunities for wage growth, promotion, or training.[23] Likewise, while the increase in service jobs affects both men and women, there is reason to think that such demographic trends hit women the hardest. According to Macdonald and Sirianni in *Working in the Service Society*, "from 1950 to 1990, 60 percent of all new service sector employment and 74 percent of all new low-skill jobs were filled by women."[24]

Scientific reports of such distressing trends in the labor market have also been given a more human face, particularly by accounts that describe the economic brutalities faced by those who work in the service sector. Barbara Ehrenreich's best-selling *Nickel and Dimed: On Not Getting by in America* (2001), for example, details the economic impossibilities she faced when trying to remain financially solvent as a waitress, housecleaner, and Wal-Mart employee. Ehrenreich's book also includes the staggering statistic that almost 30 percent of the American workforce toils for eight dollars an hour or less.[25] Similarly, David Shipler's tour de force, *The Working Poor: Invisible in America* (2004), recounts interviews with a plethora of low-wage earners throughout the country, many of whom are single mothers and single wage earners with several children. Shipler's volume also illustrates the frequency with which the new service economy assaults the working class, an attack that appears depressingly without reason. A Wal-Mart manager in rural New England reveals, for instance, that the store could easily afford to pay its employees almost two dollars an hour more.[26] Those who labor in America thus increasingly do so not as glamorized workers but rather under the auspices of decreasing wages, globalism, multinational corporations, downsizing, deunionization, and jobs lost to fledgling markets in third-world countries. As Phyllis Moen and Patricia Roehling argue in *The Career Mystique* (2005), while sociologists used to classify workers as primary (full-time workers with benefits and the possibility of advancement) or secondary (part-time employees with few skills or little education), the prevalence of corporate restructuring and downsizing has today created a risk economy, which "effectively places almost everyone in something akin to a secondary-labor market."[27] It is under *these* conditions, I argue, that the current relationship between women and work must be understood, which is to say that models predicated on working as a choice are at best the problems of a small minority.

Moreover, while abysmal employment prospects and the growing gaps between rich and poor are disheartening for both men and women, the situation is exacerbated for women by virtue of their lower pay (American women still make 76 percent of the earnings of their male counterparts) and the demands of child care, for which women still remain primarily responsible.[28] Finally, we might consider the comments made by Lawrence Summers, then president of Harvard University, in January 2005. Summers speculated in a public forum that women's paltry representation in the academic fields of science and math were perhaps due to "biological differences." While his comments drew a firestorm of criticism, he also offered as another potential explanation for the gender disparity the seemingly less controversial idea that women, cognizant of personal demands such as child care, had less interest in pursuing jobs that require eighty-hour work weeks. One might ask, however, why men were not assumed to face similar dilemmas or, more pointedly, why such an unforgiving schedule is accepted as inevitable for anyone, male or female.[29] For all the feminist response rhetoric swirling around the Summers controversy, one aspect of his remarks that was hardly questioned was his assumption that the physical, emotional, financial, and temporal brutalities of the New Economy are justifiable for both the privileged and the working classes.[30]

To locate what I think *is* a necessary critique, and one that can be found in the realm of postfeminist culture, I offer a series of cinematic texts that are surprisingly attentive to the realities of twenty-first-century labor, an investigation they offer by also interrogating the invigorating promises of marriage. I make no pretense that these texts present the best possible critique of the New Economy or the marital institution. Yet they are remarkable in the sense that their invocation of the female adultery trope identifies this set of texts as one of the few places in popular culture where one can locate a challenge to celebratory rhetorics of the female worker and to the rampant overvaluation of the marital imperative. Not all adultery texts serve this function, of course, yet I am struck by the fact that in recent years there have been at least ten female adultery films distributed in the United States, many of which have garnered considerable acclaim. These include *American Beauty* (1999), *A Walk on the Moon* (1999), *Lovely and Amazing* (2001), *The Good Girl* (2002), *Unfaithful* (2002), *The Secret Lives of Dentists* (2003), *Tadpole* (2003), *My Life without Me* (2003), *We Don't Live Here Anymore* (2004), *Closer* (2004), and *Being Julia* (2004).[31] Before turning to these films, and in particular *The Good Girl*, I would first like to address the question of why female adultery in particular might serve a mediating function with respect to the issue of female labor. I ask: what ideas does the adultery narrative, with its historical link to the issue of marriage, make available and how might this discussion also speak to the realities of female labor in the early twenty-first century? Likewise, why do we find this emphasis on the infidelity genre, typically one used to uncover the hypocrisies of a restrictive social order, at a time when postfeminist discourse seems so invested in telling women that their life choices are determined solely at their own discretion?

Women in the Workplace = Adultery All Around?

Because investigations of female adultery now so routinely arrive at, and are often causally linked to, the situation of female labor, the adultery narrative offers a surprisingly apt vehicle with which to critically interrogate the uses and limitations of the figure of the working woman. I address here the ways in which the adultery narrative bespeaks a crucial vocabulary of boredom. Although it was once used to expose the banal repetitions of the domestic sphere, this narrative has been easily transported to the modern day workplace and especially to the low-wage service sector.

Perhaps surprisingly, it is virtually impossible in the present era to talk about female adultery without also talking about work. In part, this is because the workplace is so often blamed for creating the mise-en-scène of the extramarital affair, that is, for having enabled an erotic scenario whereby, because women and men are given such easy access to one another, extramarital passions are virtually guaranteed to flourish.[32] The psychologist Shirley Glass argues in her 2004 volume *NOT "Just Friends": Rebuilding Trust and Recovering Your Sanity after Infidelity*, for example, that the workplace is today the foremost breeding ground for extramarital affairs. Glass's work was somewhat groundbreaking in that she credited the rise in infidelity not to the workplace in general but to the increased presence of women in that space. As she writes, "More women are having affairs than ever before. Today's woman is more sexually experienced and more likely to be working in what used to be male-dominated occupations. Many of their affairs begin at work. From 1982 to 1990, 38 percent of unfaithful wives in my clinical practice were involved with someone from work. From 1991 to 2000, the number of women's work affairs increased to 50 percent."[33] Glass's sentiment was echoed in part in July of 2004 when *Newsweek* ran a cover story on the issue of female infidelity. Entitled "The Secret Lives of Wives," perhaps in part to pun the film *The Secret Lives of Dentists*, the article attributes the supposed rise in women's infidelity to a host of reasons, including the temptations of the workplace, the surging use of the Internet as an erotic breeding ground, and an increase in the number of harried husbands unable to devote the time or energy to making their wives feel loved. Yet, despite its insistence on the myriad factors that pave the sordid path to betrayal, the article begins with an account of a woman in her forties who after a decade of marriage began a series of adulterous affairs only after she returned to work: "Erin started seeing other men when she went back to work after her youngest child entered preschool. All of a sudden, she was *out there*. Wearing great clothes, meeting new people, alive for the first time in years to the idea that she was interesting beyond her contributions at PTA meetings."[34] In this equation of infidelity, work is the means by which women gain access to other men, and thus female employment is implicitly credited with having provided the material and psychological shift that infuses women with the boost of confidence that in turn makes them feel more attractive, and more desirable, to men other than their husbands. In some circles, of course, this feeling of self-reliance and autonomy would be celebrated, yet such sentiments also betray a hint of patriarchal bewilderment, and perhaps even anger, at the notion that the reality of Erin's work has made it more convenient for her to cuckold her unsuspecting husband. (Neither should it escape notice that Erin is positioned as a rather superficial person, moved to cheat simply because she is finally "out there" and wearing "great clothes.")

As these popular accounts make clear, the temptation for both men *and* women to indulge in extramarital dalliances has been aided by women's increased role and relevance in the contemporary workplace, and this focus on the woman worker in particular suggests that she is somewhat responsible, if not totally at fault, for contributing to this troubling trend. The discourse on female adultery typically stops short, however, of advancing the obviously retrograde idea that women do not belong in the workplace or that the existence of female adultery should be taken as a sign that traditional divisions of labor need to be reinstated.[35] Yet the sheer prevalence of discourses on female adultery suggests that at least one strain of cultural anxiety has coalesced around the figure of the adulterous working woman, whose increased visibility has been underscored by the plethora of popular representations that showcase her as a cultural phenomenon.[36] Although these representations vary in scope and character, it remains possible that at least some of these discussions are animated by the fear that working women might outpace men in the economic or intellectual realm. At least, there is an alarmist element to accounts that suggest that the rise in female adultery has reached epidemic proportions, discussions that often include the veiled suggestion that the increase in strained marriages is perhaps too high a price to pay for women's professional autonomy.

Read in conjunction with an impulse to curb the spread of this apparently rising trend, the deployment of the female adultery narrative in the popular media might signal an attempt to displace an instance of cultural anxiety over female labor onto a highly recognizable (and typically blameworthy) figure, the female adulteress. This strategy can be most obviously detected in a film such as *American Beauty*, in which audiences are encouraged to hate everything the perfectionist real estate agent, Carolyn Burnham (Annette Bening), stands for, namely, cold calculating ambition and an utter inability to appreciate her "good" life or her sweet husband, Lester (Kevin Spacey). Clearly meant to represent a career woman whose pretension and greed render her not only a bad wife and mother but also pathetic and humorless, Carolyn's affair with a popular real estate agent, Buddy Kane (Peter Gallagher), dubbed "the King" by his fellow agents, is similarly rendered as one propelled not by desire but by ruthless selfishness. In fact, the film suggests that Carolyn has sex with Buddy, a vile narcissist, for the basest of motives, namely, to further her own career. Carolyn's female worker is thus an amalgam of bourgeois pretension whose monstrosity is further underscored by the fact that she revels in orgies of adulterous sexuality and reads banal self-help books such as *Your Money, Your Life*. For all that it pretends to offer a critique of capitalist excess, the film in fact uses an unflattering portrayal of Carolyn merely as a foil for her more sympathetic, presumably less materialistic husband. Likewise, her frequent absence from their suburban home carves a space for the film to explore its real focal point, which is Lester's trajectory of self-discovery. The film never-

In *American Beauty*, Carolyn Burnham's (Annette Bening) professional devotion to her job as a real estate agent brands her as wasteful and pathetic. Here she appears after frantically cleaning a modest suburban home in preparation for its market debut, only to be disappointed when no one attends her open house.

theless betrays a misogynist impulse thanks to its none too subtle figuring of Carolyn as a caricature of the working woman—and cheating wife—utterly lacking in humanity.[37]

Part of my argument in this essay is thus to suggest that public anxiety about female work is frequently filtered through the adultery narrative such that the narrative offers a means not only of regulating and controlling that anxiety but also of displacing it onto an easily identifiable target. Patriarchal culture's need to keep the working woman "under surveillance" lest she get too heady with power (or lust) is also an obvious animating factor in some popular representations. Of course, it should be mentioned that a number of adultery films simply punish the unfaithful outright without using the figure of the working woman to provide mystification for a symbolic displacement. In such cases, the female adultery narrative is deployed in order to explore the threat that the unfaithful woman poses, in general, to the patriarchal order. One variation on this theme explores the profound destabilization that ensues when men suspect that their wives have betrayed them, an exploration typically accomplished by focusing not on the adulteress herself but on the forms of male anxiety she instigates. In *Unfaithful*, for example, Edward Summer's (Richard Gere) confirmation of his wife's infidelity is linked to an unstoppable act of heinous criminality. Specifically, when faced with the unsettling discovery that his wife, Connie (Diane Lane) has given an anniversary present from him to her French lover, Edward brutally murders his sexual rival. The film, however, also implicitly normalizes this murder by making Edward a highly sympathetic figure, a choice that renders plausible the idea that finding out about a wife's betrayal is so profoundly disruptive that it causes an otherwise righteous and principled man to suddenly do the unthinkable.[38] Similarly, *The Secret Lives of Dentists* explores the symbolic castration experienced by a thirty-something dentist, David (Campbell Scott), who is robbed of his well-being and even perhaps his sanity when he suspects but cannot confirm that his wife, Dana (Hope Davis), has been unfaithful. Because David struggles to fashion an appropriate response to his wife's perhaps wholly imagined betrayal, he is rendered in more sympathetic terms than is his emotionally distant spouse. Yet to the film's credit it insists on the obtuseness of Dana's reasons for straying and fails to decisively confirm or deny her adultery. Both of these films are notable, however, for having turned the tables on traditional gender typology since they position the male character, rather than the female, as the hysteric.[39]

Read in this framework, it is possible, though perhaps difficult, to find any feminist potential in the female adultery narrative. Yet I am convinced one *can* find such suggestions in the infidelity tale, specifically thanks to its ability to give voice to the condition of female boredom and, notably, to do so in a way that is attentive to the sorts of economic arrangements that have increasingly come to dominate the contemporary work sphere. In historical precedent, of course, the linkage between boredom and female adultery was accomplished by the trope of having unfaithful women driven to scandalous behavior out of domestic malaise. Excluded from the sphere of waged labor, their boredom was at least partly attributable to the fact that women's duties were for the most part limited to the events of family life. Perhaps the most famous of all bored adulteresses was Flaubert's Emma Bovary, a figure whose extramarital dalliances proved paradigmatic in codifying the idea that adulterous actions might testify to the corrosive effects of marital, familial, and domestic boredom. Adultery, as a literary and historical construct, might then be understood as a mode that articulated the boredom and restlessness that were the inevitable by-product of a social order which mandated women's estrangement from the economies of public labor and productivity. Likewise, the adultery genre has been almost unique in its capacity to take seriously the forms of frustration and disappointment characteristic of women whose unhappiness seemed to matter little on the cultural or national stage.[40]

Surely, of course, women's social positioning has changed in our current day thanks in part, as I have argued, to the changing landscape of the contemporary workplace. What has remained constant, however, is the ability of the female adultery narrative to speak about female boredom, a potential that has changed surprisingly little despite the new demographic realities of work. This consistency might be explained precisely with recourse to the specificities of the current work sphere, for as I have argued, the low wage service sector, with its plethora of deskilled labor, has increasingly come to dominate the new American economy. According to George Ritzer, author of *The McDonaldization of Society* (1996), and *The McDonaldization Thesis* (1998), the labor process is characterized by its adoption of the organizing principles of a fast-food restaurant. As Ritzer argues, workplaces are increasingly structured around the objective of offering routinized services in the interest of emphasizing efficiency, calculability, predictability, and control, yet these rational systems are "unreasonable systems that deny the humanity, the human reason of people who work within them or are served by them."[41] Thus, although highly skilled jobs that require autonomy and intelligence are the kinds most often represented in media culture, in real life many female workers find themselves performing tasks that are, in many cases, not unlike those demanded by and housed within the domestic sphere. Many low wage jobs are characterized by repetition, routine, and a focus on emotional rather than intellectual labor. As one prominent sociologist, Arlie Hochschild, has argued, jobs in the service sector (she focuses primarily on flight attendants) ask workers to engage in emotional labor in the sense that employees must to some extent bring themselves and their personal emotions into the work they do in order to also produce the desired emotions in others. Hochschild maintains, therefore, that because workers become alienated from the parts of themselves that are doing the labor they risk becoming alienated from their own emotions.[42]

This understanding of service labor as emotional labor is crucial to the argument I wish to make about boredom because boredom can be read, I believe, as an act of *emotional resistance* in that bored workers in effect refuse to mimic the idealized demeanor of the service worker as friendly, affable, and eager to help customers. At the same time, however, the presence of workplace boredom evidences the dehumanizing effects of such industries. If workers are asked to increasingly follow routinized scripts that predetermine everything that happens to them in the workplace, one logical effect of such standardization is to remove all vestiges of human creativity and autonomy from the work sphere. We must understand service jobs, then, as those which attempt to take control of workers' emotions and yet often produce a situation wherein workers are effectively dehumanized. Workplace boredom is thus both a *symptom* of this condition and a possible *cure* for it both exists as an effect of the labor and also, in some respects, allows workers to register their awareness of, and displeasure with, such conditions of labor.

By staging the event of an extramarital affair in a workplace setting, the contemporary adultery narrative reveals itself as one attuned to the conditions of both workplace *and* marital boredom. Such representations thereby capitalize on the adultery narrative's long-standing status as a paradigm for articulating female malaise; however, by suggesting that such disappointments are produced in a public workplace setting (rather than solely inside the confines of the domestic arena), the adultery tale persuasively connects an exploration of marital boredom to the equally, if not more exigent, objective of investigating and interrogating working conditions in the low-wage sector. The adultery narrative, already well able to debunk marital mythology, thus presents itself as a likely vehicle through which to *also* energize a workplace critique.

That adultery, as a cultural construct, can problematize contemporary configurations of labor is an argument I borrow in part from Laura Kipnis, whose groundbreaking essay "Adultery" appeared in a 1998 issue of *Critical Inquiry*. Using a Marxist theoretical framework, Kipnis introduces the term *surplus monogamy* in order to argue that marriage in contemporary formulations is, for lack of a more elegant phrase, "like work" (Kipnis terms it "intimacy labor" or "relationship labor") and that those plugging away at their marital relationships are conjugal workers operating in the "marital gulag," putting in their time to feed the marital machinery even as they become further and further alienated from the fruits of their own labor. Specifically, Kipnis posits that adultery functions as a protest against marriage, which it filters through an implicit critique of capitalism; she insists on the relation, as she says, "between the prevailing social organization of sexuality and the grander designs of capitalist patriarchy."[43] That adultery can be understood as an implicit rejection of the disciplinary effects of a capitalist society (and especially a service economy) is an animating principle of my essay as well, although *The Good Girl* shifts the terms of this debate slightly. Whereas one of Kipnis's foundational observations is that adultery functions as a protest against work because marriage, in many forms, operates just like a modern workplace, *The Good Girl* is often more explicit about the extent to which the workplace, rather than even the marriage, becomes the driving force behind an adulterous protest. Thus, while Kipnis notes that marriage seems like work, *The Good Girl* does the seemingly obvious, which is to make *work* seem like work, a reality that is surprisingly scarce in popular cinematic representations.[44]

Stagnation, Sex, and Small Town Inertia in *The Good Girl*

I begin this section by invoking Martin Ritt's *Norma Rae* (1979), a film about a small North Carolina town in which Norma (Sally Field), an uneducated, sexually promiscuous, divorced, and remarried laborer succeeds in fighting class inequality by lobbying for unionization in the textile factory that is her town's largest employer. A film about what I am calling "real" work, *Norma Rae* suggests that Norma's political awakening is spurred in equal parts by her rising sense of the injustices perpetrated by the factory owners against the workers and by an obvious sexual attraction to Rueben (Ron Liebman), the union organizer from New York with whom she begins to collaborate. Her story is underpinned, in fact, by the presence of extramarital desire (although it is never consummated), an observation that the film sidelines in the interest of exploring Norma's widening public and political commitments. Norma's trajectory, however, presents itself as an important backstory to my analysis of *The Good Girl* for it suggests a historical precedent wherein, channeled in productive ways, extramarital attraction can segue to a richer and ultimately more meaningful tale of class injustice.[45] The same cannot necessarily be said for *The Good Girl*, although I think the film is equally persuasive about the need to be conscious of class as a category of identity and the dire necessity of combating the dehumanizing effects of low-wage labor. (The setting of *The Good Girl* is a retail store rather than a factory, a juxtaposition that nicely illustrates the transition from industrial to service labor that took place in the United States over the latter half of the twentieth century.) *The Good Girl* is unwilling, however, to risk offering any solution to this disquieting pattern besides cynicism, a reluctance that may represent another distressing commonplace in our contemporary postfeminist era. I suggest that *The Good Girl* is in some ways equally insistent on collapsing a film about women's work into a film about extradomestic desires and extradomestic spaces, although, unlike *Norma Rae*, it stops short of the suggestion that in the deadened emotional locales of small town America extramarital attraction can provide anything other than simply more of the same.

The Good Girl centers on the story of Justine (Jennifer Aniston) a thirty-year-old retail service worker who is married to a good-natured but ineffectual pot-smoking painter, Phil (John C. Reilly). In this depiction of small town inertia, Justine's marriage and her job exist in synergistic relation in the sense that each seems to exacerbate the mediocrity of the other. That is, the film creates a symbolic corollary between the boredom of Justine's life in rural Texas, the routine monotony of her marriage, and her mind-numbing job at Retail Rodeo, a cross between Wal-Mart and a more old-fashioned retail store.[46] Justine's working environment is thus similar in many respects to the low-wage service sector I have been describing throughout this essay. Although perhaps not as routinized as the "McJob," Justine's position as a retail assistant in a massive warehouse store in many ways exemplifies low-wage labor in the New Economy: it is an unskilled or deskilled position with little opportunity for growth or advancement. Similarly, Justine's work as a makeup counter assistant has a clear domestic subtext. She purveys a private service that has now been transferred into the commodity marketplace, yet her position as a beautifier is somewhat perverted—the film offers the satiric suggestion that Justine and her coworkers' customers, once slathered with the moisturizing creams, garish eye shadows, and rouges the employees are peddling, often emerge looking tawdry rather than improved.

The opening scene of the film presents perhaps the best verification of its intention to establish a relationship between Justine's job, her marriage, and her life in general. It opens in darkness, with a voice-over in which Justine states, "As a girl you see the world like a giant candy store, filled with sweet candy and such, but one day you look around and see a prison, and you're on death row." A shot of the outside of Retail Rodeo interrupts this sentence, and in momentary succession there appear images of Justine inside the store at the makeup counter, rubbing lipstick across her lips with a look of total apathy; of a security guard, who is using his foot to play with the automated

Cheryl (Zooey Deschanel) and Justine (Jennifer Aniston) pass the time in the Retail Rodeo in typical fashion—standing around looking blankly at the space of their discount employer.

door; and finally of the store manager, who is surreptitiously eating candy in the aisles. Justine's voice-over continues, "You want to run or scream or cry, but something's locking you up. Are the other folks cows, chewing cud, till the hour comes when their heads roll, or are they just keeping quiet, like you, planning their escape?" Justine's opening monologue narrates a tale of devastating substitution whereby the candy store of a young girl's hopeful reveries has given way to the Retail Rodeo of a young woman's present. The store is stocked with candy, but it is hardly the penny candy, dime store version that Justine's girlhood fantasy promised. Rather, Retail Rodeo's overly lit aisles boast a mass-produced sea of KitKats and Milky Ways, which are being nonchalantly pilfered and thoughtlessly consumed by the store manager. The monotony that characterizes this atmosphere is also satirized by the female announcer's virtually pornographic incitement for women to clean their "filthy pipes" with Liquid Drano, an announcement that is accompanied by overhead shots of the store and its customers.

The paralyzing banality of this setting is, of course, most literally personified by Justine, whose thoughtless, almost crude rubbing of lipstick back and forth across her lips not only implicates her surroundings but also suggests that she barely transcends them. *The Good Girl* thus stakes its claim to stage an exploration of the effect of labor on consciousness for Retail Rodeo's evacuation of personalized meaning is also Justine's and recalls in part Fredric Jameson's compelling notion that under late capitalism one finds a waning of affect in people whereby there is "no longer a self present to do the feeling."[47] While Retail Rodeo's environment renders its workers virtually comatose, one might also observe that Justine's boredom affords her a way to refuse to participate fully in her life since her lack of affect registers a displeasure so strong that it is tantamount, in fact, to an utter rejection. Yet the terms of this rejection rest unmistakably on an act of self-immolation: in comparing herself and her fellow workers to prisoners on death row and cows waiting for slaughter, Justine suggests that inside a store that looks like so many others dotting America's small towns she and her fellow workers willingly continue their death march as they approach their inevitable (and perhaps quickly approaching) demise. This threat is realized, in fact, during the film's diegesis; by its end, one of Justine's coworkers, Gwen, and her lover, Holden, are both dead.[48]

The implications of *The Good Girl*'s death scenario are thus decisively linked to the Retail Rodeo, a fact that the film underscores with a close examination of service work. The first scene, for example, evokes the disciplinary conditions that one faces while laboring in a service environment; under surveillance by a bustling coworker intent on lining up lotions in perfectly symmetrical order, Justine is reminded snidely that perhaps she should try working sometime. Immersed in this supposedly friendly, "neighborhood" store, which is really simply a bastion of mass-produced goods and manufactured emotions, Justine's curiosity is piqued by her observation of a worker who seems similarly unwilling to participate in the corporate charade. Holden (Jake Gyllenhaal) is a new worker at the Retail Rodeo who stands at his cash register reading, either entirely indifferent to or in flagrant defiance of, the capitalist dictum that one must at all times look busy. At the age of twenty-two, Holden (his real name is Thomas Worther, as in the eternally suffering romantic) has renamed himself after J. D. Salinger's cynical and angst-ridden teenage hero in *Catcher in the Rye*, and after Justine approaches him they discover that they share a mutual disdain for their surroundings. After facing a customer who accepts a makeover and then haughtily announces that she will not buy anything that day, Justine reports to Holden over lunch, "I hate my job. I hate everybody here. . . . I'm starting to understand why maniacs go out there and get shotguns and shoot everybody to pieces." When Holden asks her how long she has worked there, Justine replies that it has been "forever and a day." Likewise, the scene that sparks their attraction is a conversation wherein Justine reveals her hatred for her husband and her sense that Holden also shares her disdain for life. She tells him, "I was looking at you in the store, and I liked how you kept to yourself. I saw in your eyes that you hate the world. I hate it too." Shortly thereafter they begin their affair.

Given the link the film establishes between boredom, anger, and infidelity, it is perhaps not surprising that a number of the reviews of *The Good Girl* equate Justine's plight with that of Emma Bovary, Flaubert's petulant and impressionable, adulterous heroine.[49] Yet in contrast to Emma Bovary's naive longings, which are ignited by her consumption of romantic narratives, Justine often appears to be simply numbed, incapable perhaps of even the misguided claims that Emma makes on her own happiness. As Justine tells Holden, "I used to lie in bed and imagine other lives, other cities, other jobs I could have, other husbands. Now I don't even know what to imagine anymore." Justine's description of her imaginative failures has an interesting resonance with Adam Phillips's comment that boredom presents "two impossible options: there is something I desire, and there is nothing I desire."[50] As an explanatory framework, Phillips's definition suggests that Justine's utterance that she no longer knows what to imagine, and by implication what to desire, is an indecipherability triggered, and also exacerbated by, her boredom. Adultery presents the bored woman with an available object, giving her something *to* desire. This interruption of mind-numbing stagnation in the form of a romanticized love object is also an interruption of, and act of resistance against, her working environment. In other words, while the McDonaldization ethic works precisely to standardize spaces and the workers that populate them, Justine's affair with Holden suggests an impulse to resist the corporate disciplining of body and soul or at least to wake that soul from the stupor imposed by the requirements of repetitive labor.

One quite elegant passage in the film associates the budding emotions of Justine's and Holden's affair, through imagery, with a reinvigoration of emotions such as hope and happiness, which seem to have been long drained out of this contemporary workplace. In quick succession, the film offers shots of Justine at work, where, instead of the vacant facial expressions that have comprised her entire emotional register, she is seen smiling at Holden, talking with Holden, flirting with Holden at the makeup counter, and finally in the bathtub reading. The accompanying voice-over narrates, "After living in the dark for so long, a glimpse of the light can make you giddy. Strange thoughts come into your head, and you better think 'em. Has a special fate been calling you and you not listening? Is this your last, best chance? Are you gonna take it? Or are you going to the grave with unlived lives in your veins?" With the exception of the bathtub shot, all of these scenes locate Justine and Holden in the Retail Rodeo, which thematizes the idea that their discovery of one another has made the unbearable monotony of the workplace a bit more palatable. Moreover, the image of Justine in the bathtub positions the affair as a sort of spiritual rebirth, for it suggests that there might indeed lie ahead for her a new life if she is able to forget this one and embrace the one yet "un-lived."

Justine's extramarital activity must also be understood, of course, as an implicit rejection of her marriage, wherein, although her husband is sweet, he is also lazy and fairly obtuse. Justine cannot get him to stay sober long enough to fix the TV set much less engage in an interesting conversation. She tells Holden, for example, that Phil doesn't "get her," that he's a "pig" who "talks but doesn't think." Interestingly, this view is proven to be something of a falsehood when, after he discovers her affair, Phil tells her he needs to get high in order to "escape" and then miserably, asks her if she sometimes needs the same thing. Here it becomes clear that he is not entirely inoculated from the same despair that consumes Justine but rather uses pot in much the same way that she uses adultery, as a brief but ultimately unsatisfying escape. Yet to read Justine's adultery as a mere protest against her marriage does not fully encompass the myriad structures of disappointment that inform her betrayal; more pernicious, perhaps, is the seeming small-mindedness of her town and the picayune trivialities and deadening boredom that characterize her job and thus most of her waking existence.[51]

In the context of the film's satiric logic, Justine's affair offers a momentary reprieve but no real answer to this staggering series of disappointments. It is difficult, then, to read Justine's adultery as a genuine attempt at revolt because her adultery is not an event of passionate abandon nor does it express a concretized plan for change. Instead, it might simply represent, as she says, her "last, best chance." The circumstances of her affair are frequently more laughable than romantic. Justine and Holden have sex while on the job, in the Retail Rodeo storeroom, an act that Laura Kipnis might characterize as "stealing time" from the capitalist employers but one that nevertheless does little to alter their working conditions. Similarly, although one might regard Justine's and Holden's active sex life as racy, it is also equally possible to read it as debased; like clichéd paramours, they meet in cheap hotels and even arrange their first rendezvous in the parking lot of a Chuck E. Cheese restaurant. Further, when Justine's husband's best friend, Bubba, finds out about the affair, he demands a piece of the action. Relegated to a sexual economy wherein she must exchange her body for Bubba's silence, Justine succumbs to him in the numbed state that characterized her affect prior to her affair.

Justine's affair is ultimately both disappointing and humiliating for, like Emma Bovary, she is distressed to find in adultery the same platitudes she experiences in her marriage. Holden, she realizes, is not simply a brooding teenager but a deeply disturbed young man who becomes so possessive of her that he steals fifteen thousand dollars from Retail Rodeo and plots their escape into the great unknown. As she reveals, "Holden was at best a child, at worst a demon." Similarly, Justine's life becomes consumed by hypocrisy, her newfound lack of morality distinguished by halfhearted attempts to kill Holden and her decision to pass off the baby she has conceived with him as her husband's. The film obviously parodies this "good girl's" turn to lawlessness and her increased capacity for cruelty, but more important is what it suggests about the choices available to her. In a crucial scene at the end of the film, Justine stops at an intersection and must decide, at that moment, whether to join Holden and run away or return to her job at Retail Rodeo. Significantly, the film sets this up as a choice not between her lover and her husband but between her lover and her job, although choosing her job, she knows, means "days upon days of lipstick and ticking clocks, dirty looks and quiet whisperings and burning secrets that just won't ever die away." When Justine chooses her job and turns Holden in to the police, which leads to his suicide, her decision may seem perplexing insofar as the film sites the locus of boredom more in her job than in her marriage. Yet, by collapsing the public and private in this way, the film suggests not only the interdependence of these two experiences but also their intractability.[52] Moreover, Justine's decision to return to her dead-end job (and, by implication, to remain in her dead-end marriage) seems to stem more from a tired resignation than any sort of intentional choice. This failure of imagination is thematized in the appealing but ultimately rejected image of the open road, which Justine visualizes as a dusty desert strip and describes as "the blue sky, the desert earth, stretching out into the eerie infinity, a beautiful, never-ending nothing." Yet, for all its poetic potential, the lure of the unknown cannot compete with the known quality of the everyday. It is thus the strength and not necessarily the appeal of the everyday that wins out, a parable, it might seem, for why America marches toward a grimmer and grimmer future for its underclass, all the while suggesting that its salvation lies in the familiar triumvirate of work, family, and religion. This decision, however, remains a death wish fulfillment for the provinciality the film satirizes is still Justine's fate.

The Good Girl closes, interestingly, with a happy ending that seems to "wink" at its viewers for it features Justine's voice reading the words of a story Holden wrote about them, a working-class fairy tale wherein a girl who is "put upon," whose job is "like a prison," whose life has lost all meaning, and who is misunderstood by her husband falls in love with a boy who is also put upon. Instead of imagining Justine and Holden living out this wish fulfillment, however, the images flash between visions of Justine at work, applying cosmetics to customers, and eating at a restaurant with Phil, Bubba, and Bubba's girlfriend, scenes that are clearly meant to illustrate her return to "normalcy" following Holden's suicide. The sequence then cuts to a shot of the vacant lot outside the couple's bedroom window, a scene Justine often stares at as she lies in bed, and then finally to a shot of Phil joining Justine in bed with "their" new baby, which audiences know is in fact Holden's. The wink of this ending seems to be its insistence on exposing the lie of this happy vision for in its shadows lies the adulterous affair that created this baby and the absent presence of the boy whose suicide ensured that Justine's falsifications will remain undetected.

This is, to be sure, an ironic and even biting conclusion, dependent in equal parts on Holden's sacrifice, Phil's forever believing in the deception of his false paternity, and Justine's questionable commitment to a marriage she once flagrantly betrayed. The searing rot at the core of this fantasy of domesticity, then, is not exactly dismissed or denied by the film for the sordid truth that underlies this family's precarious hold on stability is sublimated but clearly not eradicated. This scene is striking also for what it omits for the film does not end with what would seem the most obvious choice: the site of the Retail Rodeo, the locale that has provided the imaginative landscape for virtually the entirety of the film. What this departure suggests, I believe, is that an arrival at this admittedly compromised vision of marital harmony is a more preferable resolution than is a return to a workplace with little or no redemptive potential. For all its burning secrets, the family still represents an available site of fantasy, whereas the low-wage job site remains irrevocably locked in a ceaseless cycle of hopelessness and despair. That the film locates the source of disappointment more in the workplace than the marriage but then retreats to the marriage at its close confirms the paralysis produced when one tries to reimagine or reinvigorate the concept of waged labor. Similarly, it reminds us of the dire need to theorize work, especially as it exists for the many women for whom work is a necessity rather than a stab at feminist fulfillment.

Biding Time: Adultery in a Postfeminist Context

The Good Girl achieves a symbolic collapse between marriage and public laboring because it addresses the situation of an extramarital affair conceived and even consummated in the workplace. Whereas, as I have argued, recent postfeminist cinema typically focuses on unrealistic visions that either mythologize or offer reactionary accounts of female professionalism, this film provides a refreshing departure from such polarizing concepts in order to expose a number of troubling aspects of waged labor. Such reminders are made all the more necessary in the current climate pervaded by the Wal-Marting of America and an incipient rise in the service economy. Likewise, the exposure of such unsettling realities reminds us of the need to rethink the economies and ethics of low-wage labor, practices whose disturbing qualities are too easily papered over in accounts that view the mainstreaming of the working woman as feminism's greatest achievement.

While postfeminist discourse insists on lauding the "many options" women now have, the adultery narrative provides, in counterpoint, a far more pessimistic account of the ways in which so many of the sites of female fantasy—the job, the marriage, the family—are still institutions with their own problematic histories. This is not to say that the instances of female infidelity present in such representations offer a panacea for the inequities that characterize such institutional sites; if anything, female affairs are often as infantilizing and self-negating as are the marriages in which women participate and the jobs at which they work. This point is made even more bluntly by *Lovely and Amazing*, a film that also narrates a tale of an unlikely adulterous relation spurred in part by workplace resignation, a thematic it establishes by setting the adulterous heroine's affair within the confines of her workplace, the cramped spaces of a one-hour PhotoMat. A frustrated artist with a passion for creating specialized and miniaturized designs, Michelle (Catherine Keener) turns to a job that not only offers little opportunity for advancement or status but also requires her to participate in a service whereby images are mass produced by technological means rather than fashioned with hands or skills. Michelle's symbolic demotion to the PhotoMat (surely an industry that would fit Ritzer's categorization of a McJob) confirms that once her aspirations for productive and fulfilling labor have been cast aside she is left with the brutal reality of an hourly job working alongside, in this case, a high school student.[53] Michelle's affair with this student, also ironically played by Jake Gyllenhaal, seems to adopt this infantile valence for it begins thanks to Michelle's need to be reinstated within a sexual economy from which her marital status and age have disqualified her. Her subsequent arrest for statutory rape (her lover is not yet eighteen) indicates that her method of working out such staggering disappointments is more symptomatic that curative. In the debased trifecta of Michelle's brief adultery, her emotionally abusive marriage, and her mindless job one finds not a hierarchy but rather a constellation of offenses since all are made to signal the desperate, abject condition at which she has arrived.

That *Lovely and Amazing* equates all three of these realities suggests that the contemporary adultery trope hinges on a demystification of multiple sources of disempowerment and disillusion, although, unlike *The Good Girl*, it offers no narrative denouement that inscribes the adulterous woman back within the heteronormative family structure. In the film's penultimate scene, for example, Michelle visits a McDonald's restaurant following her arrest. This return to the site of saccharine familial sentimentality and childish indulgence only underscores Michelle's infantalization for there she finds Annie, her eight-year-old half sister, who has snuck out of the house for a midnight snack. Reminding us of the ease with which, in a commodity culture, corporatized chain eateries (and the processed emotions they purvey) present a simulacrum of domestic harmony, the scene suggests that the comfort Michelle seeks will surely not be found in the empty calories of her "Happy Meal," a poor substitute for the spiritual nourishment she craves. Michelle's retreat to this location of childish familiarity in fact offers no real solution to her marital woes, her domestic disappointments, or her stale ambitions. My point is not that the adultery narrative as it appears in its contemporary formulations offers itself as a magical elixir to right the wrongs of waged labor or compulsory hetero-sexuality but rather that its appearance is often symptomatic of precisely the types of degradation that so often accompany such institutions. The fact that Emma Bovary's modern-day counterparts find that work and marriage traffic in similar forms of stagnation suggests that the adultery narrative continues to offer a convenient and powerful paradigm for problematizing postfeminist refusals to look critically at marriage and work, issues that remain sources of disappointment and even despair for many women.

Notes

1. For more on the dialectical relation between the feminist movement and media images of working women, see Dow, *Prime-Time Feminism*.
2. The rise in numbers of American working women was most pronounced in the era following World War II. According to the U.S. Department of Labor, in 1950, 34 percent of women participated in the paid labor force. By 2003, the rate had risen to more than 60 percent. See "Facts about Working Women" at the Web site www.aflcio.org. Despite these dramatic increases, we should resist the impulse to credit the women's movement entirely for this shift. As the historian Stephanie Coontz explains, married women's presence in the labor market rose throughout the twen-tieth century thanks to structural and demographic changes such as the maturing of industrial capitalism, the rise in wages, greater education for women, and better control over childbearing (*The Way We Never Were*, 157).
3. Lower- and working-class women have always constituted a greater percentage of the labor pool than have affluent women, and according to Coontz it was working-class women who pioneered married women's employment in the 1950s and 1960s (ibid., 163). Yet the "ideological revolution" that promoted the idea that work was an important component of life satisfaction for women was instigated in the 1960s by "upper-middle-class, college-educated" women (163). The spike in women's labor in the latter half of the twentieth century is thus generally associated with this image of the upper- or middle-class woman who works primarily in the interest of self-determination.
4. Radical second-wave feminists were vehement, in fact, in their assertion that the fight for paid female labor could not be won without also tackling the economics of the marital institution. In 1971, Sheila Cronan wrote in *Notes from the Third Year* that "since marriage constitutes slavery for women, it is clear that the Women's Move-ment must concentrate on attacking this institution. . . . As long as women are working for nothing in the home we cannot expect our demands for equal pay out-side the home to be taken seriously" (65).
5. In addition to a plethora of wedding-themed magazines and books, there has been

a marked rise in television representations of weddings, including the Learning Channel's *A Wedding Story* and *For Better or Worse*, a reality show in which a couple leaves all the decisions pertaining to their wedding to their friends. In addition, networks such as the Style Channel regularly feature shows on celebrity weddings, do-it-yourself weddings, and weddings executed on a low budget. For a comprehensive materialist analysis of the wedding industry as both economic force and media event, see Ingraham, *White Weddings*. For a sociological history of weddings, see Otnes and Pleck, *Cinderella Dreams*.

6. Other shows that dramatize the courtship process include *Married by America, Who Wants to Marry My Dad, Race to the Altar, Till Death Do Us Part: Carmen and Dave*, and, perhaps the most sensational, Fox's *The Littlest Groom*.

7. For a comprehensive overview of the myriad ways in which society colluded in the 1990s and early 2000s to reprioritize marriage and domesticity for women, especially through discourses that attempt to discipline single and/or working women, see Negra, "Quality Postfeminism?" Especially striking about this account is the plethora of popular films, social policies, and journalistic reports Negra cites; she writes, "American women are bombarded in a variety of forms from advice literature to reality programming with neoconservative logic that defines their primary if not sole interest as (heterosexual) romance and marriage."

8. For an update on the conservative movement to strengthen the marital commitment, see Crary, "Conservatives Urge Broader Look at Marriage."

9. For a trenchant analysis of the reasons behind marriage's evaporation as a feminist cause, see Brook, "Stalemate," in which she observes that "in this climate of conjugal diversity, feminism's long and illustrious history of marriage critique seems to have lost much of its potency. Feminists no longer seem to care very much about marriage, and the passion with which our political foremothers rallied to decry marriage seems as obsolete as hooped skirts" (145).

10. There is, however, an important distinction to be made between third-wave feminism and postfeminism. Whereas postfeminism is best approximated as a cultural tendency that is either openly hostile to feminism or simply takes its precepts for granted, third-wave feminism is a self-conscious activist movement defined by its attempt to reformulate a feminist politics less restrictive in terms of class, race, and sexuality than was second-wave feminism. For an overview of the third wave, see Henry, *Not My Mother's Sister*.

11. Baumgardner and Richards, *Manifesta*, 37. Whereas Baumgardner and Richards suggest that their support for the institution of marriage has emerged because the reality of marriage has changed, other young feminists use their desire for marriage as an opportunity to position themselves against second-wave feminists, who they see as trying to "spoil" their lives by restricting their choices. In "The Feminist Wife?" for example, Patricia Payette characterizes her decision to marry as an example of her refusal "to submit to outmoded paradigms that tell us what we should and shouldn't desire for ourselves" (141). Payette's view is somewhat commonplace in a postfeminist culture that works to position second-wave feminism as a monolithic

and humorless entity intent on telling women what to do. Yet, by framing the debate in terms of individual choice, Payette both misrepresents second-wave feminism and sidesteps crucial political and social implications of the marriage debate. For a discussion of how the rhetorical positioning of second-wave feminism as dogma intent on making "ordinary" women feel bad functions as a complex means of back-lash, see Whelehan, *Popular Culture and the Future of Feminism*, especially chapter 1, "Retro-Sexism and the F-Word."

12. Negra, "Quality Postfeminism?"

13. In *The Mommy Myth*, Susan Douglas and Meredith Michaels explore how the mass media have contributed to the trend of overvaluing motherhood. Notably, they claim that this tendency, which they refer to as "the new momism," is the central justifying ideology of postfeminism.

14. Lynn Spigel has recently located the female media worker, as she appears in both contemporary formulations and historical precedent, as a productive voice for feminism. I would simply add that the role of the media worker is a rather rarified position in American society. Specifically, this type of labor confers an enormous degree of cultural if not economic capital. See Spigel, "Theorizing the Bachelorette."

15. This particular image of the postfeminist working woman has already had some critical purchase within media studies, wherein she is sometimes read as a legacy of the famous Helen Gurley Brown. Brown's hallmark 1962 text, *Sex and the Single Girl*, reassured female readers that working in order to purchase nice clothes and cosmetics was essential not only to advancing their careers but also to ensuring their desirability (and eventual marriageability) in a male-dominated world. Some modern analyses of working girls in postfeminist culture thereby attend to this figure by noting her compliance with the logics of presentation and consumption advanced by Brown. For an analysis of working girls in a specifically postfeminist culture, see Radner, "Pretty Is as Pretty Does." See also Brunsdon, "Post-feminism and Shopping Films." For a more comprehensive account of the various versions of working women presented in Hollywood films in the 1980s and 1990s, see Tasker, *Working Girls*.

16. One possible exception to this claim can be found in the genre of reality TV. Heather Hendershot argues that because shows such as *The Apprentice* and *The Simple Life* ask their stars to partake in the physical necessities of work, "reality TV is the first genre to emerge that is obsessively focused on labor." See Hendershot, "Belaboring Reality."

17. Projansky, *Watching Rape*, 87.

18. Belkin, "The Opt-Out Revolution," 42. This trend has also been explored by Mary Blair-Loy in her sociological study *Competing Devotions: Career and Family among Women Executives*. In this examination, Blair-Loy interviews women who have remained highly devoted to demanding careers in the financial industry and those who have left such positions altogether.

19. Hewlett and Luce, "Off-Ramps and On-Ramps."

20. Elspeth Probyn, in "Choosing Choice: Images of Sexuality and 'Choiceoisie' in

Popular Culture," refers to this postfeminist tendency to frame all personal and political decisions in terms of personal choice as "choiceoisie." She is cognizant, however, of the generalities that such conceptions often invite, writing that "one could rightly argue that at a material level the great majority of women still have very little to choose from and that all these representations that fill the air with alluring options are but ideological manifestations" (282). Sarah Projansky has elaborated on this trend in relation to the critical conversation about women's work, noting that what she calls "equality and choice postfeminism" generally "consists of narratives about feminism's 'success' in achieving gender 'equity' and having given women 'choice' particularly with regard to family and labor" (*Watching Rape*, 67).

21. Sidler, "Living in McJobdom," 26.

22. Bernhardt et al., *Divergent Paths*, 171.

23. Ibid., 176.

24. Macdonald and Sirianni, *Working in the Service Society*, 14. One obvious corollary to this trend is the increased feminization of work in the service industry. As Macdonald and Sirianni report, the fact that more women have joined the workforce has produced greater demand for the services once provided free by housewives, such as cooking, cleaning, and child care, which in turn has created the need for more service jobs, vacancies that are predominantly filled by women (2). Moreover, such jobs are frequently staffed by women of color, often from third-world countries. For more on these demographic shifts in the labor pool, see Ehrenreich and Hochschild, *Global Woman*.

25. Ehrenreich, *Nickel and Dimed*, 3.

26. Shipler, *The Working Poor*, 64–65. Censorious statements about Wal-Mart's labor policies appear in a number of books that chronicle economic disparities in the United States, including Bill Quinn's *How Wal-Mart Is Destroying America and the World and What You Can Do about It*. See also Liza Featherstone's *Selling Women Short: The Landmark Battle for Workers' Rights at Wal-Mart*, which recounts how a sex discrimination suit was brought against Wal-Mart on behalf of 1.6 million female employees. Despite the myriad accounts of Wal-Mart's discriminatory practices, strong-arm economic tactics, substandard wages, and fervent religiosity, the colossal dominance of this company continues virtually unfettered.

27. Moen and Roehling, *The Career Mystique*, 7.

28. The wage disparity between men and women was reported most recently by the 2004 U.S. Census. For women of color, the figures are even more abysmal: African American women make sixty-six cents on the dollar while Latinas earn only fifty-five (www.pay-equity.org).

29. For more on the increasingly unforgiving nature of the American workplace, see Schor, *The Overworked American*.

30. Interestingly, formal examinations of the "brain drain" created by women's exodus from the workforce have led to surprisingly progressive suggestions regarding how such brutalities might be minimized. Citing women's claims that when they returned to work they were interested in pursuing jobs that might help the commu-

nity, Hewlett and Luce end "Off-Ramps and On-Ramps" by urging companies to find better ways to put women's skills to uses that are altruistic rather than simply profit driven.

31. The topic of female adultery has also been featured on the international stage, appearing in foreign films such as *Innocence* (Belgium, 2000), *Faithless* (Sweden, 2000), *The Lover* (Russia, 2002), and *Facing Windows* (Italy, 2003).

32. Adrian Lyne's *Fatal Attraction* is perhaps the cinematic benchmark for this trend, although in this erotic scenario it is the man, Dan (Michael Douglas), who commits adultery with Alex (Glenn Close), a woman he meets at a work function.

33. Glass, *NOT "Just Friends,"* 1–2.

34. Ali and Miller, "The Secret Lives of Wives," 47.

35. One might attribute the lack of such traditionalist discourse to the fact that the woman worker has been folded so neatly into the capitalist economy thanks in part to her often sizable disposable income. As Elizabeth Cagan argues in "The Selling of the Women's Movement," 5–12, capitalism has always needed the woman consumer. Thus, contemporary celebrations of the New Woman (a term generally used to refer to working women) are in fact quite consistent with the capitalist imperative to encourage the highest possible levels of consumption. The figure of the working woman might signal an economic triumph to feminists, but she also looks a lot like a willing consumer, and even a profitable market category, to capitalists. For more on the production of the New Woman as a category created by the changing demands of a capitalist society, see Hennessy, *Materialist Feminism and the Politics of Discourse*.

36. In addition to the films cited earlier, one can find a number of representations of unfaithful women on television. In 2004, for example, *The Sopranos'* long-suffering Carmela Soprano finally strayed from her chronically unfaithful husband, Tony, and her betrayal came, perhaps not coincidentally, after her would-be lover recommended that she read *Madame Bovary*. Lifetime also ran a made for television movie entitled *Infidelity*, which linked an accomplished psychotherapist's extramarital affair to her reluctance to have children. Both were causally attributed to her failure to accept her "rightful" maternal role, a pathology instigated by her father's chronic infidelity. The steamy ABC television drama *Desperate Housewives*, which began airing in the fall of 2004, also won 2005 and 2006 Golden Globes for Best Comedy thanks to its satiric exposé of the graphic exploits of a number of gorgeous suburban housewives, some of whom channel their domestic boredom into sexual promiscuity. Interestingly, at the urging of conservative groups, which cited the show's racy content and assault on family values, a number of advertisers, including Tyson and Kellogg's, decided to withdraw their funds from the show just a few weeks after it began airing. Other contemporary television offerings include the Style Network's first-person reenactment of both male and female infidelity aptly titled *Diary of an Affair*.

37. Kathleen Rowe Karlyn has also commented on how Carolyn's status as an economically autonomous woman renders her a threat. Although she does not address Carolyn's affair per se, Rowe argues that "as an emblem of the independent woman whose ambition and drive enable her to provide materially for her family, Carolyn

bears the resentment of a culture angry about her power and unable to disentangle strong women from fearful images of castrating phallic mothers" ("Too Close for Comfort," 83).

38. There is also a certain amount of xenophobia in this portrayal. Although her French lover, Paul Martel (Olivier Martinez), teaches Connie about "passion," which is itself a cliché, Paul is also figured as a bit of a rake. After his death, for example, Connie learns that he was married. Paul's expulsion from the film thereby succeeds in defending the American family against the intrusion of the amoral French other. I thank Diane Negra for this suggestion.

39. Interestingly, this strategy borrows something from feminist literary history. In both Kate Chopin's "Her Letters" (1895) and Virginia Woolf's "The Legacy" (1944), a husband's posthumous discovery of his deceased wife's long-term infidelity discredits his previously unwavering conviction that he knew everything there was to know about her. In their renderings of these husbands' subsequent befuddlement and distress, both Chopin and Woolf convey the sense that these men's ignorance was somewhat criminal. A more contemporary example of male crisis over a wife's suspected adultery occurs in Jane Smiley's *The Age of Grief* (1987), on which *The Secret Lives of Dentists* is based, although its feminist goals are significantly more tempered.

40. For a discussion that historicizes boredom, and especially points out the way female boredom has traditionally been undervalued, see Petro, "Historical Ennui, Feminist Boredom," 82–94.

41. Ritzer, *The McDonaldization of Society*, 121. See also Ritzer, *The McDonaldization Thesis*. For more on the increasing standardization of service work, see Robin Leidner's *Service Work and the Routinization of Everyday Life*. For a filmic exploration of similar issues, see *Fast Food Women* (1992).

42. Hochschild, *The Managed Heart*, 6–7.

43. Kipnis, "Adultery," 307.

44. As Yvonne Tasker notes in *Working Girls: Gender and Sexuality in Popular Cinema*, the "world of work is only rarely represented in popular cinema in terms of its mundanities (routine, repetition)" (25). She also argues that the status conferred by work *is* nonetheless ever present and is displaced onto signifiers such as costume, speech, or gesture.

45. I do not mean to offer a wholly uncritical celebration of *Norma Rae* for the film's flaws clearly include the fact that its quasi-Marxist sensibilities are muted by its re-inscription of the individualist ethic all too common in American film. Indisputably, *Norma Rae* is the story of *one* woman whose triumphs are almost as personal as they are political. For a fuller explanation of this critique, see Kuhn, *Women's Pictures*, especially chapter 7. I nevertheless value the film because it distinguishes itself in its commitment to the politics and policies of a class-conscious feminism. Similarly, *Norma Rae*'s emergence and popularity marked a historical moment of dialogue that effectively acknowledged that the question of the woman worker, and especially her relation to the cause of social justice, was an issue worth taking seriously.

46. In thinking about this film as a star vehicle, it is interesting to note that Aniston also had a supporting role in *Office Space* (1999), which has become something of a cult classic for its portrayal of the petty and mind-numbing qualities of corporate bureaucracy. In *Office Space*, Aniston appears as a waitress at a chain restaurant who is fired for refusing to wear "flair," sloganistic buttons meant to bespeak a commitment to customer satisfaction.

47. Jameson, *Postmodernism; or, the Cultural Logic of Late Capitalism*, 15.

48. This interlocution between the death drive, adultery, and low-wage labor is also explored in *My Life without Me* (2003). While the looming death of its working-class protagonist, Ann (Sarah Polley), at the age of twenty-three is physical rather than solely spiritual—she suffers from an aggressive form of uterine cancer—the film suggests that her impending demise is in some senses her only form of imaginable freedom. Ann's death perversely affords her an escape from multiple sites of disappointment, including her dead-end night job as a janitor at a local college, her adored but initially unwanted children, her marriage to the first boy with whom she ever slept (an act that resulted in the conception of her first daughter when Ann was seventeen), and their cramped trailer park home. The film thus affords Ann the opportunity to "die" out of her life and reconstruct it according to fantasy, which is also why she is granted a pass to have a sexual affair with Lee (Mark Ruffalo), a handsome stranger, sans retribution. I am grateful to Gregory Jay for recommending this film to me and for sharing his interpretation of it as a death-wish fulfillment.

49. For reviews of *The Good Girl* that explicitly compare it to *Madame Bovary*, see Hoberman, "Hungry Hearts"; French, "The Good Girl"; and Petrakis, "Wasteland, Texas," 47. These reviews may also have taken a cue from the film's production materials since Fox Searchlight's official Web site for *The Good Girl* describes Justine as "a present-day suburban Emma Bovary." See www.foxsearchlight.com.

50. Phillips, *On Kissing, Tickling, and Being Bored*, 76.

51. Retail Rodeo provides an instructive, if satiric, microcosm of small town life, including its propensity to facilitate zealous religiosity, petty provinciality, and rampant gossip.

52. When Holden is trying to convince Justine to leave her marriage, he says to her: "You hate your job. You hate your husband. You love me," as if the decision to leave a marriage requires only the realization that one hates one's husband and job equally.

53. It should be noted that *Lovely and Amazing* is less a tale of working-class malaise than one of stalled middle-class ambition. Whereas the poignancy of *The Good Girl* is earned though its frank descriptions of working-class life, Michelle is rendered as a woman whose racial and class privilege enables her to indulge in frequent bouts of self-pity.

Anna Feigenbaum

5

Remapping the Resonances of Riot Grrrl

FEMINISMS, POSTFEMINISMS, AND "PROCESSES" OF PUNK

Through women-oriented shows, conventions, and the circulation of zines, the 1990s Riot Grrrl movement foregrounded visions of punk feminism.[1] Locating what they deemed "mainstream" society's conflicting demands and values, Riot Grrrls spat critiques of patriarchy and spoke of the contradictions women face. Mimi Nguyen, the editor of the zine and producer of the Web site Worse Than Queer, and contributing columnist for *Punk Planet*, argues that "beyond a distinctive musical styling, Riot Grrrl was "an informal pedagogical project," a kind of punk rock "teaching machine . . . that existed in and sometimes replaced the classroom as the most meaningful context for the transmission and production of knowledge among its body of participants."[2]

Spreading through various media, from independent zines to local arts reviews, glossy magazines, and national newspapers, Riot Grrrl became visible as an infusion of punk and feminism. But as mainstream media got hold of Riot Grrrl the grrrls lost control of their words and actions. The grassroots movement became a spectacle, and the focus quickly shifted from reports on the feminist content and production values espoused by Riot Grrrls to features on their punk fashion sensibilities. Many journalists dismissed the Riot Grrrls as juvenile and their music as angsty noise.[3] A media blackout was called by some members and Riot Grrrl chapters in 1992, but this only sparked further commentary and profiles.

While the popularization of Riot Grrrl helped spread the word and at first led to the start of new Riot Grrrl chapters and legions of fan mail for early zinesters and bands such as Bikini Kill, eventually the movement dispersed. Reported dead circa 1995, Riot Grrrl suffered the fate of what Jennifer Pozner has termed the "false feminist death syndrome," in a media environment that attempts "to discredit and erase young feminists from the political landscape."[4] As report after report located the failure of Riot Grrrl within the movement itself, the relationship between independent and corporate production remained absent from the debate. And, perhaps unsurprisingly, the media failed to address its own accountability for Riot Grrrl's purported death.

Today the term *Riot Grrrl* still circulates, mapping a variety of women writers, poets, musicians, Web designers, hackers, and even pornographers.[5] The term continues to be used to designate everything from emergent consumer demographics to grassroots feminist activists. In this essay, I analyze some of the various ways in which the Riot Grrrl movement has influenced, informed, and inspired—both positively and negatively—feminist and postfeminist sites of creative production. Superimposing a spatial mapping on a retracing of Riot Grrrl history, I discuss Riot Grrrl at times as a catalyst, a feeling, an experience, a memory, and a journalistic convention.

Throughout this essay, I analyze young feminists' articulations that are often absent from documentations of the Riot Grrrl movement. In navigating this remapping, I turn to zine and Web site writings in addition to other academic scholarship on Riot Grrrl histories because it is in these sites that one can locate a different set of articulations about the political meanings of Riot Grrrl. As a scholar, a young feminist activist, a Riot Grrrl fan, a consumer, and a producer of feminist punk culture, my writing is infused with and influenced by my personal and political investments and engagements in this culture. Thus, my analysis privileges sites and processes of production and distribution that resist corporatization and commodification, highlighting the perspectives performers take in their own analyses of the political economics of cultural production, distribution, and circulation. I privilege these sites and voices not to discredit the impact and influence of "popular" performers and producers on major labels but rather to draw attention to the importance of political economic issues in the analysis of postfeminist media.

In what follows, I look specifically at the cultural productions of four off-shoots of Riot Grrrl: protogrrrls, pop "punk" girls, antiracist grrrls, and Web gurls. I then move to address the recent anxiety around Kathleen Hanna, the Riot Grrrl founder, and her move to Universal Records with her band, Le Tigre. The controversy surrounding Le Tigre's decision to sign with a major record label is distinctively marked by contemporary political economic concerns and conditions and current debates within recent feminist writing about the conditions of cultural production. Raising questions about the relationships between corporate, punk, and feminist production processes throughout this analysis, I end with a look at ongoing Riot Grrrl cultures.

Protogrrrls

Women have been involved in punk bands and the transatlantic punk scene since its inception in the 1970s, but it is the 1990s Riot Grrrl movement that is most frequently credited with bringing punk and feminism together. The contributions of the 1970s punk icons Chrissie Hynde, Patti Smith, Siouxsie Sioux, Poly Styrene, and Joan Jett—to name only a few—left their mark on the scene, but as punk diffused some bands signed corporate deals, some vowed to remain "underground," and some went defunct, high on disillusion. This proliferation of punk resulted in the further marginalization of women in punk scenes. As "hard-core" acts took over local venues, punk spaces became increasingly hostile and at times dangerous for punk girls. As Jennifer Miro of the Nuns famously stated in late 1977, "There were a lot of women in the beginning. . . . Then women didn't go to see punk bands anymore. . . . It was so violent and so macho and that was repulsive. [We] just got squeezed out."[6]

Rather than serving as an origin or point of lineage, the label Riot Grrrl—and at times just grrrl—is now used to describe women who were directly, indirectly, and sometimes barely associated with the 1990s Riot Grrrl movement. Analyzing how the term maps associative connections between various feminist cultural producers, I argue that this marker constructs feminist histories and lineages. While at times these associations offer accounts of feminist alliances, creating positive connections between seemingly disparate feminists, they also group women together with little concern for their political, cultural, and personal conflicts.

For example, the avant garde feminist author Kathy Acker was labeled a "theoretical grrrl" in an homage after her 1997 death from cancer. The article claims that Acker was "a riot girl ahead of her time."[7] Likewise, the 1980s punk pop performer Joan Jett is often heralded as "the original riot grrrl,"[8] while the novelist and poet Marge Piercy deemed herself "an early grrrl" in the title of her 1999 book of poems expressing her admiration for contemporary Web-based gurl feminism and noting that she has since created her own Web site.[9] Yet Kim Gordon, the bassist of Sonic Youth, and Courtney Love are also often cited as protogrrrls, even though Gordon maintained a peripheral and mildly supportive position toward Riot Grrrl and feminism more generally, while Love has publicly voiced scathing critiques of Riot Grrrl and Kathleen Hanna in particular.

Journalists' mobilization and employment of the word *grrrl* (which officially entered the Oxford English Dictionary in 2001) creates, in this way, a retrospective genealogy. However, this mapping can function to contain, as well as celebrate, these "popular" women. Often employing the terminology of motherhood and sisterhood, the mark of Riot Grrrl carries with it matriarchal or familial connotations that are all too common in discourses about feminism. This is perhaps most visible in the case of Courtney Love. Tagged a "bad mother" for her heroin use and perceived maternal deficiencies, Love is also deemed a bad mother for abandoning her grrrls. This was exemplified in the media's portrayal of the 1995 "catfight" between Love and Kathleen Hanna at the Lollapalooza music festival. Media coverage of the altercation between Love and Hanna made an event out of these women's failure to fulfill their falsely constructed relational ties. As Astrid Henry writes, "Whether dutiful daughters or insolent ones, we all appear unable to leave feminism's 'family.'"[10]

While some young feminists do take up a language of rebellion, seeking to resist the "rules" or "victim model" purportedly espoused by second wavers, most of this familial language fails to accurately represent the disassociative and associative moves that young feminists make in their performances, writing, and activism.[11] For example, academic activists such as Emi Koyami and Kimberly Springer have gone to great lengths to rearticulate such divides.

While Koyami insists on discussing the third wave of feminism as "outside of but not after the Second Wave,"[12] Springer has worked to renarrativize feminist histories, complicating the second-wave mother/third-wave daughter binary by focusing on the roles of women of color and postcolonial theorists in the shaping of young feminists' thought.[13]

The employment of a "familial" vocabulary, as these young writers and others have pointed out, traps women within a restrictive set of predefined female relationships, precluding a more complex discussion about women's various friendships and conflicts. At the same time, it also functions to obscure and depoliticize feminist history. When critics and journalists chart "rebellion" by mapping only the work of "famous" white feminists—be it Andrea Dworkin, Catharine MacKinnon, Gloria Steinem, Germaine Greer, Naomi Wolf, Katie Roiphe, Jennifer Baumgardner, or even Courtney Love—they leave too little room to debate and discuss other connections between feminists. The political, everyday work of feminists that falls below the media radar leaves in its path what Gloria Anzaldúa calls "los desconocimientos" or ignored knowledge.[14]

Kathleen Hanna has reflected on this, stating, "Even though I paid bullshit lip service to the feminism of the past, I don't think I knew my history like I do now."[15] Hanna's 1999 track "Hot Topic" with Le Tigre works to rearticulate a feminist genealogy in this light. The band shouts the names of influential feminists such as Yoko Ono, Ani DiFranco, the Butchies, Angela Davis, Dorothy Allison, Gertrude Stein, Nina Simone, and Joan Jett. Each name unfolds over the next while Hanna sings:

> You're getting old
> That's what they say
> But I don't give a damn
> I'm listening anyway . . .
> (chorus) Don't you stop
> I can't live if you stop.[16]

Le Tigre's ode draws these women together, intentionally meshing and juxtaposing feminist-identified writers and musicians from the last eighty years. Seen as an alternative articulation of feminist histories, "Hot Topic" acts as an archive that disrupts linear narratives while reimagining the potential and futurity of feminists' associative connections.

As mentioned above, some of the women Le Tigre lists, such as Joan Jett and Kathy Acker, have worked directly with the Riot Grrrl movement as well as with other feminist punk bands. Jett's collaborations with Hanna, Kat Bjelland (Babes in Toyland), and Donita Sparks (L7) have led to her iconicization by the third-wave feminist magazine *Bust*, which recast the aphorism "What Would Jesus Do?" as the basis for a parody clothing line, "What Would Joan Jett Do?" The relationship between Hanna and Acker also gives way to a narrative that bridges rather than divides feminist performers. Reportedly, Acker told Hanna fifteen years ago, "If you want to be heard . . . you should be in a band," after which Hanna went home and started Bikini Kill.[17]

Associative connections like these chart positive influences and partnerships, expanding our knowledge of women's popular histories. Rachel, the guitarist and singer of the (former) British band Pixie Meat, explains that Riot Grrrl "help[ed] me discover amazing bands practically ignored by . . . rock family trees."[18] However, unfortunately and all too often the *feminist* family trees we construct function similarly—rooted in false narratives and branching out only as far as the mainstream press can see.

Pop "Punk" Girls

Emerging "girl" groups and performers are also frequently marked as part of an ever expanding new Riot Grrrl order. Constructing everything from these maternal lineages to stylish singing sororities and "chirping chick" categories of women, rock critics and discourses of rock criticism often group artists in order to familiarize readers with them.[19] John Charles Goshert argues, "While the mass media label of punk may be applied indiscriminately . . . it is precisely because of punk's local production and consumption, as well as the geographic specificities in musical forms, style of dress, and political practice . . . that it cannot be reduced simply to a musical or otherwise stylistic genre."[20]

Following from this, broadly terming women artists "punk" or new "grrrls" often indiscriminately groups them together. No matter what the production ethos or articulations of these artists (be they anticorporate, anti-misogyny, or anti–Britney Spears), they are left undifferentiated. As *NME* declared in its 2003 "Women in Rock" issue—which featured, among others, the "pop" punk performers Avril Lavigne and The Donnas—"All Hail the Heroines of the No Cock Revolution!"[21] Only the heroines aren't having a revolution, and the same critics who hail these young women also mobilize discursive conventions that confine, demean, and marginalize them.[22]

Moreover, as both the punk and feminist movements have historically been grassroots, locally organized endeavors, their emergence as "popular" may render them apolitical or already co-opted. Goshert writes that "it is precisely when punk becomes popular culture that it ceases to be punk," while Catherine Driscoll asks in *Girls*, "Can feminism be a mass-produced, globally distributed product, and can merchandized relations to girls be authentic?"[23]

This concern resonates in the criticism of artists such as Gwen Stefani, Avril Lavigne, the Donnas, and Pink, who are commonly discussed as "punks," "punky," or (my personal favorite) "pop punkettes." However, these women's aggressive performances at times demand that the content of their songs be considered. *Feminism*, a word one rarely reads in the mainstream press in regard to popular music, is explicitly addressed. So, while Pink belts "neofeminist anthems" demanding "power, choice and halter tops," Stefani sings "like a little riot grrrl lost," Avril Lavigne has a "charming punk attitude," and the Donnas are "punk-rock debutantes" who cite L7 and the Riot Grrrl bands Bikini Kill and Bratmobile (among others) as inspiration.[24]

The intersections of punk and postfeminism can be readily mapped onto any of these performers. However, while discourses around Stefani, Pink, Lavigne, punk, and feminism are ripe for commentary, the trajectory of the Donnas' career appears ready-made for an analysis of post–Riot Grrrl, postfeminist punk. In 2001, the Donnas, an all-female "pop" punk act from Northern California, signed a deal with the multinational conglomerate Atlantic Records. A staple of their local, small venue circuit for over five years, the Donnas' corporate backing has taken them onto the mainstream airwaves, on tour with the traveling rock festival Lollapalooza, and to the pinnacle of all that is American pop — the gatekeeping MTV program *Total Request Live*.

Before signing with Atlantic, the Donnas were backed by Lookout! Records — a moderate-sized noncorporate label run out of Berkeley, California. Founded in 1987, Lookout! began and continues to function as a profit-sharing label that preserves artist control over records and marketing. Although Lookout! has maintained its position on the fringes of the multinational industry, it has also become a vehicle through which bands can rise to conglomerate fame. As the name Lookout! suggests, artists and repertory

(A and R) men do just that, monitoring "underground" success and campus airwaves in search of untapped (fan-base-intact) talent.

It is perhaps no surprise that a major label would be on the lookout for the commercial possibilities, the niche market eagerly but unknowingly awaiting the shrill sound of the Donnas' kitsch rhymes and quippy social commentary over speedy rifts. Based on the success of previous performers, the marketing potential of four conventionally attractive, young white women is clear (although the heaviest is always positioned in the back). The Donnas soon became the poster girls for the Pantene Pro–voice (no need to write your own songs) singing competition—in addition to their radio commercial for Budweiser, a Levi's fashion spread, and music licensed for Sprite and Target advertisements.[25]

Kristen Schilt writes that "the appropriation and packaging of Riot Grrrl Politics" has contributed to the dispersal and depoliticization of the Riot Grrrl movement. She cites the success of such major-label women performers as prominent examples of the corporate packaged girl power that morphed out of Riot Grrrl's success.[26] Yet narratives of co-optation and commercialization often overlook too soon the legions of young girls who now have access to the Donnas' assertive, sex-positive music. The Donnas is one of the most popular all-girl rock bands whose members play their own instruments and write most of their own songs. Often compared to the Runaways and the Ramones (in part because each member of the group uses the stage name Donna), over the last few years the Donnas have received positive attention from the music press, establishing them as a "legitimate" pop act—critical praise that is rarely lavished on any band with an overwhelming majority of young female fans.[27]

Articulating a common response to claims of selling out, band member Donna R. (Allison) comments, "Women deserve to have a female rock band that is accessible for people. Not everybody lives in towns where they can find independent labels."[28] In 1999 and 2001, the Donnas toured with the original Riot Grrrl act, Bratmobile, only rather than opening the Donnas headlined the tours, causing critics to comment on the "irony" of this fan and role model reversal. Reviewing a 2001 concert at the Bowery Ballroom for NY-Rock.com, Jeanne Fury writes, "Watching Bratmobile open for the Donnas is kind of like watching your older, wiser sister open for you. . . . You know full well you'd be nowhere without big sister, but her time to shine has passed and now you're the one the masses want to see."[29] As Fury suggests, the Donnas frequently voice appreciation for their Riot Grrrl predecessors.[30] And, although they may be articulating "minimart feminism" with lyrics such as "Need your love 123 / Stop starin' at my D cup / Don't waste time just give it to me"[31] shouted over heavy guitar, the group does offer the attraction of "thrills, hard, fast rock music, drugs, and alcohol," which, as Holly Kruse argues, is rarely acknowledged as part of adolescent girls' identification with popular music.[32]

However, as critics such as Schilt note, these overtly sexualized articulations are far from the explicit critiques of "staring at one's D cup" made by Riot Grrrl bands such as Bikini Kill.[33] And, although Donna R. certainly has a point about the accessibility of independently produced and distributed music, "what the masses want to see" is largely determined by what the massive record labels make visible. Unlike the Donnas, Bratmobile continues to release LPS on independent labels such as Kill Rock Stars and Lookout! Records, which perhaps contributes, even more than their aging (at over thirty!) to this smaller fan base.

Articulating a common neoliberal position, in *She's a Rebel* Gillian Gaar argues, "The Donnas chose to sign with Atlantic; [Riot Grrrl band] Sleater-Kinney chose to stay with Kill Rock Stars. Neither choice was "better"— each group simply had an equally valid way of defining success on their own terms."[34] Comments such as Gaar's, which appear to be complacent with— or at least uncritical toward—the corporate conglomerate structure of the music industry, are quite common in anthologies and histories of women in rock music. Many texts of this type celebrate women's success while attempting to neatly sidestep issues of political economy. In doing so, they uphold statements such as Donna R.'s, and, although they often offer in-depth information on feminist music practices, their refusal (or perhaps reluctance) to address global market conditions speaks to the need for both "a friendly alliance" between feminist theory and political economy and an analysis that documents manifestations of punk's economic opposition to capitalism.

My analysis of the cultural location of bands such as the Donnas does not simply lend itself to, but demands a consideration of, the pathways of capital that inform and produce any feminist politics that is subsumed in their performance. In the remainder of this section, I offer a critique of "girl band feminism" waged from a vantage point that moves beyond textual analysis in order to work through the political economic aspects of such major-label performers' engagements with feminist issues and specifically with the embrace of "female" pleasure. Gaar and Fury's comments, as well as the Donnas' disassociation from the anticapitalist ethos of former feminist punk acts, obfuscate feminist histories while promoting a collectivization of women in rock and a universalization of female expression.

While speaking about these "pop punkettes" through the familial connotations of Riot Grrrl can expand on and inform our memory of (post)feminist culture, I seek to locate political and economic differences in the production and distribution processes of these performers. Just as women of color are written out of many journalistic and academic histories of women's contributions to both punk and feminism, anthologies of "women in rock" also tend to chart only the popular successes of white acts and to define "female expression" in white, middle-class terms. This is largely due to the domination of the pop punk genre by white acts resulting from cultural and musical histories marked by pervasive exclusion and oppression of nonwhite feminists and punk performers.[35] As discussed in the section that follows, it is crucial to raise questions from a political economic perspective about the production and distribution structures of "the popular" that exclude and render invisible nonwhite acts and performers.

My remapping of Riot Grrrl thinks through the lens of feminist political economic analysis in order to create a new canon of feminist punk that privileges the tenuous relationships between performers and structures of race, class, and gender relations, making space for more informed critiques and ways of (re)telling women's "popular" histories. Furthermore, this remapping makes visible linkages that complicate mother-daughter binaries and the universalizing language of sisterhood, positioning girls (and grrrls) at the center of the debate without eschewing their many political, as well as performative, differences.

Antiracist Grrrls

The Riot Grrrl revolution formulated many of its positions from an investment in gender and sexual difference, leading many participants to feel alienated from the movement because of its failure to acknowledge how class and race construct the oppression of many women. For example, Kathleen Hanna's appeal for "girl love" in many ways could be interpreted as an extension of a second-wave feminist rhetoric that has been criticized for promoting a myth of "universal sisterhood" that treats gender oppression as the dominant oppression of *all* women.

Pseudonymous spaceblaster writes on her Web page, "There are no overt gestures of racism. no crosses are burned. no dolls of me are hung in effigy from trees outside clubs. but . . . i am not regarded as fully female, and this, i attribute to my race."[36] Articulating a similar response, Leah Lilith, the creator of the zines *Patti Smith* and *Sticks and Stones*, writes, "I was coming to realize that the reality of [Riot Grrrl] groups was far less than their reputation, and much of the time they did not understand or respect my colored girl, leather-dyke, femme, survivor self."[37]

Although Riot Grrrls sang about racist, misogynist "white boys" and sent these messages of girl love across racial divides, they were often not actually engaged in dialogue with the women of color they sought to include. Middle-class whiteness often subsumed all social difference without much interrogation, leaving out or glossing over the experiences of many young punk women of color. However, these critiques were often leveled from within the community, and many of the women critiquing the movement identified themselves with it or in proximity to it. As spaceblaster writes, "i completely support the ideals of the punk feminist movement. . . . i simply believe that there needs to be total honesty about the fact that . . . just because you call yourself a feminist does not absolve you of the responsibility of your racism."[38] Mimi Nguyen, in the zine collection *Evolution of a Race Riot*, articulates a similar position informed by an antiracist, feminist standpoint. She writes, "I truly believe that riot grrrl was—and is—the best thing that ever happened to punk. . . . Unfortunately, riot grrrl often reproduced structures of racism, classism, and (less so) heterosexism in privileging a generalized 'we.'"

Briefly drawing attention to such covert racism in the Riot Grrrl movement, Stacy Thompson argues in *Punk Productions* that critiques of Riot Grrrl "mimicked historically earlier ones aimed at the Second Wave." However, he quickly claims that these failures of inclusion were a "shortcoming" common to punk scenes. Stressing the gender empowerment that Riot Grrrl provided young women, within the span of four sentences race not only disappears as a problem in Thompson's narrative but it is explicitly coded in efforts to purify the grrrls' historical contributions.[39]

While I support Thompson's desire to document the potential of anticapi-

talist punk productions, reading racism out of social movements' histories maintains systems of racial privilege while it eclipses the critical voices of people of color whose thoughts—and bodies—are often at the forefront of radical social change and transformation. By attempting to engage rather than eschew criticisms of Riot Grrrl's implication in upholding structures of privilege and racialized oppression, a more dynamic and honest account of punk productions can be developed by reflecting on these failures in our current efforts to document and construct antiracist, feminist knowledges, communities, and movements. In order to map this crucial dimension of Riot Grrrl's politics, one can look at the e-zines and print zines that emerged throughout the 1990s and offered critical and self-reflexive assessments of race and racism in Riot Grrrl culture. These media allowed women identified with Riot Grrrl to construct their own critiques of the movement.

For example, Mimi Nguyen, among many other grrrls, including Leah Lilith and Sabrina Margarita Alcantara Tan, the editor of *Bamboo Girl*, outlines a sophisticated critique of how Riot Grrrl often perpetuated race and class privilege in its attempts to counter gender and sex oppression. Lilith and Tan acknowledge that Riot Grrrls' claims to be nonracist, nonhomophobic, and nonmisogynist differ from an engagement in an active, affirmative process of inclusion and self-reflection that insists on "making whiteness strange" and working with and through questions of social difference.

As critiques such as those of Lilith and Tan were circulated within Riot Grrrl communities, many grrrls—of all races—began to think more critically and self-reflexively about social difference. Although these Web sites and zines were fostered as a reaction to Riot Grrrl's perpetuation of race- and class-based exclusions, as many of these women continue to write, the political tensions that first prompted their texts have carried them far beyond issues of racial identity. While there is still much work to be done in remapping the effects of racism in feminist punk, these issues occupy the minds and meetings of many (punk) feminists more and more frequently. As Leah Lilith explains, "I left Riot Grrrl. . . . But I will always remain grateful to grrrl-punk and zine culture for teaching me to speak the truth, love my freakishness and make my own freedom."[40] It is in this way that Riot Grrrl can be said to resonate, as part of a process in which, as Adrienne, vocalist for the Riot Grrrl splinter group Spitboy, sings, "We try to figure this one out."[41]

Web Gurls

Turning to the Internet, Riot Grrrl is often also cited as a catalyst for Web-based gurl feminisms. The Internet site Webtalkguys.com links these two movements, stating, "RiotGrrls [are] taking on the male dominated world of rock and WebGrrls [are] taking on the internet."[42] Discussing the role that technology played in the Riot Grrrl movement, Ednie Garrison mobilizes the term *technologics*, arguing that it articulates an awareness of "the ways our cultural repertoire of discourses, objects, ideas and modes of resistance merge and regroup in a cultural milieu that is proliferatively technologically saturated and mediated."[43] To engage technology, as Garrison points out, is not simply to travel the terrain of cybergeography. But neither is it only to utilize a "tool kit" or "master technology" as Garrison suggests. For many grassroots Riot Grrrl organizations, bands, and other cultural producers, having a Web site both resulted from and generated a greater circulation and distribution of goods and ideas.

Rather than operating with technologics, I suggest that employing technologies involves shifting interactions between users and machines that are crucial for an investigation of the technological resonances of the Riot Grrrl movement. In this section, I look at how gurl producers are embedded in nonlinear pathways established by Riot Grrrl's rhizomatic structure, which, as Marion Leonard argues, "matches the idea of an underground culture multiplying via lines of connection which are not controlled from a primary location." This, she writes, "splits apart any concept of [Riot Grrrl] as a unified progression."[44]

In what follows, I also address how Web mediation is criticized for cutting down on the face-to-face communication that Riot Grrrl concerts and conventions offered, often further rendering—for better or worse—the "bedroom" as the site of girls' cultural production.[45] This has led critics to either reformulate Web-based activism as something that can take place from within the private sphere or claim that the potential for collective action automatically decreases in the face of Web proliferation. As the chorus for one of Le Tigre's tracks goes, "Get off the Internet, I'll meet you in the street, destroy the right wing."[46]

Both this position vis-à-vis Web-mediated feminist activism and Garrison's view that feminists have developed a mastery over technology fail to address the shifting interactions that take place when users engage "new" technologies. For example, in 1996 Rebecca Odes, the former bassist of a punk band and proclaimed riot grrrl,[47] along with Esther Drill and Heather McDonald, founded www.gurl.com, the largest Web site for teenage girls. In 1999, these three women edited a softcover book, *Deal with It! A Whole New Approach to Your Body, Brain, and Life as a Gurl*,[48] which offers frank advice on sexuality, development, sexually transmitted diseases, and reproduction. Its content, made up in part of girls' comments from the Web site's pages, is informed by feminist theory. And, while it was published by a corporate subsidiary, Pocket Books, its layout is inspired by the do-it-yourself aesthetics associated with punk and Riot Grrrl zines. With lower-case lettering, line drawings, and a description of Adrienne Rich's "lesbian continuum," the nonconformity of *Deal with It!* was dealt with by concerned parents and politicians, who relegated the book to "self-help" sections and pulled it from public library shelves in Florida.

In print form, the book's content was susceptible to censorship and surveillance. But at the same time this Web-inspired print text became accessible to non-Internet users. Many young women familiar with the Web site eagerly awaited the book's arrival, ordering numerous copies for adolescent girls and mothers. In fact, the press coverage that *Deal with It!* received after protests (in the street) for and against its availability in stores and libraries spread the word about the text. This points to the rhizomatic—or nonlinear and multidimensional—circulation patterns of Riot Grrrl production, as well as to the constant dialogue that exists between technologies, institutions, and political positions that render information more and less accessible, sometimes seemingly at once.

Riot Grrrl Reconsidered

When I learned in 2004 that Le Tigre had signed a deal with Universal Records after the closure of their previous label, Mr. Lady Records, I was angry at Kathleen Hanna for going back on her words, words that functioned to demarcate what appeared to be a clear distinction between indie and corporate affinities. And so, after hearing this news, I went back through this article, retaining Hanna's aesthetic and discursive articulations of feminism while reconsidering her thoughts on the political economics of feminist punk production. One omitted excerpt from a previous draft of this essay comes from Hanna's *Punk Planet* interview, published in 2001: "We need to earn a living, but the ultimate goal is to change the entire system. But unless we build models—even small little lego ones in our houses—we're not going to figure out how that's going to come about."[49] How Hanna planned to change the system by making a corporate deal with Universal Records—part of Vivendi Universal's Universal Music Group (UMG)—was not only beyond my essay's analysis but beyond my comprehension. How was I going to figure this one out?[50]

In his introduction to *Punk Productions* Stacy Thompson asks, "Can the commodity form be taken up and used against capitalism?"[51] This question appears to me to be at the crux of the debate over the political potential of utilizing corporate venues and corporately produced media forms to promote feminist punk agendas. In fact, it is precisely this question that Le Tigre's members asked their fans and critics to reconsider in interviews and press releases surrounding the move to Universal. Le Tigre member Johanna Fateman told Northeastern News, "There were no feminist voices at all in the mainstream [media] and we felt like it would be really great if we could have some kind of a presence to a larger audience."[52]

Claiming that the pop musical form ensures listeners' engagement with a song, Le Tigre's major label debut album, *This Island*, bops and rhymes—as well as screams—its punk and feminist investments. Le Tigre's 2003 participation in the Bands against Bush tour and tracks from their album such as "Seconds," a song about President Bush with a vehement chorus that repeats,

Handbill from a 2003 Le Tigre show in Montreal with the opening acts Lesbians on Ecstasy and Les Georges Leningrad

"You make me sick sick sick sick," and "New Kicks," which contains sound bites from Iraq war protests, are marks of the band's commitment to oppositional politics and positions. In its concert performances, Le Tigre's video for "Seconds" flashes pictures of Bush interspersed with the word *sick*. Hanna also frequently speaks of her intense disdain for the current president during intervals between songs.

These political articulations can certainly engage listeners, but if the alternatives Le Tigre's members propose are in the product and not the production of their music, what kind of feminist transformation is being imagined? As my analysis of Riot Grrrl has argued, I think it is important that we ask questions about the messages articulated in postfeminist media, as well as the political economics of feminist punk production. As Annalee Newitz writes in an article for AlterNet, "I know Le Tigre deserve a big cash injection, and lead singer Hanna has been a dedicated champion of underground culture for almost a decade and a half. I don't actually believe there's anything wrong with selling out if it will help liberate an artist from a crappy day job or give her access to better resources. And yet—isn't there another way?"[53]

Newitz articulates a distinction between corporate conglomerates and independent labels, but in doing so she problematizes proscriptive notions of "selling out" that create an authentic-inauthentic binary, particularly in considerations of punk and feminist cultures. Newitz's commentary leaves room for considering the contextual specificities of artists' decisions while maintaining the desire for a less corporatized, mainstream cultural industry. Newitz, like Hanna in 2001, wants models of alternative economic practices to begin in our living rooms. Such a desire does not render every articulation Le Tigre makes irrelevant, irrational, or inauthentic. Rather, the band's corporate backing forces those who consume and engage with its punk feminism to renegotiate the linkages between economic production and political articulations. The conclusions one comes to may differ as political investments and ideas about the functions of capitalism diverge among critics and fans. However, whatever conclusions—or even partial conclusions—one draws, it remains crucial that analyses address, rather than avoid, the complex and often ambiguous alliances between feminism and the political economy. As my remapping insists, documenting the movements of Riot Grrrl demands that we acknowledge the various economic, as well as aesthetic, forms that feminist punk assumes.

Riot Grrrl Resounding

While Le Tigre can no longer be heralded for its noncorporate feminist punk, young women committed to anticapitalist processes of production and distribution continue to find it increasingly difficult to build infrastructures that make their music and media accessible and their incomes sustainable without amending their political values. In the face of an ever-infringing, profit-motivated industry, the ability to think realistically and transformatively is continually in jeopardy. Yet grrrls across the globe are finding ways to connect and build communities without signing with corporate labels or selling shampoo.

Kill Rock Stars (Sleater-Kinney) and Lookout! Records (Bratmobile) continue to produce and release albums influenced by Riot Grrrl while even small, local labels such as Lucky Madison navigate the music business, releasing the work of Riot Grrrl bands such as the Roulettes. Riot Grrrl chapters still exist, with local activist efforts based in cities across North America and Europe, while Ladyfest, a series of performances and workshops organized by Bratmobile's Allison Wolfe in Olympia, Washington, in August 2000, continues to expand in cities throughout the world, including Monterrey, Mexico; Malmö, Sweden; Brighton, England; Melbourne; Bielefeld, Germany; Ottawa; and Denver. Ottawa's 2004 Ladyfest held sessions on topics ranging from punk rock aerobics to the politics of menstruation.[54] Ladyfest Europe discussion boards contain news and information on international Ladyfests and provide a space for young feminists to make connections, linking participants and organizers, as well as offering a "start your own" Ladyfest guide.[55] This ongoing festival carries out Riot Grrrl's punk feminist tradition of do-it-yourself production and grassroots organization.

The Grrrl Zine Network, a Web site run by the Austrian feminist and zine writer Elke Zobl, is one of the most prominent examples of how grrrls have created a sustainable infrastructure that allows for the circulation of goods and ideas. Serving as both an active forum and an archive of feminists' work, this "network" provides links to zine distribution outlets (called distros), as well as articles by feminist academics and interviews Zobl has conducted with other zine writers and distributors. The Web site includes young feminists' work and writing from across Europe, North America, Australia, New Zealand, Southeast Asia, and parts of the Middle East, fostering transnational dialogues about contemporary feminist issues.

These sites point to the ways in which Riot Grrrl lingers and expands. Although the term has been appropriated by major media corporations and profit-driven marketing industries, it has not faded into oblivion or collapsed as an apolitical assignment of a once meaningful term. Rather, Riot Grrrl is unfinished and fluid, and its residual effects can be found in new manifestations of feminist and postfeminist punk. While the term can be mobilized to excuse or obfuscate exploitive and commercialized versions of (post)feminism and punk production, it also maps a politics in process that engages in constant and shifting interactions with institutional and capitalist structures and technologies that delimit and determine its content and accessibility. One grrrl based in the United Kingdom, Cassandra Smith, captured this idea when she wrote, "Riot grrrl was not so much a culturally specific phenomenon as [a] mindset or form of energy. As we all know energy is neither created nor destroyed, but rather passed on."[56]

Perhaps what is most important is precisely this "passing on" of energy. Riot Grrrl continues, resounding in the echoes of young feminists' knowledges, reverberating against the walls of concert halls, classrooms, and girls' bedrooms. The term *Riot Grrrl* charts a genealogical history of women's activism and engagement with punk forms of cultural production. Riot Grrrl is, in this sense, a cartography of punk feminisms' successes and failures, exclusions and inclusions, as they continue to resonate in print, online, and over the airwaves. As a remapping of Riot Grrrl suggests, the political is always a shifting site of potential, of the words not yet on our lips.

Notes

1. A zine is a small magazine with very low production costs usually assembled by an individual or a small group of people.
2. Nguyen, "Punk Planet 40."
3. Schilt, "A Little Too Ironic." See also Press and Reynolds, *The Sex Revolts*.
4. Pozner, "The 'Big Lie,'" 35.
5. See, for example, Tomlin, "Sex, Dreads, and Rock 'n' Roll."
6. Quoted in Klatzker "riot grrrl."
7. Carr, "The Legacy of Kathy Acker, Theoretical Grrrl," 49.
8. Gill "The Original Riot Grrrl Keeps It Pure," 10.
9. Seaman, "Piercy, Marge," 959. The oldest grrrl I've found to date is nearly two thousand years old. The remains of a female gladiator discovered in London were named Gladiator Grrrl in Dalai, "Gladiator Grrrl."
10. Henry, "Feminism's Family Problem," 211.
11. Both Katie Roiphe and Naomi Wolf are frequently critiqued and discussed in terms of the mother-daughter (and consequently the feminist-postfeminist) divide, while newspaper headlines such as "Not Your Mother's Feminism" have also become commonplace, proliferating the disjunction between feminist "mothers" and "daughters."
12. Koyama, "On Third Wave Feminisms."
13. Springer, "Third Wave Black Feminism?" I use the term *women of color* throughout this essay with some reservations. While I think it remains, for now, a useful term for affirming the presence of women who are racialized, it cannot capture the intersections and complexities of oppression or undo the hegemony of whiteness. For a discussion of how this term often functions to reaffirm the invisibility of whiteness and efface differences of privilege and power among and between women of color, see Carver, "I Am Not a Person of Color."
14. Anzaldúa and Keating, *This Bridge We Call Home*.
15. Hanna, interview with D. Sinker, in Sinker, *We Owe You Nothing, Punk Planet*, 65.
16. Le Tigre, "Hot Topic," *Le Tigre* (Mr. Lady Records, 2001).
17. Carr, "The Legacy of Kathy Acker, Theoretical Grrrl," 19. Notably, Ann Cvetkovich's book, *An Archive of Feelings: Trauma, Sexuality, and Lesbian Public Cultures*, begins with a discussion of Le Tigre and Tribe 8, perhaps unwittingly ending with a Kathy Acker quote, "Keep on living," which is the chorus to one of Le Tigre's tracks. Cvetkovich moves on in the second chapter to discuss the writer Dorothy Allison's

work. Her methodology throughout attests to the possibilities for reimagining non-linear associations between feminist texts.

18. O'Brien, *She Bop II*, 161.

19. Feigenbaum, "Some Guy Designed This Room I'm Standing In."

20. Goshert, "'Punk' after the Pistols."

21. "Women in Rock," *NME*, 22 March 2003, cover.

22. Feigenbaum, "Some Guy Designed This Room I'm Standing In," 37–56.

23. Goshert, "'Punk' after the Pistols," 85; Driscoll, *Girls*, 272.

24. Chonin, "Diva Demands Power, Choice, Halter Tops," 30; "Play That Punky Music," *People*, 9 September 2002, 41; Dunn, "Punk-Rock Debutants," 35; Kat, "The Donnas," 58.

25. Martens, "The Donnas Keep Building with Move to Atlantic," 17; "Pro-Voice Party with the Donnas," www.pantene.com, 15 April 2003.

26. Schilt, "A Little Too Ironic," 5–16.

27. See Wald, "Just a Girl?"; and "I Want It That Way."

28. The comment was made on www.teenmusic.com, 20 March 2004.

29. Fury, "The Donnas and Bratmobile at the Bowery Ballroom."

30. In the occasional interview, the Donnas speak of going to a Bikini Kill concert and handing the band a tape, only to find it in shreds on the venue floor later that night. Calling the event "disappointing," Donna R. told the "indie" magazine *ROCKRGRL*, "If those people had just said something nice to us, it would have totally made our day. But nobody ever did" (ibid.). The Donnas also opened for Joan Jett in 2000.

31. The Donnas, "Take It Off," *Spend the Night* (Atlantic Records, 2002).

32. Kruse, "Abandoning the Absolute," 145.

33. Schilt, "A Little Too Ironic," 5–16.

34. Gaar, *She's a Rebel*, 484.

35. For an in-depth discussion of racism in the punk scene and the experiences of punks of color, see James Spooner's documentary *Afropunk* (2003).

36. "Race and Riot Girl," Spaceblaster.com, 22 February 2004.

37. Lilith, "Sticks and Stones May Break My Bones," 3.

38. These comments appeared on Spaceblaster.com.

39. Thompson, *Punk Productions*.

40. Lilith, "Sticks and Stones May Break My Bones," 4.

41. Spitboy, "Word Problem," *Mi Cuerpo Es Mio* (Allied Recordings, 1994).

42. www.webtalkguys.com. 22 February 2004.

43. Garrison, "U.S. Feminism-Grrrl-Style!"

44. Leonard, "Paper Planes," 111.

45. It is important to note that, although Internet access is on the rise, the ability and money required to run and finance a Web site are very different from the know-how, "leisure" time, and resources needed to produce a narrowly circulated paper zine. Even do-it-yourself zine culture is criticized for overlooking the "privilege" involved in access to photocopiers, free time, and materials. However, both of these forms of production have been utilized by a wide demographic of girls. See, for example, Green and Taormino, *A Girl's Guide to Taking over the World*.

46. Le Tigre, "Get off the Internet," *From the Desk of Mr. Lady* (Mr. Lady Records, 2001).

47. Lange, "Deal with It," 102.

48. Drill, McDonald, and Odes, *Deal with It!*

49. Hanna, interview, 67.

50. In 2003, Universal Music Group was the world's largest music company, operating in seventy-one countries with an estimated global market share of 23.5 percent. It lists Polydor, Decca, Verve, and Mercury Records among its sixteen principle labels. Its owner, Vivendi Universal, also owns 18.5 percent of NBC Universal, as well as large shares of the telecommunications industries of France and Morocco. Vivendi Universal's revenues for 2004 were 21,428 million euros ("Vivendi Universal," www.vivendiuniversal.com, 27 June 2005).

51. Thompson, *Punk Productions*, 3.

52. Hankinson, "Le Tigre Talks Song Writing, Politics, and *Spin* Magazine."

53. Newitz, "Suck My Left One."

54. "Workshops!!" Ladyfest Ottawa, 2004, www.ladyfestottawa.com, 24 April 2005.

55. "Homepage," Ladyfest Europe, www.ladyfesteurope.org, 24 April 2005.

56. Smith, "Riot Grrrls."

Lisa Coulthard

6

Killing Bill

RETHINKING FEMINISM AND FILM VIOLENCE

In a climate shaped by long-standing concerns about the ill effects of viewing violence, discussions of film violence tend to concentrate less on the theorization or analysis of violence itself (its definitions, forms, structures, ramifications, and modes) and more on the seeming legitimacy (or gratuitousness) of its presence; moreover, because only a very few accounts of violence address the spectacular effects of explicit gore or brutality, most often this legitimacy is judged according to the role of graphic violence in the construction of empathetic characters and the verisimilitudinous, classical, and genre-based narratives in which they are found. In feminist contexts, this focus on character tends to stress either the subversive or disruptive identification with the perpetrator or the ethical, feminist, and political significance of identifying with depictions of victims of violence, an emphasis usually framed as a progressive concern (from political, feminist, and ethical standpoints) but one that can lead to encompassing and exculpatory assessments of portraits of victimization, on the one hand, and celebrations of female power in images of violent women on the other. Both render the place of represented violence obscure or insignificant.

With the advent of third-wave and postfeminism, the concerns of violence, gender, and representation have shifted in favor of the latter critical framework as a new emphasis on "postvictim" feminism has transferred attention toward debates about the presence of violent women in cinema and popular culture and away from women as victimized subjects *to* violence.[1] While there have always been images of violent women in fiction and art, as well as discussions of women who enact violence (from *Medea* to *Hedda Gabler* to the film noir femme fatale), recent debates have coalesced around the presence of a certain kind of very popular and often very violent heroine of the contemporary action film. Marked by popular appeal, narrational centrality of active female characters, genre hybridity, and sophisticated fight choreography, a number of recent films have foregrounded the presence of violent women in genres usually associated with male characters, actors, and audiences. Contemporary action and martial arts films as diverse as *Elektra* (Bowman, 2005), *Lara Croft: Tomb Raider* (West, 2001), *Charlie's Angels* (McG, 2000), *Crouching Tiger, Hidden Dragon* (Lee, 2000), *Mr. and Mrs. Smith* (Liman, 2005), and the spectacularly violent and postmodern double feature *Kill Bill*, volumes 1 and 2 (Tarantino, 2003 and 2004), all feature women engaged in violent action as a central part of their stories and structures. Of these films, Quentin Tarantino's *Kill Bill* (for ease of discussion and methodological reasons, I refer to parts 1 and 2 as a single film) stands out for its excesses of length (two parts, four hours, and twelve minutes), graphic violence, genre hybridity, and visual spectacle. Varied and contestatory, media, critical, and audience responses to *Kill Bill* consistently refer to its excess, attacking or celebrating the film's extreme and arguably gratuitous use of blood and gore; its stylistic referentiality; its lack of character depth, emotion, or psychology; and its use of female figures (and young female figures in particular) as both agents and victims of violence. *Kill Bill* foregrounds violence and gender, doing so in a way that emphasizes its own commodification, stylistic extravagance, superficiality, and cultural appropriation. Displaying and emphasizing its generic and cultural excesses, the film offers a spectacle of gender and aestheticized violence that simultaneously deflects and invites or provokes our critical attention to its discourses of gender, race, power, authenticity, and tradition.

It is not surprising, then, that for many critics the central question to be asked when faced with the excessive violence of *Kill Bill* is one of its relation to feminism and in particular of its construction and reflection of images and role models for women. As a *New York Times* article phrased its criticism of

Kill Bill is organized around an iconic image of female violence in a narrative of "justified" revenge.

what it viewed as *Kill Bill*'s regressive politics: "You've come a long way baby. Now kill someone."[2] With violence as the new smoking, this clever phrasing adapts a 1970s cigarette advertisement to the ultraviolence of Tarantino's film, inviting a connection to feminist politics, capitalist consumer culture, and dominant patriarchal ideology. Pursuing this connection begs a fundamental question: if the original ad can be critiqued for replacing the actual political and social imperatives, achievements, and drives of the women's movement with a superficial, individualistic, and consumerist marker of an empty and potentially lethal habit, can *Kill Bill* be critiqued for offering equally empty discourses of false liberation through the representation of violent, active women onscreen? Suggestive in its associations, this analogy invites us to query current discourses of progress and to question whether these contemporary images of violent women are anything more than an attempt to expand the mostly male audience of action films to a new female consumer population. As popular and prominent displays of violent women, films such as *Kill Bill* suggest the importance of identifying trends in violent representation and asking what these trends indicate, disavow, or articulate. What is the relation among the popularity of these images of violent women, postfeminist culture, and feminist theory and criticism? Is the violent heroine of contemporary popular action cinema merely a symptom and product of a postfeminist cultural context that elevates postpolitical commodification and capitalistic success under the guise of progress? And what kind of new approaches and questions might these questions invite and what relations might be forged or desired among popular culture, postfeminism, and feminist theory through the analysis of violence?

These are, of course, complex and difficult questions that cannot be answered or even fully addressed in the course of this essay; by asking them, however, I hope not only to approach *Kill Bill* and the debates about its violence from a different tack but also to emphasize and signal the importance of investigating representations of violent women in ways that take account of the ambivalence, complexity, and disruptive and consoling dimensions of violence in cinema. Violence in cinema takes many forms, is approached and defined in a multitude of ways, and is inseparable from style, theme, narration, and reception; in this diversity and plurality, it is important not to approach it as essentially or ontologically either subversive or regressive regardless of the gender of its agent or object. Interrogations of violence and gender have always been a significant part of film, feminist theory, and film criticism. As a limit and excess that emphasizes the social, political, and ethical dimensions of film reception and representation, violence provides a particularly loaded entry point for questioning shifts, trends, or tropes of gender representation or transgression. It is also arguable that it is the excesses, shifts, or reconfigurations of violent display that are at the heart of many debates about gender and representation. Discussions about the potentially regressive or subversive force of representations of female violence have played a part in both film and feminist theory, and the yoking of debates about spectacular displays of film violence in popular culture to the analysis of gender construction and representation more generally should not be a surprise, especially to those of us familiar with the ways in which feminist theory (especially the psychoanalytically informed work driven by Laura Mulvey, Linda Williams, Gaylyn Studlar, Teresa de Lauretis, and Kaja Silverman) has anchored many of its central tenets and positions through concepts of sadism, masochism, power, and the body. The representation of female violence in particular has occupied a significant contestatory place in film analysis with films such as Marleen Gorris's 1982 *A Question of Silence*. That film's portrayal of a seemingly unmotivated murder of a male shopkeeper by a group of three women shoppers occasioned intense activity, antagonism, and division in discussions about the possible or desired relation between feminism and violence. In addition to questions regarding the ethical and political dimensions of depicting a murder without apparent narrational justification, these discussions addressed the issues of treating violence with irony and humor and the possible feminist strategies involved in using laughter as a mode of community and political resistance.[3]

Eschewing graphic violence and politically, ideologically, and ironically engaged with its material on a complex stylistic and thematic level, Gorris's film and its concomitant debates would seem to have very little in common with the popular, graphic, kinetic, and stylish mass media images of violent women in contemporary genre cinema and television. This is not to say that these kinds of debates have completely disappeared: with the advent of an increasing number of images of violent women and popular discourses of postfeminism, recent years have seen a proliferation of representations and discussions of women and violence, an intensification that has both reified and redefined binary divisions between masculine and feminine action but has not yet impacted or shifted debates and theorizations of film violence.[4] As J. David Slocum points out in his introduction to *Violence and American Cinema*, violence "tends to be employed as a lazy signifier, conspicuous but typically unexamined,"[5] and while Slocum's volume goes some way in redressing this lack, there is still very little work on violence and cinema that offers a theoretical methodology, orientation, or framing for film violence, a situation compounded and made problematic by the ethical, political, and social imperatives that seem concomitant to any discussion of violence. As the very terms *gratuitous* and *excessive* indicate, violence in film is somehow essentially questionable or suspect; framed by ethical and social responsibilities and issues, the presence of graphic violence is thus frequently thrown into a discourse of justification or condemnation based on its perceived relation to actual violence, audience identification, and response or character, narration, and style.

In keeping with this approach to violence as a catalyst for narration or identification or as stylistic and aesthetic spectacle, many of the debates on violent action heroines investigate female violence on film through its relation to character and representational trends. Viewed as either a marker of anti-feminist recidivism and masculinization or of feminist power and progress, female violence is approached through its connections to issues of feminism. While a few recent works on violence and women in film attempt to problematize notions of gender and genre by emphasizing historical precedents or stressing the complex interweaving of gendered (and generic) tropes of vulnerability, invulnerability, sexualized representation, and violence, much research focuses only on discourses of postfeminist girl power, utopic subversion, and viewer pleasure. For example, working from important feminist interventions in gender and the action cinema such as Yvonne Tasker's

Spectacular Bodies, recent books such as Jacinda Read's *The New Avengers: Feminism, Femininity, and the Rape-Revenge Cycle*, Sherrie A. Inness's *Women Warriors and Wonder Women in Popular Culture* (as well as her more recent edited volume *Action Chicks: New Images of Tough Women in Popular Culture*), Martha Mc-Caughey and Neal King's edited volume *Reel Knockouts: Violent Women in the Movies*, and Dawn Heinecken's *Warrior Women of Television* have attempted to address the construction, reception, and significance of the intensification of images of violent women and girls in contemporary popular culture but often do so in ways that address only explicit and often superficial markers of power and strength.[6]

However, more than indicating mere physical prowess, representations of female acts of violence and victimization suggest the importance of considering the ramifications and gradations of representational codes and modes of film violence, modes that might be potentially transgressive but might also present regressive or dominant ideological constructions of violence and gender under the guise of liberatory or subversive fantasies of omnipotence. This is not meant in a programmatic way but to indicate the importance of interrogating and investigating the ways in which violence is understood, defined, represented, and made visible. What does culture construct, recognize, and signify by the term *violence* (e.g., where do partner abuse, psychological violence, more passive acts of violence, and forms of neglect such as starvation fit into this understanding)? Further, what are the fantasies, symbols, allegories, and narratives with which violence is aligned and through which it is framed? And how are its various forms, tropes, modes, enactments, and representations linked to visibility, politics, community, gender, the body, ideology, and constructions of injury, trauma, evil, or subjectivity?

Provocative and challenging, these kinds of questions indicate the difficulties or obstacles involved in reading hybrid and contradictory postmodern texts such as *Kill Bill* as unambiguous representations of feminist empowerment. Although the images of femininity and violence the film seems to offer are presented as complex and ironic, they can also be seen as ideologically, stylistically, and narrationally unified fantasies of femininity: the film's depiction of female violence is entwined with discourses of idealized feminine whiteness, heterosexuality, victimhood, sacrificial purity, maternal devotion, and eroticized, exhibitionistic, sexual availability. On the surface, and clearly *Kill Bill* is a film that invites attention to surfaces, the spectacle and iconicity

Images of violent women have achieved a position of high-profile marketability in popular media culture, as this full-page advertisement from *Entertainment Weekly* suggests.

of femininity that is primary in the film is reconfigured so as to present its violent action in a putatively gender-neutral zone. Most of the fight scenes in the film are between women and are choreographed and filmed in a way that is stylistically similar to those of any masculine-centered martial arts film or western. These are duels, battles between equals; women fighters are never inferior to men.

This gender play works in conjunction with the explicit intertextuality of the film to highlight contradictory and complex generic combinations. Throughout the film, the Bride (Uma Thurman) controls the action, including the physical action of violent spectacle, and the costuming, roles, settings, and choreography confirm both the spectacular nature of the violence and the excessive referentiality of the pastiche: the Bride's yellow tracksuit references Bruce Lee; the opening fight between the Pasadena housewife Vernita Green/ Copperhead (Vivica Fox) and the Bride reveals the ironic and extreme incongruity between a Disneyfied, toy-house-like domesticity and a racially coded tough street fight (complete with posturing and knives); and the fight at the House of the Blue Leaves moves from a grand scale kung fu fight to an almost delicately feminine Japanese sword fight (borrowing stylistically from the Japanese film *Lady Snowblood* [Fujita, 1973]) in a serene garden (matched incongruously with Spanish guitar music). Each fight scene, and in fact each segment of the film, has its own stylistic signature and generic and cultural references, and throughout the Bride forcefully and skillfully carries the action toward resolution. As with most martial arts films, the fight scenes vary in setting, choreography, and success (as the hero/heroine trains, overcomes obstacles, and moves toward a final battle), but in *Kill Bill* each of the fight scenes has an additional function in exploring an aspect of the Bride's revenge: the fight between equals with Copperhead; the professional, stylized battle against O-Ren Ishii's (Lucy Liu) employees and then the ritualized fight with O-Ren herself; the more intensely motivated revenge fight with Elle Driver (Daryl Hannah) (for killing her master as well as her association with Bill); and the final battle with Bill (David Carradine).

Emphasizing the overarching revenge structure and presenting significant information on characters, themes, and narration, the differences in these scenes are more than mere shifts in style and genre. In particular, each fight places gender (that of the heroine and that of her opponent) at the forefront. Fights with single women, collective groups, or male adversaries make use of unique fighting styles and weapons (knives, swords, martial arts) and offer particular outcomes. Further, although it is significant that near defeat comes at the hands of a male opponent, Budd (Michael Madsen), it is also important to note that the fights between women occupy more screen time and are more developed in terms of choreography and style. Moreover, these fight scenes all feature moments of female bonding (connections made over the shared feminine concerns of children, pregnancy, lovers, mentors, or business success) that are conjoined with graphically violent action. Intense bloodshed in *Kill Bill* is reserved for female opponents, and each of the personally motivated battles occurs within enclosed, domestic, or at the very least quiet and incongruous spaces for violence (home, garden, trailer). Varied in tone, theme, narrational style, and context, all of these fight scenes are defined by the strong kinetic action of the heroine. In opposition to this action, there are three points in the two parts of the film during which the Bride is passive: when she is presumed to be dead on the floor of a church, when she is unconscious on a hospital bed, and when she is bound and gagged in a coffin. In each instance of passivity, the Bride is objectified and eroticized as her appearance is given diegetic (in each instance, the male characters offer comments about her attractiveness) and stylistic (each involves an overhead shot) attention. Set in opposition to the Bride's active violence, these scenes stand out in a way that both potentially reinforces and ironically critiques the eroticization of victimized, powerless, and silent female bodies. At least on the surface, the Bride is set apart from these discourses of eroticized passive femininity: only when she is dead or gagged is this female heroine inactive.

However, for all of this apparently empowering action it is important not to adopt a language of subversion in excess, validation on the basis of pleasurable spectacle, or a postmodern excitement about new combinations. As the levels of referentiality, irony, and pastiche suggest, the issues are more complex; the layers of genre borrowing and blending alone, for example, raise significant issues involving cultural appropriation and race and class politics. For all its postmodern pastiche and ambivalence, what is most apparent about *Kill Bill* is its almost sacralizing and nostalgic homage to genre cinema and its use of a vengeance frame that accentuates and foregrounds the conservative rather than subversive functions of its stylistic violence. In addition, more than merely suggesting cultural appropriation, the generic and stylistic borrowing of already ideologically and politically problematic genres in *Kill Bill* carries with it the inherent and attendant issues of each referenced mode. The political, cultural, and ideological ramifications of the genres of blaxploitation, teensploitation, and rape revenge films have, for instance, been analyzed as problematic or at least ambivalent objects for progressive feminisms, and the mixing of pastiche does not necessarily neutralize or empty the genres of these issues. Thus, this employment of pastiche should not be excised from the constructions of race, class, violence, and gender at work in intertextuality, self-referentiality, or genre hybridity. Further, by borrowing and referencing genres as diverse as Hong Kong, Chinese, and Korean martial arts and action films, blaxploitation films, teensploitation films (especially of the contemporary Japanese variety of *Battle Royale* [Fukasaku, 2000] and *The Suicide Club* [Sono, 2002]), women in prison and rape revenge films, anime, exploitation cinema, the western (the Italian variety exemplified by the films of Sergio Leone in particular), the Japanese samurai film, and television series such as *Charlie's Angels*, *Kill Bill* replicates and reinstates traditions and tropes of representations of violence and gender excised from political, historical, and cultural contexts and implications. It could be argued that in building up its referentiality to such a degree *Kill Bill* empties the antecedent texts of their problematic associations — that in reducing the tropes and stylistic signatures to mere style and surface the film expunges ideological implications — but the shared and dominant ideological constructions of violence and gender that traverse these referent films and genres suggest that any eradication or clearing is more difficult.

Moreover, it is the excess of the violence itself that becomes paramount in these reworkings and references. In order to analyze in more detail the role of the violent woman in *Kill Bill*, it is necessary to focus on what I would argue is the central structure of the film's violence — revenge. For female avengers, the most common revenge scenario is that of rape revenge, a highly gendered narrative structure that, as Tasker argues, is characterized by a problematic binding of eroticism to violence and vulnerability to invulnerability in the victimized violent women. While many film texts take rape (actual, imagined, or threatened) as a starting point for male revenge — for example, *The Searchers* (Ford, 1956), *Straw Dogs* (Peckinpah, 1971), *Deliverance* (Boorman, 1972), *Unforgiven* (Eastwood, 1992), and *Irreversible* (Noé, 2002) the rape revenge cycle is usually discussed in reference to films such as *Lipstick* (Johnson, 1976), *I Spit on Your Grave* (Zarchi, 1978), *Ms. 45* (Ferrara, 1981), and *Extremities* (Young, 1986) in which the main female character exacts violent retribution for her own rape. As both Jacinda Read and Carol Clover suggest, these films offer ambivalent pleasures for male and female spectators and contradictory ideological positionings and pleasures for their audiences; indeed, the films themselves can be addressed as simultaneously feminist, antifeminist, classist, racist, and often even radically critical of dominant ideology. This ambivalence is striking given the simplistic nature of the films and plots. It is as if in their reduction of narrative, character, and style to eroticism and graphic, vengeful, and violent display the films address the core of these issues in all their fantasmatic and symbolic contradictions and inconsistencies.

Indeed, though classical in origin, the rape revenge film seems in some ways definitively postmodern. In the reduction of narrative to a series of loosely connected acts, cinematic rape revenge narratives can be seen to offer a depiction of violence that is particularly hospitable to the pastiche, narrative fracturing, attention to surfaces, ironic distance, and lack of affect that define postmodernism. Violent action is not tied to character arc, development, or psychology; instead the revenge film offers a series of murders and/or scenes of torture linked through a loose narrative of revenge (often justified by an equally graphic opening scene that launches the violence). However, this reduction is one that ultimately values a unified narrative, and it is in this drive that we locate an ideological coherence in the way these films address violence as instrumental, rational, and fully justified. In the revenge scenario, violence does not operate as a shock that defamiliarizes or disrupts narrative (as both Marsha Kinder and Leo Charney argue is the case in many postmodern film texts featuring graphic violence) but constitutes the narrative.[7] The emphasis on graphic bodily injury displayed in these films cannot be separated from their overarching structure, which requires and provides the visual, narrative, and ideological foundation for the violent action represented. Even when it is framed as excessive, the logic of a revenge narrative invokes, justifies, and contains the violent action depicted within a clear rationalized frame; from Roman stoicism to Renaissance drama to contemporary cinema, the revenge scenario has always been the most graphically and excessively violent of representational modes. Further, it offers an instrumental logic of violence that absorbs the gore and bloodshed within its purview.

Arguably, the conservative, purgative, and restorative functions of violence in the revenge narrative are even more exaggerated in the female rape revenge cycle, a mode that offers a dominant discourse of retribution and violent redemption and a stabilizing and nonthreatening construction of feminine victimization within the context of a potentially subversive spectacular and often erotic display of female action and violence. Its focus on closure, narrative containment, the personal (often familial) nature of public acts of violence, and the rampant individualism of the quest narrative constructs the revenge narrative so that it is ultimately an exercise in conserving, neutralizing, and containing the violence it suggests; secondary narrative, characterization, theme, or style are merely there as frameworks for the acts of violence that make up the main narrative strand of purposeful and often regenerative or redemptive acts of violent vengeance. The set of integers is frequently finite and delineated (in *Kill Bill* literally becoming a list) with a narrative closure based on some sort of violent conclusion (the murder of the last person on the "list" or the death of the avenger). In the rape revenge scenario, the violence is narrationally "used up" such that the narrative closure erases its existence after the fact and threats of socially, politically, or ideologically disruptive, radical, or revolutionary acts of female violence are not only contained but ultimately expunged from the text itself.

With its death list, cast of characters all involved in the violent action, and its utopic ending of naturalized wholeness, completion and redemption, such instrumentality, rationalization, and apolitical containment of violence are especially prominent in *Kill Bill*. As is the case in most revenge films, the avenger in *Kill Bill* is the ethical center of the universe created—there is no law, no outside world against which these violent actions are framed—and, perhaps more important, there are no innocent observers or outsiders; everyone is implicated in the violence, and those killed are either guilty parties or willing fighters.[8] In keeping with its other excesses, *Kill Bill* offers an excess of revenge. The only witness or outsider to the violent action is Nicki, Vernita Green's daughter, and it is implied that she may well develop her own future cycle of vengeful violence. For example, as the first narrationally extended and contextualized introduction to the Bride (i.e., one that offers some character psychology and backstory and stylistically invites a degree of audience identification and empathy) and the only scene in which the Bride kills someone not implicated in her past actions either directly or by association, the hospital rape scene gains a certain prominence in the film's narrative. By emphasizing this scene, as well as a form of maternal rape (the Bride's missing daughter), the film combines rape, professional, and familial revenge scenarios. In these merged revenge scenarios, the film exposes the entire tradition for what it always already was—a way of linking disparate scenes of gratuitous, graphically violent spectacle. Unambiguous and singular, the revenge narrative is here boiled down to its rudimentary core of graphic, gory, and spectacularly displayed violence against persons who deserve what they have coming to them. The violence is personal, occurring outside ethical frameworks or discourses of social or political justice. The revenge motive is depicted and enacted with clinical coldness and shrewd planning. As the Bride states very early in the film, it's "mercy, compassion, and forgiveness" that she lacks, not rationality.

Essentially, then, this is a film with a single story of female revenge (the Bride occupies a central place in all but a few scenes), but it is a narrative in which revenge becomes multiplied and figures in every aspect of narration and characterization; although O-Ren Ishii's is the only secondary revenge story given any screen time, every character has his or her own relation to vengeance, and it is primarily this relation that ties them together. The dead are not victims, and the killer is not a murderer but a victim of attempted murder; as an avenger against personal injury and outrage, the Bride claims the symbolic weight of the victim even while exercising acts of violence. As victim and wronged mother, her rage and brutality become sympathetic, productive, and pragmatic; the audience is invited to share in violent acts framed as redemptive, lucid, and even courageous. Her bloody acts of murder are thus contained and explained by a rational retribution. As the "old Klingon proverb" that opens the film states, it seems that revenge is indeed a "dish best served cold."

Reiterating this redemptive function of retributive violence, the final scene of *Kill Bill* offers a utopic and intensely feminized image of a naturalized and conventional maternal wholeness. This melodramatic ending is in keeping with the drive toward increasing domesticity that carries the final acts of the film.[9] The penultimate scene is literally one of domestic implosion: the mise-en-scène indicators of melodrama; the familial, private setting; and the death of Bill by internal heart failure rather than invasive bodily violence. As implosion, there is an extent to which Bill's death is framed as a result of masculine agency. The technique, one that leaves the edifice of the male body intact and whole, is passed on to the Bride by a male teacher; Bill is not penetrated but killed from within (a literal heartbreak), leaving his external bodily wholeness intact (a fate not shared by his ruthlessly fragmented female counterparts). The patriarch is ultimately responsible for his own demise. Completing this reorganization of the family on maternal rather than paternal grounds is the final scene of a blissful mother and daughter reunion, a state of affairs presented as natural, right, and desired.

The female violence that precedes this narrative closure is thus framed as an aberration, made necessary by circumstance and made possible by extensive training (shown in flashback), a reading that is reinforced by the depiction of female violence as artificial or unnatural that dominates the film as a whole in the images of hybrid perversity (a pregnant Bride, a geisha yakuza boss, a murderous schoolgirl, a knife-fighting Pasadena homemaker). In emphasizing the distortion inherent in each of these constructions, these figures become markers of the violation of nature and natural order wreaked by the violent woman, a point that is reiterated in the symbol of the reunited lioness and cub invoked at the end of the film. Although this ending can obviously be read ironically, given the excessive violence that has come before, given the repetition that Beatrix Kiddo/Black Mamba/the Bride is a killer and will always be a killer, and given the disturbing attraction to violence evidenced by her appropriately named daughter, B. B., this reading does nothing to reposition our response and understanding of the spectacular physical violence that has been depicted. We might recognize the circular nature of the film's ending (the possibility of Nicki seeking revenge for her mother's death), but this recognition does not shift the acceptance of the essentially redemptive and regenerative function of the violence depicted over the course of the film. The vengeful and bloody violence has been subsumed in an ending that moves farther and farther inward toward the private, the domestic, and the essentially nonviolent and moves so effectively that the opening scene of domestic invasion and murder is rewritten in the happy rebirth of the second mother-child combination. The threat of female public, violent action is subsumed by the private, essentially nonviolent domestic space.

Alone with her child in the anonymous space of a hotel room and devoid of ties to the past or community (even a community of killers), the apolitical, individualistic, and stabilized feminine construction of the Bride at the end of *Kill Bill* contains in one figure the fantasies of feminine victimization, vengeance, erotic display, maternal devotion, and sacrifice: Beatrix Kiddo/ Black Mamba/the Bride becomes quite simply "Mommy." Public and private realms are strictly divided and demarcated with the woman clearly positioned in a private, domestic, and essentially feminine habitat; there is no threat of the active, public woman or of collective action but only of reunification and ingenerate wholeness acquired through maternity. What was lost has been found, the action is over, and the lioness can return to her natural habitat of an enclosed, private, nonviolent, and passive domestic space.

The violence in the film is thus placed firmly in a restorative and redemptive dimension; it appears to reestablish an order, yet, as is the case with all nostalgia, it establishes an order that never actually existed. The strongly gendered vision we are given at the end of the film is not one that has appeared elsewhere, even in flashback. It is an idealized vision of maternal wholeness, one predicated on violent revenge but also on absolute and idealized familial feminine sacrifice. The Bride gives up everything, including her powerful, active identity as a skilled fighter (a point Bill repeats and emphasizes), for her daughter. Any crises in identity, gender, or communities of belonging are erased in the familial emphasis, and this holds despite all the rhetorical references made to the Bride's essentially violent nature (as a "Black Mamba," a "renegade killer bee," a lioness). The familial structure of the death squad (with the "Snake Charmer," Bill, as the patriarchal head) is replaced with more benign and normalized maternal bonding.

The violent deaths in the film are thus doubly rationalized as they are framed by a redemptive narrative in which they become more than the mere expressions of exacted revenge. Even though the logic is one that escapes the Bride until her confrontation with Bill, the ideological power of the ending (and the audience's knowledge of her daughter's existence) transforms the vengeful murders into required acts necessary for the rescue of a child. This emphasis on the child (and the concomitant significance of the rescue plot) is reinforced by the way in which the revelation of the child's survival marks the cliffhanger of the first film and offers a bridge between the two parts. It is ultimately the figure of the child and the significance of her reclamation that unify the film both structurally and thematically. And this reclamation is yoked to a revenge plot from which it is inseparable. The violence of revenge is merely shifted with the discovery of the child, as the Bride's motivation becomes one of maternal recovery.

Thus, although the argument could be made that the maternal melodrama and idealized familial wholeness that end the film are overdetermined, even ironic, and therefore destabilizing, such a reading is not supported by the structure of regenerative and retributive violence that organizes and anchors the film. Even if it is only temporary, as in the cyclical revenge implied at the end of *Kill Bill*, the revenge structure ends with resolution, serving as its own closed system. The structure is not a linear narrative so much as it is a series of acts of violence imprinted on the film from its very start and completed at the end; violence is merely a means to achieve this end. Rather than being an instance of ironic play, I suggest that in *Kill Bill*'s maternal avenger—who operates within a confluence of genre, cultural appropriation, and celebration of an essentially pure and nonviolent white femininity—we can recognize the dominant cultural and ideological constructions of femaleness that occupy popular culture and discourse. In particular, we can identify the tropes that construct femininity's relation to violent acts in ways that attempt to control, contain, and rationalize threats of female violence while maintaining the appearance of ironic distance from patriarchy and active gender transgression. It is not insignificant that the most dominant popular culture images of female power are those in which the violence is ideologically, visually, and fantasmically contained within some individualized, apolitical frame. The most common narrative structures and tropes in popular cinematic constructions of violent women mark the female fighter as artificial, as trained, destined, built fighters guided by male father figures, as in *La Femme Nikita* (Besson, 1990),

Buffy the Vampire Slayer (Kuzui, 1991), *The Long Kiss Goodnight* (Harlin, 1996), *The Fifth Element* (Besson, 1997), and *Crouching Tiger, Hidden Dragon*; an avenger for herself or her family, as in *I Spit on Your Grave, Ms. 45, Thelma and Louise* (Scott, 1991), *The Quick and the Dead* (Raimi, 1995), *Freeway* (Bright, 1996), *Baise-Moi* (Despentes, 2000), and *Monster* (Jenkins, 2003); or as a highly sexualized, perverse, and often materialistic murderous vixen, as in erotic thrillers such as *Basic Instinct* (Verhoeven, 1992), *Poison Ivy* (Shea, 1992), and *The Crush* (Shapiro, 1993) but also neo-noirs such as *Body Heat* (Kasdan, 1981) and *The Last Seduction* (Dahl, 1994). Although these examples or categories clearly do not exhaust the multitude of images of violent women on film and television screens, they outline a certain commonality of features that are the most prevalent and popular, the main feature of which seems to be the explanatory and instrumental functionalizing of violence as tied to singular character traits or experiences. In these texts, female violence is set apart as exceptional, as an individualized, and sometimes pathologized, action that is established in the end as both artificial or unnatural and as potentially liberating or gender transgressive.

With this in mind, it seems necessary, if simplistic, to return to the concerns outlined in the first part of this essay and to note that the presentation of female toughness, strength, violent action, or fighting is not always potentially disruptive or subversive but relies on the interplay of violence and gender in the form, style, narration, and structure of any given film text. While it is valid to argue that violent action is not traditionally a strong trope of codes of femininity, this does not necessitate a transgressive function for violence itself. Similarly, arguments of empowerment, while engaging, do not fundamentally shift, reframe, or retheorize the dominant and prevalent modes for approaching and understanding either film violence or the relation between gender and violence in representation, nor are they equipped to address the kinds of explosive, extreme postmodern and intertextual images of violence that we are currently seeing in theaters or on television. The violence of the classical genre film, which is usually framed as supportive of dominant ideology through the simultaneous disavowal and valuation of violent acts (acts that are presented as useful and necessary but ultimately nonrecuperable), becomes complex, layered, and significantly more difficult to pin down in postmodern hybrid genre films.

Moreover, as postmodern texts many of these films invite attention to their own superficiality and, in turn, to their own engagement with codes of excess and transgression. The postmodern "knowingness" of *Kill Bill*, which emphasizes its visceral and spectacular excesses of violent action and erotic feminine display, should not, however, be taken as an active critique or a transparent sign of shifts in societal and ideological constructions of gender and power. In framing themselves as self-referential and ironic play, many of these female-centered postmodern action films, such as *Charlie's Angels* and *Kill Bill*, appear to anticipate and deflect critical engagement by constantly reasserting the attention to surfaces, display, and viewing procedures shaped by consumption. For example, it is difficult to criticize *Charlie's Angels* for its presentation of idealized femininity or *Kill Bill* for its excessive violence because both the films and their audiences are fully aware that the films exist for these purposes alone. These are not hidden but overt discourses of postfeminist and postmodern superficiality and spectacle, and critical responses often reiterate these discourses in responding to the texts in these terms.

This kind of ironic but not necessarily disruptive play is clearly at work in a number of contemporary violent films. For example, rather than operating as a subtext, the relation between action cinema violence and the phallic framework of castration has been brought to the fore in any number of postmodern genre films that repeatedly make explicit anxieties about castration. The castrated and fetishized women of action films, and in particular of postmodern films that address gender and violence in excessive, ironic, and fragmented ways, have reached critical mass in contemporary films such as Rodriguez's *Sin City* (2005), which appear to revel in masochistic references to castration and phallic loss. Yet, for all its jokes about castration and explicit and brutal attacks on masculine phallic power, it can be argued that *Sin City* (or even *Kill Bill*) offers gender clarity within a stable, capitalist, and depoliticized global economy. All women are whores in *Sin City*, and, although men may not always operate as their saviors (the women protect themselves), they still desire to do so. In fact, there is throughout a strongly marked nostalgia for a world in which male chivalry and power are both possible and certain.

Similarly, in *Kill Bill* the emphasis is on a nostalgia for nuclear family unity freed from the concerns of patriarchal violence or female solidarity, community, or public action. The Bride is reconstructed as a mother and violence is justified as the world is placed in balance by the valuation and establishment of a naturalized, protective, nonviolent maternity. In its celebration of genre pastiche and maternal harmony, *Kill Bill* can thus be seen as a nostalgia film of the kind outlined by Fredric Jameson in his analysis of *Star Wars* (Lucas, 1977).

Extending the definition of the nostalgia film beyond those that use historical settings, Jameson argues for a nostalgia of sense or feeling in which the desire is not to re-create or even refer to the past or past objects but to reawaken the sensations and feelings associated with those objects.[10] As noted earlier, *Kill Bill*'s affectionate and celebratory pastiche of genres can be seen in this nostalgic and sacralizing way, but it is also important to extend recognition of this nostalgia to the film's narrative and ideological vision. In its nostalgic homage to the sexploitation, blaxploitation, rape revenge, and martial arts genres, the film offers an idealized instrumental, violent femininity seemingly unencumbered by contemporary feminist concerns or their cultural, social, and political ramifications. The Bride's violence is exceptional, personally motivated, and purposefully aimed at the reestablishment of family unity. This unity may only be partial, but its recuperative and affective impact is clear. The end of the film offers a family devoid of its patriarch, but the emotive and narrational force of the film transforms this absence into positive presence. The absence of patriarchy is an absence of violence and threat, and the female violence of the film is configured retroactively as temporary, aberrant, obligatory, and curative.

My critique of *Kill Bill* and popular images of violent women in film is not meant to suggest that all such images are equally supportive of or tied to dominant ideology, patriarchy, or postfeminism. There are a number of films that shift the depiction of the violent woman in interesting ways or engage with issues of representation directly, although often these depictions are found in films outside of genre-based, popular cinemas. For example, the theorist Slavoj Žižek posits the importance of the violent female in *Lost Highway* (Lynch, 1997) as a way of engaging with both classical and postmodern variations of the femme fatale.[11] According to Žižek, the power of the femme fatale brings us back to the roots of courtly love and the fundamental contradiction of the feminine ideal as mother, whore, and virgin. In opposition to what he argues is the outwardly transgressive but essentially regressive tendency evident in neo-noir heroines (*The Last Seduction*, *Body Heat*, *Bound* [Wachowski, 1996]), heroines who may succeed in a materialistic sense but in doing so confirm an apolitical orientation, and the more subversive but still sanctioned transgressions of the classic femme fatale, Žižek argues for the actual and radical disruption offered by films such as *Lost Highway*, which present the instability of this fascinating femininity itself. Split in two halves,

Lynch's film offers a complex, dreamlike text that on the most basic narrative level can be analyzed as the story of a failed relationship and its fantasy flip side. The film presents the stories of two couples. In the first half, Fred and Renee have a sterile marriage shaped by Fred's suspicious jealousy and Renee's emotional distance. After the apparent murder of Renee by Fred, his imprisonment, and his subsequent transformation, the film moves into its second half, which is dominated by Fred and Alice (Fred is played by two actors, and Renee and Alice are both played by Patricia Arquette), who are in fact the kind of passionate, adulterous couple that Fred feared and fantasized about in the first story. Pointing out that by splitting the film in two, with the Fred character being doubled in name but played by a different actor and the Renee/Alice character played by the same actress, Žižek notes that Lynch makes explicit the shifting constructions of "woman" that rely on fantasies of eroticism and violence. The beautiful but not fatal Renee in the first half of the film becomes the deadly and erotic Alice in the second half, thus staging what she always already was in the lead male's fantasy. In *Lost Highway*, Alice confronts desire with fantasy, and as Fred is given his fantasy projection back his message quite literally returns to and destroys him. The doubling of the woman thus effectively becomes "a kind of meta-commentary on the opposition between the classic and postmodern *noir femme fatale*."[12] It is in the disruption of coherence and in the openly staged nature of these depictions of violent femininity that we can see the cultural constructions of woman for what they are. Rather than containment, the film offers confusion, disjunction, and a potentially aporetic lack of closure, all aspects that, Žižek argues, contribute to the image of radical femininity depicted.

Clearly this kind of radical, complex, and destabilizing depiction of femininity is not common in popular genre cinema, which trades in more cohesive and totalizing ideological myths and structures. But in its use of the figure of the femme fatale, a popular and generically based character and trope, *Lost Highway* suggests the possibilities for complex, violent femininity that seem absent in much of today's action cinema, which tends to articulate an idealized, nonviolent, and stable femininity that is set in opposition to a fantasmic and contradictory complexity, nuance, politicized action, or collectivity.

The action cinema heroine is in some ways like the stable masculine figures of classical western or action cinema: her violence is rationalized and redemptive, and her acts are solitary ones. However, unlike westerns such as *The Searchers* or *Shane* (Stevens, 1953), in which masculine violence is both needed and shunned by the community, the violent female individual figures in *Kill Bill* present solitary and selfish violent action not as a necessary negative against the idealized community but as a worthy good in its own right. Violence in this scenario is instrumental, rationalized as either purposeful or perverse (in an individual, pathological way). The actions of violent women in popular cinema typically enact some form of either "positive" resolution (*Kill Bill*, *The Last Seduction*) or suicidal implosion (*Thelma and Louise*, *Mulholland Drive* [Lynch, 2001]). Only rarely are acts of female violence directed outward as protest, subversive communication, or cultural critique (as they are in Gorris's *A Question of Silence*) in the form that we get in a number of films focused on male violence (e.g., *Dog Day Afternoon* [Lumet, 1975]). Appropriating images of power and progress and enlisting them in the service of individualized action, these films provide imagistic and ideological support for the system they appear to subvert.

The action heroine and the neo-noir femme fatale ought not to be automatically read symptomatically, therefore, for hidden cultural anxieties and fears; the anxieties these figures address may be more explicit and transparent. In fact, I would argue that the explicit anxieties the neo-noir heroine signals are not those of crises in masculinity or even femininity itself but those of feminism and in particular of the public face, collective action, and political engagement of feminism. Indeed, an overwhelming number of films featuring violent women can be seen to have at their core a narrative resolution of the entry of women into the public sphere and the resulting tension between ties to the familial and the social, of woman's relation to public space and community, that is at the core of feminism. In opposition to an active, public construction of female power (of the kind we see in *A Question of Silence*) or a representation of femininity that acknowledges its own agonistic, essentially split, fraught, and disruptive ideology and fantasies (as in *Lost Highway*), the neo-noir heroines of films such as *The Last Seduction* and the contemporary action heroines of films such as *Kill Bill* articulate a postfeminist discourse of individualistic, "have it all" feminism that yokes violence to individual, personal, erotic, and financial success.

These violent heroines of contemporary popular cinema, then, are suggestive of the kind of ideological masking that is at work in both popular culture and postfeminism itself. In many of these films, the role of violence, and the revenge narrative in particular, is one of stabilization rather than excessive transgression, a situation that asks us to question the ways in which discourses of class, gender, and race are articulated through narratives of bodily dismemberment, violent action, and depoliticized, individuated, and antisocial systems of justice. Instrumentalized, justified, and rationalized within an individual rather than communal or political framework, vengeful violence becomes the primary means by which the action heroine enacts fantasies of recuperation, redemption, and ultimate omnipotence and transcendence. Although they are powerful, visually pleasurable, and appealing, it is important to recognize the role these fantasies of gendered violent action play within popular culture and to note that in many of these images of (and responses to) violent women we can recognize an apolitical, individualistic, and capitalistic celebration of the superficial markers of power that dominate much of the popular discourse of postfeminism. Seen in this way, the violent woman of contemporary popular action cinema does not upset but endorses the status quo. Unlike the classical femme fatale, she is difficult to read symptomatically because she does not so much imply or reveal society's repressions and anxieties as she offers them support in a positive valuation of individualist, self-serving action. In this way, the violent action heroine is not phallicized or masculinized through her actions (a common concern in much scholarly and popular writing on action heroines) as much as she is postfeminized; her superficial transgression and postpolitical, individual acts, and achievements become the markers for the ambivalent and problematic pleasures, regressions, and recidivisms of postfeminist popular culture. As a kind of inherent or sanctioned transgression of dominant patriarchal, capitalist ideology, the violent action heroine offers the image of innovative or even revolutionary change while disavowing any actual engagement with violence and its relation to feminism and female solidarity, collectivity, or political action. Perhaps the contemporary action heroine has not come such a long way after all.

Notes

1. See, for example, Boyle, "What's Natural about Killing"; Franco, "Gender, Genre, and Female Pleasure in the Contemporary Revenge Narrative"; Heinecken, *Warrior Women of Television*; Inness, *Action Chicks*; Inness, *Tough Girls*; McCaughey and King, *Reel Knockouts*; Owen, "Vampires, Postmodernity, and Postfeminism"; Peixoto Labre and Duke, "Nothing Like a Brisk Walk and a Spot of Demon Slaughter to Make a Girl's Night"; and Read, *The New Avengers*.
2. Leland, "Everything a Man Can Do, Decapitation Included."

3. The most prominent and influential of these articles are Fischer, "Murder, She Wrote"; Elsley, "Laughter as Feminine Power in *The Color Purple* and *A Question of Silence*"; Gentile, "Feminist or Tendentious?"; Rich, "Prologue"; Rich, "Lady Killers"; Root, "Distributing *A Question of Silence*"; and Williams, "A Jury of Their Peers." Distinct in critical position and theoretical and methodological orientation, each of these articles seeks to address the political, ethical, and representational issues at the center of inquiries into and depictions of women's violence. All, however, even when focusing on the stylistic issues of laughter, group cohesion, displaced narration, or the choruslike trial scene, address to some extent the question of whether the film depicts female violence in a manner that is tantamount to an empty exercise in gender reversal that reinscribes dominant patriarchal ideology.

4. This is indeed the case with much work on violence in contemporary popular film; there is an intensified desire to address issues of violence and representation, but many discussions tend to do so in fairly limited or circumscribed ways. As a result, many significant and insightful analyses of film violence treat it as a relatively known and stable entity, as an entry point for the examination of auteurism, genre, national cinema, race, gender, class, or history, but they do not, for the most part, engage in detail with our understandings of what violence is, how we construct and approach it, or what its modes, operations, ramifications, and tropes are. For example, in addition to articles and books on filmmakers such as John Woo, Martin Scorsese, Abel Ferrara, Oliver Stone, Sam Peckinpah, and Quentin Tarantino, influential texts on violence and cinema such as the edited collections *Mythologies of Violence in Postmodern Media* (Christopher Sharrett), *Screening Violence* (Stephen Prince), and *Violence and American Cinema* (J. David Slocum) focus to a large degree on individual films, genres, filmmakers, or national cinemas.

5. Slocum, *Violence and American Cinema*, 2.

6. This attention to bodily display is, of course, a significant part of criticism aimed at male action heroes as well, but in accounts of violent females in film there is a notable attention to superficial markers of power read as indications of subversion, and, although analyzing the function of clothing (clothing changes in particular), corporeal markers of strength or weakness (muscles and breasts or their lack), or sexuality (blatant eroticism or explicit sexual pleasure) is significant to any analysis of contemporary action film heroines, it does not necessarily address film violence or its choreography, representation, functions, effects, and narrational or structural features. Many of these analyses of female power are engaging and insightful and take on the discourse of erotic, powerful feminine display with a playful and alliterative vigor. For example, in *Impossible Bodies*, Chris Holmlund notes the "deadly dolls," "lethal lovelies," "violent vamps," and "fatal femmes" of contemporary cinema (73–74). Although Holmlund is ironically using these terms to emphasize and critique the whiteness, youth, and erotic appeal of popular images of violent women, the common usage of these kinds of catchphrases suggests that the emphasis on pleasurable surfaces that is a part of the films themselves often works its way into the analytical argumentation that reiterates this focus. For example, Inness's introduc-

tion to *Action Chicks* addresses musculature and gym culture in detail but notes the significance of erotic or aesthetic appeal in an action chick's ability to be "attractive and feminine" even though she may not "graciously accept" societal roles (7); in *The New Avengers*, Jacinda Read's analysis of *The Last Seduction* pays particular attention to shifts in costuming; and in "Things Are Different Now?" Dominic Allessio makes note of the central character's "good looks and cutting edge fashion sense" (731).

7. Leo Charney's "The Violence of a Perfect Moment" argues that moments of heightened violence do "battle with a corresponding impulse toward storytelling" (48) but that it also "depends on the narratives that enclose and defamiliarize it, that allow violence to retain its kinetic impact and prevent it from becoming a string of meaningless sensation" (48). In her "Violence American Style: The Narrative Orchestration of Violent Attractions," Marsha Kinder similarly argues that the eruption of violence in films such as *The Wild Bunch* (Peckinpah, 1969) threatens to "usurp the narrative's traditional function of contextualization" (68) in a manner similar to the performance number in a musical. This comparison of the fight scene and the musical number is especially pertinent in *Kill Bill*, which utilizes all the spectacle, space, kineticism, and bodily display of a classic Hollywood dance number.

8. These comments apply to the revenge narrative itself and not the backstory, which is usually framed within ethical, moral, and legal parameters so that the audience is clearly positioned in its response to the wrong committed and the need for revenge.

9. This domesticity is highlighted by an emphasized and unified domestic space, slower pacing, costume changes, and a color palette that highlights conventional femininity and softness and attention to routine domestic activities such as sandwich making.

10. As Jameson notes, "One of the most important cultural experiences of the generations that grew up from the 1930s to the 1950s was the Saturday afternoon serial of the Buck Rogers type—alien villains, true American heroes, heroines in distress, the death ray or the doomsday box, and the cliff-hanger at the end whose miraculous solution was to be witnessed next Saturday afternoon. *Star Wars* reinvents this experience in the form of a pastiche; there is no point to a parody of such serials, since they are long extinct. Far from being a pointless satire of such dead forms, *Star Wars* satisfies a deep (might I even say repressed?) longing to experience them again: it is a complex object in which on some first level children and adolescents can take the adventures straight, while the adult public is able to gratify a deeper and more properly nostalgic desire to return to that older period and to live its strange old aesthetic artefacts through once again" (*The Cultural Turn*, 8).

11. Žižek, *The Art of the Ridiculous Sublime*.

12. Ibid., 13.

Steven Cohan

7

Queer Eye for the Straight Guise

CAMP, POSTFEMINISM, AND THE FAB FIVE'S
MAKEOVERS OF MASCULINITY

The big hit on American cable television in the summer of 2003 was the Bravo series *Queer Eye for the Straight Guy*, airing on Tuesday evenings. Every week five gay men, collectively referred to as the "Fab Five," take on a domestically and sartorially challenged straight man. He serves as their "trade" but not in the sense of the term suggested by the double entendre of the title; rather, they do a complete makeover of the straight guy. Each member of the queer team represents what is taken as a gay-identified specialty: Carson Kressley is in charge of fashion, Kyan Douglas grooming, Thom Filicia decorating, Ted Allen cooking, and Jai Rodriguez something vaguely called "culture" but more accurately a hybrid of dating or hosting etiquette and leisure entertainment skills. Typically, each episode focuses the straight guy's makeover around a particular "mission," with the Fab Five's renovation directed toward his achieving a personal or professional goal so that he can attain "confidence" and "grow up," as is frequently said on the show. Regardless of the particulars, the Fab Five's primary objective is to teach the straight guy how to satisfy the emotional and domestic needs of a present or potential female partner.

Queer Eye adheres to the makeover show format insofar as it defines a confident, mature masculinity through consumption and then normalizes it through a heterosexual couple, leaving the queer guys out of the loop except as spectators. Just as important, though, while decidedly aimed at restoring the straight guy's cultural capital in a postfeminist marketplace, *Queer Eye* also makes a concerted effort through camp to visualize queerness in its contiguous relation to straightness. How one weighs these concerns, I am going to argue, determines what one can find in the Fab Five's makeovers of the straight guys.[1] My discussion of the first season of *Queer Eye* will thus aim to situate its legibility as a queer show in light of this collection and the conference that inspired it. I have in mind (and am, to be candid, intentionally resisting) how some formulations of postfeminism have so readily absorbed the impact of queer theory but left out the queerness. Witness how, in addressing the woman now seemingly liberated by feminism, consumer culture and the mass media have transformed the visible gay male into what Baz Dreisinger aptly describes as "the trendy accessory for straight women," namely, the "postfeminist" female's best friend and confidante, and the inspiration for her ideal consort, that hip, het "metrosexual."[2] While recognizing the extent to which *Queer Eye* encourages a highly comforting view of homosexuality as a useful accessory of postfeminist femininity, I want to examine how the series simultaneously enables a queer viewer to see past that agenda.

Good Fairies to the Rescue?

Queer Eye for the Straight Guy was Bravo's effort to exploit the popularity of makeover shows, twisting the format a bit with its five gay experts. Moreover, Bravo paired it with another gay version of a reality TV genre, the dating show *Boy Meets Boy*, to create a two-hour bloc of "alternative" programming on Tuesday nights. The intent was to establish a niche identity, thereby overcoming the blandness of this NBC-owned cable network, and possibly to find a signature show. Having gay or gay-coded hosts on a cable reality series was not new; nor did *Queer Eye* make any pretense of reinventing the makeover format. All the same, in the absence of a big, tabloid, TV event in the summer of 2003, *Queer Eye* immediately received a great deal of media coverage because, unlike *Boy Meets Boy*, it featured five gay men perfectly comfortable with their homosexuality and openly identified itself as a series respectful of queer tastes and attitudes.

Exploiting the buzz that resulted from so much attention, NBC subsequently reran episodes several times in its powerhouse Thursday night lineup during the summer months (a significant spot for advertising the opening of new movies each week), and the series' success prompted an appearance of the Fab Five on the network's *Tonight Show* in August to do a makeover of the host, Jay Leno. They performed the same job for preselected audience members on Oprah Winfrey's afternoon talk show in early autumn. In the fall as well, the Comedy Central satire *South Park* parodied *Queer Eye*, indicating how quickly this new series had entered popular culture awareness. Aside from the expected gay demographic, the series quickly attracted a strong female following, prompting a Yahoo! discussion group dedicated to this important segment of the viewing audience, "A Girl's View of *Queer Eye*." Yet the series also drew a cadre of straight men. One fan site, "Straight Eye for the Queer Shows" (now apparently defunct), featured four openly heterosexual men who rotated responsibility for writing detailed, tongue-in-cheek recaps of each week's episode. This is not to suggest that the male segment of the series' audience took its makeover lessons lightly. A December 2003 survey conducted by Jericho Communications revealed that whenever a new episode aired on Tuesday evenings it encouraged more males to go shopping with a buddy the day afterward than at any other time during the week.[3]

The currency of *Queer Eye* throughout its first season occurred at the same time that same-sex marriage became a controversial, publicly debated issue.[4] Two Canadian provinces legalized such unions in the summer of 2003, making it possible for gay and lesbian couples to travel there from the United States and marry, and in November of that year the Massachusetts Supreme Court upheld same-sex marriages, prompting local civil resistance to the federal Defense of Marriage Act in states on the East and West Coasts. This timeliness certainly contributed, if indirectly, to the attention *Queer Eye* and its five hosts received in the months following the premiere. In its year-end chronicle of events, the American Film Institute (AFI) listed *Queer Eye* as one of the two major cultural developments of 2003 (the other was the issue of film piracy). The AFI singled out *Queer Eye* because it brought "gay culture to the national fore by spoofing and celebrating stereotypes, and unlike other reality shows, it did so in a winning and genuine manner that developed a bond between the gay and straight man."[5] The AFI was not alone in applauding the series' liberal viewpoint. Oprah Winfrey expressed much the same sentiment, often tearfully, several times during the Fab Five's appearance on her show.

Alongside that liberal approval, *Queer Eye* received its fair share of negative criticism for perpetuating, not debunking, gender-sexual stereotypes. News stories on the suddenly hot new show balanced criticism and praise in their accounts of the response from gay viewers.[6] Skimming several gay-oriented discussion boards during the months following the series premiere, I found that the strongest charge against the Fab Five was directed at their "unmasculine" appearance and mannerisms, epitomized by their flamboyant personification of effeminate stereotypes, with Carson and Jai targeted in particular.

Inevitably, a comparison was made with the more attractive gay men to be found on Bravo's other new series, *Boy Meets Boy*. Its hook was that the gay bachelor did not know his dating pool included straight men. While this premise appeared to belie the distinction between gay and straight on the basis of appearance, *Boy Meets Boy* reinscribed the axiom that the most attractive gay men are those who can successfully pass as straight, and the series only proved that, when it comes to dating, gay men can be just as banal and superficial as their straight counterparts. But *Boy Meets Boy* capitalized on the thinking that motivates the many gay personal ads seeking straight-acting men, and it exploited the fantasy, a staple of gay erotica, that straight men are seducible. What stood out in the contrasting remarks about *Queer Eye*'s circulation of gay stereotypes was the discomfort felt by hostile viewers precisely because the Fab Five were not gym junkies; they did not conform to the "Abercrombie & Fitch" ethos inspiring (not to say inciting desire in) gay men of their generation, which, as Michael Joseph Gross observes, is to look like everyone else, to be "regular guys—[but] with better-than-average bodies."[7] In short, these viewers preferred the buff, twenty-something, heterosexual-looking guys on *Boy Meets Boy*. While the criticism declared that *Queer Eye* reconfirmed straight prejudices about nelly gay men, it could be reduced to the simpler question: why can't these five queers act and look more like straight guys?

When watching that first season of *Queer Eye*, my own answer at the time was: if they did, we wouldn't be able to tell the difference. True, *Queer Eye* defines the queerness of the Fab Five through their expertise as consumers, not through their sexual orientation. As Anna McCarthy points out, "The Fab Five are totally sexless. They may tease their subjects, but there is no chance that they will get to sleep with them."[8] Their queer eye is for the most part not focused through a gay gaze—it's not *that* kind of queer eye for a straight guy—but is meant to illuminate for heterosexual men what their girlfriends, wives, or mothers already know, namely, the value of "products," perhaps the most repeatedly used term on the show, as the cornerstone of heterosexual self-confidence and maturity. The five hosts function for each episode not as protagonists but in the capacity that narratology calls helper figures, serving the needs of a domesticated heteronormality; this subordinate role in the narrative of each episode enables a makeover to be focused through a decidedly straight eye for the queer guy, which is why the five hosts may encourage what is actually "the fantasy that [the series'] straight viewers gain entry into an otherwise inaccessible, unfamiliar gay culture."[9] With their homosexuality serving mainly as consumer culture's equivalent of professional counseling for the straight couple, and gay culture itself reduced to shopping, the Fab Five do end up seeming all too reminiscent of the three drag queens in *To Wong Foo, Thanks for Everything! Julie Newmar* (1995): the asexual good fairies who bring a hip Manhattanite's taste for style, flair, color, and cleanliness into a bland and dingy straight world and quickly depart as soon as they have spread their gay cheer.

As for its depiction of straights, *Queer Eye* follows the example of all the self-help relationship books that binarize the difference between men and women, depicting the genders as "different species entirely" and consequently promoting the expectation that heterosexual romance "is not a walk in the park but an arduous expedition."[10] I think it is safe to assume that the appeal of the series for many women lies in its mission of softening masculinity's rough edges for successful male-female cohabitation. Registering what Sasha Torres observes is "the incapacity of the heterosexual families that spawned the straight guys to sustain even a minimal quality of life," *Queer Eye* depicts not only the domestic rehabilitation but also the class elevation of straight men for the benefit of their women.[11] Like other makeover shows, the series teaches its viewers that this dual mission is most easily performed through one's appearance, and the urgency of such instruction is expressed every time the Fab Five obsess over men needing to shave in "the right way" and to remove all that gristly body hair, whether it's the straight guy's back hair, ear hair, or unibrow. As Torres notes, the show's preoccupation with shaving crystallizes, through the Fab Five's intervention, both the necessity of male-male tutelage in perpetuating the protocols of civil masculinity and the heterosexual family's failure to perform this crucial function for its unruly sons, much to the dismay of their future girlfriends and wives.

With successful straight coupling requiring endless negotiation between alien creatures polarized in their libidinal, emotional, and domestic needs, *Queer Eye* brings in the Fab Five to mediate heterosexual difference; their visible queerness then functions to speak for women in an unthreatening male voice. As a result, the series brings out the contradiction constructing the postfeminist female viewer being addressed from this vantage point. Straight masculinity is identified as problematic more than oppressive, and it can be remedied through a male's consumption of the same kind of products that enhance in order to regulate femininity. However, even though the makeovers serve the interests of women, *Queer Eye* concentrates on "the pleasures of companionship" between straight guys and their gay cohorts, relegating women to "a shadow presence on the show."[12] A female's main function is to nod approval at what the queer guys have achieved for her in her absence, which involves their pedagogical bonding with the straight guy as well as his makeover.

The cultural ideal of masculinity aimed for here—though it is a standard the straight guys on the series at best only approximate to provide the link between the makeovers and the advertising and product placement—is what the media has termed the metrosexual, the youngish, upscale, heterosexual male who spends so much time on his appearance (and so much money on hairstyling, fashionable clothing, and skin products) that he is readable as "gay" and too liberal to mind the mistake—but hands off, please! On the Fab Five's return visit (21 November 2003) several months after their makeover of the *Tonight Show*, Carson Kressley defined this suddenly ubiquitous yet sexually ambiguous figure for Jay Leno as the straight guy who moisturizes but doesn't have sex with other men. More accurately, the fashion guru quipped, he's "a moistrosexual."

A recent invention of marketing and the urban press, the metrosexual male gives every impression of revising how straight masculinity has traditionally been defined in opposition to feminine activities such as shopping, grooming, and cooking, as Martin Roberts points out elsewhere in this volume.[13] Such a refiguration of masculinity has a longer history, though, deriving from an earlier representation of what was termed the New Man in advertising, TV, and films of the 1980s, itself an outgrowth of the kind of marketing aimed directly at male consuming, which *Playboy* magazine perfected in the 1950s.[14] Somewhat like the metrosexual, the New Man of the 1980s was depicted as being "tough but tender, masculine but sensitive—he can cry, cuddle babies

and best of all buy cosmetics."[15] This newly styled image of a straight masculinity geared toward consuming was perhaps first signaled by *American Gigolo*
(1980), the neo-noir film starring Richard Gere that put the clothing designer
Georgio Armani on the map, and it was featured in advertising campaigns for
products such as Levi's 501 jeans and Grey Flannel cologne. By the end of the
decade, when the Liz Claiborne company introduced its own brand of men's
cologne, the marketing was specifically aimed at the New Man, "who attends
Rob Reiner romances and tipples kir royales [and] might also want to take an
introspective and vulnerable approach to the way he smells."[16]

According to Suzanne Moore, the 1980s New Man drew on the visual iconography of soft-core gay pornography, drawing attention to the male body
"as a pleasurable object [but] on condition that his pleasure can be contained
within a narcissistic/auto-erotic discourse."[17] Just as important, this image
addressed women by offering "the possibility of an *active female gaze*."[18] Moore
attributes this kind of radical shift in depicting the masculine, which blurs
the distinction between the active male voyeur and the passive female exhibi-
tionist, to popular culture's awareness of the "renegotiations over masculinity
brought about by radical political discourses," feminism, and the gay and lesbian rights movement in particular.[19] Because of the homoeroticism informing the visual representation of the New Man, however, the heterosexuality
of this image of masculinity was never fully secure. Hence paying attention
to how one smelled could signal vulnerability as well as introspection, just as
it still connoted suspicion about—and feminized as narcissistic—the type of
man who was *too* concerned with how he looked.

The 1980s New Man, in short, could always turn out to be a closet case.
By contrast, as the newer term suggests, the metrosexual willingly displays
his toned but moisturized body as a means of performing his masculinity
through his ability to consume, using his exhibitionism to assert his identity as an urban, middle-class male. While this newest incarnation of a male
attuned to the same consumerist desires as his domestic partner is presumed
to be heterosexual, he is still poised between assumptions about what makes
a man readable as "straight" and what makes him readable as "queer," which
is why he is more "metro" than "hetero." Appropriating the tropes formerly
used to identify the gay male consumer, the metrosexual reimagines masculinity from a postfeminist perspective, but the price remains this new man's
sexual ambiguity—the very anxiety that *Boy Meets Boy* appeared to celebrate

but actually fostered by keeping its gay bachelor in the dark about the sexual orientation of the men he was scrutinizing, flirting with, and sharing his feelings with in one-on-one encounters. For single straight women, even if the metrosexual moisturizes but doesn't swing with the other team, his sexual ambiguity renews the motive for the much-quoted worry that all the best men are either already married or gay—for if they aren't gay they certainly look like they are, so how is a girl to tell?

This is where the Fab Five come in: to clarify who is and who isn't. *Queer Eye for the Straight Guy* outwardly deploys their queerness to facilitate the mating of a metrosexual wannabe with his postfeminist partner, but these makeovers of the sleeping woolly beast for his date with Princess Charming are primarily structured around the opposition of "queer" and "straight," not "masculine" and "feminine." The series' humor and its potential edginess reside in this opposition. The Fab Five's queer eye slyly acknowledges the regulation and deregulation of domestic and urban spaces through that dualism, which places gay men outside straight culture yet makes them central to its successful operation. At issue is the spatial differentiation pointed out by the series' title. *Queer Eye for the Straight Guy* does something akin to what Joshua Gamson argues about daytime talk shows, which perform "an ambivalence about just who is doing what and how in public—and, more fundamentally, just to whom public space belongs." "It's not so much the *gayness* that is bothersome," Gamson concludes, "it's the *publicness*."[20] *Queer Eye* does not represent that disturbance through violent confrontations in the manner of Jerry Springer or Ricki Lake. Rather, in order to stage the queer eye–straight guy encounter as a momentary deregulation of boundaries, *Queer Eye* foregrounds the public visibility of queerness in its adjacency to straightness through *camp*, although the Fab Five do not always maintain this viewpoint coherently or consistently in each episode.

Camping with the Fab Five

Historically speaking, in the pre-Stonewall era of the closet (a crucial space for *Queer Eye* as it turns out), camp was a strategy of cultural differentiation for queers, one highly responsive to the imperative of passing—a "queer eye for the straight *guise*"—even more than it was a "sensibility" and "style" or a category of "taste," to refer to Susan Sontag's and Andrew Ross's early commentaries on camp.[21] As I have written elsewhere, "In response to that era's oppression and censorship of homosexuality, camp allowed for the ironic, self-reflective style of gay men passing as straight, who kept a 'straight face' so as not to let outsiders in on the joke, while simultaneously winking at the initiated in shared acknowledgment of it. *Camp* can be defined as the ensemble of strategies used to enact a queer recognition of the incongruities arising from the cultural regulation of gender and sexuality."[22] Despite its later appropriation by the mainstream during the 1960s and 1970s, which began to efface its history and politics, camp still works by exaggerating the homologous boundaries of the visible/straight/natural and invisible/queer/ unnatural in order to locate one side of the polarity in more direct tension with the other. This is why, as Esther Newton observes, "Camp is not a thing. Most broadly it signifies a *relationship between* things, people, and activities or qualities, and homosexuality."[23]

Today camp may seem politically incorrect because of its association with the oppressive politics of the closet, but its significance for gay culture, while reinflected according to the times, has not diminished. Camp still enables a queer perspective to be discerned through its *effect* (the ironic inflection of a witty putdown or pun, a coded allusion for those in the know, the exaggeration of artifice and theatricality) and, more profoundly, in its *affect* (the queer pleasure in perceiving, if not causing, the disruption of gender-sexual categories whether in representations of heterosexual normality, the values that reiterate it, or the commodities that derive from and reinscribe it). Although first feminism and then postfeminism have provocatively taken camp as a ground for theorizing the artifice of gender construction and regulation, and to serve as a strategy for reading against oppressive representations of women, I want to insist on what is still, to my mind, the intractable *queerness* of camp. It may illuminate the subordination of women alongside that of gay men, but because of its queer bias it is not reducible to either feminist political aims or postfeminist awareness of the interaction between feminine identities, gender performativity, and consumption.[24]

On *Queer Eye*, from Carson's double entendres to Jai's exaggeration of a drag queen in mufti to Ted's understated, straight-faced irony, the Fab Five engage in camp at the level of both effect (what they do and say to make viewers laugh at the straight people) and affect (how that laughter then yields pleasure in watching the makeovers, though a pleasure that exceeds the series' ideological purpose of recuperating heterosexual coupledom). Their camp enables them to be readily perceivable as "gay," in contrast to the straight men they remake for straight women, but it also allows them to cast a queer eye on their job of serving heterosexuality as its asexual helpers.

Rather effortlessly, yet somewhat violently, the team moves in and out of the regulatory boundaries that uphold the distinction, in private and public, between queer and straight spaces. Each episode begins with the Fab Five speeding across Manhattan in their sport-utility vehicle as they briefly describe their mission of the day. The opening credits then identify each member of the team individually according to his expertise; pictures them in a group as if they were the Mod Squad, the A-Team, and Charlie's Angels combined; and locates them at the imaginary intersection of Gay and Straight Streets. Following the credits, the first segment records them arriving at their destination like a gay brigade of terrorists or kidnappers invading the presumed sanctity of the straight guy's home and disrupting its heterosexual space. With pseudo-militaristic fervor, the five charge inside and register their offense at what they find there: disarray, dysfunctionality, and dirt. In this first segment, edited in a fast-paced montage that does not follow temporal chronology, they appropriate items from the kitchen, bathroom, or bedroom closet in order to mock the straight guy's ad hoc domesticity, indifference to sanitation, ineptitude with clothing, and, whenever the opportunity arises — for instance, if they find porn or condoms or even his underwear — his sexual prowess. The humiliated straight guy stands by watching helplessly, often laughing but rarely offering resistance to this demeaning ridicule except to avoid physical contact, while the five queer men proceed to trash the place literally as well as verbally, even going so far as to toss his furniture or clothing out a window or over a balcony.

The next set of sequences leads the straight guy through the physical makeover, which amounts to a takeover. He passively puts himself in Carson's hands for a shopping spree and in Kyan's for grooming at a salon or spa; usually there is a third outing with one of the others for furniture or cuisine. The ostensible point of these sequences is his instruction — on what clothes suit his body, what areas of his face, hair, or body need immediate attention, and how to select furniture or food. Visually and verbally, the camp humor in these sequences depends on the extent to which the team can expose how this consuming disturbs their subject's comfortable occupation of public space as a heterosexual male. These are indeed "outings." Not only is the straight guy undertaking an activity of specialized consuming presumed to be a gay man's preoccupation with his appearance for the appreciative gaze of another man, but this straight guy is doing it in public with an openly gay guy, so the act of consuming places the two together in a hybrid space that confounds a straight-queer dichotomy. Anyone who observes the straight guy in an upscale clothing store with Carson is not going to presume that these are two straight buddies—the pair identified by the Jericho Communications survey—picking up a new pair of jeans or polo shirt to replace a worn one. Flamboyantly rushing through the store with his straight guy in tow, Carson announces his queer presence at every turn by means of his camp manner. The straight guy, meanwhile, submits to a scrutinizing queer eye that is superior to his when Carson appraises his appearance; using a quick wit as well as a keen sense of style to exploit his discomfort and objectify him, Carson dresses down the straight guy while dressing him up.

Similarly, when Kyan supervises the straight guy's subjection to exfoliating, tweezing, plucking, and waxing—the work that goes into "femininity"—he also exposes him to the gaze of a queer eye. Although it does not occur in each episode, here the crossing of boundaries can most disturbingly question how *queer* and *straight* are still defined according to spatial regulation. This is most vividly apparent in episode 108, "Law and Disorder" (first shown on Bravo on 19 August 2003), which recounts the makeover of John Verdi, an Italian American cop living on Staten Island. A bald, pudgy, pasty, white man with gross toenails, John is taken to the Completely Bare spa for a spray-on tan. All he can mutter throughout is how embarrassed he is, not so much for appearing practically naked on national television as for doing so side-by-side with a gay guy. "See how he has a farmer's tan," Kyan remarks to the female attendant while pointing it out on John's chest and verifying that the process can contour and slendorize the body through the way the color is blended. John, in the meantime, has his eyes shut tight. "Dude," Kyan comments, "I have to say this is the most embarrassing thing ever done to help out a straight guy." But John seems more flummoxed: "Dude, this is so embarrassing, to be standing next to a gay guy in skivvies and . . . disposable skivvies, I might add."

Kyan: Well, you're no Prince Charming either, Big Boy.
John: I'm not—I'm not even looking at you. I don't want to look that way.

Kyan: Are you serious?

John: Dude, it's like . . . uh . . . you don't understand.

Kyan: What's gay about this situation?

John: Are you kidding me right now?

Kyan: I mean, over here it's gay. But (*pointing to John's space in the tanning booth*) what's gay about that?

John: Cause I'm in skivvies next to a gay—you don't understand.

But Kyan *does* understand. A short time later, he pressures the straight guy again, wondering to the attendant, "Can you make his penis look bigger?" "Guy," John asks defensively, "why are you looking at my penis?" Kyan laughs, and John begs, "Come on, please." Although Kyan demurs, his joke taken, the camera then focuses on crotch and butt shots of John as the tanning process is completed.

This segment questions what makes one space gay and another straight, and does so at the straight guy's expense, triggering his homophobic panic at being in such intimate proximity to a gay male body—the seminude Kyan, the member of the group whom fans and the media consider the "hottest." His gayness is for the moment defined in explicitly sexual terms as a queer eye not for products but for the straight guy's penis. This definition is then overlaid with the erotic display of Kyan's body for a gay and female viewer, as well as the camp deflation of John's endowment, which encourages one to infer that perhaps it is already looking a little "bigger." Joking about penis anxiety is an obvious sign of the discomfort that arises when heterosexual identity comes into contact with homosexual desire, harking back to the embarrassment, insecurity, curiosity, and/or excitement that characterizes all those group showers straight boys have had to take after high school gym classes. However, the John Verdi episode is more complex than this for it also brings out how this straight guy's "Guido Mumbo" masculinity, as Jai calls it later in the hour, is not only a performance of heterosexual codes for the benefit of the queer guys but is also, shall we say, blended, contoured, and slenderized by homosexual codings as the condition of his being made over in order to be more compatible with his female partner.

As happens in each episode, following the physical makeover John Verdi returns home with his new queer buddies in order to see what Thom has accomplished in his absence ("You don't feel like you live in some gay guy's apartment?"), to perform a fashion show of the clothing Carson has selected

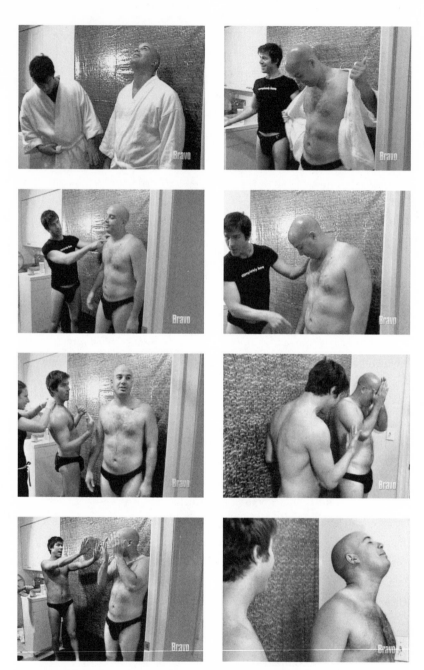

Crossing gay and straight spaces while getting a spray-on tan. (Episode 108 of *Queer Eye for the Straight Guy*.)

for him ("Hip hop with a little more class," but remember to zhuzh up the sleeves), to learn from Kyan how to establish a grooming regimen (proper use of products, which happen to vary each week, for "long-term skin care"), and to receive final instructions on preparing and serving food for the evening from Ted (in this case, a torte or quiche, though Ted reassures John that this torte is "a manly quiche, a quiche with balls"—even though it is made with eggs). Then the Fab Five depart for an apartment in Manhattan where, in the final segment, cocktails in hand and getting visibly looped, they observe how successfully the straight guy follows their tutelage on closed-circuit television (fig. 2).

Once again this episode reveals how camp identifies a distinctly queer eye for the show. John's mission has been to rekindle his romance with his live-in girlfriend, Ayana, a "hot" African American model who is tired of mothering him. As soon as she enters, John abruptly readjusts his masculine persona: "Isn't this re-mahk-able?" he asks, further showing his excitement about the makeover of his body and their home by jumping up and down and talking baby talk, all the while appreciating how her "boobages" look in her new out-fit, which was also selected by Carson. In the meantime, much as if they were watching *Sex and the City*, the Fab Five gather in front of the TV for some camp camaraderie. "He's bouncing around like a little girl, isn't he?" Kyan asks in disbelief. "He's acting gayer than I do," Carson agrees. "He was all tough guy around us, and now he's . . ." Ted cannot find the words, so he makes a flaming gesture. "He totally hopped out of the bedroom," Thom adds. Through-out this segment, the Fab Five note every potential disaster or faux pas, as well as every sign of slippage, between queer and straight in John's demeanor, as when he describes the dessert he has prepared as "divine." "Divine? He used the word *divine*," Ted exclaims, to which Carson replies, "He *is* gay." John confesses to Ayana how for a while he has been lacking confidence but now he has "a spark in his pants" again, and Thom mutters, "Don't look at me—I didn't put it there." "There's a lot of power in a pedicure and a spray-on tan," Kyan concludes, restoring the consumer orientation of the makeover. Mis-sion complete, the Five toast their success in rescuing another straight guy from drabness.

Queer Eye may deserve the critiques it has received for its endorsement of class hierarchies based on consuming, but that does not mean the overt ideological agenda of the series warrants outright dismissal of the additional

With cocktails and camp wit, the Fab Five observe how well the straight guy follows their tutelage. (Episode 108 of *Queer Eye for the Straight Guy*.)

cultural work it performs as a queer show. The series remakes straight masculinity according to bourgeois norms, but it does so through the mediation of queerness, which foregrounds the instability of both masculinity and straightness. For all their disavowals, most of the straight guys appear to realize the fragility of their heteromasculinity at some point in the hour. For instance, while shopping, John Verdi tells Carson that he'd do anything for his female partner, "even start with five gay guys and get made over." His problem, however, is that he doesn't know "what sexy is." All he knows is that he wants it and the queer guys know how to gain access to it, so he submits to their tutelage.

John's confession makes explicit the gender instability on which the series' camp outlook spins. Straight masculinity is just another cultural product and a confused one at that. As John's makeover illustrates, the series just as explicitly recognizes how a so-called normative masculinity is a performance, frequently multiple in its signifying effects; that it achieves an impression of stability by maintaining the perceived boundaries strictly differentiating between and culturally locating hetero- and homosexual male identities; and that it occurs in a consumer-oriented society that, needing to exploit the male market, overlaps these two identities (as in the metrosexual advertising image), thereby requiring the performance in the first place. The series' understanding of how straightness is organized according to its disavowed proximity to queerness is best epitomized in the opening segment, which depicts the Fab Five's invasion of a heterosexual domicile, during which they ridicule the straight guy's veneer of manliness, exposing his dirty underwear literally and figuratively, and in the closing one, which records the Fab Five's withdrawal into their own camp camaraderie, where they laugh once more at the spectacle of a straight guy's performance of his newly acquired, upscale masculinity. This framing vantage point enables *Queer Eye for the Straight Guy* to pass, in effect, as "safe" entertainment and yet display an edgier outlook, as the John Verdi episode well illustrates. The series can be read as straight or nonstraight, as noncamp or camp, depending on which eye you look with.

The central joke driving the series, it bears repeating, is that men with no sexual interest of their own in women have to be brought in from outside a clearly delineated heterosexual space in order to teach a straight guy "what sexy is," which enables heartfelt appreciation by heterosexual men and women alike of this needed queer intervention. This joke defines what the queer eye can see in the makeover because it also highlights what the straight eye fails to see. Thus, the remarks posted by females on the "Girl's Eye View of Queer Eye" Web site, right after the John Verdi episode aired, confined themselves to appreciating how "adorable" the Fab Five looked or behaved at certain points and how striking John appeared in his new clothes, making him such an attractive date. A more interesting response appeared in the recap of this episode on the "Straight Eye for the Queer Shows" fan site. The writer, "Larry," goes into great detail; he describes all the bristly interactions between the cop and the Fab Five from their entrance through each stage of the makeover, including the trip to Completely Bare (although the point seems to be what NBC edited out when it reran this episode), and he quotes much of their dialogue. However, except for noting that the gay men dwell on the size of Ayana's breasts (their response to John's appreciation of her "boob-ages"), "Larry" ignores the final segment, in which the team watches the re-sults of the makeover. Instead, as if the Fab Five's viewpoint were transpar-ent, this straight fan disregards their camp commentary and only describes what they see—John and Ayana's night out. Expressing his appreciation of John's efforts to please Ayana, "Larry" concludes:

> Now a number of people have complained how John gets such a hot chick. In his defense, he's tall, pretty fit, and strong (though he's gained some weight) and a cop. He's apparently good at the kissing (full align-ment with light tongue tizzle) and it seems like he had a good sized pack-age while being spray tanned. Many women out there want a guy who can take care of them and really love them and this guy can do it. Any man willing to stretch himself to keep his relationship fresh, is a good catch, and most women should be so lucky.[25]

The difference between queer and straight viewpoints depends on the ex-tent to which, as "Larry" typifies here, a viewer disregards the Fab Five's camp mediation and identifies primarily with the woman as the motivating force behind the straight guy's makeover—he's doing it solely for her, and she then serves as his private audience when he shows off the results of his makeover. However, in fulfilling that role for this type of viewer, Ayana is also partici-pating in the performance, which the Fab Five simultaneously watch on their closed-circuit TV. Because they filter the straight couple through their camp spectatorship, it is difficult to extract a bona fide feminine viewpoint from the closure, however much "Larry" tries to do so. The couple themselves are rarely if ever shown recognizing any camp element in their performance of heterosexuality, even when they acknowledge the performative dimension of the makeover and its subsequent test run as the straight guy shows off what he has learned for his partner's inspection and approval.

Yet, by casting his closing response to this episode through an awareness of Ayana's needs and not the Fab Five's camp, "Larry" can display the post-feminist male sensibility that, one has to assume, allows him to take pleasure in the series and coauthor the "straight guy" Web site. No doubt influenced by all those self-help relationship books, which are supposedly written in the wake of feminism but present an option other than feminism when it comes to women's relations with men, "Larry" writes as a male seemingly liberated from sexist attitudes and, what is more, since he did notice John's "package," as a male not subject to insecurity about the stability of his own heteromasculinity. To sustain this viewpoint, he has to ignore both the Fab Five's camp eye and the subordinate role of women in the makeover. For her part, Ayana knows very well her limited contribution to the makeover process; on departing the premises so that the Fab Five can take charge of John's makeover, she loudly announces, "The vagina is leaving the nest." "Larry's" summary does indicate why a woman's presence, at least in the closure of each episode, is still a crucial element in the series' success. She facilitates the more sanguine, straight male response to the Fab Five's queer intervention in heterosexuality, which Larry typifies when he in effect rewrites the John Verdi episode to concentrate solely on the couple through Ayana's point of view.

A Straight Eye for those Queer Guys

That a female figure cannot easily be removed from the series' formula stands out all the more when we look at the guest appearances of the Fab Five on the Oprah Winfrey and Jay Leno shows. Not surprisingly, given their target audience, each guest spot retains the series' premise but not its structure, more noticeably marginalizing the five gay men as outsiders for a predominantly straight female and male audience, respectively. The difference between the two spots is quite revealing. Winfrey's singling out of the female motivation for the makeovers considerably tames the Fab Five's impact, negating any jarring collision of straight and gay spaces, whereas a female's absence from the Leno makeover brings out more clearly the disturbance that the series itself manages more insightfully through camp.

On the Winfrey show (first shown in syndication on 22 September 2003), the queer makeovers of the various straight guys selected for a much-needed rescue, at least according to Oprah and the men's wives, cause members of the female audience to cry, with everyone who had a stake or hand in the renovations gathered together onstage for a big group hug at the end of the hour. One exemplary moment occurs in the final segment, when a formerly shaggy middle-aged man named Roland returns to display his new appearance, supervised by Kyan. Previously Roland had not shaved his beard or cut his hair in over twenty years, during which time his wife and two daughters had never seen what lay behind all the hair. Not only does the family break down in tears at the revelation that a well-groomed Roland is as handsome as "a movie star," but Oprah herself is open-mouthed when gazing at his dramatically different look. While Kyan, as befitting his role as product endorser, reflects that "shaving is all about preparation and products," Roland himself confesses, "I feel like I'm alive again." He grabs Oprah in a tight hug and begins to weep, and she gets caught up in the emotions too. "Let's all just have a cry," she sobs, inviting the predominantly female audience in the studio and at home to participate in the emotional outburst that confirms feminine gratitude for the queer intervention on behalf of what Oprah has earlier called "frustrated wives" who are unable to assist their "helpless husbands." The way the show is shot encourages such empathetic participation throughout the hour, and it does not involve the visual or verbal mediation of the Fab Five, despite the many times Oprah laughs heartily at Carson's camp barbs. The desperate wives who have "turned in" their husbands, as Oprah puts it, sit in the front rows as audience members, whereas the husbands stand uncomfortably onstage like wanted men; repeated close-ups of the wives' disgruntled then delighted faces equate their reactions with those of the audience members at large, fostering identification with this point of view by the home viewer as well.

By contrast, no tears are shed when Jay Leno receives his makeover. To publicize it, the Fab Five show up the night before the big reveal, appearing after Kevin Costner, who is promoting his new western, *Open Range* (2003), which was broadcast on NBC on 14 August 2003. As soon as the Fab Five make their entrance, Leno begins to bait Costner, implying that the star's heteromasculinity, not Leno's own, is in doubt because of its proximity to queerness. After describing the *Queer Eye* slogan, "Five gay men out to make

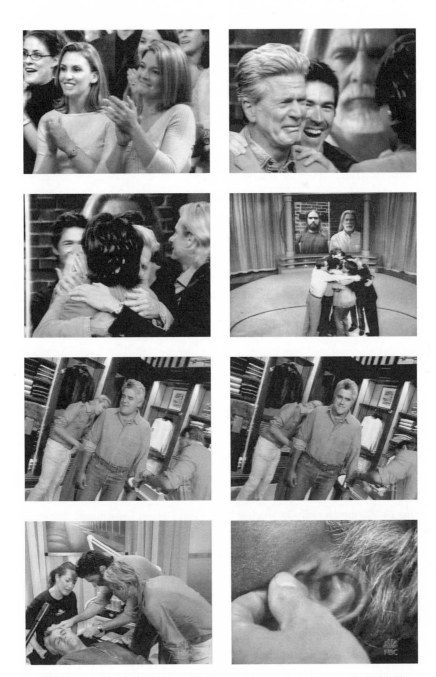

The makeover on the *Oprah Winfrey Show* results in tears and a group hug, whereas on the *Tonight Show* Jay Leno gets a booty check and has a "pubic hair" plucked from his ear.

over the world—one straight guy at a time," Leno turns to Costner, warning, "and you're next, buddy." Leno goes on to joke that Costner intentionally lowered his voice when greeting the Fab Five, to tease Costner about getting his buttocks pierced, to propose that the Fab Five should plan Costner's upcoming wedding, and to suggest that, possibly because he had already spent too much time on the open range when making his movie, Costner is now rethinking the whole marriage thing. Although at moments Costner does seem uncomfortable, especially when the Fab Five first descend on him en masse, at other times he gets into the spirit of things (asking Jai, for instance, what he means by "working a room"), but Leno repeatedly attributes discomfort to him. Additionally, Leno turns every comment made by his guests into a joke about straight masculinity that actually endorses it as the impeachable norm—just in case any one is wondering. For instance, when Thom explains that the worst offense he finds in straight domiciles is bad lighting, typically supplied by a single torchiere halogen lamp, Leno again makes a joke at Costner's expense: "Straight guys like that porno lighting," Leno explains. "See, Kevin knows what I'm talking about." When Ted comments on straight guys' insecurity about ordering fine wines at restaurants, Leno similarly reasons, "it comes from going to strip shows."[26]

Without a straight male ally onto whom he can deflect his anxiety, the following night Leno resorts to homophobic jokes about the makeover process, playing up the gayness of the Fab Five in contrast to his own resistant straightness (broadcast on NBC on 15 August 2003). Distancing himself from the makeover even while going through it, Leno repeats his worry that the process effeminizes him by forcing him to think about fashion and skin conditioning. Not deterred, the Fab Five keep their banter going, chiding Leno for his appearance and his show's decor. They anticipate his stale straight-guy jokes, beating him to the punch line or turning the jokes awry, and four members of the team have an opportunity, with their customary chat and drinks, to view the remodeled set's disclosure and Ted's gourmet spot with Leno on a TV monitor from behind the scenes.

Somewhat like the tanning booth segment with John Verdi but with less good-natured candor, what seems disturbing to Leno, because it motivates so many of his jokes during the makeover, is how intimate contact with these gay guys makes his body vulnerable to anal penetration. Indeed, the makeover edition of the *Tonight Show* begins by explicitly identifying this fear and making it central to the whole enterprise of renovating Leno. On this night, the program forsakes its usual opening credits and begins instead with an imitation of the Fab Five's own series opening. As the team discusses its new mission, making over a famous talk show host, Kyan remarks that Leno is "a spa virgin" and Jai rejoins, "You're going to pop his spa cherry." Whether improvised or scripted, this exchange predetermines how the audience will subsequently view both Leno's discomfort during the shopping and spa montages and his many attempts to go for the easy, homophobic laughs. "I feel like the new guy on his first day in prison," Leno announces as the Fab Five inspect him, a sentiment also included in the teaser for the makeover shown the night before. Kyan's discovery of "a pubic hair" growing out of Leno's ear is just the proverbial tip of the iceberg. Carson insists on doing a "booty check" when Leno tries on pants. Displaying for a whining Leno a broad pinstripe suit (the one he will wear on the show), Carson compares the pattern to racing stripes, which Leno confirms he likes but does not want up his ass. During his hairstyling, Leno complains, "These guys are putting, like, KY Jelly in my hair."

On the two *Tonight Show* appearances by the Fab Five, women are excluded from all phases of the encounter. Without a woman to motivate the makeover and safeguard the straight guy's heterosexuality, the Fab Five's difference as gay men is more homosexualized and shown to be more potentially tempting to a straight guy, though not to Leno of course. On a shopping spree to buy new furniture for the show's set, Jai does a Christina Aguilera impersonation and Thom remarks to the young salesman, "It's kinda scary when he does that. He's so good acting like a woman." Sitting on the floor, the salesman replies, "The scary thing is, it doesn't bother me," so Jai mimes, "call me," drawing a big laugh from the studio audience. While this brief encounter seems daring for the *Tonight Show*, even as it reiterates the stereotype that gay men are at heart women (both are reasons for the laughter), it actually goes far beyond that (the reason I laughed). From the return of looks, we are encouraged to see the straight-looking salesman responding to Jai with homosexual interest, and, what is more, this not so straight guy is neither attracted to nor put off by Jai's effeminacy—rather, it just doesn't bother him. The Winfrey show, on the other hand, places the makeover's value for the straight guys' wives always in the foreground, which keeps queer and straight men at a much safer distance from each other while also sentimentalizing the beneficial results of their interaction, little of which is shown to viewers. The Fab Five serve as the wives' domesticating surrogates; unable to do the work of civilizing their mates themselves, for whatever reason, these wives, like the women on the series, have to rely on the kindness of queer strangers to clean up the mess.

In contrast to the Fab Five's appearances on the Winfrey and Leno shows, their own camp spectatorship of the straight guy's makeover in the closing segment of each *Queer Eye* episode parodies the hegemony of the straight guy and his mate in order to reverse the inside-outside dichotomy that marginalizes the queer. Even more than their expertise as specialists in fashion, grooming, cooking, decor, and "culture," their camp is the sign that these five men are the true insiders—the savvy cultural observers—as far as the series is concerned. When an episode can develop its edgy camp outlook, as in the John Verdi example, *Queer Eye* skillfully engages both queer and postfeminist viewpoints but also takes care not to make them identical. The series' camp target, after all, is straight masculinity, not femininity; while the Fab Five mockingly introduce straight guys to the domesticating regimes of grooming and housework long associated with femininity, the Fab Five never challenge the validity of such protocols, instead offering women the compensation of laughing at the ineptitude and insecurity of straight men when it comes to performing the social rituals that they have had to master in order to attract the guys in the first place. This camp perspective enables queerness to be visible amid straightness, just as it distinguishes the queer eye from a postfeminist one even though both are acutely aware of the construction of masculinity and femininity alike through consumption.

As telling of the culture industry's absorption of difference, though, *Queer Eye* has been unable to sustain its camp perspective week after week with any degree of rigor or consistency. The rigid formula of the makeover structure, the budgetary restriction to Manhattan and its outlying boroughs and suburbs, the sameness of the straight guys willing to expose themselves, the necessity for seemingly endless product endorsements on the series, and the Fab Five's own gleeful emersion in popular culture as the latest media darlings all work against the camp humor that made *Queer Eye* seem more queer than one could have expected when it first aired. The Fab Five have gone on to do a music video, star in commercials, and write self-help books; their celebrity keeps their queerness visible and in circulation but homogenizes it as a product—the gay accessory—for lifestyle consumption. As success begets repetition on television, it also breeds boredom, and even camp gets dull and predictable when prepackaged as a commodity in its own right.

Notes

1. In a substantive analysis of *Queer Eye* that appeared after I wrote this essay, Beth Berila and Devika Dibya Choudhuri examine the multiple ways in which, by re-inscribing a white, middle-class bias through effacement or minimalization of racial, sexual, and class hierarchical differences, the series "contains gayness by reducing it to a commodity that services heteronormality" ("Metrosexuality the Middle Class Way," para. 4). I do not disagree with their careful and lengthy critique, which shares but develops much more fully the concerns of critics noted below; however, I think it is important to place alongside that kind of critique consideration of how the Fab Five's performance of the show's ideological agenda can at times also allow some viewers to see its transparency and laugh at it. Thus, while Berila and Choudhuri note that *Queer Eye* "troubles heteronormality on one level while reinscribing it through the commodification of gayness on the other" (para. 8), I am arguing that the series does not always manage this strategy so easily or readily and specifically that its cultural impact during its first season had much to do with the way episodes were not necessarily reducible to a single, recuperative, and heteronormative viewpoint in the makeover narratives.
2. Dreisinger, "The Queen in Shining Armor," 3.
3. "Survey Finds 'Queer Eye' Affects Shopping," Zap2it.com, 4 December 2003.
4. Gallagher, "*Queer Eye* for the Heterosexual Couple," 224.
5. "Piracy, 'Queer' on AFI Timeline," *Hollywood Reporter*, 16 December 2003.
6. During the summer of 2003, a Web search turned up articles reporting on both the positive and negative responses to the series and not only in the dailies of large urban areas. See, for example, Potts, "'Queer Eye' Makes over View of Homosexuals"; and Moon, "'Queer Eye' Opens Window to Gay Life."
7. Gross, "The Queen Is Dead," 64.
8. McCarthy, "Crab People from the Center of the Earth," 99.
9. Gallagher, "*Queer Eye* for the Heterosexual Couple."
10. Dreisinger, "The Queen in Shining Armor," 4.
11. Torres, "Why Can't Johnny Shave?" 96.
12. Gallagher, "*Queer Eye* for the Heterosexual Couple," 223.
13. See Roberts, "The Fashion Police," in this volume. Toby Miller chronicles the 1990s marketing invention of the metrosexual figure in "A Metrosexual Eye on *Queer Guy*."
14. See Cohan, *Masked Men*.
15. Moore, "Here's Looking at You, Kid!" 45.
16. Rothenberg, "Claiborne's Approach to Today's Man."
17. Moore, "Here's Looking at You, Kid!" 55.
18. Ibid., 45.
19. Ibid., 48.
20. Gamson, *Freaks Talk Back*, 201, 203.
21. Sontag, "Notes on Camp"; Ross, "Uses of Camp."

22. Cohan, *Incongruous Entertainment*, 1. The book's introduction elaborates more fully the historical understanding of camp that I am summarizing here (see pp. 1–19). For further discussion of the mainstream appropriation of camp, see pages 208–10.

23. Newton, *Mother Camp*, 105.

24. My point is that, while recognizing the affinities of camp and feminism, I do not want to erase the queer location of camp, which is crucial to understanding how it operates in practice, beginning with its ironic stance toward the regulation of heteronormality. To be sure, camp—in large part when it is solely equated with drag queens and their adoration of female stars—has a history of being read for its hostility to feminism. Camp was repudiated for its apparent misogyny in parodying "women's oppression," reflecting the tension between the feminist and gay rights movements of the 1970s, as Michael Bronski notes in *Culture Clash: The Making of Gay Sensibility* (205). Camp still bears this dubious status for many feminists. Yet, while certain instances of camp may be misogynistic, camp as a cultural strategy has another history of being quite valuable to feminism and of serving its transition into postfeminism. Although her source in camp is at best implicit, rendered through the extended example of drag, Judith Butler, in *Gender Trouble: Feminism and the Subversion of Identity*, has offered what is perhaps the most influential theorization of gender as a performance of identity through the convergence of camp and feminism. It is worth noting, however, that, even though *Gender Trouble* has become a landmark text for both queer theory and postfeminism, in her new preface to the 1999 edition Butler locates the agenda of her book in feminism, not queer theory, nor does she identify her project as a postfeminist one (rather, she cites its genealogy in poststructuralist French theory). For a different sort of example of how camp has been usefully linked with feminism as a cultural strategy taken up by women, see Robertson, *Guilty Pleasures*, though here, too, note the author's need to call what she is analyzing feminist camp in order to point out her paralleling of women's camp strategies and gay men's. From a different perspective, in *Female Masculinity*, Judith Halberstam examines the possibilities of a recent phenomenon, lesbian camp. According to her, masculinity stills tends to rely on tropes that efface its performativity, which resists the predication of camp "on exposing and exploiting the theatricality of gender," so she proposes, as an alternative to "the camp humor of femininity," a new term, *king-drag*, to designate "[lesbian] drag humor associated with masculinity" (237–38). While the enhanced theatricality of femininity has always been an easy target for camp humor and display—hence the long-standing but also somewhat limiting reduction of camp to drag—I think that camp can be sharply attuned to the performative dimensions of masculinity, as *Queer Eye for the Straight Guy* illustrates. But see also my chapter on Gene Kelly's camp masculinity in *Incongruous Entertainment* (149–99).

25. "Queer Eye #108—Law and Disorder: Special Picnic Unit," Posted by "Larry," www.straighteye.com, downloaded 21 March 2004.

26. During the Fab Five's return visit to the *Tonight Show* in November 2003, Leno baited the comedian Colin Quinn in the same way, causing the irritated guest to exclaim, "Jay, I thought it was going to be *me* and *you* against *them*!

Sarah Banet-Weiser

8

What's Your Flava?

RACE AND POSTFEMINISM IN MEDIA CULTURE

In the spring of 2003, an advertisement appeared on the children's cable television channel Nickelodeon for the Mattel toy company's recent doll line, Flavas. This ad features young girls of various races and ethnicities playing with female Barbie-type dolls characterized by ambiguous ethnic identities—with "neutral" skin color and vague facial features, the dolls could easily be Latina, African American, Asian, or white. What is clear is that the dolls are urban: they wear clothing that is hip and trendy, they carry boom boxes, and they are sold in boxes with a cardboard backdrop that resembles a concrete wall covered with graffiti. On toymania.com, a Web-based toy outlet, Mattel issued the following press release the week the dolls appeared in stores.

> EL SEGUNDO, Calif.—July 29, 2003—Flava, according to "Hip Hoptionary: The Dictionary of Hip Hop Terminology" by Alonzo Westbrook, means personal flavor or style. With the nationwide introduction of Flavas (pronounced FLAY-vuhz) this week, the first reality-based fashion doll brand that celebrates today's teen culture through authentic style, attitude and values, Mattel (™) has created

a hot hip-hop themed line that allows girls to express their own personal flava.

> Born in the world of music and fashion, the hip-hop movement has evolved into a cultural phenomenon and celebrates fearless self-expression through freestyle dance, hip-hop music, street sport and signature fashions. Flavas, for girls ages 8–10, is the hottest doll line to embrace this latest tween trend encouraging girls to show their inner flava to the outer world.[1]

The Flavas marketing campaign featured not only ads, such as the one on Nickelodeon, which featured hip-hop music and trendy dance moves, but also a sponsorship of the pop singer Christina Aguilera's tour, a singer that Mattel claims "personifies the idea of fearless self-expression." Despite the fact that the word *flava*, the culture of hip-hop, and the idea of street style all signify racially in contemporary American culture, the racial identity of the dolls is never mentioned in the ads or the press release. While this could have been an interesting opportunity for Mattel to explore issues of different skin color among African Americans, as there is a dark-skinned doll and a light-skinned doll, or racial issues in and between Latinos and African Americans, race in this context is just a flava, a street style, an individual characteristic, and a commercial product.

Like race, gender identity is constructed in the present "postfeminist" cultural economy as a "flava," a flexible, celebratory identity category that is presented in all its various manifestations as a kind of product one can buy or try on. Signified by the hip consumer slogan "girl power," postfeminist gender identity is a slippery category precisely because of the ways in which it intervenes in productive ways in traditional ideological frameworks even as it works in other ways to shore up those same frameworks. For example, Nickelodeon is widely lauded for its efforts to champion girls in what has been a historically male-dominated televisual landscape. Proudly celebrating its contributions to girl power, Nickelodeon forced the attention of parents and young people to the connection between these two concepts, "girl" and "power," a connection that has become normalized within the discourses of consumer culture. In the contemporary cultural climate, in other words, the empowerment of girls is now something that is more or less taken for granted by both children and parents and has certainly been incorporated into commodity culture, evidenced by consumer goods ranging from T-shirts to lunch boxes to dolls proclaiming that "Girls rule!" Like other brands in contemporary media culture, Nickelodeon taps into this commodity-driven empowerment by targeting aspects of personal identity (such as gender and race) as a way to be inclusive; in fact, Nickelodeon's brand identity is crafted around the way in which the network is different from other children's media in the way it "empowers" children through (among other things) its commitment to gender and ethnic representation.

On the other hand, Nickelodeon's ability to claim that diversity matters has proved strategic from a business standpoint, positioning the network as "different" in the competitive field of children's television. In other words, despite the lofty goals of the channel to empower children, Nickelodeon's carefully crafted industry identity as the "diversity channel" and a champion for girls is a lucrative business strategy. Within the world of children's television, representations of race and gender work as a kind of cultural capital, in terms of which it increases the political and social clout of a network to be able to claim that it is "diverse."[2] As is well known, historically there has been a dearth of diverse characters on children's television (in terms of both race and gender), and the few that have been represented have been depicted in highly stylized and stereotypical ways.[3] However, in the current media economy it no longer makes commercial sense to ignore girls or people of color as important characters. Nickelodeon has capitalized on the historical invisibility and exclusion of diverse characters and has framed this history as part of a shrewd business strategy. In this way, its decision to create diverse programming is often discussed in such nonspecific terms as "good business," thus distancing the channel from the political implications of embracing diversity.

These two identity categories — race as a "flava" and girl power — function together in the current media environment to produce categories of identity that are defined by ambiguity rather than specificity, ambivalence rather than political certainty. These mediated forms of race and gender are produced within the specific context of late industrial capitalism in the United States, a moment that has been characterized in racial terms as a multicultural or postrace society and in gendered terms as a postfeminist culture. My concerns in this essay focus on television programming within this "postrace" and "postfeminist" culture and are twofold. First, I explore how these two features of contemporary American media culture function together as a productive kind of tension or ambivalence. The tension resides within the acknowledgment that race and gender are important identity categories to consider in terms of representation, while at the same time the acknowledgment itself works to repudiate this very importance. Angela McRobbie, writing about how this works within postfeminism, argues that contemporary popular culture is effective in the "undoing of feminism" precisely by appearing to participate in an inclusion of feminist ideologies.[4] I argue that a similar dynamic occurs with recent popular representations of race and ethnicity. Within the contemporary climate, television and media products seem to acknowledge the historical racist landscape of television not only by featuring programming with casts that include people of color but also by incorporating nonwhite narratives in ads, programs, and merchandise. Yet these particular representations and narratives of race and ethnicity are marketed by media corporations as cool, authentic, and urban and have proven to be incredibly lucrative economic tools for marketing to broad, especially white, audiences. Contemporary marketers, selling clothing brands such as Tommy Hilfiger and soft drinks such as Sprite, have efficiently capitalized on the connection of "cool" with images and narratives of the urban so that popular culture is rife with what Herman Gray describes as the *proliferation* of difference.[5] This redefinition of the urban stands in contrast to media representations in the United States of the "urban" in the 1980s and early 1990s, which predominantly signified the dangerous "other" and indeed functions to render irrelevant and repudiate those earlier concerns about racist imagery. The representation of the "urban," like the representation of girl power, is associated with the ideological notion that contemporary American society is a multicultural, postfeminist one in which racial difference and gender discrimination are no longer salient. Race, like gender, comes to us in the contemporary context as a commodity, and as such the ideologies shaping these representational politics are necessarily rethought and recast.

Second, I examine how the contemporary definitions of *postfeminism* and *postracial culture* are framed around generational differences. In terms of gender representation, this generational difference appears most often in ideological struggles between second-wave feminism and postfeminism. This particular generational divide revolves most centrally around a general assumption (one that is supported by commercial popular culture) that the goals of feminism have been accomplished and are now history, rendering it unnecessary to continue rehashing old political issues. Regarding postracial culture, these generational differences have a more specific economic angle. That is, in what Christopher Smith calls the "New Economy" of the late twentieth century and early twenty-first the tropes of the urban and hip-hop culture are used as means to designate a particular national perspective on diversity. Despite the material realities of poverty, unemployment, and general institutionalized racism in the United States, a contemporary ideology about race casts it as a style, an aesthetic, a hip way of being. Indeed, Smith identifies the 1990s New Economy as one in which "hip-hop evolved from being the symbolic anathema of the dominant commercial apparatus to serving as one of its most strategically effective symbolic instruments."[6] Like commodity feminism or what Bonnie Dow has identified as "prime-time feminism," the commodification of the urban works to diffuse the politics from this particular racial formation, resulting in a kind of racial ambivalence that dominates the representational landscape.[7] Given the contemporary representational context, what are the consequences when race or gender becomes cultural capital—a "competency" or mode of consumption within the world of media entertainment?

I see these shifts in gender and race representation as located within the struggles between generations so that representation itself becomes an arsenal in a kind of cultural territory war. Within this particular battlefield, the struggles of the past to represent women and people of color are read through a nostalgic lens as an "old school" kind of politics. Indeed, contemporary manifestations of "girl power" and the "urban" render the language of sexism and disenfranchisement as old-fashioned and even quaint. The dismissal of the language and the politics associated with it is characteristic of "new school" politics, where commodity culture is situated not in opposition to those politics but rather provides the very means to exploit and represent these dynamics of race and gender. To demonstrate how this works in television programming, I offer a brief analysis of a very successful Nickelodeon program, *Dora the Explorer*, and argue that Dora, the intrepid, seven-year-old, Latina heroine of the show, is poised as a global citizen in the New Economy. Before I turn to Dora, however, the generational differences in how girl power and the urban are understood and used by media audiences need to be explored.

Generational Differences:
Grumpy Old Women and a New Generation of Feminists

In her discussion of contemporary forms of popular culture, McRobbie identifies the 1990s and the early twenty-first century as a "postfeminist cultural space." This space, she argues, is a context in which "we have a field

Dora, the intrepid heroine of Nickelodeon's hit preschool program, *Dora the Explorer*, with her friend, Boots the monkey.

of transformation in which feminist values come to be engaged with, and to some extent incorporated across, civil society in institutional practices, in education, in the work environment, and in the media."[8] However, this engagement most often results in a denial of those very same feminist values so that postfeminist popular culture is more accurately antifeminist in its trajectory. Postfeminism, understood in this manner, is thus a different political dynamic than third wave feminism, which is positioned more overtly as a kind of feminist politics, one that extends the historical trajectory of first- and second-wave feminism to better accommodate contemporary political culture and the logic of consumer citizens. Postfeminism, on the other hand, is as McRobbie puts it, "feminism taken into account," a process in which feminist values and ideologies are acknowledged only to be found dated and passé and thus negated.

Importantly, McRobbie sees this process of repudiation taking place in the popular media,

> where a field of new gender norms emerges (e.g., *Sex and the City, Ally McBeal*) in which female freedom and ambition appear to be taken for granted, unreliant on any past struggle (an antiquated word), and certainly not requiring any new, fresh political understanding, but instead merely a state into which young women appear to have been thrown, or in which they find themselves, giving rise to ambivalence and misgiving.[9]

Part of young female identity in this contemporary context means to engage this media narrative about new gender norms not in a traditional, politically engaged way but rather in what McRobbie calls a "ritualistic denunciation." This denunciation occurs when feminism is acknowledged but in a trivialized fashion, shelved as something that may have been useful in the past but is clearly out of date in today's world.

This denunciation of feminism thus informs the ways in which postfeminism situates issues of gender within commercial and popular culture. This commercial embrace of postfeminism is often invoked as the crucial difference between it and other feminisms because postfeminism is understood as more representative for a new generation of women. This struggle over the "ownership" of the politics of feminism seems to be the primary lens through which contemporary feminisms are understood. Indeed, one of the most impassioned discourses involving feminism lately has not been generated by differing political platforms or a specific egregious act of discrimination against women but from the arguments, contradictions, and general disavowals between different manifestations of feminisms. Within the contemporary context there are different feminisms (just as many different feminisms made up the broad second-wave feminist movement in the United States). Thus, the political focus of postfeminism is vastly different from that of third-wave feminism for the former eschews gender politics as rather old-fashioned and dreary and the latter refigures gender politics in a commercially bounded culture. There is clearly a lack of generational cohesion between the various feminisms, making it difficult to figure out one's position within feminism. And yet, as Lisa Hogeland points out, different generations are not a significant explanation. The alternative, recognizing problems within feminism, means confronting the "unevenness" of the movement itself and the "fundamental differences in our visions of feminism's tasks and accomplishments."[10] One of these differences concerns media visibility. In part because of the proliferation of media images of strong, independent female characters, many contemporary feminists seem to regard consumer culture as a place of empowerment and as a means of differentiating themselves from second-wave feminists (although empowerment itself is read differently by postfeminists and third-wave feminists). Second-wave feminism has thus tended to be critical of the misogyny of popular consumer culture.

The embrace of consumer culture is the site for tension around the concept of the individual within feminisms as well. One of the key differences between the "cultural space of postfeminism" and second-wave feminist politics in the United States and the United Kingdom is the focus on female individualism and individual empowerment. As McRobbie points out, postfeminism shifts feminism into the past—not just the ideas and values of feminism but the emancipatory politics and community activism of feminism as well.[11] Key to this shift is the fact that in work that claims to be postfeminist there is what McRobbie calls a "double failure," for, "In its over-emphasis on agency and the apparent capacity to choose in a more individualized society, it has no way of showing how subject formation occurs by means of notions of choice *and* assumed gender equality coming together to actually ensure adherence to new unfolding norms of femininity."[12]

This move toward focusing on individual empowerment rather than coalition politics or structural change forces consideration of several questions. Once feminism is represented as a commodity in precisely the mainstream it has traditionally challenged, can we still talk about it as political? Can the social elements of feminism be represented and enacted within the context of popular culture's relentless celebration of the individual or is popular culture by design hostile to feminism? Are we simply living in, as Naomi Klein claims, a "Representation Nation," where visibility in the media takes precedence over "real" politics?[13] Again, for those who consider themselves to be third-wave feminists, such as Jennifer Baumgardner and Amy Richards, the argument is made that this kind of media visibility is absolutely crucial to politics.[14] For those who position themselves as postfeminists, this kind of media visibility is precisely the evidence needed to "prove" that there is no longer a need for feminist politics. And yet, as Bonnie Dow argues, while the liberal feminist politics of equal opportunity and equal pay for equal work has been somewhat normalized (although the material reality of this politics is not always or even often achieved), it is also the case that the process of mainstreaming an oppositional politics often functions as a hegemonic strategy to diffuse that very politics. In other words, the normalization of feminism has prevented it from existing as a discrete politics; rather it emerges as a kind of slogan or generalized "brand."[15]

However, for third-wave feminism, this normalization of feminism within the media and popular culture has encouraged an embrace of feminism as political; as Baumgardner and Richards argue, the young women who make up the third wave were "born with feminism simply in the water," a kind of "political fluoride" that protects against the "decay" of earlier sexism and gender discrimination.[16] The struggle for "positive" representations in the media is certainly not over, but we also do not experience the same media that we did even ten years ago, when, as Susan Douglas contends, the most pervasive media story remained "structured around boys taking action, girls waiting for the boys, and girls rescued by the boys."[17] There has been a clear historical trajectory of incorporating feminist ideologies into mainstream popular culture, ranging, as Dow points out, from the 1970s television show *One Day at a Time* to shows in the 1980s and 1990s such as *Murphy Brown* and *Designing Women*.

As a contemporary social and political movement, then, feminism itself has been rescripted (though not necessarily disavowed) so as to allow its smooth incorporation into the world of commerce and corporate culture—what Robert Goldman calls "commodity feminism."[18] This commodity feminism has resulted in a complex dynamic that is directly concerned not only with general gender issues but also with issues of cultural territory. As part of a general self-identification, second-wave feminism is at times overly romanticized in terms of its commitment to social protest politics, and there seems to be a kind of reluctance on the part of second-wave feminists to rethink and redefine politics according to the stated needs and desires of contemporary feminism (Susan Brownmiller, in a now infamous *Time* magazine interview about third-wave feminists and postfeminists, claimed that "they're just not movement people").[19] Part of this reluctance to rethink contemporary feminism concerns the ways in which gender identity is also always about racial identity; perhaps because of the commercial "urban" context of many contemporary feminists, the intersectionality of race and gender has been acknowledged in ways that challenge the exclusionary history of second-wave feminism. For many third-wave feminists, the territorialism that surrounds some of the current politics of feminism seems to be about salvaging the term *feminism* (and presumably the politics that grounds and historicizes it). Baumgardner and Richards, Barbara Findlen, and Naomi Wolf, for example, participate in this kind of salvation project, the project of not necessarily appropriating a historical concept of feminism but widening its borders to include more contemporary manifestations of the politics.[20] While in theory this makes sense, and certainly these authors at times do justice to the legacies of feminisms, Baumgardner and Richards also insist that "underneath all of these names and agendas is the same old feminism."[21] However, it is precisely *not* the same old feminism that structures the politics of third-wave feminism. The insistence that it is stems from a range of sentiments, from nostalgic yearnings for "real" social protest movements to respectful acknowledgments of political practices that open up economic and social opportunities to a sheer base desire to "belong" to something. Without discounting these sentiments, it is also the case that lingering in this generational battle between second- and third-wave feminism has paralyzed the debate and prevented the further development and refinement of a feminist praxis and material feminist politics. In turn, this paralysis has allowed for a more conservative postfeminism to become dominant in media representation, so much so that feminist politics—be it second-wave, third-wave, or some other version—is rendered obsolete in the contemporary historical moment of hip empowerment.

The complexity of the current feminist landscape means that the idea that "we" all share a feminist politics, that we all "want the same thing," is highly problematic, as it clearly connects to history. Not only does this propagate the mistake made by many second-wave feminists, who insisted on a universal feminist standpoint, but it also functions as a kind of refusal to identify what it is we all apparently want.[22] In other words, if "we" all want the same thing in feminism, what is it: a liberal version of equality, a more radically configured understanding of liberation from patriarchy, or simply a more frequent and "positive" media appearance? And, if this is true, does contemporary feminism address other factors of identity, such as race and sexuality, in ways that challenge the exclusive nature of second-wave feminism? This struggle over territory has encouraged feminisms to exist primarily as part of a turf war. The politics of feminism is quite obviously different for different generations, and third-wave feminists and postfeminists are produced in a very different cultural and political context than were the feminists of the twentieth century. It then becomes impossible to combine contemporary manifestations of feminisms into a singular "movement"; rather, feminisms exist in the present context as a politics of contradiction and ambivalence. Rather than dismissing this politics as an elaborate corporate masquerade, one that intends to encourage an ever more vigorous consumer body politic at the expense of social change, it makes more sense to theorize how power functions in contradictory ways within the context of consumerism.

One way to do this is to situate postfeminism as an ironic configuration of power, a configuration that, as McRobbie points out, skillfully uses the language of feminist cultural studies "against itself."[23] The ironic use of oppositional language and counterhegemonic practices within mainstream commodity culture has been widely theorized. For instance, Naomi Klein understands today's brand culture to be using the language of identity politics as an effective means through which brand loyalty can be assured; Malcolm Gladwell has theorized the economic importance of "cool" in the contemporary political economy; and Joseph Heath and Andrew Potter have argued that countercultural values have always been, ironically, "intensely entrepreneurial" (in fact, as they point out, the commodification of rebellion reflects "the most authentic spirit of capitalism").[24] McRobbie theorizes a similar kind of dynamic within postfeminist consumer culture, where much of contemporary advertising and popular culture uses a particular kind of irony when representing women, as if to suggest that the "problem" of objectification of women's bodies is one of history; women "get it" about objectification, and *because* of this understanding it is acceptable—indeed, even ironically empowering—to objectify women's bodies in the most blatantly demeaning ways. Thus, popular media function as a kind of critique of mainstream culture through the strategies of irony, camp, and a kind of postmodern cynicism—but within a conventional narrative framework. Current advertising uses this kind of self-reflexivity to both critique and ultimately sell products.[25]

Thus, one of the factors that characterize a contemporary postfeminist generation is this group's finely honed sense of irony. Decades of economic seesawing, progressively more sophisticated marketing strategies, and gradually more blurry boundaries between consumption habits and political and cultural beliefs have produced, among other things, a generation that is savvy, "smart," and generally perceived to be disaffected or cynical about culture. This general ideology makes it difficult to sustain an "old-fashioned" feminist politics that involves understanding women as victims of patriarchy, the theorizing of structural impediments in terms of employment and child care, or even more general assumptions about the various ways in which women are oppressed because *they are* women in the contemporary climate. In other words, the cynicism of the current generation is not only directed toward consumer culture but also toward historical political formations such as feminism.

Part of this has to do with the fact that irony as politics is a much more personal kind of politics than a more activist, public politics. As Jeffrey Sconce says about "smart films" of the 1990s, "American smart cinema has displaced the more activist emphasis on the 'social politics' of power, institutions, representation and subjectivity so central to 1960s and 1970s art cinema (especially in its 'political' wing), and replaced it by concentrating, often with ironic disdain, on the 'personal politics' of power, communication, emotional dysfunction and identity in white middle-class culture."[26] The consumer culture that Klein characterizes as "ironic consumption" seems to evacuate politics from the landscape in one sense because of the intense focus on personal identity. And it is this focus on personal identity and the rhetoric of choice that characterizes not only postfeminist culture but also the "New Economy" of race, where representations of personal success and media visibility seem to provide enough evidence that historical struggles over the enfranchisement of minorities and minority communities were crucial interventions but are no longer necessary in the current media economy.

No More *Cosby Show*: Generational Struggles over Race in the New Economy

In his incisive study of race representation (and specifically the representation of African Americans) on American television, Herman Gray delineates televisual depictions of race as a series of discursive practices that were particularly relevant in the 1980s. He identifies these practices as three interconnected strategies: assimilationist, or invisibility, where blacks are either simply not represented or represented as white people; pluralist, or "separate but equal," where blacks are represented on television but as a discrete niche or target group; and multiculturalist, or diversity, where Gray sees the "struggle for blackness" taking place in complex and often contradictory ways.[27] The influx of racial representations in the 1980s media landscape did not necessarily reflect a progressive political consciousness about the politics of race but were the result of a convergence of political and cultural dynamics, including the increase of niche channels on cable television, the rise of brand culture, the marketing tool of lifestyle demographics, and the conservative politics of the Reagan administration. In the 1980s, it became palatable—indeed, fashionable—to be multicultural and multiracial (under certain constraints and conditions). Black representation in 1980s media was part of a conservative appropriation of discourses of "political correctness" as a specific element in brand identity development in a burgeoning brand environment and came to represent cultural capital in this context.

As Gray, Justin Lewis, Sut Jhally, and others have argued, the American sitcom *The Cosby Show*, a hit in the 1980s under the guidance of Bill Cosby and featuring an all African American cast, represents a culturally and politically significant moment in television representations of race. In fact, Gray argues that it is impossible to understand contemporary representations of blackness without a consideration of what he calls "the Cosby Moment."[28] He locates the impetus for *The Cosby Show* (as well as other programs that featured African American characters) within a context in which the cultural definition of *diversity* as a specific marketing tool was beginning to be realized in corporate America. This emergent moment is crucial to consider when theorizing the contemporary context of race and representation, but, as with the generational differences between twentieth- and twenty-first-century feminisms, there is a generational distinction not only between the representations of race on television in the 1980s and the early twenty-first century but also in what these representations mean for a larger political formation.

In other words, what Gray regards as a "struggle for blackness" that took place over representational issues of the 1980s is a different kind of struggle in the context of the early twenty-first century. To "struggle" for blackness assumes a kind of stable identity for blackness itself—something tangible and "authentic" and worth struggling over. The struggle to which Gray referred was not simply about a politics of inclusion within the media but more generally a politics of inclusion within all areas of American cultural and civic life. In the current media moment, media representations of people of color are much more commonplace precisely because of the kinds of struggles Gray details and because the connections between media visibility and American cultural life are formulated primarily within consumption practices. Thus, as a way to extend Gray's historical analysis, I see a slightly different practice occurring within the current representational landscape, a practice that might be called "postracial" or "urbanized."

Indeed, a more overt connection of race with marketing dominated in the 1990s, especially marketing the "urban" to young, white, middle-class Americans. This was a different kind of urban than the images of urban black underclass that constituted most of the representations of people of color on 1980s

American television. However, the urban image that was increasingly part of the 1990s televisual landscape also contrasted with the wholesome, "positive," Cosby image of the 1980s. Leon Wynter sees this more recent movement or shift in representation as resulting in what he calls "Transracial America," which is a "vision of the American Dream in which we are liberated from the politics of race to openly embrace any style, cultural trope, or image of beauty that attracts us regardless of its origin."[29] Of course, the notion that through a process of urbanization we have been liberated from the politics of race is clearly an illusion, but it is the case that this politics has been reframed within brand culture. Popular discourses of race and images of nonwhites have become cultural capital in the contemporary marketing world, so that, as Gray discusses, there is a proliferation of difference rather than an absence of diversity. This practice can be seen on television channels such as Nickelodeon, where programs feature "diverse characters and themes."[30] Nickelodeon, like other contemporary media companies, uses newly shaped economic models and an ethnically nonspecific, "transracial" style as a way to appeal to increasingly diverse and segmented audiences without alienating specific groups. As with postfeminist representations, the "problem" of diversity in the current climate is no longer one of invisibility and, indeed, no longer about "separate but equal" doctrine or pluralism. On the contrary, capitalism and brand culture, through the relentless narrowing of marketing niches by means of gender, sexual identity, and ethnic and racial identity, has *provided for* rather than prevented a kind of diversity. That is to say, particular definitions of diversity are recognized as significant by media outlets such as Nickelodeon because diverse images, like images of girl power, sell well in a segmented political economy. The definition of *diversity* that has the most economic potential in the current climate is one that relies on a hip, cool, urban, "postracial" style.

The danger, of course, in labeling any kind of shift in discourse or practice "post" is that this prefix implies that whatever it modifies is somehow *over*—postfeminism, for instance, suggests (and at times insists) not only that feminism is passé but also, more obliquely, that whatever goals feminism sought have been accomplished. As Sarah Projansky has argued, one form of postfeminism clearly invokes a linear, historical trajectory, insisting that if we are in an age of postfeminism then we cannot also be in a moment of feminism—the two cannot coexist within linear logic.[31] However, to call this moment in late capitalism postracial is not to suggest that race and race relations are somehow irrelevant but rather to think seriously about recent shifts in capitalism that contain and market race and diversity in the media using new strategies. More traditional cultural definitions of race have been repackaged in the New Economy in ways that further disconnect race as a commodity from race as a material and social reality. The representation of race in current media is, on the whole, "positive" and is significant to how race is interpreted and navigated in cultural politics.[32] Because of historical interventions and social change, there is clearly more public awareness concerning "negative stereotypes" of people of color. Yet the various ways in which cultural definitions of race and diversity signify a market orientation toward the "urban" has further consolidated the ways in which race is produced as a particular commodity more than a more traditional kind of engaged politics. This kind of diversity thus functions according to the logic of a different political economic model than the one that supports Gray's discussion of television images.

What has occurred in the more than twenty years since the 1984 premiere of *The Cosby Show* is that media representations of people of color have proliferated but the connection between individual and group empowerment gained by media visibility and progressive change in poverty levels, unemployment, policy, and education continues to be illusive. Words such as *identity* and *multiculturalism* were, in the 1980s, code words for race; in the early-twenty-first century, these same terms are code words (especially for the consumer market) for "hip," "urban," and "cool." Race, like gender, as a political identity has been appropriated (at least in part) in the dominant culture through the brand identity of the urban and postfeminism. Within this context, I do not want to romanticize a definition of *politics* as something stable and immediately meaningful—or, conversely, to vilify brand identity as exclusively superficial and ephemeral—but I do want to shift the cultural frame through which youth empowerment is understood.

Visions of Power: Empowerment within a Postfeminist, Postracial, Media Culture

As I've briefly discussed in this essay, one of the interesting, as well as disturbing, consequences of the increasing mainstream visibility of identity politics and multiculturalism is not simply that people of color and girls "matter" publicly through their media and policy presence but also that these groups became the target for corporate America in terms of cultivating specific marketing niches. Because of the historical connection between empowerment and media visibility within this contemporary context, empowerment cannot be theorized as separate from market strategies but is rather a *constitutive* element in these strategies. Empowerment is thus discursively figured in at least two ways in this historical moment: as media visibility and market demographic. It is true, however, that there is a particular lack of substance that supports these representations for the number of people of color living below the poverty line in the United States continues to increase, women continue to make only 78 cents to the dollar of their male counterparts, and sexism and racism seem to be as institutionalized as ever.

There is, however, no lack of the *image* of diversity and gender within media culture; images of savvy, urban individuals and empowered girls function as lucrative commodities in the media marketplace. Advertisements feature young, urban, hip people of all races and genders, the soundtracks of ads and television programs often include urban music (such as hip-hop or rap), words associated with hip-hop culture such as *bling* and *dawg* are frequently used in family television, and casts that feature strong, independent young girls in youth television are more the rule than the exception. The taboo long associated with media representations of people of color is no longer salient. As Wynter points out, "As this taboo melts in the marketplace, whether as a reflection of social reality or in spite of it, the underlying energy of desire associated with racial prohibition is being liberated for exploitation by commercial marketers."[33] This, of course, raises the question of the nature of this liberation. The process whereby images of diversity are liberated from the racist practice of invisibility only to be used for a different set of purposes yet still rooted within the capitalist structure of the media deserve examination. In other words, McRobbie's proposition that postfeminism is "feminism taken into account" can be amended in the contemporary American context to include "diversity taken into account"—and, like feminism, an institutional kind of diversity is situated within this formulation as something belonging to history.

Thus, while the contemporary visual landscape certainly shares some similarities with that of the 1980s, when the economic and political context made it profitable to include particular representations of people of color and women within popular culture, the political economic landscape has clearly shifted. Race and gender have become even more important commodities within media culture and thus have achieved a sort of status within media consumer culture. However, as I've been arguing, not just any representation of race or gender will do in the contemporary U.S. media context; rather, the *kind* of ethnicity and the *particular* gender identity need to be specified. Specific images of ethnicity and gender function effectively as marketing tools within this cultural economy and are used to sell products by appealing to consumers who self-identify as empowered individuals or are "ethnic identified."[34] Race and gender within the current media culture are inextricably tied to dynamics of the market, where segmented marketing strategies and more localized capitalist ventures lead to a consumer-based valorization of self-identity.

This commercially defined articulation of identity needs to be distinguished from other means of self-construction within the social and political world, but the distinction itself is one that is in flux and continually negotiated. That is, when a media audience is "empowered" by images of race and gender, there is no linear connection to empowering communities. Rather, the connection is based on a notion of agency that is consumer driven and thus has consequences primarily in terms of consumption habits and even specific purchases made—a T-shirt that reads "Girls Rule!" perhaps, or a CD by the popular hip-hop artist 50 Cent. The current moment is thus characterized by ambivalence rather than specificity, where an ambivalent identity category such as urban or girl power becomes dominant and is the entry point to a commercially defined "postfeminist" or "postracial" society. As Eric King Watts and Mark P. Orbe argue in their essay about the commodification of race in Budweiser television commercials, this ambivalence is experienced by media audiences as a kind of "spectacular consumption" that works, in this specific case, in particular ways to contain race representations: "As the market economy seeks to regulate and integrate 'authentic' difference, white American ambivalence toward blackness is paradoxically both assuaged by its 'universality' and heightened by its distinctiveness."[35] This focus on the universality of racially or gender-specific images marks an interesting shift from the logic of clearly defined niche markets (i.e., the African American market, the female market, etc.) to one that is more ambiguous yet still clearly "diverse."

Dora the Explorer: The Global Individual

> Finally the idea emerged to have the star be a little girl with a sidekick partner, but it wasn't until a Nickelodeon executive attended a Children Now diversity seminar in 1998 that the doors opened for Dora. Did someone say abre?[36]

While spectacular consumption works in a contradictory way to both challenge and reify dominant ideologies of race and gender in Budweiser ads, hip-hop videos, and prime-time television, I'd like to turn briefly to the children's cable channel Nickelodeon to examine the representations of postfeminism and urbanization on kids' TV. Children's television in the United States has typically been more diverse than prime-time television, primarily because of the assumed pedagogical function of shows such as *Sesame Street, Blue's Clues*, and *Dora the Explorer*.[37] Indeed, the twenty-first-century context of postfeminism and the present celebration of urban images have encouraged a lineup of children's shows that feature strong, smart girls and multicultural casts.

The use of diversity as a part of social identity, and as a more abstract narrative theme, is an important element in Nickelodeon's claim to empower kids and address its child audience as active cultural citizens. Diversity, for Nickelodeon, is part of the network's brand identity. Like other brands in contemporary culture, Nickelodeon targets aspects of personal identity such as race as a way to be inclusive. In fact, its brand identity is crafted around the way it "empowers" children through (among other things) a commitment to gender and ethnic representation.

The ability to claim that diversity matters to Nickelodeon has thus given the network a way to stand out in the competitive field of children's television. In a recent report on diversity within children's television, the media advocacy group Children Now featured an article written by Nickelodeon's then-president, Herb Scannell, on the network's success with diversity.[38] As Scannell puts it, "One of the questions we are frequently asked by the media and the advocacy community is why we've been able to present a more diverse screen when other networks are often criticized for their lack of diversity. I can only speak for Nickelodeon when I say that it really boils down to our core mission of serving all kids."[39] Scannell explicitly connects the channel's images of diversity to Nickelodeon's claims to "respect" kids, thus building up cultural capital not only with advocacy groups such as Children Now but also with parents, educators, and others in the television industry. Indeed, within the world of children's television, racial and ethnic identity works as a kind of cultural capital, and it increases the political and social clout of a network to be able to claim that it is "diverse." As cultural capital, Nickelodeon's mission to respect kids and provide a safe and secure environment connects specifically to representation. The network's claim to empower kids overtly references the historical invisibility and exclusion of people of color that has plagued television since its inception, and the inclusion of diverse casts and characters is explicitly recognized by the network as part of its mission to "respect" kids. As with the channel's commitment to girls, Nickelodeon has pledged to air diverse programming, created shows that feature nonwhite characters, and developed programming that directly invokes racial or ethnic themes. Diverse programming is, as we have seen, often discussed as "good business," thus distancing the channel from the political implications of embracing diversity.

Dora the Explorer is one of these programs. Produced for Nick Jr. (Nickelodeon's preschool lineup), the show embodies some of the contradictory discourses of race and gender celebrated within a contemporary popular culture context. Dora is an animated, seven-year-old Latina with dark skin and brown eyes who speaks both English and Spanish throughout the show. In every episode, the narrative revolves around solving a puzzle or mystery (such as how to find a frog's lost voice or how to save a baby jaguar) and encourages interactive behavior on the part of the audience. The program itself is structured like a computer game, so there is a cursor that "clicks" on the right answer when Dora asks the audience for help. There are pauses in the program when Dora looks at the audience, waiting for viewers to reply to her questions about the daily mystery, thus encouraging a kind of active engagement on the part of the preschool audience.

The emphasis on audience interaction is, of course, typical of many contemporary children's programs for which the creators have researched the pedagogical potential of television. It also speaks to a more general cultural shift — signified by postfeminism among other things — that recognizes media audiences as active, savvy consumers. Textually, the tropes of postfeminism and urbanization are evident in the overall aesthetics of the show, including featuring an intelligent girl as a lead character and celebrating a kind of racial "authenticity" through the physical representation of Dora, the names of the other characters on the show, and the general representational style of the program. The show features both human and animal characters, most of whom are recognizably Latino, in either physical representation or linguistic behavior. Dora's parents, Mami and Papi, her grandmother, Abuela, and her cousin, Diego, all speak Spanish and English, and animals on the program are gendered and racialized (e.g., as Benni the Bull, Isa the Iguana, and Tico the Squirrel). The home in which Dora resides with her parents is Spanish in style, an adobe building with a red tile roof. While the plot themes of the show are often developmental and pedagogical, the narrative of Dora also frequently references Latino culture, traditions, and styles, though not necessarily in an ethnically or geographically specific manner. All the episodes follow the same format, in which Dora solves a mystery by following a series of clues, guided by her anthropomorphized "backpack" and "map," and the clues often are framed within an ambiguous Latin American lens. So, for instance, the Latin American rain forest is a frequent destination on Dora's quest to solve mysteries, a Christmas episode features a Mexican parade called a *parranda*, and characters on the show play salsa music to celebrate Dora's successes. One episode, "El Coqui," based on a famous Puerto Rican legend, involves Dora and a *coqui* (frog) who has lost his voice and will not be able to sing unless he gets back to his island. Dora and the frog eventually make their way to the island, assisted by a bird named Señor Tucan, allowing the frog to reunite with his friends and family.[40]

The weaving of the Puerto Rican legend into the show and, more specifically, incorporating themes of migration and exile culture as the primary narrative of the episode along with Latino dances and music, are ways to employ the strategy of being racially specific but ethnically nonspecific. In the most recent episodes of the program, this strategy continues to be honed and deployed. Perhaps most overtly, the expansion of Dora's extended and immediate family has added new dimensions to her postfeminist, "pan-Latino" persona. The show's producers have added two siblings to the family, twins, and in new episodes Dora is charged with taking care of the babies. The babies, like Dora, are drawn as Latino characters and are spoken to in Spanish as often as they are in English. Dora's status as a big sister is a frequent theme of current programs (as well as a new theme for toy manufacturing), and the program has smoothly incorporated a nurturing element into Dora's adventurous personality. The babies often accompany Dora on her adventures, allowing the show's producers to both create new thematic ideas for the show and add further elements to its postfeminist framing. Dora teaches the babies to speak English and Spanish, Spanish lullabies are now part of the show, and Dora's family is featured more centrally. Another way in which the show celebrates a particular notion of "difference" occurs with the addition of Dora's bilingual eight-year-old cousin. Diego Marquez, who was introduced in *Dora the Explorer* as someone who helps animals in danger, now has his own show, *Go Diego Go!*, which is also part of Nickelodeon's preschool programming package. The program continues the theme of Dora through its celebration of "authentic" Latin American culture: the animals that Diego rescues are all indigenous creatures to Latin American rain forests, each show contains references to Latin American folktales and traditions, and Spanish is intermingled with English throughout each episode.

Diego's character furthers the initial strategy of *Dora the Explorer* where postfeminist culture and the celebration of "difference" function as effective ways to both target and create a particular community of consumers. Dora's character, as well as Diego's and others on the show, are depicted in such a way that race and ethnicity *matter*, though in particular ways, as a kind of "authentic" pleasure and an unproblematic embrace of "difference." Race, in this context, is not rendered invisible, but it is also not presented as specific and particular. Rather, Dora, like Diego, represents a marketable global citizen. Dora is pan-Latino intentionally so that as a Latina she has a wide appeal for her young audiences across the world. Indeed, her "Latinidad" has been expertly commodified in dozens of toys, books, clothes, and food items that appeal to a wide demographic of consumers, including, but certainly not limited to, American Latinos. In an article entitled "Adorable Dora Is Opening the Doors of Diversity," the producers of the show comment specifically on her panethnic representation: "'With Dora, Nickelodeon found a heroine that appeals to kids of all ethnic backgrounds' . . . [said producer Gifford,] recalling one Chinese child who said, 'She's just like me; she speaks another language.' The creators purposely do not specify Dora's ethnic background, preferring that she have a pan-Latino appeal, and revised her original green eyes to brown after content supervisor Dolly Espinal pointed out that a majority of Latinos have brown eyes and that it was important to celebrate that."[41] The difference embodied by the character of Dora allows for an ethnically informed style of politics, yet it is, in McRobbie's terms, difference "taken into account" yet not necessarily acted on. Challenging racist stereotypes by creating a new one fit for the current political and cultural economy, Dora operates as part of a strategy that motivates a commercially defined notion of diversity. As Arlene Dávila points out in her study about marketing aimed at Latinos, "To sell themselves and their products, those in [the advertising] industry have not only drawn from existing stereotypes . . . but have also positioned themselves as the 'politically correct' voice with which to challenge stereotypes and educate corporate clients about Hispanic language and culture."[42] Nickelodeon's self-identity as the "diversity station" utilizes a similar kind of strategy through which it gains cultural capital by offering diverse representations to its young audience.

Within the current market environment, a dual process of challenging and reinforcing racial stereotypes in the media is necessary in order to maintain an "ethnic" niche in the market.[43] Yet in programs such as *Dora the Explorer*, which confront stereotypes as they simultaneously reformulate them for a shifted market, the stereotype that is reconstituted is one that is not necessarily intended for an ethnic niche market but is meant to appeal to a broader (more "global") audience. Using this strategy, Nickelodeon can claim that the network is committed to diversity despite the fact that this progressive ideology works as a more general market imperative. This strategy works hand in hand with postfeminist politics, where Dora, as a strong, smart, female character, is clearly a product of a culture that recognizes the importance of "positive" gender representations yet does not call attention to any kind of feminist politics other than the politics of representation. Thus, the challenges to dominant stereotypes that *Dora the Explorer* poses are framed within normative social conventions so that the challenge is contained and made palatable for a media audience. What this means, at least for Dora, is to utilize Latino "themes" as part of the program but in a safe way so as not to alienate Nickelodeon's predominantly white, middle-class cable audience.

In the case of Nickelodeon, as demonstrated by *Dora the Explorer*, diversity is less about a specific identity in terms of ethnicity than about an identity as an empowered consumer-citizen. Indeed, the show's cocreator and executive producer, Chris Gifford, claimed he had "empowering children in mind" when he created *Dora*.[44] The construction of Dora as a global citizen whose ethnicity is specific but whose appeal is racially nonspecific makes her what one consultant, Carlos Cortes, calls "a crossover phenomenon and the product of a slow evolution in television."[45] This "evolution" in television is indicated by the construction of ethnic markets, an increasingly diverse body of consumers, and the emergence of a cool, more "multicultural" approach to making television shows that corresponds to a general youth market. Another element of this television evolution is signaled by postfeminism, which similarly celebrates the "empowered" consumer-citizen.

Conclusion

Within the current media environment, itself a product of a post-civil-rights society, race functions as an ambivalent category in which, on the one hand, race remains an important issue in terms of representation—shown by featuring people of color more prominently (as demonstrated by the Flava dolls) and crafting story lines that focus on race and race relations. On the other hand, the plethora of images of urban and cool people of color in advertising, television programs, and music videos (among other popular culture artifacts) implies that representational visibility no longer has the same urgency. Indeed, the implication is that race itself no longer matters in the same way it once did but is now simply an interesting way to feature the authentic, cool, or urban or develop a theme in a reality show. This postracial television economy is the legacy of diverse programs such as *Sesame Street* and *The Cosby Show*, but it engages these earlier representations of race within new economic models in which the connection between enfranchisement and "positive" images of diversity no longer has the meaning it did in the media context of the 1970s and 1980s. These new economic models also inform the production of postfeminist popular culture, in which "feminism taken into account" is the dominant narrative, effectively framing feminism as history even as a commodified version of feminist ideas and values is normalized.

It is not my aim to resolve these tensions or expose postfeminism or the "urban" as a commercial hoax. It is my goal, rather, to theorize how the contradictory media representations of girl power and urbanization function as a particular kind of politics and as such work to constitute audiences as particular kinds of cultural citizens. The same problems and distinctions that formulate the current postfeminist and postracial cultural space also constitute consumer citizenship: nostalgia, an imagined golden past, superficiality, a focus on the individual, rhetorics of choice reframed in terms of consumer purchases, and so on. Like consumer citizenship, postfeminist and postracial culture is profoundly, indeed necessarily ambivalent.

Notes

1. Press release, Flava Dolls, Mattel, Inc., www.Toymania.com, retrieved February 2004. Unfortunately for Mattel, Flava Dolls were not a big hit with girls age nine to eleven, and shortly after their release in toy stores across the United States Mattel stopped production. However, clearly this style of toy remains significant, as another brand of similar dolls, Bratz Dolls, produced by MGA entertainment, are immensely popular in the United States. Bratz Dolls are also multiethnic and, according to a fan Web site, are "known for having fun, detailed accessories and play sets which reflect their 'cool' (and somewhat materialistic) lifestyle—discos, karaoke and sushi bars, salons and spas, limousines, retro cafes, malls are all available" (collectdolls.about .com, retrieved June 2005).

2. Pierre Bourdieu theorized cultural capital as knowledge, or a kind of competence, about styles and genres that are socially valued and confer prestige on those who have mastered them. He distinguished between economic capital, which refers to the quantity of material goods and income commanded by an individual, and cultural capital, which refers to a kind of competency derived from education, familiarity with a legitimized cultural tradition, and modes of consumption. For more on this, see Bourdieu, *Distinction*.

3. For more on this subject, see Buckingham, *After the Death of Childhood*; Buckingham, *The Making of Citizens*; Seiter, *Sold Separately*; and Gray, *Watching Race*.

4. See McRobbie, "Notes on Postfeminism and Popular Culture."

5. Gray, *Cultural Moves*. As Gray argues, this proliferation of images does not necessarily connect with a more equitable legal system or a lessening of racist practices in the United States. In fact, the increasing presence of images of African Americans often obscures the ways in which a racist society functions.

6. Smith, "I Don't Like to Dream about Getting Paid."

7. Dow, *Prime-Time Feminism*.

8. McRobbie, "Notes on Postfeminism and Popular Culture," 5.

9. Ibid., 6.

10. Hogeland, "Against Generational Thinking; or, Some Things That 'Third Wave' Feminism Isn't," 107.

11. McRobbie discusses this shift to a more "lifestyle" type of politics in "Notes on Postfeminism and Popular Culture."

12. Ibid.," 10–11.

13. Klein, *No Logo*.

14. Baumgardner and Richards, *Manifesta*.

15. The awareness of feminist accomplishments in the areas of employment, wages, and policy led to a widespread adoption of the adage "I'm not a feminist, but . . ." As Susan Douglas argues, the comma in this statement is hugely significant, marking

the contradictions involved in feminist politics: "The comma says that the speaker is ambivalent, that she is torn between a philosophy that seeks to improve her lot in life and a desire not to have to pay too dearly for endorsing that philosophy" (*Where the Girls Are*, 270).

16. Baumgardner and Richards, *Manifesta*, 83.
17. Douglas, *Where the Girls Are*, 293.
18. Goldman, *Reading Ads Socially*.
19. Bellafante, "It's All about Me!" 57.
20. Baumgardner and Richards, *Manifesta*; Findlen, *Listen Up*; Wolf, *Fire with Fire*.
21. Baumgardner and Richards, *Manifesta*, 80.
22. See Hartsock, *The Feminist Standpoint Revisited and Other Essays*.
23. McRobbie, "Notes on Postfeminism and Popular Culture."
24. See Klein, *No Logo*; Gladwell, "The Coolhunt"; and Heath and Potter, *The Rebel Sell*.
25. See, for example, Gladwell, "The Coolhunt"; Klein, *No Logo*; and Quart, *Branded*.
26. Sconce, "Irony, Nihilism, and the American 'Smart' Film," 352.
27. Gray, *Watching Race*. While Gray recognizes the historical trajectory of these discourses, he also acknowledges that all three practices continue simultaneously.
28. Gray, *Watching Race*, 79.
29. Wynter, *American Skin*, 135.
30. Scannell, "Why Not Diversity?"
31. Projansky, *Watching Rape*.
32. See Wynter, *American Skin*, and Smith, "I Don't Like to Dream about Getting Paid."
33. Wynter, *American Skin*, 17.
34. By this, I do not mean "authentic" ethnicity (i.e., a physical relationship with ethnic identity and history) but rather a more diffused embrace of ethnic identity and the urban.
35. Watts and Orbe, "The Spectacular Consumption of 'True' African American Culture, 3.
36. Cabrera, "Adorable Dora Is Opening the Doors of Diversity."
37. Although these programs take an explicit political position on diversity, and federal regulations in the United States dictate that at least three hours a week of children's television must be "educational," there are certainly plenty of programs that are not diverse. Indeed, the enormous market for licensed character products lends itself to rigid stereotypes because simplistic hegemonic images are easier to package and sell—they have a clearer market identity.
38. The network leadership of Nickelodeon has changed since this article was written; in January 2006, Herb Scannell resigned as president of Nickelodeon and was succeeded by Cyma Zarghami.
39. Scannell, "Why Not Diversity?"
40. *Dora the Explorer*, "El Coqui."
41. Cabrera, "Adorable Dora."

42. Dávila, *Latinos, Inc.*

43. This dual function of stereotypes is not unique to Dora, of course, but is characteristic of stereotyping more generally. For more on this, see Bhabha, "The Other Question."

44. Cabrera, "Adorable Dora."

45. Ibid.

Martin Roberts

9 **The Fashion Police**
GOVERNING THE SELF IN WHAT NOT TO WEAR

Over the past decade, television has been undergoing a radical transformation in response to the forces of new media technologies, neoliberal economics, and globalization. The transformation in question is not just technological or political economic but extends to television's very role and purpose in modern society. The history of television is typically told as a tale of two systems: on the one hand, the public service model, usually embodied by the BBC, which conceives of its role as educating and informing citizens so as to enable them to participate more fully in a democratic society; and, on the other, the commercial model, which is usually exemplified by American television, which provides popular entertainment in order to maximize audiences for advertisers. In recent decades, however, privatization, deregulation, and technological change have found public service monopolies increasingly having to compete with transnational commercial networks for audiences, while those networks, in turn, lay claim to the public sphere, blurring the distinction between public and private, citizens and consumers.

Lifestyle Television and Postfeminism

The emergence of what has become known as lifestyle television is one of the consequences of this transformation.[1] Gareth Palmer suggests that "the concepts of lifestyle and surveillance are part of a new discursive formation in which appearance is of paramount importance."[2] Television plays a key role within this formation. In a world where "it is now widely agreed and understood that 'appearance is everything,'" "people now understand television as an active agent of transformation."[3] Public service television in its traditional forms saw its role as the intellectual and moral improvement of citizens; lifestyle television is no less interested in improving its audience, but the forms of improvement in this case are those proposed by a consumer society and have more to do with, say, understanding wines, where to go on holiday, or the right way to shave than political participation. They are about the self and the achievement of social distinction through consumption. Thus is lifestyle television able to position itself as performing a new kind of "public service." For what is ultimately at stake, as Palmer points out, is the very raison d'être of television itself. He writes, "While television's influence has now extended to directly fashioning people—for their own good, of course—this is also for television's sake, to keep proving that somehow 'it,' the apparatus, *works*."[4] In a similar vein, Rachel Moseley suggests that the privatization of the public sphere in recent decades has led to a shift in the ethos of public service broadcasting, with television taking on a new role in the "care of the self, the home and the garden, addressing its audience through a combination of consumer competence and do-it-yourself on a shoestring."[5] Rather than a simple shift from citizen to consumer, Moseley suggests, today's lifestyle shows "represent a complex conjunction of the two, in which the personal and the private are figured as significant spaces in which citizens can, on a small local scale, learn to make changes, make a difference, improve the person for the national good."[6] In effect, lifestyle television transforms consumption *into* a form of citizenship, a duty that we are all, as responsible citizens, required to perform for the general good. Correspondingly, as we shall see, a sizable proportion of lifestyle television is devoted to the stigmatization of those who are laggardly or recalcitrant in their fulfillment of this duty and, through a combination of public shaming and financial incentives, to inducing them to become fully participant, consuming subjects in the neoliberal economy.

The production and management of social identities conducive to the economic interests of the corporations that underwrite lifestyle television are crucial to this project, and this is especially true in those series that sustain a specifically gendered mode of address. Since the earliest days of commercial television, women have been recognized as a crucial component of the television audience because of their spending power as consumers.[7] That principle is equally valid today and is one of the key tenets of lifestyle television. In particular, as I want to argue here, the hegemonic discourse of postfeminism, which has become so ubiquitous in media culture and popular cinema in recent years, has proved an especially useful tool for lifestyle television's construction of a model of feminine identity predicated on consumption, just as lifestyle television itself has emerged as a primary locus for the articulation of postfeminist ideology. If feminism has historically aligned itself with the Marxist critique of consumer society, elaborating a critique both of the commodification of women themselves and of models of femininity inseparable from mass consumption (fashion, cosmetics, etc.), the discourse of postfeminism has proceeded to stand this critique on its head, articulating a model of feminine identity unthinkable outside consumption and constructing a logic in which "empowerment"—perhaps the central tenet of postfeminist ideology—is shown as dependent on self-confidence and sexual attractiveness, which in turn depend on the services of the fashion and beauty industries— all of which, needless to say, must be purchased.

As Moseley has also noted, in recent years lifestyle television's production of consumption-based gender identities has been increasingly extended to men, both gay and straight, most notably in that latest figment of the media imagination, the metrosexual.[8] While gay male identity in its more bourgeois forms has long been associated with consumption, reinforced by contemporary style shows such as Bravo's *Queer Eye for the Straight Guy*, until recently straight masculinity has been more defined by its resistance (or at least sullen indifference) to the traditionally feminine pursuits of shopping, fashion, cosmetics, and cooking. Much of the ideological work of lifestyle television in recent years has accordingly been directed toward changing this, through what Moseley identifies as a degendering of such activities or, to put it another way, the projection of a heterosexual masculinity no longer incompatible with an interest in fashion, "grooming," or even cooking (celebrity chefs Jamie Oliver or Gordon Ramsay) and by extension with the shopping that necessarily accompanies these.[9] In addition to the postfeminist consumer, newly style conscious, straight male designers and celebrity chefs are among the most significant projections of contemporary lifestyle television.

Governmentality

While a substantial body of cultural studies scholarship has emerged in recent years in response to the rapid expansion of lifestyle television, this scholarship has relied heavily (perhaps too heavily) on the sociology of Pierre Bourdieu. What I propose to do here instead is to examine lifestyle television within a different theoretical framework, one that has developed over the past decade around the concept of governmentality. Just as the concept of governmentality helps us to better understand lifestyle television as a disciplinary practice, as I hope to show, lifestyle television provides an equally useful case study for observing the role of mass media in the larger set of disciplinary practices known as governmentality.

First elaborated by Michel Foucault in a 1978 lecture at the Collège de France, over the past decade the concept of governmentality has become the basis for a new approach to the study of the operations of power in modern societies.[10] Understood, in Foucault's cryptic formulation, as "the conduct of conduct," the concept of governmentality has been increasingly deployed in the field of cultural studies in Toby Miller's concept of the "well-tempered self" and several anthologies devoted to the subject.[11] More recent scholarship has begun to explore the workings of governmentality in mass media: the role of television and other media in the process of what Nikolas Rose calls "governing the soul" or the production, shaping, and management of subjects useful for the purposes of the state and its associated institutions.[12]

Over the past decade, Rose has laid out a comprehensive history of the role of Enlightenment knowledge systems such as psychiatry, psychoanalysis, and psychology in the production and governance of the modern self.[13] A key factor in this process has been the rise of expertise in all its forms.

[W]e have witnessed the birth of a new form of expertise, an expertise of subjectivity. A whole family of new professional groups has propagated itself, each asserting its virtuosity in respect of the self, in classifying and measuring the psyche, in predicting its vicissitudes, in diagnosing the causes of its troubles and prescribing remedies. Not just psychologists — clinical, occupational, educational — but also social workers, personnel managers, probation officers, counselors and therapists of different schools and allegiances have based their claim to social authority upon their capacity to understand the psychological aspects of the person and act upon them, or to advise others what to do. The multiplying powers of these "engineers of the human soul" seem to manifest something profoundly novel in the relations of authority over the self.[14]

As the saturation of everyday life with the vocabularies of psychotherapy (denial, trauma, libido, passive-aggressive behavior) amply attests, such expert discourses have come to define our very way of thinking about our "self," its problems, and the solutions to them.

Rose's work is centrally concerned with tracing a historical genealogy of governmentality within modernity, but his analysis raises equally important questions about its contemporary modes of operation and how these may resemble or differ from its historical ones. One such question concerns the institutional basis of governmentality: who or what, institutionally speaking, is the driving force behind contemporary governmentality? Through what channels does it operate and in the name of whose interests? Historically, the answer to this question has been the state and its associated institutions, with the "conduct of conduct" being ultimately about securing and maintaining the control of states over their populations. A key problem within modernity, however, concerns the relationship between the state and capitalism and the notion that governmentality has been driven as much by the economic interests of capital as the political requirements of the state. While this is clearly a complex historical discussion, a strong case can be made that in the contemporary world, at least, governmentality is driven primarily by the agendas and interests of neoliberal capitalism as much as of the state, that, indeed, the state and its institutions are increasingly subject to these interests and have taken on an instrumental role in securing them. One need only think of the number of new psychological "disorders," along with the equally proliferating array of new pharmaceutical products to treat them, to find an example of the complicity between "expert" knowledge systems and the profits of the pharmaceutical industry.[15]

If we accept that governmentality in postmodern societies is driven primarily by the interests of the market rather than of the state as such, a further question concerns the role of commercial media in this process. Viewed from this perspective, lifestyle television and the new forms of expertise it deploys can be seen as performing an instrumental role.[16] The developing body of work on governmentality in media studies promises to provide a much-needed consideration of the role played by media in the governance of contemporary postmodern identities, and the present essay is accordingly intended as a contribution to that literature. The instrumental rationalities governing the postmodern self, I suggest, are less those of the state than of neoliberal capitalism, with its associated ideologies of freedom and expressive individualism linked to consumption, which lifestyle television tirelessly reinforces.

A third question that arises in relation to my earlier discussion concerns the place of gender within governmentality and vice versa.[17] A governance of identities, clearly, also involves in part a governance of gender: the shaping of gender identities for particular ends, in this case the economic interests of the lifestyle industries. The discourse of postfeminism that pervades lifestyle television can be seen from this perspective as an instrument of governance in that it naturalizes a model of feminine identity and female power inseparable from consumption. It may be further suggested that gender itself is inescapably inscribed within practices of governance in that the social subjects whose conduct they seek to direct are always gendered subjects and therefore require different strategies and the mobilization of different rationalities depending on the identity of the subject in question.

What Not to Wear

> Your best friends won't tell you what not to wear, but we're not your friends. And we will.— WHAT NOT TO WEAR

In what follows, I will elaborate the preceding points through a discussion of the popular BBC fashion makeover show *What Not to Wear* (2001–), which I see as a paradigmatic example of the operations of governmentality in lifestyle television and the role of postfeminist ideology in that process. Currently in its fifth series in the United Kingdom, to date the show has generated five spin-off books and a DVD,[18] while its hosts, Trinny Woodall and Susannah Constantine, have become media celebrities, engaging in such ancillary activities as performing cameos on other popular shows, such as *Top Gear* and *The Kumars at No. 42*, and hosting London Fashion Week and the BAFTA (British Academy of Film and Television Arts) awards.[19] Like the home makeover show *Changing Rooms*, *What Not to Wear* has inspired numerous clones on American lifestyle

what not to wear

NEW SEASON
Tuesdays 9 pm e/p

Your best friends won't tell you what not to wear.
But we're not your best friends.

And we will.

BBC AMERICA
Watch on digital cable or satellite.

The British fashion makeover program
What Not to Wear has achieved significant
visibility in the United States via
BBC America. The tagline used here is
consistent with the series' rhetoric,
which stresses that participants will be
subjected to an unfriendly (even sadistic)
process of transformation.

channels, including the Learning Channel's series of the same name; the Style
Network's *Fashion Police*, *Style Court*, *How Do I Look?* and *The Look for Less*; and
Bravo's *Queer Eye for the Straight Guy* (and now the *Straight Girl*).[20] The British
series has aired in Australia and New Zealand, while a local Australian version has also been produced. *What Not to Wear* merits attention because it exemplifies some of the key characteristics of contemporary lifestyle television,
most notably its naturalization of consumption, of a postmodernist model
of self predicated on outward appearance rather than interiority, and of one
of the central tenets of postfeminist ideology: that sexual attractiveness is a
source of power over patriarchy rather than subjection to it.[21]

Gareth Palmer has noted the increasing ubiquity of surveillance footage
on British television exemplified by *Big Brother*, a tendency that he sees as
related to the pervasive presence of closed-circuit television (CCTV) cameras
in British society at large.[22] Elsewhere, Nick Couldry has expressed concern
about programs such as the BBC's *Crimewatch*, which in turning television into
an instrument of law enforcement blur the boundary between the state and
media and thereby undermine the media's purported role as the representative of the general public.[23] *What Not to Wear* is clearly related to such developments, but it is only one of a number of shows on British and American
lifestyle television that use the fashion-police metaphor such as the aforementioned *Style Court*, *Fashion Police*, or E! Entertainment's *101 Most Sensational*

Crimes of Fashion. Such shows are themselves only part of the growing number of television shows organized around the policing of social and sexual identities, from HGTV's *Garden Police* to the much-maligned *Cheaters* (Bobby Goldstein Productions).

What Not to Wear essentially reproduces the narrative structure of a cop show, following the successive stages of law enforcement from surveillance and arrest through interrogation, conviction, and release to ultimate rehabilitation. The process begins with the "setup," in which the sartorially impaired suspect (or "victim," in the show's parlance) is reported to the "authorities" by a network of informers—her own family, friends, or coworkers—and placed under observation.[24] After hidden-camera footage of the suspect in various forms of unflattering attire has established her guilt beyond a reasonable doubt, she is apprehended, in the company of those who have set her up (as the hosts never fail to mention, "you've been set up!"), and summoned to appear with her offending wardrobe in return for a kind of reverse fine (*bribe* might be a better word) in the form of a check for two thousand pounds for the purchase of a new one. At the first meeting, the detainee's clothing is submitted to a thorough inspection and most of it summarily disposed of in spite of protestations about sentimental value and the like. She is required to perform a compulsory self-inspection in the show's signature 360-degree "chamber of mirrors," shot from above from the classic surveillance-camera viewpoint. Issued with a set of preliminary guidelines, she is released on parole (or payroll) to begin shopping for her new wardrobe at a nearby mall—cue product placement for high-street shops such as French Connection, Zara, and Monsoon. Meanwhile, the experts monitor their protégée's progress as she gamely tries to put into practice (or often willfully ignores) the rules prescribed for her, intervening to scold fashion faux pas and provide on the spot training in the "right" choices. Interspersed with these sequences are black-and-white video diary segments in which the subject reflects, often tearfully, on the transformation process. Through a combination of coaxing and coercion, she is induced to choose the "right" look and duly emerges, in most cases visibly satisfied with her new image. Returned to her former life, she remains under surveillance, albeit approving this time, which confirms her successful rehabilitation, and the episode concludes with the enthusiastic responses of husband, family, and friends and footage of the preening fashion butterfly.

For Gareth Palmer, whose analysis draws extensively on the work of Bourdieu, shows such as *What Not to Wear* are primarily about naturalizing middle-class tastes and inculcating them in their petit-bourgeois subjects and audiences, teaching them how to pass "as citizens in the republic of taste."[25] In this sense, *What Not to Wear* has much in common with *Faking It*, another contemporary BBC show organized around the transformation of identities, which usually involves "passing" in a higher professional or social position than one's actual one. I would argue, however, that *What Not to Wear* goes to some lengths to suppress the class-based nature of its taste hierarchies, a suppression in part achieved through the device of the "rules." Rules are central to *What Not to Wear*'s discourse of expertise. They figure prominently not just in the show itself but in the *What Not to Wear* books and Web sites, while one of the series' most recent spinoff books, *What Not to Wear: The Rules*, explicitly foregrounds them. What kind of rules are we talking about? Ever since Roland Barthes's semiotic analysis of *Elle* magazine, theoretical analyses of fashion have been dominated by the Saussurean linguistic model in which fashion is conceived as a system of signs organized into cultural codes.[26] This semiotic model, in which fashion styles are understood as a signifying system encoding class, gender, race, ethnicity, age, and other social variables, has become almost taken for granted in postmodern consumer culture. From this perspective, what is striking about the rules taught by *What Not to Wear* is that they are based not on semiotics but on the body itself. In the commonsense world of *What Not to Wear*, choosing what (not) to wear begins and ends with the body and can be summed up in two key principles: flaunt your natural "assets" and hide your "defects": "It's about dressing to show off what you love and hiding what you loathe about your body."[27] The process begins by listing ten "problem areas," each the subject of a chapter of the first *What Not to Wear* book: "big boobs," "no boobs," "big arms," "big butt," "no waist," "short legs," "flabby tummy," "saddlebags," a "short neck," and "thick ankles and calves." The solution to these problems is, quite simply, to hide them, and *What Not to Wear* is permeated with a rhetoric of disguise, deception, of covering up. The "golden rules for big arms," for example, are as follows.

> Fat arms must always wear sleeves.
> Capped sleeves are an absolute no—they strangle big arms.
> Small prints cover a multitude of flabby flesh.
> Be ruthless—chuck out the clothes that don't suit you and treat yourself to some new ones that do.[28]

The injunction simply to "chuck out" ill-suited clothes and replace them with new ones occurs in no less than five of the book's ten sets of rules, exemplifying how self-renewal is synonymous with consumption in the show's worldview; how readers are to afford to "treat" themselves is never addressed. While the show does often reference semiotic meanings, usually in negative contexts ("She's dressed like a Ferrari mechanic"), it is the body and its appearance that remain the central reference point. This insistence on the body enables a universalist discourse that transcends class difference and makes even the social meaning of clothes foregrounded by semiotics seem irrelevant. No matter who we are socially and economically, the show seems to suggest, we are all equals when standing naked in front of a three-way mirror. While, as Palmer (via Bourdieu) has pointed out, the norms of taste enforced by the show are predictably upper-middle-class ones, the strategy of ideological "outing" neglects the larger point that by fixing attention on the (classless) body the show disavows class and can present its choices simply as the "natural" ones for the body in question. The very language used to talk about bodies on the show evidences a strategy of blurring class difference, with recognizably working-class terms ("arse," "tits," "bum," "knickers") being used ubiquitously along with middle-class ones ("boobs," the transatlantic "butt").

As in actual cop shows, much of the drama of *What Not to Wear* stems from conflicts between the representatives of law enforcement and their detainees. Typically, subjects begin by vehemently rejecting the "expert" assessments of their fashion style and denying any need for reform. The show thus becomes a narrative about overcoming resistance, as the subject, like the suspect in the interrogation room, has to be broken down and eventually acquiesces to the rule of law. Much of the interest of the show accordingly lies in seeing how resistant the subject will be, with the most entertaining shows being those in which the subject proves most recalcitrant. Some subjects (most notoriously Jane Anderson in series three) may prove exasperatingly tough nuts to crack, and their resistance can lead to heated exchanges, resulting in only an uneasy truce at the end. Ultimately, though, the show is about achieving consensus, a compromise between expert knowledge and personal quirkiness through a rational process of honest self-examination and disinterested, objective advice.

One of the reasons why the breaking-down process may prove so difficult is that it amounts to nothing less than a breaking down of the subject's sense of her own identity and the literal fashioning of a new one in its place. As the video diary segments attest, the process can often be disorienting; as one subject remarks, "I feel like I'm looking for clothes for someone who isn't me at the moment" (Julie Nicholson, 3:1). Crucial to the project's success, however, is the subject's understanding that the "new" self is preexistently latent within herself. This new self must be liberated rather than being imposed from the outside ("There's a sexy woman in there that's trying to get out!"). This imaginary self must not only be "discovered" but experienced, paradoxically, as more authentic than the previous one, which henceforth comes to be regarded as inauthentic ("I feel like I've discovered the real me!"). The supposedly more authentic self, however, bears the unmistakable hallmark of the postfeminist, consumer-oriented self. It is, above all, a *sexier* self in which sexual attractiveness has been magically transformed from an oppressive imperative of patriarchy into a source of power *over it*, a brave new postfeminist self requiring continual self-monitoring and investment in salons and spas, fashion stores, and regular visits to the gym.

In his study of enhancement technologies, *Better Than Well*, Carl Elliott notes how those engaging in various forms of technological self-transformation, from body building to sex reassignment surgery, tend to experience this not as the creation of a new self but the discovery of a more authentic "true self" and therefore as a project of self-realization, of becoming who they "really are."[29] While such essentialist conceptions of self are easy to dismiss, for millions of people around the world they provide a basis for self-understanding and for decisions about the remodeling of their bodies and, increasingly, their minds.[30] The enhancement technologies deployed by *What Not to Wear* may seem benign compared to the procedures Elliott discusses, but they raise the question of how far one may be prepared (or allowed) to go in the discovery of the "true self."[31] What if the achievement of the true self involves more radical procedures than just a new wardrobe? An answer is already being provided by the current generation of American "extreme makeover" shows (Fox's *The Swan*, MTV's *I Want a Famous Face*, FX's fictional *Nip/Tuck*), which have turned cosmetic surgery into a new form of voyeuristic entertainment. The experts on such shows are no longer interior designers or fashion gurus but white-coated cosmetic surgeons and solemn-faced psychologists whose role is to support their often traumatized subjects through the painful surgical procedures leading to the mirror-phase ritual known as the "reveal." While such shows clearly go several steps beyond those of the *What Not to Wear* variety, they are arguably informed by similar ideologies of personal transformation and expressive individualism, as well as highlighting how those ideologies coincide with the economic interests of the cosmetic surgery industry, not to mention commercial television.

It may come as no surprise that *What Not to Wear*'s preferred subjects are middle- and lower-middle-class professional women in their thirties and forties, many of whom are balancing a job with the demands of raising a family and at some point have given up on the imperative of perpetual attractiveness to their partners or men in general. The brief biographical sketches at the beginning of the shows and on the Web sites generally identify them by first name (full name in later series), age, number of children, and (less often) profession. Motherhood becomes a focus of particular attention in the fourth series. The Web site for the British series lists episodes entitled "Mums with Babies," "Mums with Glam Teens," "Mr. Commitment," and "Menopause," as well as a link to a page on "What to Wear in Pregnancy." This foregrounding of pregnancy and motherhood in a fashion show is unusual, and while it is no doubt related to the fact that both of the show's hosts were themselves very visibly pregnant at the time it is also connected to the show's postfeminist ideology.[32] The point being made, it could be suggested, is that, contrary to common assumptions, motherhood and fashion need not be mutually exclusive. One *can* have it both ways. One can both be a mother and continue to dress stylishly, even sexily, or, to put it in less "empowering" terms, being a mother, middle-aged, or menopausal does not mean that women can neglect their obligation to be stylish and simply let themselves go.

While men generally occupy a marginal role in *What Not to Wear* (usually in the form of dissatisfied partners), they remain implicitly present throughout, and their approval at the end of each show validates the transformation project. An episode of the second season, however, turns the tables on the usual complaining husbands by featuring the spouse of Maria Barraclough (1:4) from the first season, who had allegedly nominated his wife because he had "had enough" and wanted a "sexy wife" (BBC America Web site, episode guide 2:6, "Matthew"). The show was welcomed by female viewers (BBC America Web site, episode review 2:6), and several episodes of the third series were subsequently devoted to men and male fashion. Significantly, however, the men in question were all celebrities (or ex-celebrities) in contrast to the anonymous women who are usually featured: Mick Brown (3:5) is a former host of *Top of the Pops* and a radio disc jockey, David Baddiel (3:3) is a popular TV comedian, and Jamiroquai (3:3) is the lead singer of the band of the same name. Predictably, male subjects tend to be more resistant than their female counterparts, which skews the dynamics of the show considerably. While they do end up looking a lot sharper, they do not take the show and its hosts all that seriously. Woodall and Constantine themselves also tend to be more deferential and are surprisingly upbeat about male fashion (or at least male celebrity fashion).[33] Still, the show's very attempt to bring men under its authority is symptomatic of lifestyle television's project of extending the boundaries of straight masculinity to include the traditionally "feminine" concerns of personal appearance and the domestic sphere, with the potentially lucrative implications for markets in the beauty, fashion, design, and food industries that this entails.

If *What Not to Wear* is concerned with policing middle-class norms of taste and promoting a postfeminist model of identity, it can also be seen as a characteristic example of the default (or what Glen Creeber calls "hideous") whiteness that has traditionally dominated British television programming in spite of the presence of significant immigrant communities in the wake of decolonization in the 1950s.[34] The fact that the overwhelming majority of its participants have been white is ironic given the larger shifts that have been taking place in British culture around it. Paul Gilroy has written recently of the grudging acceptance of immigrants that has taken hold in the country in recent decades, a condition for which he uses the term *conviviality* in preference to the largely outdated ideal of multiculturalism.[35] One consequence of this gradual process of integration has been the growing visibility of racial minorities in mainstream media culture, from the South Asian comedy series *Goodness Gracious Me* and its successor, *The Kumars at No. 42*, to the films of Gurinder Chadha. Gilroy comments in particular on the role of lifestyle television in this context.

> Reality TV has unwittingly done a great deal to transmit the idea that racial and ethnic differences are unremarkable contingencies of social life. Instead of adding to the premium of race, viewers discover that in consumer culture the things that really divide them are much more profound: taste, lifestyle, leisure preferences, cleaning, gardening, and child care.

Changing Rooms, *Wife Swap*, and *Big Brother* reveal that what matters is how quickly your tasks are completed, how frequently you clean or redecorate your house, how often you chastise your children, and how much time you spend with your spouse. Alongside those habits, racial and ethnic differences appear mundane, even boring.[36]

An episode from the second series of *What Not to Wear* (2:3), which features a South Asian woman identified only as "Meeta," provides a good example of what Gilroy has in mind. Significantly, it is differences of class and taste, rather than race or ethnicity, that are the primary sources of conflict in the episode. While Meeta's cultural otherness is acknowledged (with references to saris and so forth), it is treated as purely incidental. Like most South Asians on British television, Meeta speaks apparently native English, while her accent connotes a regional British class identity (lower-middle-class, southern) rather than an Indian one. Just as the show's postfeminism has little time, it seems, for "boring" forms of political feminism, it takes a similarly no-nonsense approach to racial and cultural difference. Meeta is as British as the rest of us, the show seems to imply; as with postfeminism, the assumption is that we have somehow moved beyond the issue of racial and cultural politics. Another case in point was Woodall and Constantine's appearance on the 2004 Christmas special of *The Kumars at No. 42*, in which Sanjeev Bhaskar plays a South Asian amateur chat show host who interviews celebrities in his family's living room accompanied by his Indian grandmother and parents on the sofa. The guests themselves are iconically white British celebrities (Michael Parkinson, Patrick Stewart, Boy George), but what the show seems to be about is not so much a turning of the tables as the projection of a multicultural "conviviality," as Gilroy puts it, in which the imperial past, while continually acknowledged, is something we can now all poke good-natured fun at.

Theoretical discussions of governmentality have focused almost entirely on its workings in modern societies. The question of governance in postmodern societies, on the other hand, remains underexplored. It seems clear, nonetheless, that the pervasiveness of media representations takes on a far greater importance in this context, while the example of lifestyle television suggests that significant shifts have taken place in both the objectives and the strategies of governmentality and that the concept itself is in need of revision. At first sight, much of what Nikolas Rose writes about governmentality seems quite applicable to contemporary television.

Through self-reformation, therapy, techniques of body alteration, and the calculated reshaping of speech and emotion, we adjust ourselves by means of the techniques propounded by the experts of the soul. The government of the soul depends upon our recognition of ourselves as ideally and potentially certain sorts of person, the unease generated by a normative judgment of what we are and what we could become, and the incitement offered to overcome this discrepancy by following the advice of experts in the management of the self. The irony is that we believe, in making our subjectivity the principle of our personal lives, our ethical systems, and our political evaluations, that we are, freely, choosing our freedom.[37]

Rose's reference to "experts in the management of the self" clearly calls to mind the endless parade of experts across contemporary lifestyle channels.[38] Similarly, his discussion of the paradoxical "compulsory freedom" that governmentality requires of its subjects seems especially applicable to *What Not to Wear*. What the show seems to require of its subjects, indeed, is that they freely choose a new, postfeminist image *for themselves*, albeit within the prescribed guidelines. This is most clearly on view in the sequences in which the subject is provisionally "released" into retail stores to begin shopping for her new wardrobe under the watchful eye of the experts. The point, repeated ad nauseam, is that she has to learn to make the "right" choices *herself*. As the frequent interventions that are necessary make clear, this contradictory objective is by no means easy to achieve, but it remains the object of the exercise because it enables the subject's transformation to be presented as a *self*-transformation, freely accepted and undertaken, rather than a form of social discipline. Thus is governmentality able to erase its own operations in the freedom of its subjects.

Where lifestyle television problematizes Rose's model of governmentality is in the latter's characteristically modernist emphasis on interiority. Rose's primary historical concern is with the governance of the inner life, of what he calls the "soul," which later becomes the "psyche," and the transfer in jurisdiction over it, within Western modernity, from Christianity to the secular knowledge systems of the Enlightenment, notably the psychological sciences.[39] Clearly, much of contemporary television, from Channel 4's *Supernanny* to Dr. Phil (whose hectoring, tough-love style of therapy in many ways anticipates Trinny and Susannah's), can be seen as a continuation of this process of governing the self through the normative discourses of psychotherapy, but lifestyle television suggests that governmentality in its contemporary forms is no longer concerned just with the psychological domain. Theories of postmodernity and postmodernism have often emphasized their preoccupation with surfaces, coupled with a suspicion of the modernist privileging of depth over surface, reality over appearance. For Palmer, on the contrary, lifestyle shows such as *What Not to Wear*, bbc2's *Would Like to Meet . . .* , or the aptly titled *Faking It* are characterized by an emphasis on appearance as the basis of identity.

> Rather like the home transformations, the model being proposed here is that emphasis can and should be laid on the surface, on the *look*, for that is the dominant feature. A concern with style has become fundamental to who we are. In many senses it is what we are. In this information age appearance becomes precious while effective symbolism becomes priceless — you are what "you appear to be." The pain of transformation is worth it to feel better about "you."[40]

For all its rhetoric of interiority, *What Not to Wear* is preeminently about the production and management of appearances. This is not to posit the existence of a putatively real, authentic self *behind* the superficial mask of the fashion self. In the world of *What Not to Wear*, the goal is the externalization of a supposedly more authentic inner self: you *are* what you wear. Arguably, it is this that makes it possible for the show's participants to believe that they have "found" who they really are rather than accepting a prefabricated identity from outside. In such a world, where how we look is meant to define who we are, modernist distinctions between surface and depth, representation and reality, become increasingly blurred. The governance of postmodern subjectivities, then, no longer works — or at least no longer just works — at the interior level of the psyche; the management of appearance, whether that of the home or that of the body, becomes the key to maximizing consumption.

Writing on the continuing pervasiveness of psychological expertise in contemporary media, Rose suggests:

> On every subject from sexual satisfaction to career promotion, psychologists offer their advice and assistance both privately and through the press, radio, and television. The apostles of these techniques proffer images of what we could become, and we are urged to seek them out, to help fulfill the dream of realigning who we are with what we want to be. Our selves

are defined and constructed and governed in psychological terms, constantly subject to psychologically inspired techniques of self-inspection and self-examination. And the problems of defining and living a good life have been transposed from an ethical to a psychological register.[41]

While much of what Rose says is no doubt valid, it could be suggested that in the contemporary world what he here calls "defining and living a good life" has been increasingly taken up not just in a psychological but also in an aesthetic register. If in the world of religious belief the ethical domain is the principle of governmentality, and in the modern world of Enlightenment rationality the psychological, in the postmodern world the domain of aesthetics has become one of the primary arenas for postmodern forms of governmentality. The discourses of expertise deployed in *Changing Rooms*, *What Not to Wear*, or *Project Runway* are forms of aesthetic expertise; the new lifestyle experts are designers, journalists, or performers, certified by their professional training and experience in the artistic practices of the contemporary culture industries. In the face of such expertise, television seems to teach us, our only option is to listen humbly as our design skills, sense of style, or musical talents are scrutinized and dissected, our homes remodeled, our identities reformatted, and our intimate histories laid bare on back lawns for inspection, sorting, and disposal. Yet, as incontrovertible as it may seem, the authority of the lifestyle experts ultimately remains contingent on our assent and is therefore open to challenge. As Foucault reminds us, since governmentality depends on consent, the option always remains to throw off the selves that lifestyle television creates for us, to be who *we* want to be, to think for ourselves. For this reason, the most inspiring episodes of *What Not to Wear* are arguably those that feature the most strong-willed, confident subjects, who refuse to be intimidated and defend their personal taste under considerable pressure from the "experts."

Desperately Seeking Fashion

Feeling desperate? Watch Sundays starting July 17.

—BBC AMERICA WEB SITE AD FOR THE SERIES
FOOTBALLERS' WIVES

From Rosanna Arquette's portrayal of Roberta Glass in *Desperately Seeking Susan* (Seidelman, 1985) to the ABC series *Desperate Housewives* and the remake of *The Stepford Wives* (Oz, 2004), the figure of the desperate housewife is one of the most pervasive images of postmodern media culture. But, whereas the source of female desperation in these and similar examples is typically the suburban hell of bourgeois everyday life and the oppressiveness of patriarchal gender roles, the fourth season of *What Not to Wear* opened with a different kind of female desperation.

> In contrast to previous seasons, the girls no longer pounce on unsuspecting victims. Instead, crowds of female volunteers who are *desperate* for some style compete for the duo's brutally honest wardrobe dissection. . . . From hundreds of applicants eager for the girls' cruel-to-be-kind treatment, Trinny and Susannah meet with a select few to learn more about their daily challenges. Then they choose two of the most *desperate* cases for the complete *What Not To Wear* transformation. . . . With full access to the women's lives for a day, Trinny and Susannah visit their workplaces and homes and talk to their friends and family. (BBC America Web site, my italics)

The narrative here elaborates a recognizably postfeminist ideology of female emancipation through *embracing* bourgeois gender identities and the consumer culture that goes with them in contrast to the feminist rejection of them. Rather than having to be coerced into participating, it seems, the show's would-be participants are now *turning themselves in* to the authorities en masse. Correspondingly, the latter take on a less disciplinary, more nurturing role, visiting the workplaces and homes of their charges like the social workers created by the modern welfare state. Where the first three series placed the subject's home and workplace under video surveillance but confined their disciplinary practices to public spaces outside these, the fourth goes a step further, entering the home and workplace for extended periods as an ostensibly benign but potentially more controlling presence. Again the parallels with Foucault's history of policing and Rose's history of the strategies of governance of the modern state are all too obvious, but they should lead us to consider the degree to which contemporary reality and lifestyle television have taken on the role of policing identities and behavior and their success in reconfiguring these in accordance with the economic interests of neoliberal capitalism.[42]

For those who continue to believe in narratives of media manipulation and false consciousness, the developments outlined above may seem all too familiar if no less depressing. For followers of Bourdieu, they no doubt attest to the inexorable power of lifestyle media in securing the subservience of the lower classes to the symbolic authority of the socioeconomic elite and in reacquainting the habitus with the practice of consumption. For followers of Foucault, they may seem to suggest a similar ineluctability in the operations of governmentality. Before we fall into the gloom of a sociological fatalism, however, it is useful to remember that one of the most important flaws of Marxist media analysis, and in different ways of both Bourdieu and Foucault, is that of determinism and the failure of their theoretical models of power to account for the possibility of resistance. In contrast, Gramsci, de Certeau, and Hall have persuasively argued over recent decades that resistance is always possible, that no power can be absolute, and that all power is at best provisional and precarious. As we see time and time again in *What Not to Wear*, the imposition of the will of the authorities requires a constant, often wearisome struggle with the resistance or simply the inertia of their subjects and with little assurance of long-term effectiveness. From this perspective, the image of desperate housewives clamoring for the advice of the experts can be read as just another hegemonic strategy, a kind of propaganda or self-fulfilling prophecy (if this many people think the experts can help them, maybe you should too), or merely wish fulfillment — the media's dream of its own transformative power. Similarly, *What Not to Wear* and other shows that detail the media's magical powers of transformation arguably serve a primarily ritualistic purpose whose function is to convince their audiences (and, more to the point, sponsors and advertisers) that, as Gareth Palmer has suggested, they do actually *work* and *are* capable of producing substantial, lasting change in the everyday lives of their chosen subjects. Yet to date lifestyle television has produced little evidence that its transformative magic lasts any longer than the day on which it takes place. We can only speculate on how many women resume their former bad clothing habits, how many couples revert to the design of their former living rooms, and how quickly homes again fill up with clutter after the cameras have left. What we really need, of course, is a follow-up series depicting the subjects of such shows a week, a month, six months, a year, or five years after the makeover process, but to date lifestyle television has remained more interested in the quick fix than in documenting its own long-term effectiveness. The inertia of everyday life and the undertow of resistance, it would seem, are apparently less easy to overcome than the hosts of *What Not to Wear* and shows like it would have us believe.

Notes

1. On lifestyle television, see Brunsdon, "Lifestyling Britain"; Palmer, "The New You"; and Bell and Hollows, *Ordinary Lifestyles*. On the concept of lifestyle itself, see Chaney, *Lifestyles*.
2. Palmer, "The New You," 173.
3. Ibid., 184, 189.
4. Ibid.
5. Cited in ibid., 174.
6. Cited in ibid.
7. See Spigel, *Make Room for TV*.
8. Flocker, *The Metrosexual Guide to Style*; Hyman, *The Reluctant Metrosexual*.
9. Moseley, "Makeover Takeover on British Television."
10. Foucault, "Governmentality." For a useful overview of the concept of governmentality and its application across a variety of disciplines in the social sciences, see Mitchell, *Governmentality*.
11. See Miller, *The Well-Tempered Self*; Burchell, Gordon, and Miller, *The Foucault Effect*; and Bratich, Packer, and McCarthy, *Foucault, Cultural Studies, and Governmentality*.
12. Palmer, "*Big Brother*"; Palmer, *Discipline and Liberty*; Palmer, "The New You"; Ouellette, "Take Responsibility for Yourself."
13. Rose, *Governing the Soul*; "Assembling the Modern Self"; *Powers of Freedom*.
14. Rose, *Governing the Soul*, 3.
15. For more on the relationship between psychotherapy and the pharmaceutical industry, see Rose, "Neurochemical Selves."
16. Rose has surprisingly little to say on this subject. Curiously for a work published as recently as 1990, his *Governing the Soul* does not include television among its index listings (although it does list the telegraph). References to film and television, whose role in the governance of the modern self arguably extends from the Mass Observation project in 1930s Britain to contemporary reality shows, are few and far between, and where television is mentioned at all it appears either entirely undifferentiated or in generic allusions to "soap operas" or "talk shows." On Mass Observation, see Highmore, "Mass Observation."
17. A good place to start is the gendered nature of the field itself: the literature on governmentality is overwhelmingly male dominated, and, while a few of the authors of contributions to the existing anthologies are female, the only article that directly considers governmentality in relation to gender is Lisa King's "Subjectivity as Identity: Gender through the Lens of Foucault." Mitchell Dean's introductory study, *Governmentality: Power and Rule in Modern Society*, does not address questions of gender difference in governmentality, and its index includes no listings under "gender," "women," or "feminism." While I am unable to speculate here on the reasons for this state of affairs, there is clearly a need for further consideration of the

place of gender in governmentality and vice versa, to which this essay is also in part addressed.

18. Woodall and Constantine, *What Not to Wear*; *What Not to Wear: For Every Occasion*; *Trinny and Susannah: The Rules*, DVD (Video Collection International, 2003); *What Not to Wear: The Rules*; *What You Wear Can Change Your Life*; *What Your Clothes Say about You*.

19. Woodall and Constantine began their collaboration in a regular "Ready to Wear" section of the *Daily Telegraph*'s weekend edition, which resulted in their first book, *Ready 2 Dress: How To Have Style without Following Fashion*, and an ill-fated Web site, Ready2Wear.com. For an overview of the background to *What Not to Wear*, see Merritt, "Yes, Your Bum Looks Big in That . . ."

20. The American *What Not to Wear* is culturally very different from the BBC show, not least because the show's style "gurus" (as they are called), Stacy London and Clinton Kelly (Wayne Scott Lukas in the first season), and their assistants take a kinder, gentler approach than their authoritarian British counterparts do. A comparison of the cultural differences between the more collaborative, team-oriented American show and its British model would no doubt be interesting but is beyond the scope of this essay. The hour-long length of the American show's episodes, in contrast to the half-hour format of the BBC show, also produces a more leisurely (if tedious) pace.

21. Like the cultural studies literature on lifestyle television in general, analyses of *What Not to Wear* have relied heavily on Bourdieu. See Gareth Palmer's discussion of the show in "The New You" (182–85); Angela McRobbie's "Extended Notes" on *What Not to Wear*, which accompanies her chapter on Bourdieu in *The Uses of Cultural Studies*; and her "Notes on *What Not to Wear* and Post-feminist Symbolic Violence." McRobbie's argument that the show is about inflicting symbolic violence to bring it back into line with the functional requirements of a consumer-based economy is quite similar to my arguments about governmentality, albeit using a different theoretical idiom.

22. Palmer, "The New You."

23. Couldry, *Media Rituals*, 112–13.

24. The use of the female pronoun here is deliberate. The victim in most cases is female, although some episodes in later series feature men and male fashion, which I will be discussing later.

25. Palmer, "The New You," 185.

26. Barthes, *Système de la mode*.

27. Woodall and Constantine, *What Not to Wear*, 7.

28. Ibid., 51.

29. Elliott, *Better Than Well*. See, in particular, the second chapter, "The True Self" (28–53).

30. See ibid. (chap. 2) on how users of drugs such as Prozac experience their emotional transformation as the discovery of who they "really" are.

31. See, for example, Elliott's astonishing chapter on voluntary limb amputation ("Amputees by Choice," ibid., chap. 9, 208–36).

32. Both have since given birth, Susannah Constantine to her third child and Trinny Woodall to her first (Erin Oates, BBC America forum, www.bbcamerica.com, 22 October 2002).

33. The Baddiel episode concludes with a strangely eulogistic photographic homage to the "Seven Tribes of Man."

34. Creeber, "Hideously White."

35. Gilroy, "From a Colonial Past to a New Multiculturalism." See also his *After Empire*. I am grateful to Diane Negra for bringing the article to my attention.

36. Gilroy, "From a Colonial Past to a New Multiculturalism."

37. Rose, *Governing the Soul*, 10–11.

38. So institutionalized has the television lifestyle expert become that s/he has recently (and perhaps inevitably) been transformed into camp in the form of the Style Network's Brini Maxwell, a drag queen whose deadpan delivery spoofs contemporary nostalgia for 1960s "retro" style with the earnestness of Martha Stewart.

39. Rose's preoccupation with psychological depth still seems tied to an essentially literary model of selfhood rooted in the nineteenth-century realist novel rather than the relentless superficiality of the contemporary image world.

40. Palmer, "The New You," 184.

41. Rose, *Governing the Soul*, 10–11.

42. See Foucault, *Discipline and Punish*.

Kimberly Springer

10 Divas, Evil Black Bitches, and Bitter Black Women

AFRICAN AMERICAN WOMEN IN POSTFEMINIST AND POST-CIVIL-RIGHTS POPULAR CULTURE

Much of feminist theory recognizes the contributions of women of color, particularly 1980s and 1990s demands for attention to intersectionality as fundamental to social, political, economic, and cultural transformation. To date, studies of postfeminism have studiously noted that many of its icons are white and cited the absence of women of color, but the analysis seems to stop there. Whiteness studies, a field that started with such a bang, appears to have dwindled to a whimper when it comes to thinking about how, say, Miranda, Carrie, Samantha, and Charlotte exact racial privilege while they have their sex in the city. The arrival of postfeminist discourse in popular culture, especially, needs to be interrogated about how race is always present. Even when they are not on the screen, women of color are present as the counterpart against which white women's ways of being—from Bridget Jones to Ally McBeal to Carrie Bradshaw—are defined and refined. Although there are black women in successful business, intellectual, and cultural industries, there are also, critically, not so new manifestations of racism and sexism impacting black women in popular culture.

This essay attempts to examine both African American women's presence and absence in postfeminist manifestations of popular culture. Some critics believe that we must expand campaigns for representational inclusivity to address underlying industrial practices, particularly given the expansion of culture industries from nationally owned entities (e.g., the Big Three networks, ABC, NBC, and CBS) into the global market (e.g., Viacom, NewsCorp, and Vivendi).[1] Undoubtedly the ability of business to capitalize on niche markets continues to evolve beyond American borders. Susan J. Douglas draws our attention to the political stakes of postfeminist culture, noting that "the seemingly most banal or innocent or peripheral media fare play a central, crucial role in the weekly and monthly engineering of consent around an acceptance of postfeminism as the only possible subjective stand and political position for women to inhabit in the early twenty-first century."[2] Seemingly harmless cultural representations of black women are incorporated into institutional enactments of discrimination, including racist, sexist, classist, and heterosexist social policies. My analysis situates postfeminist and post-civil-rights discourses as retrograde and contrary to the interests of women in general and black women specifically. The potential political implications of these two discourses for popular culture pick up where misogynistic and racist stereotypes, often now implicit, left off, taking them to a new level of identity construction.

Integrating Multiple "Post-" Positions: Postfeminism and Post–Civil Rights

Examinations of postfeminism have defined it as a cultural and political move against feminism and contrary to the goals of the women's movement.[3] It is also emerging that postfeminism includes claims of feminism's demise and accusations that feminism is antisex.[4] Based on content analysis of ninety popular and academic sources, Elaine J. Hall and Marnie Salupo Rodriguez established the following four claims as central to postfeminism: support for feminism decreased from 1980 to 1990; antifeminism has increased among young women, women of color, and full-time homemakers; feminism is irrelevant because it has successfully achieved equality for young women, who feel they experience only personal, not institutional, sexism; and women who agree with feminist ideals of equality may refuse to claim a feminist identity.[5] They then surveyed public opinion polls to test these claims, finding that: levels of support increased or remained stable from the late 1980s to the early 1990s; women of color and young adults view the women's movement favorably while homemakers did appear disinclined toward feminism; from 1980 to 1999, half of their respondents considered the women's movement still relevant; and the "I'm not a feminist but . . ." position was prevalent, with the potential to depoliticize feminism.[6]

These findings and emerging definitions indicate, more generally, a back-lash against the gains and goals of feminism defined broadly as solely rooted in a liberal, pluralist, feminist framework of equality. Amber Kinser, in her exploration of third-wave feminism, observes that today's young women live in a world where, curiously, "feminist *language* is part of the public dialogue, but authentic feminist *struggles* are not accounted for in that dialogue except in terms articulated by the mainstream, which still perpetuates a conservative and sexist status quo."[7] This distinction between language and struggle is crucial because it is this difference that allows postfeminism, perhaps more insidiously than antifeminism, to appropriate feminist language and exploit liberal feminism's key weakness, namely, a call for equality without includ-ing racial analysis. Liberal feminism and postfeminism exclude revolutionary visions of feminism that continue to ask the question "equal to what?" Femi-nists of color long maintained that being equal to men of color, who experi-ence disproportionate incarceration compared to white men, more unem-ployment, and so on, would mean merely a different kind of oppression. Why would women choose this capitalist fantasy of equality when the reality in-cludes further gender segregation in the burgeoning American service econ-omy, the rapid rise of women of color as incarcerated labor, and the closing of the welfare state? Instead, they argue that feminism needs to fight for radical social transformation, particularly in the United States, where equality dis-course is rooted in a founding national document crafted by slaveholders and begins with the words "all [white] men are created equal."

It is on this basis that I would expose postfeminism's racial agenda. Post-feminism seeks to erase any progress toward racial inclusion that feminism has made since the 1980s. It does so by making racial difference, like femi-nism itself, merely another commodity for consumption. Amber Kinser remarks, "Part of the genius of postfeminism is to co-opt the language of feminism and then attach it to some kind of consumer behavior that feeds young people's hunger for uniqueness."[8] Similarly, postfeminism takes demands for racial inclusion on the feminist agenda and makes race consumable in the form of "ethnic" clothing, mainstreaming the fetishization of a "big, black booty," promoting year-round "bronzed" (brown) skin, and encouraging consumption of fair trade goods without questioning the conflation of commerce and democracy. Racialized postfeminism does not move very far from bell hooks's assertion that particular forms of cultural engagement merely amount to "eating the other": a "commodification of otherness" in which "ethnicity becomes spice, seasoning that can liven up the dull dish that is mainstream white culture."[9]

As Imelda Whelehan notes, control became a catchphrase of one 1990s manifestation of postfeminism, power feminism, but this control "always seemed to be about the right to consume and display oneself to best effect, not about empowerment in the worlds of work, politics, or even the home."[10] Women could once again be universalized under the assumption that they all want to "have it all." If, as Diane Negra maintains, "One of the key premises in current antifeminist postfeminist constructions of women's life choices . . . is the need to abandon the overly-ambitious 1980s program of 'having it all,'" does this apply across racial categories?[11] The discourse of having it all has always been a bit lost on black women and anathema to black feminism, which aimed, in the 1970s, to dismantle the idea that black women could be superwomen. The icon of the black superwoman or strongblackwoman is not the racialized equivalent of having it all.[12] Having it all discourse implies that women are lacking something that they need to go out and get: career and family. Superwoman/strongblackwoman discourse assumes that a black woman has *too many obligations* but she is expected to *handle her business*. Thus, while postfeminism proposes that white women cannot have it all, racialized postfeminism, at least for black women, means continuing to be everything for everyone else *and* maintaining a sense of self. Postfeminism, though, has begun to assimilate black women into the rhetoric of having it all. For instance, Veronica Chambers's *Having It All? Black Women and Success* accepts the terms of the having it all conceptualization and reflects a postfeminist vision of middle-class and aspiring upper-class black women's lives. This vision treads a perilous line of a depoliticized *black* postfeminism, calling on black feminist theorists such as bell hooks and incorporating paragons of white beauty such as Audrey Hepburn and Grace Kelly. While I am not implying that black women can only look to black women for inspiration, the reliance on staple icons such as Kelly and Hepburn does not advance black feminist calls, and feminist calls generally, for seeking out role models that do not fit into postfeminism's version of white, upper-class, slim, and traditionally attractive femininity.

In addition to postfeminism, there is another "post" to be reckoned with in this essay: post–civil rights. As part of a racialized discourse, one must grapple with postfeminism's place in the post-civil-rights era. Like critiques that expose the postfeminist fallacy that all of feminism's goals have been achieved, therefore rendering the women's movement unnecessary, post-civil-rights language would seem to imply that the goals of the civil rights movement were achieved starting with the Supreme Court desegregation legislation in *Brown v. Board of Education* (1954), extending through the passage of the Civil Rights Act (1964), and ending with the rise of a significant black middle class in the 1980s. However, it is more accurate to conceptualize post-civil-rights discourse as a commentary on the drastic rollbacks, or, to be consistent with criticisms of postfeminism, backlash, against the achievements of the civil rights movement. Patricia Hill Collins outlines the contours of that backlash against efforts to dismantle institutional racism: "In the 1980s, Republican administrations set about dismantling enforcement efforts for equal opportunity, cutting funding for urban programs, incarcerating growing numbers of African Americans in the burgeoning prison industry, shrinking the social welfare budget through punitive measures, and endorsing historical labor market patterns."[13] The Clinton administration's dismantling of the welfare system, shifting from Aid to Families with Dependent Children to state-administered welfare-to-work programs, and the second Bush administration's aggressive stance against affirmative action fall well within the definition of a countermovement to a progressive agenda of racial equality.

The social counterpart to institutional post-civil-rights racism was the welfare queen. Poor black women were vilified as mammies and jezebels under slavery and again in the 1970s as matriarchs destroying the black community with their female-headed households and playing the welfare system for undue gain.[14] The 1980s welfare queen image implied that black women not only cheated the system but also lived extravagantly on the proceeds. Integrally tied to reproduction, the welfare queen's trump card lay in her alleged disregard for birth control and propensity for having more children than she could afford. In its most perverse transformation yet, racist ideology maintained that, while white slave masters no longer profited from black women's offspring, black women now claimed public tax dollars for their profligacy. The incongruity of a black woman living the high life in some of the worst public housing in the world was lost on fiscally conservative American taxpayers. Welfare queen iconography remained solidly prevalent until the Clinton administration ended additional benefits for additional children. While it was not completely eradicated, the image of the welfare queen morphed into that of the crack-addicted mother, who became a mainstay of late 1980s and 1990s political rhetoric linking race and gender to the war on drugs.

Black women, the subject of racially gendered prejudices from the antebellum period through the 1980s, faced the iconography of the mammy, the jezebel, the sapphire, the matriarch, the welfare queen, and the crack-addicted mother in popular culture and social policy. As I have indicated, these stereotypes still exist, but they have also morphed into new ones more appropriate to the postfeminist, post-civil-rights era. If we are beyond discriminatory behavior, how do we account for the diva, black lady, and angry black woman images that populate the current cultural landscape?

The remainder of this essay explores representations of black women in selected television programs and films. The range of texts discussed here is by no means comprehensive, but it is meant to provide a general theory of black femininity within postfeminist and post-civil-rights discourses and illustrate examples of backlash representation.[15] Starting with popular culture more generally, I tackle the usage of the term *diva* as it relates to black women and consider what it has come to signify about "black women with attitude." I also note Patricia Hill Collins's theorizing on the black lady and modern mammy images in popular culture representations. Both in political life and on television, the modern mammy and black lady maintain a striking convergence whether found in the White House or on our television screens. Next I analyze reality television's often *unreal* depictions of black women and responses to these sexist and racist evocations of black womanhood. Finally, I examine postfeminism and films of the post-civil-rights era about black women and their contradictory messages about black women's race, gender, and class. *Waiting to Exhale* (1995), *Down in the Delta* (1998), and *Diary of a Mad Black Woman* (2005) offer fruitful areas of inquiry for locating postfeminism's racialized agenda.

Deploy the Diva!

Much like other stereotypes bestowed on African American women, the journey of the appellation *diva* is undertheorized and begs the question of how the term changed from denoting a heralded opera singer to its late-twentieth-century embodiment: a powerful and entertaining, if pushy and bitchy, woman. In thinking about how a label once applied to Maria Callas is now applied to Mariah Carey, we need to ask how the diva fits into the postfeminist, post-civil-rights agenda.

The association of the diva with singers has continued but recently changed genres. Hypothetically speaking, it is possible that a film facilitated the term's crossover from opera to R & B to hip hop. The French film *Diva* (1981) is structured around a twisting plot that was meant as a tribute to the French New Wave. The diva in question is Cynthia Hawkins (Wilhemina Wiggins-Fernandez), a reclusive black American opera singer who refuses to be recorded. A fan records one of her performances, setting off a stylized thriller with a number of interested parties all chasing after the same bootleg tape for various reasons—from adoration to criminal intent. For a generation of college-attending third-wave feminists, women and men, the film is a cult classic, with the diva, even as a recluse, driving the film's action.

If we also consider the career of another soprano, we can begin to make the leap from the black opera singer to the black R & B singer. Diana Ross was preceded by a number of talented black women singers who commanded respect in their own ways, but it was Ross who owned the 1960s and 1970s with her music and films. Topping the charts with the Supremes, she was an integral part of the distinct Motown sound. Although there were three group members, who all signed with Motown in 1961, in 1964 the record label head, Berry Gordy, designated Ross the permanent lead singer of the group—a move that generated ten number-one hit singles, making the Supremes the most successful black group of the 1960s. Notably, in 1967 the group was renamed Diana Ross and the Supremes, highlighting Ross's central role and creating tensions in the group that are still commented on whenever there is talk of a reunion.

Ross left the Supremes behind and embarked on a solo singing career in 1970. It got off to a rough start until Gordy and Motown's new film production unit showcased Ross as Billie Holiday in *Lady Sings the Blues* (1972). This garnered Ross an Academy Award nomination for Best Actress, and she won a Golden Globe award for Best Newcomer. With this new cachet and a stunning soundtrack of Billie Holiday cover songs behind her, Ross received another Oscar nomination for her glamorous role as a poor project girl turned supermodel in *Mahogany* (1975). It is no wonder that she ended the decade with a critically acclaimed 1979 album appropriately titled *The Boss*.

I highlight Ross as the focus of the transition of the term *diva* from opera to R & B because in her life (at least the media-generated one), her music, and her films she became the template for contemporary notions of the diva as immensely talented but selfishly driven and difficult to deal with. It is hard to separate legend from fact, but with her ascension from group singer to lead singer in the Supremes and the larger than life aspects of her film roles it is nearly impossible to tell the difference between Diana and the Diva. Then and now, although she is still considered the Boss and a diva, her reported behavior demonstrates the dual nature of divadom. She inappropriately touched the rapper Lil' Kim's already exposed breast at the 1999 MTV Video Music Awards. At London Heathrow Airport, she vehemently opposed an airport body search she found intrusive by grabbing the security guard's breast. Convicted for drunk driving in 2004, Ross served only a fraction of her time because it was alleged that a guard let her have the run of the prison. Her later antics only fueled her reputation as a diva and facilitated the continued (d)evolution of the term.

Just as the diva label is bestowed, women and some gay men claim to be divas as an honorific. A 2002 review of *Cry*, an album by the country artist Faith Hill, in *Time* magazine opined, "By definition, a diva is a rampaging female ego redeemed only in part by a lovely voice. It's hard to imagine why anyone would want to be one, but a new generation of female talent appears to be weirdly enamored of the word and the idea."[16] And, indeed, this was true when the adult video music channel VH1 launched its series of *Divas* concerts in 1999. Linking high glamour and a revue format to a charitable cause, VH1 capitalized, if not spearheaded, the latest incarnation of the cult of celebrity by designating new divas for each show. The first concert, *Divas Live*, featured Celine Dion (the romantic diva), Gloria Estefan (the Latina diva), Shania Twain (the pop-country diva), Mariah Carey (the R & B diva), Aretha Franklin (the truly talented diva), and special guest Carole King (the singer-songwriter diva).

Each successive *Divas* concert has followed this generational pattern: lesser-talented diva wannabes supported by genuinely talented, older women who have both style *and* substance. One might argue that truly talented women do not need pop culture entities such as vh1 to certify their abilities, nor do they feel the need to proclaim their greatness. This distinction and that between generations is evident in the number of older female singers who decline the diva label. The Motown hit maker and singer Gladys Knight insisted, "Don't call me diva. Diva has become something else now. Now they're throwing the word around. It's supposed to mean some kind of grandeur and that kind of stuff, but some of these people who they call divas have not been here long enough anyway. No, don't call me diva. I'm just here to sing. . . . I am not all that. And when I start thinking that it's me, then I get into trouble. It's not about me."[17]

In a post-civil-rights and postfeminist context, the diva label would appear to be a dubious homage. Today's divas are unreasonable, unpredictable, and likely unhinged. When a woman is called a diva or accused of exhibiting diva behavior, she is usually a woman of color. Jennifer Lopez's extravagant on-set demands; Mariah Carey's highly publicized, if disputed, nervous breakdown; Mary J. Blige's early reputation as a drink- and drugs-fuelled hellion; Whitney Houston's erratic behavior in private and in an interview with abc's Diane Sawyer; constant attempts to compare the contemporary pop group Destiny's Child (especially the group's early lineup upheavals) with the Supremes, including casting Beyonce Knowles in the film version (2006) of the Broadway tribute to Diana Ross and the Supremes, *Dreamgirls*—these incidents are regularly featured in celebrity news venues as evidence of a woman whose financial success has yielded excess. Clearly, the line of postfeminist reasoning would go, these women do not know how to be humble about their talents and use them in the service of others. While a tug-of-war over the empowering or negative connotations of divadom might be fought, it seems the label is ultimately just another form of categorization that classes women according to how well they adhere to race, class, and sexuality norms.

Black Ladies and Modern Mammies

In an "In Focus" section of *Cinema Journal*, Yvonne Tasker and Diane Negra observe, "Within contemporary popular culture, it is clear that certain kinds of female agency are recognizably and profitably packaged as commodities.

Typically, texts of this form are directed at a female audience even while covertly acknowledging male viewers/voyeurs."[18] They go on to note the ways in which postfeminism operates on the basis of inclusion and exclusion, all the while assuming gender equality that allows for politically decontextualized racial and ethnic diversity. Much like early feminist generalizations, postfeminism assumes a universal category of women—or so it would seem. I maintain, however, that popular culture narrowcasts its representations of women to appeal to audience segments. In other words, racial and gender stereotypes are the commodity and discourse that make difference legible in popular culture.

The image of the angry black woman has always been present on television, particularly in the form of a mouthy harpy. Media critics and African American historians duly note the image of the nurturing mammy, the loud-mouthed Sapphire, and the oversexed Jezebel as staples of television genres from situation comedies to family dramas to comedy sketch programs.[19] Thus, reality TV adopted this stereotype rather than originating it. In the post-civil-rights era, and with the rise of a black middle class, Collins believes we now have cultural representations and stereotypes of black women stratified by class. If poor and working-class women are defined as bitchy, promiscuous, and overly fertile, these "controlling images . . . become texts of what *not* to be."[20]

Becoming middle class, then, relies on a politics of respectability.[21] Echoing ancestral mandates passed down from the nineteenth century, black professional women must adhere to the role of the black lady, a role designed to counter accusations of black female licentiousness and one that can accommodate the ascension to middle-class status through work outside the home. Since black women were, and continue to be, necessary to the workforce, postfeminist representations make it clear that "they cannot achieve the status of lady by withdrawing from the workforce" like white women.[22] An enduring example of the black lady is Clair Huxtable, the upper-middle-class wife, mother, daughter, and lawyer of the most successful post-civil-rights black television show, the *Cosby Show* (1984–92). As she was never shown at work like her husband, Heathcliff, Clair's skills as a lawyer usually only emerged in her approach to mediating her children's squabbles. In an effort to maintain the black lady's status, Collins claims, "the image of Mammy, the loyal female servant created under chattel slavery, has been resurrected and modernized as a template for middle-class Black womanhood. Maneuvering through this image of the modern mammy requires a delicate balance between being appropriately subordinate to White and/or male authority yet maintaining a level of ambition and aggressiveness needed for achievement in middle-class occupations."[23]

George Walker Bush's secretary of state, Condoleezza Rice, is the real life example of the black lady. Disavowing affirmative action, claiming success solely based on merit, and determinedly asexual, Rice epitomizes the black professional lady at the height of her success. As the highest-ranking African American woman ever to serve in a presidential administration, Rice attempts to, paradoxically, depoliticize her presence there as a political actor. Narratives of her Birmingham, Alabama, childhood and current success are consistently separated from the struggle for civil rights. She insists on a personal and family history of self-reliance but denies privileges derived from black liberation struggles that accrued to a small but emerging black middle class long before the Cosbys.

Rice embodies postfeminist and post-civil-rights discourses in her adamant adherence to the conservative Republican Party values of individual achievement and empowerment through money. To date, one of the most revealing and extensive articles on her attitudes appeared in the 9 September 2001 issue of the *Washington Post Magazine*. In the article, Rice is reported to have said that in her family "liberation came not through a movement but from generations of ancestors navigating oppression with individual will, wits and, eventually, wallets—long before King or the federal government took up the cause. It is one of her frustrations," the article continues, "that people routinely assume she was beaten down or deprived as a child until the civil rights movement arrived. 'My family is third-generation college-educated,' she says with proud defiance. 'I should've gotten to where I am.'"[24] In Rice's logic, those who are part of America's underclass are undeserving, but her achievements are based solely on merit. Hers is a post-civil-rights mentality conditioned by defensiveness against affirmative action and rewarded for maintaining the privileges of the meritocracy.

As a high-ranking woman, Rice's sexuality has also fallen under scrutiny. In the modern mammy role, it is assumed that Rice is asexual, as would be appropriate for a woman of her rank in a presidential administration. Neither the mammy nor the black lady are thought of as sexual or having sex, but

Rice poses a conflicted dilemma for leftists who pride themselves on their antiracism and antisexism. Previously advocating positions that argue against assumptions about black women's sexuality as licentious, supposedly progressive activists and thinkers will not hesitate to make unseemly comments about Rice's sexuality. Just as Anita Hill's single status and sexual harassment claims against Clarence Thomas were pathologized as "erotomania," speculation about Rice ranges from accusations of lesbianism to innuendo that she has an intimate relationship with George W. Bush. In November 2004, the British newspaper the *Guardian* made these observations.

> As national security adviser for four years, Ms Rice has been indispensable and constantly available. She has no other life, has never married and a handful of dates with eligible men organised by well-meaning friends have led nowhere romantically.

> She spends many of her weekends at Camp David with the president, watching baseball and football and doing jigsaws with the first family. Her only time off appears to be occasional sessions playing the piano with a classical music group in Washington.

> At a dinner party with some senior journalists in spring this year, her dedication was revealed in an extraordinary Freudian slip. "As I was telling my husb-" she blurted, before correcting herself. "As I was telling President Bush."

> It says a lot about the prim reputation of both that hardly anyone in gossip-ridden Washington interpreted the slip as a sign of a romantic connection.

The Washington newspapers and blogs may have steered clear of interpreting Rice's slip of the tongue, but black liberal news sources ran with it. The Web site BlackCommentator.com was already deriding Rice as "The Borg Queen" and ran a controversial cartoon in 2003 that implied that she, in addition to being a gatekeeper, might have a more intimate relationship with the president.

The most notable black liberal ire toward Rice was exhibited in a series of cartoons by Aaron McGruder that ran in November 2004. The strip in essence contends that perhaps if Rice got some "good old fashioned lovin'" she would not be "hell-bent" on destroying the world. Possible suitors included Darth Vader as the one man in the universe who Rice might find compatible.

It is noteworthy that black men generated both depictions of Rice; black women academics and activists have been notably silent about her. Their views echo those in e-mail discussion groups and blogs contending that Rice, like Clarence Thomas, is a sell-out to African Americans. Interestingly, though, it is somehow considered just to raise Rice's sexuality as a rationale for her conservative politics. She either simply needs to get laid or, because she is an unmarried, successful woman in highly male echelons, she is a lesbian. In this postfeminist, post-civil-rights era, Rice is in a no-win situation: in the eyes of conservatives, she is totally devoid of sexuality, as a black lady should be; to liberals, she is a modern mammy (i.e., a race traitor à la Sally Hemings, an unfortunate spinster, or a lesbian).

Rice poses a dilemma in that her achievements are consistently linked to a conservative agenda for which she appears to be but a prop. Indeed, her position in the most powerful government in the world is impressive, particularly as she grew up in the midst of racist violence. And yet, when contextualized in the prevalent stereotypes of the day, it is difficult, if nearly impossible, to view Rice as a success of the feminist and civil rights movements. And she would not want that. Instead, she embraces ideologies that claim the end of racism and sexism. While she may not want to be a representative of black achievement, she enables postfeminist and post-civil-rights agendas by serving as both the good black lady and the modern mammy.

Collins cites *Law and Order*'s police lieutenant, Anita Van Buren, and *The District*'s Ella Farmer as examples of television characters that, while respectable, cannot evade the strictures of the modern mammy and the black lady. They may face sexist and racist discrimination, but "they both remain loyal to social institutions of law and order that are run by White men."[25] The same assertion is one possible explanation for the ubiquity of black female judges in television crime dramas. Failing to accurately represent the number of black women in the legal profession or the disproportionate rise in the number of black female inmates, and perhaps fearful of accusations of racism, black lady judges are preferable to 1970s and 1980s representations of black women as prostitutes or drug addicts in television courtrooms.[26]

The Editing Made Me Do It! The Evil Black Woman

> If you've ever seen a reality TV show, chances are you've seen her: a perpetually perturbed tooth-sucking, eye-rolling, finger-wagging harpy, creating confrontations in her wake and perceiving racial slights from the flimsiest provocations. At the very sight of her, her cast mates tremble in fear. And no wonder. She's the Sista With an Attitude.[27]

Reality TV "is a catch-all term, a convenient shorthand for many kinds of television."[28] This genre, borrowing the situationist approach from psychology and applying it to television ("what would happen if . . . ?"), includes programs that film people in everyday situations, in unusual situations, in game show competitions, on talk shows, and in docusoaps. What all these formats have in common is "the comprehensive monitoring of the unscripted rhythms of daily life" for both advertiser and audience consumption.[29] And just as reality TV is a catchall, its modes of operation, including casting, are a catchall for socially constructed identities.

Media critics, reality television aficionados, producers, and especially participants in the genre all acknowledge the stock trade in two-dimensional representation. Reality TV shows are not far removed from unsupervised social psychology experiments that create controlled environments using identity as mere prop.[30] Writing for the *Washington Post*, in an article entitled "The Evil Sista of Reality Television" Teresa Wiltz notes the use of "recognizable stereotypes" as "visual shorthand" in the genre.[31] In "Race and Reality . . . TV," the media critic L. S. Kim observes that, while there may be more "characters" of color than ever before on television due to the reality genre, editing creates "characters in what can best be described as an 'ensemble cast.'"[32] Omarosa Manigault-Stallworth explains, "Minorities have historically been portrayed negatively on reality TV. . . . These types of show thrive off of portrayals that tap into preconceived stereotypes about minorities (i.e. that we are lazy, dishonest and hostile). Reality TV's 'angry black woman' portrayal strikes again!"[33]

And Manigault-Stallworth should know. In 2004, she became the most infamous black woman on television. For viewers of Donald Trump's reality series *The Apprentice*, Manigault-Stallworth epitomized the angry black woman, the evil black bitch, and every other variation on that particular racist and sexist theme. During her tenure on the show in its first season, and after she was "fired" as a Trump apprentice, she was (and continues to be) vilified as difficult, lazy, obstructive, manipulative, and unnecessarily hostile to her fellow contestants.

Commensurate with Collins's update of stereotypes of black womanhood, in unscripted programming Manigault-Stallworth fell afoul of scripts for black female behavior. She was *The Apprentice*'s antiblack lady. She failed to be the modern mammy. She "played the race card" when she took offense at another cast member telling her "that's calling the kettle black." She was less than nurturing to other women on the show. She appeared to intentionally sabotage the efforts of the other African American, Kwame Jackson, participating in the show. Although Jackson came in as runner-up at the end of the competition, Manigault-Stallworth's actions played into divisive perceptions of a black woman trying to hold a black man back. She even beat out Paris Hilton for the title "Most Appalling Reality Show Star of the 2003–2004 Season."[34]

Trump offered contradictory assessments of Manigault-Stallworth. On the show, he berated her: "You were rude. You *are* rude. I've seen it. . . . It was very repulsive to me."[35] Yet, in an interview with the infotainment program *Extra*, Trump was bewildered, stating, "Omarosa is very smart. She's very beautiful, and she's got an attitude and some of the women have gotten to just hate her. The level of hatred for Omarosa is so unbelievable that I've never seen anything like it."[36] Manigault-Stallworth confounded reality TV's visual codes for women in general and for black women specifically. She's beautiful, but beautiful women are supposed to be dumb. For a man, a take-no-prisoners attitude in business would usually be just the thing he needs to succeed in the cutthroat corporate world, but a black woman with attitude has no place in Trump's or any other white-dominated institution. Both her supposed attitude and her uncompromising nature canceled out any black lady or modern mammy roles she might have assumed.

Manigault-Stallworth held her own during an appearance on *Dr. Phil*.[37] Dr. Phil McGraw, a clinical psychologist, met Oprah Winfrey while running a business that focused on providing trial lawyers with psychological expertise for mock trials and jury selection. He soon became a regular fixture on *Oprah*, known for his straight-talking, Texan manner. With his catchphrase "Get real," he launched his own advice talk show in 2002 and took on both

Manigault-Stallworth and Donald Trump in May 2005. During the broadcast, Manigault-Stallworth admitted to both playing to the cameras ("I quickly learned that as a black woman on reality television, if you want to get camera time, then you've got to be quite naughty. I knew that if I was naughty, I could certainly dominate most of the show, and I did. Guilty as charged!") and being manipulated by the editing process ("The Omarosa that America saw is a character. Out of every three hundred minutes that they shot, there was only one minute that the American people saw. You don't see the manipulation behind the scenes. You don't see a systematic pattern of how they portray people. I am cast on these shows to be naughty."). Dr. Phil accused her of complaining and being a victim, but Manigault-Stallworth characterized her experience as research and critical analysis. She readily accepted partial responsibility for her actions but only as the performance of a preexisting role. Her position is a conflicted one that is mired in "the pornography of the performing self."[38] She raises objections to a double standard that paints her and other black women as liars and bitches, but white contestants as smart and shrewd. Yet her concerns are less tailored toward fair representation than they are focused on how those projections impact her fiscal bottom line.

Audiences and critics are attuned to producers' and show participants' motivations, but that does not make them more accepting of the prejudices perpetuated. After a week of racist slights—from the overt to the covert—a student press writer, Melanie Sims, in a review of reality TV imagines she is being stalked by television producers with hidden cameras intent on catching her out "finger-wagging, neck-popping, eye-rolling, [and] disgruntled."[39] She refuses to play this role, saying, "The EBW [evil black woman] is a persona—not a person. For as much as she is respected, she is vilified. She represents only a fraction of the black female consciousness and even less of the black female population as a whole. Reality TV's angry black woman is merely a product of selective studio editing."[40]

But how much can we blame on the editing? Camille McDonald, a contestant in series two of *America's Next Top Model*, claimed that her perceived arrogance, petulance, discord with other contestants, and rudeness was "a media created, or media infused personality due to editing."[41] This disclaimer has become a standard one regardless of identity for reality TV show participants and might be evidence of a widespread postmodern sensibility about constructions of truth and reality. To blame the editing avoids directly accusing television producers of manipulation, absolves reality TV show participants of accountability for their actions, and keeps them in the good graces of producers, who might want to use them in yet another reality TV series.

Yet, in a moment of candor, McDonald admits, "It's a reality show, so I can't sit here and say that we were given characters. Nothing was scripted. Everyone said what they said and did what they did, but it was how it was put together in the editing. You also have to keep in mind that there are other people besides Tyra [Banks, series producer and supermodel] who have a say in how the contestants are portrayed. The bottom line for them is that if it doesn't make dollars it doesn't make sense." McDonald and other reality TV participants pretend to do the public a favor by cluing them in to what audiences already know: that even a genre claiming to be unscripted and true plays tricks and manipulates sound and image to craft a saleable product. It is an open secret that reality TV participants are also culpable since they, too, are concerned about the bottom line: future fame and fortune in a celebrity-fueled, "famous for being famous" culture.

Blaming the editing also allows reality TV participants to explain their consent to misrepresentation. In reality TV logic, a signed consent form assumes that participants are fully informed; thus, Manigault-Stallworth and McDonald implicitly agreed to negative representations of black women. Jennifer Pozner, the executive director of Women in Media and News, writes, "Apologists claim reality TV isn't sexist because no one forces women to appear on these shows."[42] Male rap music video directors and artists use the same rationale to dismiss accusations that they exploit women, making them just another part of the scenery like cars and money. Although audiences are often treated to the hard luck stories of reality TV participants (particularly for the eighteen to twenty-four age demographic there is often an assumed narrative of absent fathers and single mothers incapable of providing for their children), it is more difficult to refute the claim of agency denied for reality TV contestants than it is for women in rap videos. Whereas there are clear financial benefits in rap video performance, lap dancing, and other related industries that surpass working in the American service economy, the incentives for black women and men to play to type are more dubious in reality television.[43]

Brenton and Cohen contest the idea of consent in reality TV environments that are often structured, with the help of staff psychologists, around a disorienting audition process, manipulation of feelings of guilt, appeals to competitive spirit, and a sense of responsibility to see a given task through to its end. Consent, then, is a deeper issue than the mere act of a participant signing up for an experience might suggest. Consent also raises ethical questions for psychologists and legal and intellectual property issues for producers.[44] Manipulating consent, as well as reality TV participants' sense of having consented, is integral to the genre's structure and the manipulation of audiences' gender, race, class, and sexual orientation prejudices.

Although audiences have yet to see the evil black woman, or her counterpart the angry black man, win a reality TV competition, blacks have progressed through these competitions, but at what cost? For contestants across race, Kim defines the following criteria as integral to winning: a show of gratitude ("A Successful or compelling player must be grateful for the text, e.g. by praising and thanking the show [or God] for the once-in-a-lifetime opportunity to see his/her dream come true"); and a sympathetic backstory ("S/he must have a good pre-existing story, one that follows a Horatio Alger and/or immigrant tale," e.g., *American Idol* winner Ruben Studdard lived in a car with his single mother); and a good work ethic ("American viewers must see these people exerting energy and emotion in order to be worthy of becoming the winner or hero of a reality television text").[45] The stock characters that cater to audiences' prejudices benefit from what Jon Dovey calls reality TV's "regime of truth . . . the foregrounding of individual subjective experience at the expense of more general truth claims."[46]

Crucially, reality TV participants benefit from this regime of truth only to the extent that they adhere to dominant ideas about race, class, gender, sexuality, and physical ability. Thus, Studdard's sympathetic backstory is authenticated because of dominant assumptions about black single mothers as incapable of providing for their children. However, when it comes to racism and sexism, subjective experience is usually discounted as paranoia and outside the regime of truth. When confident black women such as McDonald and Manigault-Stallworth, refusing to conform to these criteria, as well as rejecting historical perceptions of black women as only existing to make white lives better, do appear in reality TV competitions, not only do they lose but they also end up maligned. Camille, a student at Howard University (a historically black school), characterizes her toughness and high self-regard as honoring her parents' sacrifice as immigrants from the Caribbean and refuses to apologize for her pride: "People have asked me 'why didn't you cry [when you were eliminated]? You're so cold; so distant. You have no emotions.' But I'm like 'cry fi wah?' If I was to cry my grandmother would be like 'yuh wan mi gi yuh sup'm fi cry about?' I have the entire West Indies riding on my back. If I make it, they make it."[47] Her use of dialect in an interview following her *America's Next Top Model* experience reflects a connection to heritage and values that did not make it into the show. As she notes, "The show portrayed my confidence as cockiness."[48] Camille, like other people of color raised similarly, is the product of parents who raised their children to hold their heads high in the midst of racism and to persevere in spite of efforts to hold them back. Reality TV cannot accommodate black women who do not fit the few sanctioned contemporary roles (e.g., the ubiquitous black woman judge, the abusive single mother, or the police captain without a capacity for significant action).

One must question black feminism's progress in dismantling images of "the black bitch," "the loud black woman," "the sistah with attitude," and a host of other stereotypes if these cues are still considered easily recognizable. There is also the notable failure of societal transformation in eradicating these images. A connected question asks whether we can hold black women who behave badly on reality TV accountable for perpetuating an image detrimental to black women. Do we just as readily recognize and remember the names of those who represented black women as kind, generous, and likable on reality TV?

Although we cannot assume that any of these women claim feminist politics, we can presume that they enter into the genre aware of black women's construction in the popular imagination. Like the negative version of the barely talented diva, do reality TV women believe their own hype? Does the reality TV diva take ideas about black women's strength to a perverse extreme, playing to those constructions to succeed at the audition stage? In a bid for celebrity or progress in their field, be it modeling, corporate enterprises, acting, sports, or any number of other professions that thrive on effective public relations, some black women in reality TV shows choose to manipulate retrograde prejudices about black womanhood. Some celebrities reject the idea that they are role models, and I am not claiming that black participants in reality TV should assume that role. However, no matter how much we adamantly maintain that no one black person should have to be representative of the race, we need to be aware that television disseminates these representations nationally and internationally.

The question very rarely asked, though, is *why* these black women are so angry. The answer lies where postfeminism meets post–civil rights: both discourses erase history and claim equality as today's norm for women and people of color. Much like 1970s feminism's failure to recognize that black women were already "liberated" in the sense that they have always worked outside the home (if this was the meaning of liberation) since slavery, post-feminism situates black women as always already angry, carrying a chip on their collective shoulders and ready to go off at the least personal slight.

This provides the context for reality TV's evil black woman. Reverting to the days before feminism declared the personal as political, postfeminism re-trenches women's grievances, especially those of black women, as personal—not structural or institutional. How, after all, can racism and sexism be built into the structure of unscripted television? By denying the fabricated nature and ensemble-cast character of reality TV, producers can recast their blatant use of racist, sexist, heterosexist, and classist iconography as creating an ensemble that represents one version of a diverse America. In the post-civil-rights vision of the world, inclusion means merely having a presence, not empowerment in terms of self-definition.[49]

Bitter Black Women

It has been suggested that postfeminism "mask[s] the persistence of a sexual double standard, the persistence of racial stereotyping, and the persistence of efforts to re-domesticate women by insisting that their place, first and foremost, remains in the home and subservient to men."[50] Do these conditions apply to all women? After all, black women historically have rarely been in *their own homes* as full-time homemakers. Now, more than ever, black women are in the workforce. Chambers notes, "Between 1976 and 2006, the number of black women in the workplace will have increased by 35 percent. This is in comparison with white women, up by 10 percent in the same 30 years."[51] Although black women are being displaced by other groups of women of color, particularly immigrant populations, they continue to earn advanced degrees at a rate faster than that of black men and "in some fields, such as sales and administrative support roles . . . black women are beginning to earn slightly more [than white women]."[52] Given black women's presence and success in the workplace, what does it mean for postfeminism to redomesticate them with the assistance of racial stereotyping and a sexual double standard?

Postfeminism's racialized narrative takes assumptions about white women's lives and turns them on their heads. Thus, the few films that deal with middle-class African American women, call for them to remain in the workplace but in racially prescribed ways. As was seen with Manigault-Stallworth, attempting to climb higher than one's racially prescribed station, exhibiting characteristics usually lauded in men, results in a violation of the modern mammy and black lady stereotypes. The post-civil-rights narrative in these films relies on the assumption that integration means assimilation and therefore a loss of culture. Presumptions in these films are based on problematic notions of racial authenticity. The story usually begins with a black couple that has worked its way up from poverty or the working class. The wife supported her husband through medical, law, or dental school or while he developed his business from a small enterprise to a large, successful corporation. The marker of the black man's success in this trope, in line with some 1970s black masculinist discourses, is a white or light-skinned black female secretary who inevitably becomes his lover. In the most callous way possible, the black man reveals to his black wife that he will shortly be moving his lover into their home and she should pack her things and go.

At this point, the story usually follows the postfeminist script of "retreatism." Analyzing a range of examples of films featuring white female protagonists, Negra concludes that "retreatism has become a recognizable narrative trope. Accordingly, both film and television have incorporated fantasies of hometown return in which a heroine gives up her life in the city to take up again the role of daughter, sister, wife or sweetheart in a hometown setting."[53] Films featuring black women protagonists also portray retreat, but filmmakers attempt to make their departure points and destinations seem racially authentic. The black female heroine goes in one of two directions: she either returns to her family and the black community that she has neglected or she turns to a tight network of sister-friends. In the case of *Waiting to Exhale* (1995), the husband of one of the four central protagonists leaves her for his white assistant, and she burns most of his expensive belongings in a fit of rage. She later calmly sells off the rest of his possessions in a yard sale. She turns to her friends for comfort and support, noting that she left her own dreams behind to support her now wealthy husband's ambitions. The 1998 film *Down in the Delta*, directed by Maya Angelou, finds a mother sending her two granddaughters and drug-addicted daughter away from Chicago to live with her brother in Mississippi. It is there that the prodigal daughter learns about ancestral struggles and her heritage—a connection with land and family that restores her self-esteem and facilitates her recovery from addiction. In a slight variation, in *Beauty Shop* (2005) Queen Latifah returns from the white world, specifically a high-end hair salon, to an urban neighborhood where she can own her own salon and hang a picture of the first black female millionaire, Madame C. J. Walker.

Postfeminism's retreatist narrative is in effect most clearly in *Diary of a Mad Black Woman* (2005), a compelling film in the postfeminist, post-civil-rights era because of its production and narrative. The film is based on one of a series of Tyler Perry gospel stage plays. Other titles include *I Can Do Bad All by Myself* (2000), *Madea's Family Reunion* (2002), *Madea's Class Reunion* (2003), *Meet the Browns* (2004), and *Madea Goes to Jail* (2004). These typically play on the "chitlin'" or "urban theater circuit," a colloquialism for the mainly African American venues, such as nightclubs and theaters, that host the productions. The lucrative potential of these plays should not be underestimated; according to Perry, he grossed over 50 million dollars writing and producing plays for urban theaters.[54] *Diary of a Mad Black Woman* surprised the industry and critics—when it grossed over 22.7 million dollars and was the number one film on its opening weekend.

The mad black woman in question is Helen (Kimberly Elise), a woman who has always lived in the same city where she was raised—Atlanta—but she has moved to an affluent suburb with her husband Charles (Steve Harris) (fig. 1). Helen has emotionally and racially left home, though. In the presence of his light-skinned mistress—she will be moving into his home with her infant son, who he has clearly fathered—Charles literally throws his wife out of the house. The mover who rescues her will eventually become the love of her life, although Helen is angry and cast as "one of those bitter black women." Ashamed and disheveled, she returns home to her grandmother, Madea.[55] Helen exacts her revenge on her ex-husband by sadistically neglecting and humiliating him after he is paralyzed in an accident and his mistress, who has turned into another stereotype, the evil mulatto, abandons him.

It is only through the religious guidance of the church, her new lover's spiritual nurturance, and her pistol-packing Granny's wisecracks that Helen

Recent popular culture has generated a set of typologies of postfeminist black femininity. Helen in *Diary of a Mad Black Woman* is pictured here first as a supportive wife and then in a short-lived period of rage and vengefulness after her husband leaves her for a lighter-skinned woman. By the close, she will establish a new sense of self tied to a rejuvenated notion of community and a "coming back to blackness."

once again learns to stand on her own two feet and knows that she can only rely on four men for sure: the Father, the Son, the Holy Ghost, and a good black man.

In *Waiting to Exhale*, *Down in the Delta*, and *Diary of a Mad Black Woman*, each heroine has sacrificed her standing as a strongblackwoman, but the end of the film finds her redeemed. *Down in the Delta* uses drug abuse and urban living to mark a loss of self for its working-poor heroine that can only be regained by getting back in touch with her roots. For middle-class women, like those in *Waiting to Exhale* and *Diary of a Mad Black Woman*, the retreat to family or sister-friends is actually a coming back to blackness—the implication being that when a black female protagonist has it all she becomes a snob and is in danger of no longer being authentically black. Eventually, the middle-class heroine returns to a true sense of herself through an appropriately black, small business enterprise (e.g., a beauty shop or soul food restaurant), her family and friends' nurturance, a good black man, and *always* a new haircut. Thus, the markers of change for these women are both stylistic changes of appearance and clearly marked as having to do with identity.

How do these films function in the postfeminist era in which they were produced? On the one hand, they can be characterized as black women's films, an updating of the 1930s and 1940s woman's film genre: black women suffer but are ultimately triumphant, having returned to a place from which they drifted, and black family and community are regained. This would seem to be a positive message for black women. Yet, within the context of postfeminist, post-civil-rights discourse, what are we to make of black women's position in American society as suggested by the deployment of the diva, the race-inflected fiction of reality TV, and the black "chick flick"?

I propose that, for African American women, the postfeminist message is that black women need to know their place within the racial and gender hierarchy even if they are permitted, in small numbers, to assume places in the middle class. For the films discussed in this essay, when black women leave work and become homemakers they lose themselves and their connection to being black. Are black mainstream filmmakers and authors in a growing area of black chick lit and flicks advocating a feminist position that black middle-class women should remain in the world of work because without work they will lose their freedom? Or are they saying that black women are incapable of choosing to stay in the (opulent) home because it is considered lazy and indulgent and will make them soft—something black women are not allowed to be if they are to continue to uphold the race? The implication is that educational and career achievement is black women's twenty-first-century racial uplift work.

Contemporary film and television representations of African American women offer two racially gendered variations of postfeminist discourse. In relation to white women, still to be defined as the other, black women continue to be denied access to the pedestal (in this case the option of not working) designated by nineteenth-century ideals as the sole province of white women. Instead, black women are expected to remain in the workplace performing emotional, if not physical, labor for whites. Black women on reality TV, if they step away from the roles of the modern mammy or the black lady, clearly exceed their place as subservient to whites. Unless it is being mimicked or appropriated by white, mainstream popular culture ("You go, girl!"), any demonstration of pride or refusal to act like a black lady is characterized as being difficult or having an attitude.

In relationship to black men and black communities, post-civil-rights and postfeminist discourses require black women not to have it all but to continue to do it all. Black women's agreement with feminist principles and continuing resistance to increased numbers of black women being incarcerated, sexual exploitation, and a host of other oppressive factors are erased because in the post-civil-rights worldview they are racial success stories.[56] Middle-class black women are marginally afforded status as women, or ladies more specifically, if they conform to a politics of respectability. If they do not conform, they are relegated to the evil black woman category along with poor and working-class black women.

Postfeminism, post–civil rights, postmodernism—linguistically all these "posts" might seem excessive and merely indulgent jargon. After all, how might a constant critique of backlash politics and culture limit visions for social transformation? To always be in the defensive position and reacting can sometimes leave little room or energy for thinking and behaving proactively. As feminist, critical race, and queer critics, the prospect that we will find ourselves only able to articulate everything that is wrong with popular culture and unable to give credit to those positive aspects that create a pathway to transformative visions is worrisome.[57] As feminists making incursions into the terrain of postfeminism, recognizing those culture makers forging ahead because of and in spite of oppression is as important, if not more important, than highlighting those forces counter to ending oppression. Yet, when forces determined to maintain the status quo use "post" formulations to attempt to make us believe we are beyond particular forms of oppression or liberation struggles, the work of critique continues.

To bring current Audre Lorde's metaphor, the master's house has not, in fact, been dismantled but instead has added additional rooms and annexes in which to harbor oppressive variations of racist, sexist, classist, and heterosexist themes. This move makes interrogating postfeminism and post-civil-rights culture necessary. Critiques of these concepts make visible the political, social, and economic changes that shape discriminatory practices and our responses to them. As modes of exploitation change to continue to accommodate oppression, our critiques also need to adapt in language and practice, making "post" political configurations critical sites of analysis.

Notes

1. Herman Gray offers a compelling critique of continued media activism around representation and offers new directions for race and media studies, noting that we no longer live in a world in which media are controlled by local, state, or even national forces. Media activists concerned about racial representation, in his opinion, will need to look for the global implications of media production and distribution and how these impact representation. See Gray, *Cultural Moves*.
2. Douglas, "Manufacturing Postfeminism."
3. Kinser, "Negotiating Spaces for/through Third-Wave Feminism," 134–35.
4. Aronson, "Feminists or 'Postfeminists'?"; Projansky, *Watching Rape*.
5. Hall and Rodriguez, "The Myth of Postfeminism," 879.
6. Ibid., 886–99.
7. Kinser, "Negotiating Spaces," 135.
8. Ibid., 144.
9. hooks, "Eating the Other."
10. Whelehan, *Overloaded*, 4.
11. Negra, "Quality Postfeminism?"
12. Joan Morgan runs the words *strong*, *black*, and *woman* together to signify the entwining and seeming inextricability of these words in the lives of black women and expectations of them; see her *When Chickenheads Come Home to Roost*.
13. Collins, *Black Sexual Politics*, 78–79.
14. See Moynihan, *The Negro Family*.
15. The idea of backlash, of course, assumes that there was momentary progress in the representations of black women before the backlash.
16. Tyrangiel, "The New Diva-Disease."
17. "Gladys Knight Talks about 'At Last,' Her First Album in Six Years, and Why She's Not a Diva."
18. Tasker and Negra, "In Focus," 108.
19. Gray, *Watching Race*; Smith-Shomade, *Shaded Lives*.
20. Collins, *Black Sexual Politics*, 138–40.
21. Higginbotham, *Righteous Discontent*.
22. Ibid., 139.
23. Ibid., 140.
24. Russakoff, "Lessons of Might and Right."
25. Collins, *Black Sexual Politics*, 142.
26. Oprah Winfrey, Collins posits, is a successful reflection of the black lady and mod-

ern mammy through her nurturance of predominately white female talk show guests and her avocations of personal, individualized transformation. Anita Hill, on the other hand, violates the tenets of black ladyhood and the modern mammy. Although she exhibited all the traits of respectability, once she accused the Supreme Court nominee Clarence Thomas of sexual harassment she challenged the social order and was punished for it.

27. Wiltz, "The Evil Sista of Reality Television."

28. Brenton and Cohen, *Shooting People*, 8.

29. Andrejevic, *Reality TV*, 8.

30. Brenton and Cohen (in *Shooting People*) cogently delineate the devolution from documentary film with social purpose to unsupervised psychology experiments (especially Philip Zimbardo's 1971 Stanford Prison experiment in which ordinary citizens took their roles as guards and prisoners to a psychologically damaging degree) and contemporary psychology professionals' dubious ethical relationships with reality TV productions as series contestants.

31. Wiltz, "The Evil Sista of Reality Television."

32. Kim, "Race and Reality . . . TV."

33. Wiltz, "The Evil Sista of Reality Television."

34. "The 2003–2004 Tubey Awards, Part Two," www.televisionwithoutpity.com.

35. Wiltz, "The Evil Sista of Reality Television."

36. Daniels, "Africana's Reality TV Recap."

37. "Reality Check," *Dr. Phil*, www.drphil.com, May 2005.

38. Brenton and Cohen, *Shooting People*, 53.

39. Sims, "Angry Black Woman."

40. Ibid.

41. Butler, "Camille McDonald Dispels Rumors and Sets the Record Straight."

42. Pozner, "The Unreal World."

43. Thomas, "The Power of Women." Applicable to most reality TV shows is *The Apprentice*'s tagline: "This isn't a game. This is a thirteen-week job interview." Landing a job with Donald Trump on *The Apprentice*, a recording contract, speaking engagements on college campuses, or hosting *MTV's Spring Break* are all possibilities, but the fickle world of reality television does not promise a long and lucrative career.

44. Brenton and Cohen, *Shooting People*, 135–44.

45. Kim, "Race and Reality . . . TV."

46. Dovey, *Freakshow*, 25.

47. Butler, "Camille McDonald Dispels Rumors and Sets the Record Straight."

48. Ibid.

49. Tellingly, of the monographs on reality TV consulted for this essay, only one indexed *racism* and none indexed *race*, *whiteness*, or any other racial grouping. This indicates a failure of the literature, to date, to adequately grapple with race and its role in the genre.

50. Douglas, "Manufacturing Postfeminism."

51. Chambers, *Having It All?* 3.

52. Ibid.

53. Negra, "Quality Postfeminism?"

54. Hughes, "How Tyler Perry Rose from Homelessness to a $5 Million Mansion."

55. Madea, an abbreviation for the endearment "Mother Dear," is Tyler Perry in drag portraying a feisty, gun-waving grandmother.

56. Hall and Rodriguez, "The Myth of Postfeminism."

57. One might, for example, examine more closely and through an academic lens the performance art of Sarah Jones or the productions and performances of hip hop impresario Missy Elliott.

Sadie Wearing

11 Subjects of Rejuvenation

AGING IN POSTFEMINIST CULTURE

If old people show the same desires, the same feelings and the same requirements as the young, the world looks upon them with disgust: in them
love and jealousy seem revolting and absurd, sexuality repulsive and violence ludicrous.—SIMONE DE BEAUVOIR

Our grandmothers painted in order to try and talk brilliantly. Rouge and
esprit used to go together. That is all over now. As long as a woman can
look ten years younger than her own daughter, she is perfectly satisfied.
—OSCAR WILDE

When Harry Sanders tells Erica Barry, in the film *Something's Gotta Give* (Meyers, 2003) that she's "the funniest
girl [he] ever had sex with," he articulates a growing preoccupation of postfeminist culture, the desire for and the limits
of "girling" the "older woman."[1] Is she a funny girl because,
played by Diane Keaton in a romantic comedy, she makes
him laugh? Or is she a funny girl because there is something
a little uncomfortable (even uncanny) about the appellation of
"girl"—in terms of both gender and generation—to a woman
in her fifties?[2] I want to ask here what kinds of "funny girls"
are being produced in recent popular culture's representations

of aging female bodies.[3] While age and aging have, of course, interested scholars, writers, and cultural commentators of all persuasions for centuries, discursive production around the question of age and aging does appears to be proliferating in popular culture.[4] This essay aims to explore some of the ways in which this increased visibility might be understood. My readings of recent examples of popular film and television in which the aging process is foregrounded examines the ways these texts illuminate the cultural work the aging, gendered, body is expected to perform. With respect to the British television makeover series *10 Years Younger* (Channel 4, 2004–), drawing on recent considerations of both postmodern "lifestyle" culture and the culture of cosmetic surgery, I suggest that, while ostensibly offering the construction of a "new" self, a "magical" transformation, "rejuvenation" in this series, is simultaneously bound by a highly conservative, equivocal understanding of the limits of such temporal impropriety, a characteristic that also informs its (re)production of gender.[5] In my reading of the American film *Something's Gotta Give*, I highlight the way that (emphatically hetero) sexuality functions in the narrative, as in wider cultural discourses around aging and gender, as a device of (covert) rejuvenation and how the film's desire to imagine the possibilities of a postfeminist life course entails an emphasis on chronological decorum, here figured as a policing of intergenerational sexuality. Thus, both texts, despite the different national, cultural, and media contexts in which they appear, offer a fantasy of escaping (or evading) time but one that places clearly defined limits on that escape. To put this another way, I am interested in how "rejuvenation" is figured in popular culture as simultaneously necessary and impossible.[6] Necessary because in complex ways the aging body is pathologized and disavowed; impossible because, as both examples discussed here demonstrate, deference to quite rigid demarcations of the appropriate, the decorous, and the "natural" still exerts a profound influence over representations of age and aging. Similar influences can also be seen in representations of feminism and feminists as dated irrelevances to young women's lives. Thus, before discussing *10 Years Younger* and *Something's Gotta Give*, I want to look briefly (and selectively) at the role generational differences have played in recent feminist debates about popular culture.

Postfeminist Time and Age

Generational politics, particularly in relation to sexual conduct, is the explicit theme of *Something's Gotta Give*, but generational politics are equally central to

Generationally appropriate coupling is reinforced by romantic iconography in *Something's Gotta Give.*

representations of the past and the future of feminism. In particular, feminist analysis of contemporary postfeminist media culture has become drawn to contested questions of age and generation. Reflecting the Anglo-American culture industries' preoccupations, the primary focus has, to date, been on the "young" women who make up "new," "third-wave" or iconic figures of postfeminist discourse. The *post* of postfeminism has included a recognition, or perhaps more properly a narrative, of the necessity for young women to, in Angela McRobbie's phrase, "disidentify" with the previous generation of feminists.[7] My interest is in how such disidentification is predicated on and in turn reproduces complicated assumptions of both age and time.

In her passionate discussion of the cultural invisibility of the aged, Simone de Beauvoir identifies the poverty, both economic and representational, faced by older people in Western societies. She also highlights the threat to identity that age entails, noting that "in the old person that we must become, we refuse to recognize ourselves."[8] Such a (desired) recognition entails questioning the very idea of "difference" since de Beauvoir's analysis indicates the imaginative leap needed to meet the "other," the "someone else" that we become over time. Kathleen Woodward, too, emphasizes that this "difference," and, crucially, its representation, is one "we all have a stake in."[9] Both Woodward and de Beauvoir refer to an older cohort than I will be focusing on in this essay. However, their understanding of the cultural and psychological complexity of responses to aging is highly relevant for my purposes. In drawing attention to the negative associations of age as it appears in the postfeminist debate I do not mean to ignore or devalue the specificities of generational experience.[10] Rather, my aim is to question the link between the "aging" of feminism and culturally authoritative narratives and anxieties over age more generally. Aging for women, particularly white women, in Western culture has been understood as "trauma."[11] This construction is linked to a prevailing but increasingly, if problematically, contested understanding of age primarily in terms of decline and disintegration rather than accumulation and growth.[12] As Patricia Mellencamp writes, "In our culture, youth is imagined or represented as a lost object rather than as a process or passage through time. . . . [A]ge [is] portrayed as series of losses rather than achievements, gains or successes for women."[13] As McRobbie suggests, the production of a generational conflict has "aged" feminism and indeed heralded, as Mary Hawkesworth states, its "premature" demise.[14] This process also entails a perception or production of "anachronism," a concept that, as Mary Russo eloquently puts it, "is a mistake in a normative systemization of time."[15] It is normative in that it symbolically confines the subject to developmental models of linear progression through "birth, reproduction and death," attempts to escape which run the risk of "scandal." This formulation is close to Judith Halberstam's description of "family time," which she contrasts with the possibilities opened up for cultural existence(s) outside of the dominant developmental paradigm: "Queer subcultures produce alternative temporalities by allowing their participants to believe that their futures can be imagined according to logics that lie outside of those paradigmatic markers of life experience—namely birth, marriage, reproduction and death."[16] In postfeminist popular culture, however, such refiguring is (unsurprisingly) elusive; here anachronism defines the continued presence of an "attitude and ideology" that properly belongs in another time, and, given that this temporality is relentlessly developmental, linear, and "progressive," that means "out" of time. Russo explicitly links anachronism to age where, for women, "Not acting one's age . . . is not only inappropriate but dangerous, exposing the female subject, especially, to ridicule, contempt, pity and scorn—the scandal of anachronism."[17] The scandalous presence of the inappropriate is then a feature of both popular representations of the aging body *and* postfeminist representations of feminist critical positions.

Many recent studies have demonstrated the ways in which postfeminist popular culture has invested a great deal in the figuration of feminism as "old" and hence, in line with women's bodies more generally, ripe for the ritualized public display of "makeover," where "the new" and "youth" are characterized as virtual synonyms.[18] Angela McRobbie's discussion of the relationship between postfeminism and popular culture suggests that "one strategy in the disempowering of feminism includes it being historicized and generationalized and thus easily rendered out of date."[19] Hilary Hinds and Jackie Stacey make it clear that this "out of date" characterization chimes easily with the preoccupations of postfeminist culture.[20] In the texts I look at here, these preoccupations translate into not only the widely noted emphasis on appearance but also a marked reliance on the temporal foregrounded in both the "before and after" discourse of lifestyle and makeover and in the emphasis on age. A related point is made by Mary Hawkesworth, who argues that while globally feminism "has experienced unprecedented growth" the labor of feminist activists is rendered increasingly invisible by a press suspiciously anxious to announce its "death," and she links the "rhetorical burial of contemporary feminism" to an effort to eliminate its "perceived danger" and "undermine feminist struggles for social justice."[21]

One aspect of this struggle plays out in terms of a generationalized response to popular culture; the feminist/postfeminist divide has often been represented as a familial affair, a struggle for autonomy between "mothers" and "daughters" often fought over the ground of culture and representation. Kathleen Rowe Karlyn's analysis of the *Scream* franchise, for example, discovers a central preoccupation in those films with the generational "tension" that occurs at the level of a contested relationship with both popular culture and feminism more widely.[22] This preoccupation occurs in a number of critical contexts, including work by black feminists who question the universal relevance of models of generational difference.[23] But what exactly is at stake and what are the risks of this reliance on the tropes of inevitable generational conflict being played out within popular narratives and feminist criticism? If we take seriously some of the assumptions about age and time behind these conceptualizations, we might want to question both the danger of infantilizing *and* rendering obsolete positions that become mired in the language and constraints of dictates taken from a narrowly conceived reliance on chronological and familial models. As Kathleen Woodward has argued, overreliance on "Oedipal" models, themselves implicated in anxieties about aging and death, can be read as another instance of the prioritizing of the concerns of the "young" and result all too often in a concomitant invisibility of "older" women. Woodward regards feminism as culpable in "internalizing" cultural "prejudices against aging."[24]

Generational Difference and Cultural Critique

To illustrate some of these concerns, I want to look, briefly, at an apparently minor incident in *Something's Gotta Give*, which offers an example of a generational dispute over popular culture and its social meanings. In a postfeminist terrain in which the "mother" is likely to be either absent or a source of conflict for the daughter, who is narratively and culturally central, the film's concern to broadly stress the similarities between mother and daughter is itself interesting; this "dispute," however, appears to complicate the mirroring of mother and daughter that elsewhere the film underscores.[25] Erica is coded as a "feminist" by the language she uses to describe both popular culture and men; she describes Harry as "chauvinistic" and the rap music his record company produces as "a tad misogynistic."[26] The music she finds so objectionable is understood by her daughter, Marin, as unproblematic; "wrong," she tells her mother can be "fun." However, Marin's perspective is not the only association between youthful femininity and "misogynist" African American popular culture that the film offers. The film, in fact, opens with a credit sequence set to a rap song, "Butterfly," performed by Crazytown, and so it could be argued to have already schooled the audience to read feminist critiques as anachronistic and beside the point.

The sequence cuts between images of eight young women (many of whom are recognizable "supermodels") in an urban setting entering nightclubs, hailing cabs, walking the streets, and socializing in bars, their catwalklike bodily deportment suggesting both complete self-possession and a very public validity and visibility, which bespeaks the (unquestioned) centrality of youth to both subcultural spaces and popular film narratives. Indeed "validation" is literalized by a close-up of the velvet ropes in a VIP area of a nightclub being lifted (significantly by a black male and white female couple) so that the girls may enter. The opening shot in this sequence is of a young, blonde woman who looks directly into the camera and then tosses her hair over her shoulder as she walks toward us with the recognizable fluid-hipped gait of the fashion model. Furthermore, the opening highlights youthful gatherings as racially mixed while the subsequent narrative (set in the exclusive Hamptons) is anything but. "Feminist" concerns, then, are covertly represented as linked to an implicitly white, staid sense of culture. This opening is significant in light of Erica's definition of rap as misogynistic because it precisely problematizes the critical position she adopts; the bodies of these "girls" are on display, "to be looked at" in Laura Mulvey's terms, but the look into the camera and the utter self-possession of these bodies seem to complicate, in recognizably "postfeminist" ways, their status as "objects of the look" and their subordinate position in regard to the music. I am not primarily concerned here to argue whether or not these women's bodies are subject to an objectifying "look" or whether their apparently assertive sexuality is evidence of a new kind of pernicious sexual "subjectivity" as identified by Rosalind Gill, important though those debates are.[27] My point is that the narrative works in *generational* terms to establish the essential *difference* between young women who appear to turn "misogyny" to their own advantage and older (feminist) women who "merely" critique it. However, crucially and unusually, the narrative concerns of this film reside less in the conflicts between mother and daughter than in their connection. The voice-over ("ahh, the sweet uncomplicated satisfaction of the younger woman") that ends this sequence is that of Harry (Jack Nicholson), whose narration is typically unreliable.[28] His appreciative, not to say lascivious, voyeurism is, in narrative terms, on display in this opening, as well as the bodies of these young women. Indeed, these beautiful bodies may even *be* his fantasy. The editing, framing, and slowing down of the sequence taken together with the only voice-over in the film all situate the sequence in a different aesthetic register than the subsequent narrative. Harry is destined during this film to be reformed (or made over); by the end, he will have overcome his desire for younger women, symptomatic of a fear of older women, and be subject to a series of humiliating reminders that he is "old, old, old" (the inverse of Christine Holmlund's analysis of the public aging of Clint Eastwood, Harry is "rotting" rather than "ripening").[29] He will, later on, leave another party scene, literally turning away from both the music that has made him rich and the young bodies he has desired.[30] In retrospect, the spectator can appreciate, together with Harry, that the centrality of these youthful bodies is, in fact, illusory. The "real" focus of the film is a woman with a different relationship to both popular culture (as producer and critic rather than as consumer, participant, or performer) and the body.

In *Something's Gotta Give*, Erica's body is narratively and visually investigated and exposed. In the process, the possibility for its "difference" to be rendered acceptable is, perhaps, compromised (or disavowed) by the film's endorsement of the codes of heterosexual romance and sexuality and also in the fostering of points of connection rather than disjunction between mother and daughter. The film's understanding of the aging process corresponds to a wider concern of twenty-first-century culture to eliminate visually and metaphorically the corporeal "signs" of aging coupled with a marked emphasis on consumption and heterosexuality.[31] *Something's Gotta Give*'s breaching of the taboo of sexuality in the older woman figures rejuvenation as tied to heterosexual romance, while rejuvenation in other postfeminist texts, such as the makeover series *10 Years Younger*, is closely tied to consumption. The older female body is expressly figured in both as a problem, which, in generically characteristic ways, these texts explore, investigate, and subject to the processes of renewal.

The iconic figures of postfeminist popular culture are, as the editors of this collection point out, girled, often stretching that category into age ranges that would previously have been understood as unambiguously adult. The extension of the attributes of "girlishness" or girliness, as has been widely noted, are closely related to traditional (but recouped, updated, and highly sexualized) versions of white femininity.[32] The relationship between feminism and femininity has been considered as directly implicated in the question of postfeminism,[33] mainly in terms of a generational divide between a censorious feminism that fails to engage young women who embrace femininity (in however knowing and ironic a mode).[34] However, what I want to stress here are the often unexamined links between "femininity" and youth that are presupposed to coexist but from the point of view of the *other*, *older* end of the "life course" or age spectrum rather than the younger. If the "waves thesis" as Lynn Spigel puts it, "works to place old feminists on the beach — washed up like a fish on the shore," what happens to the "postfeminist logic that embraces femininity and 'girliness' in the name of enlightenment and female empowerment" when the older female body *is* represented in popular culture?[35] What risks do the accomplishment of girliness and femininity run when performed by older bodies?

Gender Identity and the Process of Aging

In order to make these connections a little clearer, I want to first question the relationship between the production of gendered identities and age, briefly linking the early work of Judith Butler on performativity and gender and

Kathleen Woodward's theorization of age as "youthfulness as masquerade," whereby the attributes of "youth" are adopted by those no longer chronologically young.

Using Joan Riviere's analysis of the substantive creation of the feminine self by adoption of the gestures and accoutrements of femininity, Woodward highlights the way in which performing "youth" is a psychological attempt to forge links to "past selves," a spectacle that reveals not the wished for continuity with the former body but rather "the desire for youth and the unimpeachability of death."[36] She explicitly questions any easy equivalence between the achievement of gender (a femininity that Riviere analyzed as a mask to conceal a "masculine" accomplishment) and that of youth, noting not only the almost inevitable failure of "passing" but also that, while aging may entail an "apparent collapse or convergence of sexual difference," this cannot be understood in simple terms as a "loss." Rather, using Freud, she suggests that in fact the performance or masquerade of youth might be read as less a desire to mask the loss of femininity (masquerade appearing as prosthetic femininity) than an unconscious need to disguise the desire for "the return of the repressed . . . the return of the other sex." This analysis highlights the complex psychic processes that may accompany the production of gendered identities as we age. Woodward's insights into the youthful masquerade highlight the relationship between the body, time, and the production of subjectivity. In *Gender Trouble*, Judith Butler, too, stresses the importance of *temporality* to the production of (an always fraught) gender identity: "If the ground of gender identity is the stylized repetition of acts through time and not a seemingly seamless identity, then the spatial metaphor of a "ground" will be displaced and revealed as a stylized configuration, indeed, a gendered corporealization of time."[37]

Butler's theorization of the "performative" nature of gender identity is clearly not primarily concerned with age. However, the centrality of the temporal, the necessity for constant repetition, and the possibility that repetition will "fail" are highly suggestive for considering the relationship between age and gender as is it culturally signified in the narratives and fictions that in contemporary British and American culture concern themselves with the question of gender "in" the older body. For Butler, the "embodying of norms" that constitute "the practice by which gendering occurs" is both "compulsory" and "forcible" but also temporally bound, unstable; the "de-formity" that she locates as offering a glimpse of the "regulatory fiction" of gender might also be read in terms of age as a moment when the "sustained social performances" of gender are at some risk.[38] Butler points out in *Bodies That Matter* that the "embodying" of gender in the service of compulsory heterosexuality is an assignment that is peculiarly threatened precisely because of the necessity for repetition: "One might construe repetition as precisely that which *undermines* the conceit of voluntarist mastery."[39] The relationship between the "iteration" over time of gender norms and the processes of aging raises questions that would repay analysis. At the very least, Butler's point about gender and time might make us pay close attention to the moments in popular culture when the older body is diagnosed as problematic in terms that are, precisely, gendered. Examples from the texts I look at here include Harry's remarks about Erica in *Something's Gotta Give* as "twice the man I'll ever be," his description of her as "macho," and his comment that she's the "funniest girl he's ever had sex with," as well as the erasure of any hint of androgyny that *10 Years Younger* perpetrates on the bodies of its participants. Like aging, gender can be understood as a process; furthermore, the processes of aging, as Woodward's discussion of masquerade shows, draw attention to the complexity of the achievement of a stable and coherent gendered identity over time.

10 Years Younger: Makeover as Masquerade?

Patricia Mellencamp suggested some fifteen years ago that in the United States "chronological age" is "television and the nation's gendered obsession."[40] In this section, I want to discuss the British series *10 Years Younger* to explore the particular, and complex, direction this obsession, shared by the two national contexts, has recently taken. One aspect of the show's complexity is its reliance on the trope of "premature" aging and its exposure of, even delight in, "passing" or masquerade. A further complexity lies in the competing presence of two, apparently contradictory, discourses on aging in postfeminist culture. On the one hand, we find a vibrant, even utopian, celebratory insistence that age need not mean loss — of femininity, of fun, of "girlhood," perhaps, finally, of "self." At the same time, however, a more cautionary note is sounded, which suggests less that age "need not" and more that it "must not" be allowed to relax the hold of "youth" on the body and that responsibility for maintaining a youthful appearance lies in making the right consumer choices, including undertaking surgical procedures.

As its title suggests *10 Years Younger*'s ambition is to "make over" its showcase participant during the course of the program so that at the end the subject appears to be a decade younger than at the start. A poll of "passersby" is taken to establish the apparent (or public) age both before and after the transformation. The signature transformation emphasizes the production of "the self" through the practices of beauty and (related) consumption,[41] thus connecting it to a wider cultural shift that links, in Foucault's phrase "care of the self," to both rhetorics of consumer choice and discourses of aging.[42] The rhetoric of choice, as several critics have recently noted,[43] sounds a somewhat hollow note when applied to the aging body and the surgical subject.[44] The choice is, after all, to risk the surgeon's knife for an inevitably temporary solution to what has become increasingly conceptualized as the pathology of aging.[45] Susan Merrill Squier, for example, demonstrates that both fictional and scientific discourses have increasingly individualized understandings of the aging process: "With the turn to a modern notion of the body seen as a project, the way each person experiences aging has shifted from being universal and ineluctable to being something particular and *chosen*, and the medical response to the experience of aging is increasingly grounded not in the notion of acceptance but in that of cure."[46]

This conceptualization of aging as something that can be "cured" can also be found in *10 Years Younger*, wherein aging is imagined less as an inevitable, natural process than as a moral failing. This "ethical" position conforms to the rigid standards set for the maintenance of the body in consumer culture. For Mike Featherstone, appearance is now so crucial that "the penalties of bodily neglect are a lowering of one's acceptability as a person as well as an indication of laziness, low self esteem and even moral failure."[47] In *10 Years Younger*, this individualized "ethical" perspective is found in the role of the narrator, who makes barbed comments on the lifestyle failings of the makeover subject. In the episode I will concentrate on here (episode 1, series 2, broadcast 12 January 2005), the participant is a "wife and mother," Debbie Ashcroft, forty-six years old, who the narrator describes as "a woman who likes her vices . . . not a huge surprise then that she's losing her battle to stay looking younger." The narrator's performance of critical, disgusted (but in typical postfeminist fashion simultaneously "ironic") appraisal is underscored by the ritual poll. The poll is conducted in a public space (usually, and not coincidentally given the show's stress on the transformative and rejuvenating power of consumption, an urban shopping center). Here one hundred "passersby" call out a number (ritualizing Althusser's model of interpellation, the participant is thus "hailed" into a specifically temporal form of subjectivity). The number called is always older than the participant's "real" age. The figures are "averaged," usually coming out around five years or so over the actual age of the participant (in this case, the average was fifty-six).

This "premature" aging allows the program to legitimate its rejuvenation via the invocation of a restoration of chronological propriety. Furthermore, the age range of the participants (in the first series all were between thirty-five and forty-five) exemplifies the ways in which, as Stephen Katz and Barbara Marshall show, "the promotion of successful aging lifestyles has problematized midlife decline at increasingly younger ages despite the irony that people are actually living longer."[48] Interestingly, however, the premise of the program ignores the enormous variation in age given by the members of the public. This "ritual" is a crucial part of the narrative, generating often cruel and sometimes absurd judgments.[49] In Debbie Ashcroft's case, the "public" declared her to be anything from forty-four to seventy. Each week this discrepancy draws attention to the limitations of using "witnesses" to fix the (evidently arbitrary and subjective) relationship between the body and time. And yet this visual validation is a crucial component of the wider policing of the body in time with which the program can be seen to be complicit, a "policing" that coexists uneasily with the "therapeutic" discourse that the series simultaneously mobilizes.

It is worth dwelling on the scene of the poll as it touches on some of the serious issues produced by a "surgical" culture. Fundamental to the logic of cosmetic surgery in general, and antiaging regimes in particular, is, as Sander Gilman makes clear, the question of "passing." Without a witness to the achievement of becoming "differently visible," there would be no point in enduring the process.[50] Gilman sees passing as mired in a complex psychological desire to organize a world that is demonstrably out of our control. It is in this model that he locates the happiness associated with aesthetic surgery: "The happiness of the patient is the fantasy of a world and a life in the patient's control rather than in the control of the observer on the street."[51] In *10 Years Younger*, the successful manipulation of the "observers on the street" is almost carnivalesque, but Gilman's comments should alert us to the nature of the psychological pain revealed by this device. Equally, and perhaps inadvertently, the reliance on the judgment of (in television terms) "ordinary people" suggests something of the class dynamics of "premature" aging. The socially privileged are, as Virginia Blum observes, the most able to afford, but also the least likely to require, cosmetic intervention, specifically because they hold "advantages that shield their self-esteem from the rude and inquisitive opprobrium of strangers."[52] The show's format, then, calls attention to chronological uncertainty over the recording of time, and sensitivity to that record, on different bodies.

In an apparently direct response to the critique of the "observers," Debbie Ashcroft tells the presenter (Nicky Hambleton-Jones, the "lifestyle expert," a phrase that resonates with Foucault's analysis of the power/knowledge nexus), "I'm menopausal, but my friends and I all called it mental pause-al because that's the way we feel, and I just don't feel very happy in my own skin at the moment, I absolutely hate my neck, I'd love to be able to wear a bulldog clip at the back of my neck when I go out because it really tightens it up, and I've just lost my way somewhere really and I'm looking for some help." The logic of both makeover narratives and cosmetic surgery is predicated on the assumption of a psychic split between the "inner self" and the body, which can be rectified by expert (surgical or lifestyle) intervention. This model of therapeutic intervention is an inversion of psychoanalytic concerns with the body/psyche split. Where psychoanalysis reads the body as a symptom (e.g., in hysteria) of (frequently culturally determined) suffering, cosmetic surgery (psychosurgery) locates that suffering in the body and so (perfectly logically) treats the body in an attempt to achieve a new, "happier" inner self. Ashcroft's call for help can only be understood by this logic as a call for surgical intervention. "If we're going to make a difference," the surgeon tells the presenter, "we're going to have to be quite radical."[53] This understanding corresponds to Deborah Covino's account of the "aesthetic surgical imaginary," which she defines as the "contemporary development of a bodily imaginary that gathers our concepts of psychological health and community around aesthetic considerations."[54] She links this to both surgical culture and the makeover paradigm (on which surgical culture is visually and visibly dependent), drawing attention to the economic limitations of its "universal" appeal "to bridge the gap between an aging body and a youthful state of mind," which coexists with a knowing hint that "better relationships and higher incomes come to those with youthful good looks."[55] However, in *10 Years Younger*, despite a general reliance on matching the inner to the outer self, the show stresses that it is not, in fact, attempting to defy "real" time; rather, its claim is to match appearance to chronology, despite its own evidence as to the arbitrary nature of such judgments.

This restoration of chronological propriety is important in a cultural context that is still hugely ambivalent about the desire to efface the signs of aging on female bodies. This resistance is perhaps being eroded as cosmetic surgery becomes more and more "everyday" and as recognition that the "politics of life itself," as Nikolas Rose puts it, has altered to the point where "posthuman" bodies need to be analyzed in new ways.[56] I want to stress that there remains a resilience in the critiques of rejuvenation and that, while the discourse of responsibility for the maintenance of the optimal body is important, we shouldn't overlook this residual resistance. *10 Years Younger* taps into an existing cultural ambivalence around cosmetic surgery in general but antiaging regimes in particular through its use of the "premature" motif. As the quotation from Oscar Wilde that appears at the beginning of this essay shows, hostile skepticism toward age defiance has a long history. *10 Years Younger* rather neatly bypasses this scornful opprobrium (neatly summed up by Ashcroft's anxiety that she not end up looking like "Mutton dressed as lamb") by insisting that the mobilization of all these experts will restore her to looking her *real* age. A very familiar double standard seems to be in operation in a culture that finds the signs of age in female bodies grotesque, laughable, and fearful (and makes a spectacle out of them) but equally mistrusts the efforts to efface those signs.[57] This seems to me to be neatly summed up in television's schizophrenic preoccupation with both performing makeovers and, often viciously, reversing them, "exposing" the enigma of surgical intervention,[58] as happens on, for example, *Celebrity: Who's Had What Done?* (ITV, Carleton Television, 2005–). Significantly, the effort to unmask the celebrity who has had surgery is often justified by recourse to the ethics of exposing the duplicity of the subject in failing to "admit" to having had it performed. Moreover, the "exposure" utilizes the generic conventions of the makeover; it is similarly reliant on a team of experts, analysis of before and after photos, and lurid descriptions of the processes undergone. The often highly sadistic exposure of the processes of rejuvenation gone "wrong," and the investigation of the body for signs that it has attempted to "cheat" time are typical of long-standing critical positions that consider them either signs of typically feminine vulgarity (Baudelaire and Wilde) or symptomatic of the culture industry's manipulation (Adorno). The difficulties for feminism of holding onto a critical position on rejuvenation while not writing off (as cultural dupes) the women who participate in it remain acute. As Davis argues in her equivocal defense of the "subjects" of cosmetic surgery, such surgery belongs to a "broad regime of technologies, practices, and discourses that define the female body as deficient and in need of constant attention."[59] Nonetheless, as she also suggests, recognizing this cannot justify a refusal to listen to the voices of those contemplating such procedures, and she argues that surgery offers a model of simultaneous, everyday "compliance and resistance." Virginia Blum's succinct characterization of the debate highlights the "critical distinction" for feminists between what is done "for pleasure" or "out of shame."[60] In *10 Years Younger*, pleasure for the audience is precisely generated out of a scene of shame.

10 Years Younger places the responsibility for Debbie Ashcroft's "premature aging" on the "choices" she has made, providing further evidence of the need for feminist television criticism to be vigilant to the rhetoric of personal responsibility and choice. Her self-diagnosis that she has "lost her way" is reiterated in the public exposure of her "shame." The passersby observe that she "probably smokes a few two many" and note "the jowls and the hoods on the eyelids." "She has got that over fifty-five hairstyle" and "her neck is a little bit pouty—it's like a duck's pouch." Under these very public conditions the (only?) "choice" is to undergo the "radical" option—a brow, neck, and eyelid lift at a cost of twelve thousand pounds, which takes five hours to perform. The recovery period for this kind of radical surgery could be as much as six months, but the fetishization of time management effected by the program limits Debbie to "a few days in bed and a hundred packs of frozen peas." While aging is publicly exposed and attenuated, antiaging occurs privately and its time duration is contracted. This contraction is crucial, as Vivian Sobchack points out, to the wider cultural "disavowal" that takes place more generally over the amount of time plastic surgery actually takes.[61] Indeed, the makeover paradigm itself relies on the same temporal coexistence of images themselves bespeaking time. "Before and after" imagery by its very nature disavows the actual duration of time, the labor that occurs between the two images, effecting a spectacle of instantaneous transformation.

The costs of this surgery (in terms of real pain and real money) appear palatable, even necessary, perhaps in part due to this effacement, but they also seem to be a "reasonable" response to the very public nature of the exposure of Debbie's failure to conform to the strictures of "aging well," the "ethicopolitical" demands that are placed on the body via a number of discourses that stress personal responsibility for the optimization of health (and health includes psychological well-being).[62] This exposes the dilemma faced by women aging in postfeminist culture; in this environment conformity begins to look like a psychological and social necessity rather than a "choice." As Deborah Covino points out, "Within a cultural atmosphere that increasingly sees aesthetic surgery as affordable, available and effective, the choice not to have a surgical makeover will be more and more striking and odd."[63] But I want to emphasize also the pleasures offered here, which do not cast either the participant or the audience as the "cultural dupe" or victim of "false consciousness"; there are in the series elements of playful as well as surgical "masquerade." Indeed, one of the central pleasures offered here is the mobilization of the narrative enigma over whether the makeover subject will successfully "pass" as younger than the audience knows her to be. The pleasures of the text include setting up the passersby as enforcers and surveillance operatives, but also, in the end, the program's willing "cultural dupes." Creating and resolving a narrative enigma around successful passing and enacting a fantasy of overcoming the cultural manifestations of time on the body coexist in this television series with a coercive, and normalizing, imperative to make the responsible "choice" to maximize corporeal and psychological health. The "ethics" of lifestyle and makeover reflect a more general, and gendered, cultural preoccupation with maximizing the body and the "self" utilizing the language of empowerment and choice, which, as Sarah Projansky demonstrates, renders feminism obsolete, and which, as Covino shows, has a sinister edge of compulsion, where the celebration of "choice" and the upbeat reliance on a rhetoric of possibility to become your own "best self" exist alongside a concomitant edge of "responsibility."[64]

This apparently democratic but in fact highly classed preoccupation with rejuvenation as a lifestyle "choice" corresponds to a wider cultural debate over the "positive" aging of a generation found in magazines aimed at the newly identified "middle youth," a perspective on aging succinctly summed up in the editor's letter to readers of the British women's magazine *Red* to mark the magazine's own makeover.

> When *Red* was launched seven years ago, the time was right for a magazine for women who had grown up without growing old and who wanted to enjoy the best things in life. After all, just because you've hit/passed your

thirties, doesn't mean you suddenly have a sense of humour bypass or enter some bizarre style time warp. And so the middle youth generation was born and I'm glad to say that in 2005 we're still wearing fabulous shoes, spending far too much on gorgeous things for our homes and enjoying nights out with our girlfriends.[65]

Several things interest me about this passage. First, this (classed) call to consumption as a technique of rejuvenation can be read as part of what Katz and Marshall have identified as "the new aging," a buoyant and optimistic cultural imagery around which marketing and consumerism have rallied.[66] Drawing on Rose's work, they note the contemporary "ethopolitical" "demands that one act to improve oneself . . . [wherein the] idea of health is reconfigured to encode an 'optimisation' of an individual's corporeality." In terms of aging, this results in the "impossible ideal that people live outside of time."[67] Aging is currently being redefined as the "chronological and generational boundaries which had set apart childhood, middle age, and old age, are becoming blurred and indeterminate."[68] This indeterminacy, in *10 Years Younger* at least, seems to be both celebrated (in the emphasis on "passing" as younger) and rigorously "policed" in the stress the program places on public scrutiny and "anonymous" identification of chronological age (whatever its relation to the actual number of years the person has "clocked up"). The *Red* editorial, too, seems to demonstrate this contradictory impulse to maximize the self as a project to which age is irrelevant but at the same time curiously and insistently present. The editorial is marked by the use of persistent, if somewhat confusing, generational and temporal metaphors. It notes the disjunction between chronological age and appropriate behaviors as obsolete but in the process deploys further temporal references. In the reference to a "time warp," for instance, the social "backwardness" or anachronism of the thirty-plus woman is presumed (and corrected). The generational and gestational metaphor is elaborated further in the reference to the "birth" of the "middle youth generation." This reference conforms to the proliferation identified by Katz and Marshall of "an explosion of popular demographic terms such as 'boomers,' 'empty nesters,' and 'third agers' that gloss over the negative realities of poverty and inequality in old age."[69]

"Middle youth," a gendered and classed designation, is heralded in a number of recent media discourses, which have noted the advent of the independent, sexy, glamorous older woman. Economic independence is, for example, a crucial component of the "disco" woman (discerning, increasing years, stylish, and comfortably off) identified in a piece for the *Observer*.[70] The "contemporary" woman is defined in this piece precisely by the perception of a disjunction between the paradigms of acceptable age-appropriate attitudes ("If they are 40 or 50 they feel 30 or 40") and behaviors and the "demands" of a generation of women accessing the language of empowerment ("They had all the fashion choice in their twenties and they are not prepared to give that up in their thirties and forties") to the practices of consumption summed up in an interviewee's quote: "It's not about age any more. It's about attitude." Interestingly, though, it appears from the article that in fact it is very much about age. Chronological age is returned to again and again, and the non-fit of the existing paradigms of aging is accompanied by a paradoxical reliance on those selfsame paradigms tied resolutely to chronological age. This is a feature of recent magazine discourse on positive (i.e., invisible) aging. In the British weekly magazine *Grazia*, for example, a feature entitled "Why It's Suddenly Hip to Be 40" asks, "How is it that Sarah Jessica Parker can swan into her fortieth birthday bash looking so radiantly youthful?" Having established that "youth" is no longer tied to chronological age, the article goes on to contradict its own proposition in its insistence that its review of celebrity icons demonstrates that "40 is the new 30."[71] Redefining age in these discourses seems to rely exclusively on the "girling" of older women; attributing glamour to older bodies is linked to rejuvenating them. It seems too obvious to state, but younger women are not encouraged in these discourses to "aspire" to age. To put this slightly differently, if chronological boundaries are indeed blurring, this only happens in one direction.

The codes of glamour, sexual availability and attractiveness, and a responsible attitude toward limiting the corporeal markers of increasing years are a feature of these discourses shared with *10 Years Younger*, but here I want to make the rather obvious point that these are highly ideological strictures demanding a clear investment on the part of women to perform the roles of youthful femininity driven by consumption whatever their age. Not only is "youth" procured by patterns of consumption, but also the possibility of escaping the necessity to conform to its "girlish" precepts is fast eroding. There is no space here for the "serenity" of escape from sexual objectivity described by Germaine Greer, who sees the invisibility traditionally associated with aging for women as a "freedom" that "mass culture" obscures in its relentless celebration of celebrities who "remain youthful," thus enticing audiences to "spend enormous sums of money in the attempt to fashion themselves into ghastly simulacra of youthful bodies."[72] Whether such displays are desirable or not, it is important to note the economic aspects of this "rejuvenated" generation and the specter of inequality being displayed on the body in a new way. This is closely linked to Patricia Mellencamp's observation that money as much as "sexual difference" might divide the "postmodern subject," and thus economics needs to be central to a "theoretical foundation for cultural analysis."[73] Class and the concomitant economic wherewithal to shape transformation marks bodies, and may increasingly do so, but in *10 Years Younger* class is effectively effaced by the invocation of a discourse of individual responsibility for "having" a body that has experienced time (a "cultured" body). Debbie Ashcroft's "failures" are listed by the narrator in a manner that recalls the bossy (even infantilizing) strictures of magazine discourse but also, more equivocally perhaps, calls attention to the taste culture of the program, which equates some "care of the self" (crudely bleached hair and sun beds) with the televisually unacceptable: "Older doesn't mean wiser, and if you don't want to see the results of a lifetime of sun beds and ciggies look away now. Debbie's skin is sallow and saggy, her brow is heavy and haggard, her jaw line is hidden by her giant jowls and, here's the science bit, her hair's knackered from too much bleach. Add to all this a dress sense that says sixty rather than sexy, and this is one sad mother who needs all the help she can get."

Here the participant's investment in sun beds and bleach (an investment she has made in the multi-million-pound beauty industry, which sponsors the program) is revealed not only as misguided but as irresponsible and "aging." The invocation of a discourse of responsibility is complicated by a consideration of class with that of age.[74] The program never directly addresses class, and yet it is a feature of makeover programming more widely that it employs "bossy" middle-class women whose unspoken assignment is to eradicate any visible markers of being working class.[75] Bland, "tasteful" (in the sense of adhering to middle-class notions of decorum) and unequivocally feminine is equated by *10 Years Younger* with "young."

The lifestyle imperative to take personal responsibility for rejuvenation is especially pronounced in the book that accompanies the series, a book that reveals the classed preoccupations of rejuvenation. While the television series features those, like Debbie Ashcroft, coded by television's conventions as working- or lower-middle-class women (in terms of regional accent, occupation, style of speech, and so on), the book imagines a very different ideal reader. The class and economic bias of the book's apparently "universal" approach to its reader is demonstrated by references to the author's clients, "women who have swapped city careers for the school run" and the advice on energy levels, which includes, "Tackle the things in your life that are draining your energy. If the house is really getting you down, get a cleaner." An exemplary "equality and choice" postfeminist text, the book gleefully heralds the coming of the "new aging," explicitly linking the achievements of second-wave feminism to the shifting of boundaries around age: "Women have never had it better. We're more empowered and successful than ever before; we have a wealth of opportunities open to us and genuine life choices to make. Not so long ago we were considered on our way out at 40. Now women in their 50s and 60s are looking great, are sexually active, enjoying fantastic careers and embracing life to the full."[76] "We" here is highly exclusive; on the whole the women on *10 Years Younger* do not conform to this model of "'fantastic careers" (the first series featured a prison officer, a former flight attendant working at a market stall, a shift worker, and a part-time student). Drawing attention to the selective ability to transcend temporal limits entails inadvertently revealing the inequalities of postfeminist culture.

Grasping the possibilities of this "new aging" involves, as I have stressed, the utilization of discourses of responsibility, and this extends to the fashioning of a suitably gendered self; specifically, and recalling the earlier discussion of gendered identities and aging, it is femininity that is invoked as a weapon in the battle against age. Hambleton-Jones's commentary on Debbie Ashcroft's clothes makes this point explicitly; when told that Ashcroft has "never worn a skirt," Hambleton-Jones's displeasure is clear, announcing, "Well we're going to have to work on that." This "work" is literally to install the missing "femininity"; the "new look" is all about clothes that are fitted and "feminine." In her book, Hambleton-Jones emphasizes that women's happiness is largely dependent on their ability to locate and reproduce "femininity." Referring to mothers who do not work outside the home, she scolds: "Their idea of femininity and style has got lost somewhere amid the nappies and the muslins."[77] The potential costs of not finding this "lost object" are (none too subtly) hinted at in the book's references to the film *The First Wives Club* (in which the three principal characters are left by their husbands for younger women) and in the thinly veiled warnings of the dangers of becoming "frumpy" (i.e., comfortably dressed): "Frumpy looks old no matter what age you are. . . . It's tough but true. Just because your partner and kids don't say anything doesn't mean they don't notice how you dress. Silence doesn't mean approval."[78] While the disco women alluded to earlier are marked by their financial and social independence, a much more fearful specter of the consequences (rejection, divorce, poverty) of the failure to remain youthful (and hence recognizably feminine) is at work here.

The yoking together of youth and visible femininity is particularly clear in the case of Kerry Fender (series 1, episode 7), whose premature aging is presented as something of a "mystery": "There are no wrinkles, thick hair and bright eyes." Unlike the case of Debbie Ashcroft, the series doesn't hold her responsible for her "frumpy, defeated and definitely middle aged" looks, expressly commenting on "all her good habits." This program's diagnosis of premature aging is hugely misleading, I would argue, because what seems to be key is in fact the elimination of the participant's notably androgynous self-styling. This episode thus substantiates, despite its focus on techniques of rejuvenation, Mellencamp's claim about American television that "TV's bodily codes adhere to sexual difference and a fundamentalist propriety, particularly when it comes to the ideology of age and gender."[79]

At the start, Fender's hair is cropped and she wears "John Lennon" glasses, jeans, and a white T-shirt. By the end, her need for the glasses has been lasered away (in a procedure she is clearly frightened by) and her hair has been extended; despite the lack of wrinkles, her face has been "filled" and her high-heeled red shoes and denim skirt replace the jeans with a recognizably "girly" sartorialism. The problems with locating exactly "what is 'aging' Kerry Fender" might also account for the bizarre amount of dental treatment she receives. First, in quite a long sequence, her teeth are "whitened," and then (even whiter) veneers are placed over the newly whitened teeth. This visual redundancy seems symptomatic of the overdetermined anxiety to name "age" when actually the makeover seems concerned with "gender." *10 Years Younger* thus conforms to Halberstam's identification of the "multiple sites" in which any manifestation of female masculinity is "challenged, denied, threatened, and violated," which might, from a critical perspective, negate its knowing emphasis on a contingent and fabricated "identity" based on the parodic fetishization of chronological age.[80] The "feminization" of the problematically "androgynous" body is also apparent in *Something's Gotta Give*, where it is explicitly sexualized.

Chronological Propriety in *Something's Gotta Give*

Aging in postfeminist culture, then, seems marked by both a gesturing toward utopian desires to transcend time and chronology evident in makeover paradigms and a concurrent tendency to emphasize time, chronology, and generational (and sexual) difference. I have already suggested that one way in which this paradoxical reliance on discourses that transcend but also rely on temporal constraints plays out on women's bodies is in the negotiation of the ethics of cosmetic surgery, wherein hiding the signs of aging sometimes becomes the spectacle rather than the aging body itself. Further, at least in *10 Years Younger*, the ethical dilemmas of failing to "age well" are negotiated via a discourse of "premature" aging, neatly bypassing the complexity of constructing overly youthful bodies (bodies that have too obviously evaded time).

In *Something's Gotta Give*, the aging body achieves a centrality unusual in popular films and a similar negotiation of the ethics of aging in contemporary culture is produced. Here the emphasis is, once more, on the "appropriate," but, whereas the women who opt for makeover appear to be working (hard) on "the self," here the emphasis is on romance, on temporally "correct" bodies finding one another, and on rehabilitating the central characters into a generationally suitable sexuality. On the one hand, then, the film stands out as a popular narrative that represents the older woman, grants her a sexual life, and addresses the male fear of the aging female body (almost literally) head on. On the other hand, the reliance on chronological decorum and propriety limits the possibilities for either generation of women (mother or daughter) to finally escape the paradigms of age and generation as sexually and perhaps culturally exclusive; virility and vitality are linked in the deliverance of a "natural" rather than artificial, commodified sexuality for the male body. For the female body, the rewards of sexual and emotional "undoing," as the daughter describes it, are a little less clear. If "invisibility" is a trope long associated with older women in contemporary culture, then attention needs to be paid to the specific forms visibility might take.

Marshall and Katz have drawn attention to the centrality of sexuality to the discourses of aging in contemporary culture. They argue that sexuality, and specifically the gendered dynamics of ensuring that heterosexual intercourse successfully take place, is central to a wider reinvention of models of maturity to emphasize the "positive" lifestyle and consumer choices made by "ageless" consumers, a reinvention made possible by a "convergence of consumer society and professional expertise."[81] Indeed, they emphasize that "active sexuality," for which read heterosexual intercourse, has become the single indicator of "positive and successful aging." They note an unholy alliance among health management, commercial concerns, and the development of the "post human body," which all emphasize the "impossible burden of growing older without aging, with a fundamental part of this burden attributed to the maintenance of sexual functionality and fitness." Holmlund's analysis of *Basic Instinct* and *Fried Green Tomatoes* demonstrates that popular film, too, often reveals a great deal about the psychology of aging and its attendant fears and anxieties, fears and anxieties in which, again, sexuality plays a central role. Holmlund's analysis uncovers the "age spots as blind spots" of both critics and films where aging characters are marginalized or killed off and narratives of investigation and sexual performance "mask" midlife anxieties in specifically gendered ways.[82] Holmlund's analysis demonstrates the importance of "reading" age despite the textual concerns to erase the specter of an association between death and dying and age, a concern that, in *Basic Instinct*, locates sexuality in the youthful body of the younger woman, recourse to which (in both sexual and investigative terms) ensures the suppression of specifically male anxieties over aging. *Something's Gotta Give* requires no such uncovering on the part of the critic, but its concerns with sexuality and age are no less gendered. The film's narrative stresses both the association between sexuality and the fear of aging and death for men and offers sexuality as the "signal indicator" of positive and successful aging for women. In the process, it also demarcates limits to the "project" of "timelessness," specifically in its invocation of chronological decorum.

I suggested earlier that both postfeminist popular culture and critical commentary on that culture characteristically emphasize generational struggle. In *Something's Gotta Give*, as we saw, these discourses are mobilized but in quite complex and even critical ways. Feminist readings of popular culture and social mores are, in fact, subtly endorsed by the film, which locates much of its (quite conventionally ageist) horror at the spectacle of the aging *male* body rather than the female and is quietly celebratory of the similarities, rather than conflicts, between mother and daughter. In the restoration of chronologically appropriate sexual coupling, the film even goes some way toward obscuring the temporal differences between them, rejuvenating the mother and maturing the daughter. This stress on similarity culminates in the "generation" of a new "girl"—a baby girl—who, in the final, familial tableau, literalizes the connection between mother and daughter into one of sameness over difference, a connection that, as I suggest below, has already been established visually by an emphasis on resemblance in both their clothes and, crucially, their bodies. In narrative terms, then, there is an explicit recognition of the "continuum" between the "polar opposites" of youth and age.[83]

In the process of stressing both continuity and generational propriety, the explicitly feminist critique of the male fear of the older woman's body is overcome, though not before much of the comedy of the film has been played out in exposing and investigating it. There is a "symbolic exchange" of sexual partners during this film, an exchange or traffic that, as Eve Sedgwick and Gayle Rubin have amply demonstrated, usually occurs "between men" and is implicated in the continuity of patriarchy. Here, however, the exchange is between women, moreover between mother and daughter; any threat to heterosexual power relations that this exchange might conceivably pose is evaded by the emphasis on chronology, the symbolic "rescue" of the central character, Erica, from (feminist) sexual isolation, and (albeit comic and wrongly ascribed) the transformation of ambiguous gender into (postfeminist) feminine, emphatic heterosexuality.

The narrative patterning of romantic comedy and romantic fictions more generally conform to a logic not dissimilar to the makeover paradigm discussed earlier. *Something's Gotta Give* is a romantic comedy about the reformation of a sixty-three-year-old man who never dates women over thirty and Erica Barry, a "woman of a certain age" who, though rich, successful, and "accomplished" (as her sister Zoe tells us early in the film), never dates at all. The narrative offers a series of transformations for its lead characters. Erica, who is described (by Harry) as a "tower of strength, flinty and impervious . . . formidable" and (by herself) as a "high-strung . . . controlling, know-it-all neurotic," learns through the course of the film that satisfying sex is not confined to youthful bodies and to modify her monochrome outlook on both men and popular culture. Harry Sanders begins the film dating Marin, Erica's daughter, but learns via a series of humiliating encounters with mortality, in the form of a heart attack and attendant physical vulnerabilities, to conform to chronological propriety and to appreciate the assets (figured here as both material and fleshly) of a woman of his own generation (though not quite his own age).[84] In the process, significantly, he learns to conform to the "self-vigilance" required by various discourses that make up the profile of responsible management of the body in contemporary culture succinctly described by Rose as "the will to health."[85] Marin, Erica's daughter, is "made over" from a commitment-phobic career girl intent on having "fun" with the "old, chauvinistic, wrong" Harry to motherhood and domesticity with the appropriately aged Danny. Only Zoe, Erica's feminist sister, and Julian Mercer, the thirty-six-year-old doctor who treats Harry for his heart attack and later initiates him into the sensibilities of postfeminist masculinity (he recognizes Erica from the start as both "beautiful" and "a fantastic writer"), are immune from the inexorable narrative drive toward generationally appropriate, heterosexual makeover that the film provides for its other lead characters.[86]

Visually the film reinforces this makeover narrative logic with a focus on Erica's clothes, which, as the film progresses, reflect her sexual reawakening. The transformation of Erica's wardrobe from turtlenecks and high-collar T-shirts topped with cardigans in various shades of white, which represent her "untouchability" and present her as a sort of perversely virginal figure, is ritualized in the symbolic and literal cutting away of the turtleneck by Harry when they have sex. By the following scene, she has embraced "feminine" pastels and V-necks, exposing the same part of her anatomy that Harry has insisted she register as "beautiful" against his (and presumably the audience's) expectations to the contrary. When the romance falters, Erica is left (albeit temporarily) gesturing to her now exposed lower neck and wondering what she is going to do with "all this." Marin also goes through a wardrobe makeover, her clothes throughout representing her relationship to femininity, youth, and her parents. As important to understanding Marin's narrative trajectory is attention to the removal of clothes at significant moments, once for Harry's benefit and later in her workplace when faced with the "betrayal" of her father ("beyond creepy") for a sexual relationship with a younger woman. Here, as Marin gets ready to "sell forty-three million dollars worth of art," her distraught stripping and dressing exemplify both her emotional and professional state/status. As her mother acquires sexual and then professional fulfillment, Marin's own relationship to maturity becomes more emphatic; her successful career in auctioneering is presented as a virtuoso "performance" for which she, significantly, "dresses up." But such dressing up is somewhat double-edged, emphasizing the "play" at the heart of her apparent professionalism. Accordingly, when Marin is successfully married off she appears three months pregnant in her mother's "uniform" of high white turtleneck, a "growing up" that is also a growing into the role of motherhood that her mother has just grown out of. This "continuity" stresses both their essential similarity and the centrality of "family" time and developmental paradigms to the film's negotiations of aging and chronology.

The "unnaturalness" of Erica's pre-Harry wardrobe (and by implication her more general status as a "problem" to be solved by the romance narrative) is evidenced in a key sequence in the film in which Harry probes the meanings behind her "inappropriate" attire, asking "Never get hot?" The sexual overtones of his question are clear: while she gives him a resounding "never" (followed by a barely audible "not lately"), she then literally "rewrites" her response to a more flirtatious (signaled in a suggestive gesture at the keyboard where she is writing what will turn out to be a vengeful version of their romance) "I wouldn't say never." Checking that she is alone, she then closes the laptop, straightens her back, and undresses, underscoring both her age and the discomfort of her attire (she is, indeed, "hot"). Significantly, this is not the first time in the film that a woman has stripped, and the scene mirrors an earlier strip by Marin for Harry's benefit. I have called this a "mirroring," but in fact attention to the similarities and differences between the two women's exposure of their bodies to Harry's gaze is instructive in the understanding of the body and more precisely gendered understandings of the young and less young body that the narrative of the film is eager to rectify. Harry's reaction to seeing Erica's body in this scene might, in fact, be seen as performing the ideological work of the film: to rehabilitate the middle-aged female body into heterosexual visibility and hence activity.

Harry is, we are explicitly told, "afraid" of older women. We know this because Zoe, the film's voice of feminist critique, has, "diagnosed" Harry as an exemplar of a wider cultural phenomenon in which older men date younger women because they "are threatened and deadly afraid of productive older women."[87] We also know this because Harry's initial reaction to Erica is to cast her in the role of an authoritarian killjoy significantly registering her economic independence as both threatening and "impressive." His reaction to

Zoe, Erica, and Marin confront the unreconstructed Harry in *Something's Gotta Give*.

her Hamptons beach house is akin to the famous scene in *Pride and Prejudice* in which Elizabeth Bennet first sees Darcy's splendid stately home, just one of a number of references in the film to his taking on the role of the "girl" in this romance. When she mistakes him for a burglar and calls the police, her relationship to authority seems, for Harry at least, to be assured. As they clear up the misunderstanding, he tries to compliment her on her actions, referring to her performance as "strong" and "macho," and declaring that he hopes faced with "a burglar in his refrigerator that he'd be half the man" she was. Clearly these sentiments are played for comedy, and it is possible to overstate their significance. Nevertheless, it is the task of the narrative to restore chronological propriety to Harry's sex life by providing an explicit rejoinder to his fear that older women are less "feminine" than younger women and, further (and it is perhaps significant also that Zoe wields a large kitchen knife in this scene), that his anxiety and fear of them are explicitly likened to castration anxiety. In Laura Mulvey's classic psychoanalytic model, scopophilia famously overcomes anxiety over sexual difference, but here this foundational anxiety seems to be displaced, or at least complicated by, another anxiety linked to the woman's body, the "spectacle" of the aging body provoking a new fear. Recalling Woodward's analysis of aging as a potential site of changed or challenged gendered identities, we might speculate on the possible psychic processes at work in this narrative.

This is the context in which we understand Harry's reaction to coming across Erica's naked body: fear (he falls backward against a wall, apparently

recoiling in horror) and subsequent relief (he smiles and looks again in evident pleasure). Not so "different" after all, that is to say, not so different from
the familiar youthful female body. This revelation ironically enables him to
find romantic sympathy (sameness) along generational lines but only once this
anxious probing of Erica's "gender" has been overcome. Perhaps, if sexual
difference is conventionally understood as a site of anxiety, it has here been
displaced, at least momentarily, by an anxiety that such difference might be
less than total, less than permanent. However, it is not just Harry but also the
audience that is being schooled in the essential continuity between women of
different generations; after all, it is the audience, not Harry, that is privy to
the removal of Erica's clothes in this scene, clothes that are identical (white
jeans) to those Marin divests herself of in the earlier scene, where the younger
woman tempts Harry into the long awaited consummation of their relationship. This relationship is destined to remain asexual, however; indeed, its
dangers are literalized in the heart attack that results from their thwarted attempts to make love. Harry's fear is demonstrably misplaced as his relationship with Marin not only requires the "support" of Viagra (suggesting that it
is fundamentally "unnatural") but also threatens his life.[88] The film hugely
ironizes Harry's fear of the castrating feminist, but it is also ironic that in fact
it is male potency that the film is interested in restoring to Harry through
Erica, ironic because at the same time that it restores a symbolic measure of
sexual prowess it schools him in renouncing his signature hypermasculinity
for a more empathetic, "feminized" version.

Disciplining Time: Rejuvenation, Gender, and Sexuality

The foregoing discussion has highlighted some of the questions raised by
the changing visibility of the older body literally in popular culture and figuratively in feminist criticism and theory. If, as I have suggested, representations are becoming increasingly ubiquitous in expressing desires to thwart
the "old" negative associations of age, it remains critical to be sensitive to the
sexual, economic, and gender politics thereby produced in the "new aging."
Equally, it is interesting to note examples of moments in which an under-
current of "ageism" is, perhaps surprisingly, tenaciously reproduced, for instance, as indicated here, in popular representations of feminism as an outdated anachronism, ripe for a makeover. Makeover paradigms are a crucial
feature of postfeminist popular culture; making over the aging body emphasizes the utopian annihilation of signs and markers of age, but, as analysis

of *10 Years Younger* shows, it limits the possible defiance of "nature" to highly circumscribed norms demonstrably conformist in terms of class, body management, and gender. The program manages to "have it both ways," to offer the fantasy of therapeutic rejuvenation while remaining firmly entrenched in a coercive and moralizing policing of aesthetic and gender norms. Similarly, while offering a rare challenge to the centrality of youth in romantic narratives, *Something's Gotta Give* deploys a mixture of hostile and celebratory imagery to investigate the sexuality of those over fifty. (Hetero)sexuality in *Something's Gotta Give*, a narrative of aging in postfeminist culture, is simultaneously mobilized as a reminder of mortality and held out as a conduit for rejuvenation. The film offers a careful and cautious negotiation of the "new aging," which, even as it appears to liberate the characters into life-affirming sexual habits, places definite constraints around what constitutes appropriate sexual relationships and gender identities in time. What both texts seem to stress is a connection between "rejuvenation" and highly conventional forms of femininity and sexuality that set the standards of both chronological decorum and time defiance regulating other contemporary bodies.

Notes

1. The epigraphs that open this essay are from de Beauvoir, *Old Age*, 3; and Wilde, "The Picture of Dorian Gray," 47.
2. For a detailed discussion of the conceptualization of "girls," see Whiteley, *Too Much Too Young*, 65–70. In her discussion of *Sex and the City*, Diane Negra notes the complexity of how the iconic postfeminist series attributes "perpetual girlhood to thirty something women," which "can be celebrated by an ageist culture even while it also becomes a strategy for dismissing such women as not having attained full adulthood" ("Quality Postfeminism?").
3. The concerns of this essay are narratives and representations that purport to be sympathetic to the older female. Conventional representations of the older woman as abject, crone, and grotesque are explicitly critiqued in some of these representations, although, one might argue, the very "positive" nature of these representations is predicated on their "absent presence."
4. A survey of representations of aging in popular culture is outside of the scope of this essay, but, while my argument is that there is an increasing, and specifically inflected, visibility to the question of age and aging, it is useful to note that certain genres of both film and television have traditionally explored aging, particularly soap opera and situation comedy.
5. As Virginia Blum puts it, "In contrast to the protracted process of development and aging, surgery feels like magic" (*Flesh Wounds*, 4).
6. In his history of aesthetic surgery, Sander L. Gilman makes a distinction between

two competing models of age defiance: "rejuvenation," in which the whole body is returned to youth in a complete transformation; and the model of surgery, the piecemeal techniques of covering up, masking, or hiding aged features. He goes on, however, to describe the process by which aesthetic surgeons in the 1920s "evoked the idea of rejuvenation of the spirit," a conceptualization that has subsequently gained in currency, as I discuss below, thus blurring the boundary between the two models. I use *rejuvenation* here in a more general way to signal the mobilization of fantasies of escaping the negative associations of aging in contemporary culture via the appropriation of attributes (appearances or behaviors) previously or routinely associated with youth (*Making the Body Beautiful*, 295, 304, 311). See also Susan Merrill Squier's fascinating discussion of the transition from "replacement to regeneration" in fictional and scientific discourses on aging and the links between rejuvenation and reproductive medicine (*Liminal Lives*, 146–67, 214–52, 272).

7. McRobbie, "Post-feminism and Popular Culture," 255. In foregrounding the generational aspects of the highly contested term *postfeminism*, I do not intend to redefine or reductively limit it to this encounter but rather to call attention to correspondences between popular culture's representations of aging bodies, temporal and chronological uncertainties, and feminist scholarship's often uneasy relationship with its recent history.

8. de Beauvoir, *Old Age*, 4.

9. Woodward, "Youthfulness as a Masquerade," 127.

10. For a thoughtful discussion about these issues in relation to academic feminism, see Detloff, "Mean Spirits," 76–99.

11. Kaplan "Trauma and Aging," 172. It will become clear from the analysis that the whiteness and overwhelming heterosexuality of these representations are of central importance, colluding in, or even generating, the impression that postfeminist representations of older women follow the internally critiqued white, privileged feminism that Amanda Lotz and Anne Brooks, for instance, want to distance themselves from in their definitions of *postfeminism*. For them, postfeminism is a reflection of the "epistemological break" that "the posts" (poststructuralism, postcolonialism, and postmodernism) and the critiques of women of color, feminists of the global South, and others have made resoundingly, burying the notion that feminism can claim the category of "women." I understand postfeminist popular discourse to, in quite precise ways and as the analysis here shows, if not eradicate then at least to be highly limiting of this exact project, positing a centrality for the white, heterosexual, privileged female body and equating that very precisely with feminism, but it seems significant that this white, heterosexual, feminist woman is also older. So, whereas I understand (broadly speaking) the insights of deconstruction in various guises to be *feminist* insights and that it is unhelpful to label these postfeminist, I take postfeminist cultural representation to be implicated in a representational system that is exclusionary in the ways highlighted by Judith Butler in "Contingent Foundations." It is also important to note that the crisis and "trauma" of aging—the anxieties over an aging population—are, as Ann Kaplan points out, precisely *white* traumas and

anxieties. See Lotz, "Postfeminist Television Criticism"; Butler, "Contingent Foundations"; Kaplan, "Trauma and Aging"; and Brooks, *Postfeminisms*.

12. As I discuss below, discourses of glamour and economic independence combined with imperatives to take a responsible attitude toward the body to bypass the visible markers of increasing years are increasingly prevalent. These discourses, which Stephen Katz and Barbara Marshall identify as "the new aging," are marked by their limited socioeconomic reach. Also prevalent as perhaps a "structuring absence" of these discourses is the specter of poverty among the aged. Economic differences between aging bodies are a reminder of the difficulties and exclusions of generational groupings. For a discussion of these issues in relation to American cinema and the representation of aging masculinity, see Holmlund, *Impossible Bodies*, especially 153–56.

13. Mellencamp, "From Anxiety to Equanimity," 314.

14. Hawkesworth, "The Semiotics of Premature Burial," 2.

15. Russo, "Aging and the Scandal of Anachronism," 21.

16. Halberstam, *In a Queer Time and Place*, 2.

17. Russo, "Aging and the Scandal of Anachronism," 21.

18. In particular, in the British context Imelda Whelehan discusses the disavowal of feminism along these lines in her critique of Rene Deneld's *The New Victorians: A Young Woman's Challenge to the Old Feminist Order*, and Katie Roiphe's *The Morning After: Sex, Fear, and Feminism*. See Whelehan, *Overloaded*, 28–30.

19. McRobbie, "Post-feminism and Popular Culture," 258.

20. Significantly, in writing about the 1993 press coverage of the "gorgeous new feminist" Naomi Wolf, the author of *The Beauty Myth*, Hilary Hinds and Jackie Stacey note, "So-Called 'new feminism' is . . . billed as the glamorous make-over of the old-fashioned, drab and over-serious 'women's liberationists' of the past" ("Imagining Feminism, Imagining Femininity," 153).

21. Hawkesworth, "The Semiotics of Premature Burial," 1.

22. Karlyn, "*Scream*, Popular Culture, and Feminism's 'Third Wave.'"

23. Springer, "Third Wave Black Feminism?" 2. In the same issue, see Guy-Sheftall, "Response from a 'Second Waver' to Kimberly Springer's 'Third Wave Black Feminism?'"; and Hill, "Keepin' It Real." Another exception to the conflict model of generational difference can be found in Charlotte Brunsdon's television criticism. See her "Lifestyling Britain," 84.

24. Woodward, *Figuring Age*, xi.

25. Examples from the last decade of "chick flicks" and teen movies include *Clueless* (Heckerling, 1995), *10 Things I Hate about You* (Junger, 1999), the *Legally Blonde* franchise (Luketic, 2001; Herman-Wurmfeld, 2003), and *Raising Helen* (Marshall, 2004).

26. As I discuss later, Erica's position as a feminist is mediated by the presence of her sister, Zoe, who is coded through dress and career (she teaches women's studies) as the "voice" of feminism. Zoe's presence allows the articulation of a critique of patriarchy at one remove, and she is conspicuously absent from the final, familial tableau of appropriately aged couples and generational continuity.

27. See Gill, "From Sexual Objectification to Sexual Subjectification."

28. The casting of Nicholson in the role of Harry connects in interesting ways with a number of his previous roles in which he has played either wolfish or malevolent sexual predators (e.g., *The Witches of Eastwick* [Miller, 1987], *Batman* [Burton, 1989], and *Wolf* [Nichols, 1994]). Also particularly interesting in this context are Nicholson characters who experience dislocations in identity due to age or professional failure or both (e.g., *The Pledge* [Penn, 2001], *As Good as It Gets* [Brooks, 1997], and *About Schmidt* [Payne, 2002]).

29. Holmlund, *Impossible Bodies.*

30. I should perhaps clarify here that there is no sense of critique in the film's symbolic use of rap music. Harry's successful exploitation of musical tastes is evidence of his overinvestment in youth, but the film quietly revels, through a foregrounding of lavishly furnished interiors, in the economic success of both its leading characters.

31. Sexuality and consumption are indeed linked by the (gendered) politics of "successful aging," as Katz and Marshall have shown in "New Sex for Old."

32. Girlishness and girliness are quite differently figured, though both can be understood in terms of white femininity. *Girlish* has infantalizing overtones, as well as links to vitality and renewal, whereas *girly* has connotations of pornographic representations. See Gill, "From Sexual Objectification to Sexual Subjectification," for a discussion of young women's "pernicious" new sexual "subjectification" in place of old modes of objectification. See Whelehan *Overloaded*, 37–57, for a discussion of the limits and "whitewash" of "girl power" in the British context.

33. For example, see Hollows, *Feminism, Femininity, and Popular Culture*; Probyn, "New Traditionalism and Post-Feminism"; and Brunsdon, "Identity in Television Criticism."

34. Brunsdon refers to the way in which validating the "accoutrements of femininity" works to "remake the cultural memory of the censorious feminist" in "Feminism, Postfeminism, Martha, Martha, and Nigella," 113.

35. Spigel, "Theorizing the Bachelorette," 3.

36. Woodward, "Youthfulness as a Masquerade," 122.

37. Butler, *Gender Trouble*, 179.

38. Butler, *Bodies That Matter*, 231.

39. Ibid.

40. Mellencamp, *High Anxiety*, 281.

41. For a related discussion of another British makeover series, see Roberts, "The Fashion Police," in this volume.

42. Foucault, *The Care of the Self*, vol. 3.

43. For example, see Blum, *Flesh Wounds*, 271; Covino, *Amending the Abject Body*, 97–98; Sobchack, "Scary Women"; and Weber, "Beauty, Desire, and Anxiety."

44. See Blum, *Flesh Wounds*, 48. For a feminist discussion of the issue of cosmetic surgery from the perspective of feminism and its relationship to agency, empowerment, and feminist critique, see Kathy Davis's "rejoinder" to Susan Bordo's critique in *Reshaping the Female Body* in Davis, *Dubious Equalities and Embodied Differences*, 8–17.

45. See Blum, *Flesh Wounds*, 75–80; and Featherstone, "Post-bodies, Aging, and Virtual Reality," 228.
46. Squier, *Liminal Lives*, 216.
47. Featherstone, "The Body in Consumer Culture," 186.
48. Katz and Marshall, "New Sex for Old," 16.
49. This part of the program is broadly played for comedy. The "real" judgments are made by the team of "experts," the surgeons, hairdressers, and stylists who will deliver the rejuvenation, while the lighting and camera work highlight the isolation of the participant in the expert session.
50. Gilman, *Making the Body Beautiful*, xxi.
51. Ibid., 331.
52. Blum, *Flesh Wounds*, 132.
53. "Radical" here refers to the extent of the surgery deemed "necessary" but is suggestive in its evacuation of the political sense of the term and its incursion into the private real, which is implicitly understood as apolitical.
54. Covino, *Amending the Abject Body*, 2.
55. Ibid., 87.
56. Rose, "The Politics of Life Itself."
57. In celebrity discourse, unsurprisingly, this takes the form of some confusion over the desire to extend the life span of glamour. An article in *USA Today* (20 January 2005) entitled "The New 'It Girls': Gray and Glamorous," appears to reiterate the identification of glamour and aged bodies using "Hollywood's Hottest" over-forty Oscar winners as proof that "you can be beautiful at any age." In this article, however, the resistance to any obvious demonstration or application of the techniques of rejuvenation is also voiced; "wrinkles and lines were not removed," we are told, and the actress Shirley Jones states that "fifty and older is young today" but "lines, wrinkles, face falling—all of that. That's part of aging."
58. Blum argues that the phenomenon of stardom and celebrity in the twentieth and twenty-first centuries has been instrumental in the production of what she terms "surgical culture" and vice versa (*Flesh Wounds*, especially 220–61).
59. Davis, *Dubious Equalities*, 117.
60. Blum, *Flesh Wounds*, 294. Although writing in the very different context of public response to the death of Princess Diana and coverage of the "child murderer" Mary Bell, the program seems to me to correspond to Jacqueline Rose's analysis of the "cult of celebrity," which she identifies as being marked by a sadistic "seek[ing] out of people to carry our own shame" ("The Cult of Celebrity," 214).
61. Sobchack, "Scary Women," 207.
62. Rose, "The Politics of Life Itself," 1–30.
63. Covino, *Amending the Abject Body*, 90.
64. Ibid., 89.
65. Editorial, *Red*, March 2005, 7.
66. Katz and Marshall, "New Sex for Old," 13.
67. Ibid., 13.

68. Ibid., 4.

69. Ibid., 5.

70. "How DISCO Women Set Pace for Fashion Trends," *Observer*, 30 January 2005. I'm grateful to Diane Negra for bringing this piece to my attention.

71. "Why It's Suddenly Hip to Be 40," *Grazia*, 11 April 2005.

72. Greer, "Serenity and Power," 266.

73. Mellencamp, *High Anxiety*, 278.

74. There is a link here, perhaps, to recent exposés of the fast food industry such as *Super Size Me* (Spurlock, 2004) and *Jamie's School Dinners* (BBC TV, March 2005), which, while certainly critiquing the food industry, visually register their disgust by displaying working-class bodies and preferences in an unsympathetic, grotesque light.

75. Brunsdon, "Lifestyling Britain," 78.

76. Hambleton-Jones, *Ten Years Younger*, 9.

77. Ibid., 216.

78. Ibid.

79. Mellencamp, *High Anxiety*, 264.

80. Halberstam, *Female Masculinity*, 19.

81. Katz and Marshall, "New Sex for Old," 1.

82. Holmlund, *Impossible Bodies*, 85.

83. Woodward, quoted in ibid., 145.

84. While the audience is told on three occasions Harry's precise age, of which he makes no secret, Erica's chronological age is left somewhat vague, in keeping with the everyday decorum (or denial) of ascribing age to female bodies denoted in, to use Kathleen Woodward's description, the "figuring" of "women of a certain age." We are told she is over fifty but also only "almost" twenty years older than her thirty-six-year-old love interest, Dr. Julian Mercer. The film draws to a close over the celebration of Erica's birthday, and yet we are still not given a number. This seems to me to be interesting, as the film wants us to accept Harry and Erica as bound by generational ties and yet obscures the ten-year age gap between them.

85. Rose, "The Politics of Life Itself," 6.

86. There is an unresolved enigma around Julian's relinquishment of Erica at the end of the film; without motivation, the character's absence seems merely to be evidence of the film's inability to countenance transgenerational couplings. The only other couple in the film, Erica's ex-husband and his "new" fiancée, who is only two years older than his daughter, are represented in entirely conventional ways as merely evidence of the "epidemic" of couplings between older men and younger women. The romance between Julian and Erica is represented in a much more sympathetic light and yet has to end.

87. Here Zoe echoes Susan Sontag's analysis of "the double standard of aging," which "for most women means a humiliating process of gradual sexual disqualification" ("The Double Standard of Aging," 20).

88. For a discussion of the "cultural event" of Viagra, see Marshall, "Hard Science."

BIBLIOGRAPHY

Ali, Lorraine, and Lisa Miller. "The Secret Lives of Wives." *Newsweek*, 12 July 2004.

Allen, Sandra, Lee Sanders, and Jan Willis. *Conditions of Illusion: Papers from the Women's Movement.* Leeds: Feminist Books, 1974.

Allessio, Dominic. "'Things Are Different Now?' A Postcolonial Analysis of *Buffy the Vampire Slayer*." *European Legacy* 6:6 (2001): 731–40.

American Association of University Women. *How Schools Shortchange Girls: A Study of Major Findings on Girls in Education.* Researched by the Wellesley College Center for Research on Women. Washington, D.C.: AAUW Educational Foundation, National Education Association, 1992.

Andrejevic, Mark. *Reality TV: The Work of Being Watched.* Oxford: Rowman and Littlefield, 2004.

Anzaldúa, Gloria, and AnaLouise Keating, eds. *This Bridge We Call Home.* London: Routledge, 2002.

Arnot, Madeleine, Miriam David, and Gaby Weiner. *Closing the Gender Gap.* Cambridge: Polity Press, 1999.

Aronson, Pamela. "Feminists or 'Postfeminists'? Young Women's Attitudes toward Feminism and Gender Relations." *Gender and Society* 17:6 (December 2003): 903–22.

Ashby, Justine. "Postfeminism in the British Frame." *Cinema Journal* 44:2 (winter 2005): 127–32.

Badley, Linda C. "Spiritual Warfare: Postfeminism and the Cultural Politics of the Blair Witch Craze." *Intensities: The Journal of Cult Media* 3 (2003), http://davidlavery.net/Intensities/PDF/Badley.pdf.

Banet-Weiser, Sarah. "Girls Rule! Gender, Feminism, and Nickelodeon." *Critical Studies in Media Communication* 21:2 (2004): 119–39.

Barthes, Roland. *The Fashion System.* New York: Hill and Wang, 1983.

———. *Système de la mode.* Paris: Seuil, 1967.

Battema, Douglas, and Philip Sewell. "Trading in Masculinity: Muscles, Money, and Market Discourse in the WWF." In *Steel Chair to the Head: The Pleasure and Pain of Professional Wrestling,* ed. Nicholas Sammond. Durham: Duke University Press, 2005.

Bauman, Zygmunt. *The Individualised Society.* Cambridge: Polity Press, 2001.

———. *Liquid Modernity.* Cambridge: Polity Press, 2000.

Baumgardner, Jennifer, and Amy Richards. *Manifesta: Young Women, Feminism, and the Future*. New York: Farrar, Straus and Giroux, 2000.

Beck, Ulrich. *Risk Society*. London: Sage, 1992.

Beck, Ulrich, and Elisabeth Beck-Gernsheim. *Individualisation*. Cambridge: Polity Press, 2001.

Belkin, Lisa. "The Opt-Out Revolution." *New York Times Magazine*, 26 October 2003.

Bell, David, and Joanne Hollows, eds. *Ordinary Lifestyles: Popular Media, Consumption, and Taste*. Maidenhead, Berks.: Open University Press, 2005.

Bellafante, Gina. "It's All about Me!" *Time*, 29 June 1998.

Beltrán, Mary. "Mas Macha: The New Latina Action Hero." In *Action and Adventure Cinema*, ed. Yvonne Tasker. London: Routledge, 2004.

Bendelow, Gillian, and Simon J. Williams, eds. *Emotions in Social Life: Critical Themes and Contemporary Issues*. London: Routledge, 1997.

Berila, Beth, and Devika Dibya Choudhuri. "Metrosexuality the Middle Class Way: Exploring Race, Class, and Gender in *Queer Eye for the Straight Guy*." *Genders OnLine Journal* 42 (2005), http://www.genders.org/g42/g42_berila_choudhuri.html.

Berlant, Lauren. *The Queen of America Goes to Washington City: Essays on Sex and Citizenship*. Durham: Duke University Press, 1997.

Bernhardt, Annette, Martina Morris, Mark S. Handcock, and Marc A. Scott. *Divergent Paths: Economic Mobility in the New American Labor Market*. New York: Russell Sage, 2001.

Bhabha, Homi. "The Other Question." *Screen* 24:6 (1983): 18–36.

Blair-Loy, Mary. *Competing Devotions: Career and Family among Women Executives*. Cambridge, Mass.: Harvard University Press, 2003.

Blum, Virginia. *Flesh Wounds: The Culture of Cosmetic Surgery*. Berkeley: University of California Press, 2005.

Bourdieu, Pierre. *Distinction: A Social Critique of the Judgement of Taste*. Cambridge, Mass.: Harvard University Press, 1987.

Boyle, Karen. "What's Natural about Killing: Gender, Copycat Violence, and *Natural Born Killers*." *Journal of Gender Studies* 10:3 (2001): 311–21.

Bratich, Jack Z., Jeremy Packer, and Cameron McCarthy, eds. *Foucault, Cultural Studies, and Governmentality*. Albany: State University of New York Press, 2003.

Brenton, Sam, and Reuben Cohen. *Shooting People: Adventures in Reality TV*. London: Verso, 2003.

Bronski, Michael. *Culture Clash: The Making of Gay Sensibility*. Boston: South End Press, 1984.

Brook, Heather. "Stalemate: Rethinking the Politics of Marriage." *Feminist Theory* 3:1 (April 2002): 145–66.

Brooks, Ann. *Postfeminisms: Feminism, Cultural Theory, and Cultural Forms*. London: Routledge, 1997.

Brown, Helen Gurley. *Sex and the Single Girl*. New York: Random House, 1962.

Brown, Lyn Mikel, and Carol Gilligan. *Meeting at the Crossroads*. New York: Ballantine, 1992.

Brown, Wendy. "The Impossibility of Women's Studies." *Differences: A Journal of Feminist Cultural Studies* 9:3 (1997): 79–102.

Brunsdon, Charlotte. "Feminism, Post-feminism: Martha, Martha, and Nigella." *Cinema Journal* 44:2 (2005): 110–16.

———. *The Feminist, the Housewife and the Soap Opera*. Oxford: Clarendon, 2000.

———. "Identity in Television Criticism." In *Feminist Television Criticism*, ed. Charlotte Brunsdon, Julie D'Acci, and Lynn Spigel. Oxford: Clarendon, 1997.

———. "Lifestyling Britain: The 8–9 Slot on British Television." In *Television After TV: Essays on a Medium in Transition*, ed. Lynn Spigel and Jan Olsson. Durham: Duke University Press, 2004.

———. "Pedagogies of the Feminine: Feminist Teaching and Women's Genres." *Screen* 32: 4 (winter 1991): 364–81.

———. "Post-feminism and Shopping Films." In *The Film Studies Reader*, ed. Joanne Hollows, Peter Hutchings, and Mark Jancovich. New York: Oxford University Press, 2000.

———. *Screen Tastes: Soap Opera to Satellite Dishes*. London: Routledge, [1991] 1997.

Buckingham, David. *After the Death of Childhood: Growing Up in the Age of Electronic Media*. London: Polity Press, 2000.

———. *The Making of Citizens: Young People, News, and Politics*. London: Routledge, 2000.

Budgeon, Shelley. "Emergent Feminist Identities." *European Journal of Women's Studies* 8:1 (2001): 7–28.

Budgeon, Shelley, and Dawn H. Currie. "From Feminism to Postfeminism: Women's Liberation in Fashion Magazines." *Women's Studies International Forum* 18:2 (1995): 173–86.

Burchell, Graham. Colin Gordon, and Peter Miller, eds. *The Foucault Effect: Studies in Governmentality*. Chicago: University of Chicago Press, 1991.

Butler, Adika. "Camille McDonald Dispels Rumors and Sets the Record Straight." *Where Itz At: The Pulse of the Caribbean People*. www.whereitzatlive.com. N.d.

Butler, Judith. *Antigone's Claim: Kinship Between Life and Death*. New York: Columbia University Press, 2000.

———. *Bodies That Matter*. New York: Routledge, 1993.

———. "Contingent Foundations: Feminism and the Question of Postmodernism." In *Feminists Theorise the Political*, ed. Judith Butler and Joan W. Scott. New York: Routledge, 1992.

———. *Gender Trouble: Feminism and the Subversion of Identity*. New York: Routledge, 1999.

Butler, Judith, Ernesto Laclau, and Slavoj Žižek, eds. *Contingency, Hegemony, and Universality*. London: Verso, 2000.

Byers, Michelle. "Gender/Sexuality/Desire: Subversion of Difference and Construction of Life in the Adolescent Drama of *My So-Called Life*." *Signs: Journal of Women in Culture and Society* 23:3 (1998): 711–34.

Cabrera, Yvette. "Adorable Dora Is Opening the Doors of Diversity." *Orange County Register*, 13 September 2002.

Cagan, Elizabeth. "The Selling of the Women's Movement." *Social Policy* 9:1 (May–June 1978): 5–12.

Carney, Sarah K. "Body Work on Ice: The Ironies of Femininity and Sport." In *Construction Sites: Excavating Race, Class, and Gender among Urban Youth*, ed. Lois Weis and Michelle Fine. New York: Teachers College Press, 2000.

Carr, C. "The Legacy of Kathy Acker, Theoretical Grrrl." *Village Voice*. 6–12 November 2002.

Cartier, Carolyn. "San Francisco and the Left Coast." In *Seductions of Place: Geographical Perspectives on Globalization and Touristed Landscapes*, ed. Carolyn Cartier and Alan A. Lew. London: Routledge, 2005.

Carver, Akiko. "I Am Not a Person of Color: Re-thinking Racial Identity." In *Evolution of a Race Riot*, ed. Mimi Nguyen. Self-published zine. N.d.

Chambers, Veronica. *Having It All: Black Women and Success*. New York: Harlem Moon Press, 2004.

Chaney, David. *Lifestyles*. London: Routledge, 1996.

Charney, Leo. "The Violence of a Perfect Moment." In *Violence and American Cinema*. ed. David J. Slocum. London: Routledge, 2001.

Chin, Elizabeth. *Purchasing Power: Black Kids and American Consumer Culture*. Minneapolis: University of Minnesota Press, 2001.

Chonin, N. "Diva Demands Power, Choice, Halter Tops." *Rolling Stone*, 25 July 2002.

———. "Play That Punky Music." *People*, 9 September 2002.

Chopin, Kate. "Her Letters." In *The Awakening and Other Stories*. Oxford: Oxford World's Classics, 2000.

Christ, Carol. *Woman Spirit Rising*. San Francisco: Harper Collins, [1979] 1989.

Cohan, Steven. *Incongruous Entertainment: Camp, Cultural Value, and the MGM Musical*. Durham: Duke University Press, 2005.

———. *Masked Men: Masculinity and the Movies in the Fifties*. Bloomington: Indiana University Press, 1997.

Cole, C. L. "Suburban Icons/Communist Pasts." *Journal of Sport and Social Issues*. 26:3 (2002): 231–34.

Collins, Patricia Hill. *Black Sexual Politics: African Americans, Gender, and the New Racism*. New York: Routledge, 2004.

Coontz, Stephanie. *The Way We Never Were: American Families and the Nostalgia Trap*. New York: Basic Books, 2000.

Couldry, Nick. *Media Rituals: A Critical Approach*. New York: Routledge, 2003.

Covino, Deborah Caslav. *Amending the Abject Body: Aesthetic Makeovers in Medicine and Culture*. Albany: State University of New York Press, 2004.

Coward, Rosalind. *Female Desire*. London: Paladin, 1984.

Crary, David. "Conservatives Urge Broader Look at Marriage." Associated Press, 22 November 2004.

Creeber, Glen. "'Hideously White': British Television, Globalization, and National Identity." *Television and New Media*. 5:1 (2004): 27–39.

Cronan, Sheila. *Notes from the Third Year: Women's Liberation*. New York: n.p., 1971.

Currie, Dawn H. *Girl Talk: Adolescent Magazines and Their Readers*. Toronto: University of Toronto Press, 1999.

Cvetkovich, Ann. *An Archive of Feelings: Trauma, Sexuality, and Lesbian Public Cultures*. Durham: Duke University Press, 2003.

Dalai, Anaga. "Gladiator Grrrl." *Ms.*, December 2000.

Daly, Mary. *Beyond God the Father: Towards a Philosophy of Women's Liberation*. London: Women's Press, 1973.

Daniels, J. Danielle. "Africana's Reality TV Recap." *AOL Black Voices*. www.archive .blackvoices.com, 23 January 2003.

Davies, Owen. *Witchcraft, Magic, and Culture, 1736–1951*. Manchester: Manchester University Press, 1999.

Dávila, Arlene. *Latinos, Inc.: The Marketing and Making of a People*. Berkeley: University of California Press, 2001.

Davis, Glyn, and Kay Dickinson, eds. *Teen TV: Genre, Consumption, and Identity*. London: British Film Institute, 2004.

Davis, Kathy. *Dubious Equalities and Embodied Differences: Cultural Studies on Cosmetic Surgery*. Lanham, Md.: Rowman and Littlefield, 2003.

Dean, Mitchell. *Governmentality: Power and Rule in Modern Society*. London: Sage, 1999.

de Beauvoir, Simone. *Old Age*. Trans. Patrick O'Brian. London: Andre Deutsch, 1972.

de Lauretis, Teresa. *Technologies of Gender: Essays on Theory, Film, and Fiction*. Indianapolis: Indiana University Press, 1987.

Detloff, Madelyn. "Mean Spirits: The Politics of Contempt between Feminist Generations." In "Third Wave Feminisms," special issue of *Hypatia* 12:3 (1997): 76–99.

DeVere Brody, Jennifer. "The Returns of Cleopatra Jones." *Signs: Journal of Women in Culture and Society* 25:1 (1999): 91–121.

Douglas, Susan. "Manufacturing Postfeminism: Race, Youth Cultures, and the Boundaries between Feminism and Post-feminism in American Mass Media." Panel abstract. International Communications Association Annual Meeting, 2003.

———. *Where the Girls Are: Growing Up Female with the Mass Media*. New York: Times Books, 1994.

Douglas, Susan, and Meredith Michaels. *The Mommy Myth: The Idealization of Motherhood and How It Has Undermined Women*. New York: Free Press, 2004.

Dovey, Jon. *Freakshow: First Person Media and Factual Television*. London: Pluto, 2000.

Dow, Bonnie J. *Prime-Time Feminism: Television, Media Culture, and the Woman's Movement since 1970*. State College: Pennsylvania University Press, 1996.

Dreisinger, Baz. "The Queen in Shining Armor: Safe Eroticism and the Gay Friend." *Journal of Popular Film and Television* 28:1 (spring 2000): 2–11.

Drill, E., H. McDonald, and R. Odes. *Deal With It!* New York: Pocket Books, 1999.

Driscoll, Catherine. *Girls: Feminine Adolescence in Popular Culture and Cultural Theory*. New York: Columbia University Press, 2002.

Dunn, K. "Punk-Rock Debutants." *Rolling Stone*, 11 June 1998.

Durham, Meenakshi Gigi. "The Girling of America: Critical Reflections on Gender and Popular Communication." *Popular Communication* 1:1 (2003): 23–31.

Dyer, Richard. "White." *Screen* 29:4 (1988): 44–64.

Ehrenreich, Barbara. *Nickel and Dimed: On Not Getting by in America*. New York: Henry Holt, 2001.

Ehrenreich, Barbara, and Arlie Russell Hochschild, eds. *Global Woman: Nannies, Maids, and Sex Workers in the New Economy*. London: Granta, 2002.

Elliott, Carl. *Better Than Well: American Medicine Meets the American Dream*. London: Norton 2003.

Elsley, Judy. "Laughter as Feminine Power in *The Color Purple* and *A Question of Silence*." In *New Perspectives on Women and Comedy*, ed. Regina Barreca. Philadelphia: Gordon and Breach, 1992.

Faludi, Susan. *Backlash: The Undeclared War against Women*. London: Vintage, 1992.

Featherstone, Liza. *Selling Women Short: The Landmark Battle for Workers' Rights at Wal-Mart*. New York: Basic Books, 2004.

———. "Wal-Mart Values." *Nation*, 16 December 2002.

Featherstone, Mike. "The Body in Consumer Culture." In *The Body: Social Process and Cultural Theory*, ed. Mike Featherstone, Mike Hepworth, and Brian Turner. London: Sage, 1991.

———. "Post-bodies, Aging, and Virtual Reality." In *Images of Aging: Cultural Representations of Later Life*, ed. Mike Featherstone and Andrew Wernick. London: Routledge, 1995.

Feigenbaum, Anna. "'Some Guy Designed This Room I'm Standing In': Marking Gender in Press Coverage of Ani DiFranco." *Popular Music* 24:1 (2005): 37–56.

Findlen, Barbara, ed. *Listen Up: Voices from the Next Feminist Generation*. New York: Seal Press, 1995.

Fischer, Lucy. *Shot/Countershot: Film Tradition and Women's Cinema*. Princeton: Princeton University Press, 1989.

Flocker, Michael. *The Metrosexual Guide to Style: A Handbook for the Modern Man*. Cambridge, Mass.: DaCapo, 2003.

Forman-Brunell, Miriam. "Truculent and Tractable: The Gendering of Babysitting in Postwar America." In *Delinquents and Debutantes: Twentieth-Century American Girls' Cultures*, ed. Sherrie A. Inness. New York: New York University Press, 1998.

Foucault, Michel. *The Care of the Self: The History of Sexuality*. Vol. 3. Harmondsworth: Penguin, [1984] 1990.

———. *Discipline and Punish: The Birth of the Prison*. Trans. Alan Sheridan. New York: Pantheon, 1977.

———. "Governmentality." In *The Foucault Effect: Studies in Governmentality*, ed. Graham Burchell, Colin Gordon, and Peter Miller. Chicago: University of Chicago Press, 1991.

Franco, Judith. "Gender, Genre, and Female Pleasure in the Contemporary Revenge Narrative: *Baise moi* and *What It Feels Like for a Girl*." *Quarterly Review of Film and Video* 21:1 (2004): 1–10.

Frank, Thomas. *One Market under God: Extreme Capitalism, Market Populism, and the End of Economic Democracy*. London: Secker and Warburg, 2000.

Freeman, Elizabeth. *The Wedding Complex: Forms of Belonging in Modern American Culture*. Durham: Duke University Press, 2002.

French, Phillip. "The Good Girl." *Observer*. 12 January 2003.

Fury, Jeanne. "The Donnas and Bratmobile at the Bowery Ballroom." *NYROCK.com*, April 2001.

Gaar, Gillian. *She's a Rebel: The History of Women in Rock & Roll*. New York: Seal Press, 2002.

Gallagher, Mark. "*Queer Eye* for the Heterosexual Couple." *Feminist Media Studies* 4:2 (2004): 223–26.

Gamson, Joshua. *Freaks Talk Back: Tabloid Talk Shows and Sexual Nonconformity*. Chicago: University of Chicago Press, 1998.

Garrison, Ednie Kaeh. "U.S. Feminism Grrrl-Style! Youth (Sub)Cultures and the Technologics of the Third Wave." *Feminist Studies* 26:1 (spring 2000): 141–70.

Gateward, Frances. "Bubblegum and Heavy Metal." In *Sugar, Spice, and Everything Nice: Cinemas of Girlhood*, ed. Frances Gateward and Murray Pomerance. Detroit: Wayne State University Press, 2002.

Gaunt, Kyra D. "Dancin' in the Street to a Black Girls' Beat: Music, Gender, and the Ins and Outs of Double-Dutch." In *Generations of Youth: Youth Cultures and History in Twentieth-Century America*, ed. Joe Austin and Michael Nevin Willard. New York: New York University Press, 1998.

Gentile, Mary C. "Feminist or Tendentious? Marleen Gorris's *A Question of Silence*." In *Issues in Feminist Film Criticism*, ed. Patricia Erens. Bloomington: Indiana University Press, 1990.

Giddens, Anthony. *Beyond Left and Right*. Cambridge: Polity Press, 1995.

———. *Modernity and Self-Identity*. Cambridge: Polity Press, 1991.

———. *The Third Way*. Cambridge: Polity Press, 1998.

Gill, C. "The Original Riot Grrrl Keeps It Pure." *Guitar Player*, 19 October 1994.

Gill, Rosalind. "From Sexual Objectification to Sexual Subjectification: The Resexualisation of Women's Bodies in the Media." *Feminist Media Studies* 3:1 (2003): 100–106.

Gilman, Charlotte Perkins. *Women and Economics: A Study of the Economic Relation Between Men and Women as a Factor in Social Revolution*. Boston: Small, Maynard and Co., 1898.

Gilman, Sander L. *Making the Body Beautiful: A Cultural History of Cosmetic Surgery*. Princeton: Princeton University Press, 1999.

Gilroy, Paul. *After Empire*. New York: Routledge, 2004.

———. "From a Colonial Past to a New Multiculturalism." *Chronicle of Higher Education*, 7 January 2005.

———. *Postcolonial Melancholia*. New York: Columbia University Press, 2005.

Gladwell, Malcolm. "The Coolhunt." In *The Consumer Society Reader*, ed. Juliet B. Schor and Douglas B. Holt. New York: New Press, 2000.

"Gladys Knight Talks about 'At Last,' Her First Album in Six Years, and Why She's Not a Diva." *Jet*, 5 March 2001.

Glass, Shirley. *NOT "Just Friends": Protect Your Relationship from Infidelity and Heal the Trauma of Betrayal*. New York: Free Press, 2003.

Goldman, Richard. *Reading Ads Socially*. New York: Routledge, 1992.

Goshert, J. C. "'Punk' after the Pistols: American Music, Economics, and Politics in the 1980s and 1990s." *Popular Music and Society* 23 (spring 2000): 85–106.

Gray, Herman. *Cultural Moves: African Americans and the Politics of Representation*. Berkeley: University of California Press, 2005.

———. *Watching Race: Television and the Struggle for Blackness*. Minneapolis: University of Minnesota Press, 1995.

Gray, Mary L. *In Your Face: Stories from the Lives of Queer Youth*. New York: Harrington Park Press, 1999.

Green, Karen, and Tristan Taormino, eds. *A Girl's Guide to Taking over the World: Writings from the Girl Zine Revolution*. New York: St. Martin's, 1997.

Greer, Germaine. "Serenity and Power." In *The Other Within Us: Feminist Explorations of Women and Aging*, ed. Maralyn Pearsall. London: Westview, 1997.

Grieveson, Lee. "Policing the Cinema: *Traffic in Souls* at Ellis Island, 1913." *Screen* 38:2 (1997): 149–71.

Griffin, Christine. "Good Girls, Bad Girls: Anglocentrism and Diversity in the Constitution of Contemporary Girlhood." In *All about the Girl: Culture, Power, and Identity*, ed. Anita Harris. London: Routledge, 2004.

Gross, Michael Joseph. "The Queen Is Dead." *Atlantic Monthly*, August 2000.

Guy-Sheftall, Beverly. "Response from a 'Second Waver' to Kimberly Springer's 'Third Wave Black Feminism?'" *Signs: Journal of Women in Culture and Society* 27:4 (2002): 1091–94.

Halberstam, Judith. *Female Masculinity*. Durham: Duke University Press, 1998.

———. *In a Queer Time and Place: Transgender Bodies, Subcultural Lives*. New York: New York University Press, 2005.

Hall, Elaine J., and Marnie Salupo Rodriguez. "The Myth of Postfeminism." *Gender and Society* 17:6 (December 2003): 878–902.

Hall, Stuart. *The Hard Road to Renewal*. London: Verso, 1989.

Hambleton-Jones, Nicky. *Ten Years Younger*. London: Channel 4 Books, 2005.

Hankinson, Bobby. "Le Tigre Talks Song Writing, Politics, and *Spin* Magazine." *Northeastern News*. www.nu_news.com, 10 October 2004.

Haraway, Donna. *Simians, Cyborgs, and Women*. London: Free Association Books. 1991.

Harris, Anita M. *Future Girl: Young Women in the Twenty-First Century*. New York: Routledge, 2003.

Harris, Anita M., ed. *All About the Girl: Culture, Power, and Identity*. New York: Routledge, 2004.

Hartley, John. "Situation Comedy—Part One." In *The Television Genre Book*, ed. Glen Creeber. London: British Film Institute, 2001.

Hartsock, Nancy. *The Feminist Standpoint Revisited and Other Essays*. Colorado: Westview, 1998.

Hatch, Kristen. "Fille Fatale: Regulating Images of Adolescent Girls, 1962–1996." In *Sugar, Spice, and Everything Nice: Cinemas of Girlhood*, ed. Frances Gateward and Murray Pomerance. Detroit: Wayne State University Press, 2002.

Hawkesworth, Mary. "The Semiotics of Premature Burial: Feminism in a Postfeminist Age." *Signs: Journal of Women in Culture and Society* 30:1 (2004).

Heath, Joseph, and Andrew Potter. *The Rebel Sell: How the Counterculture became Consumer Culture*. London: Capstone, 2005.

Heinecken, Dawn. *Warrior Women of Television: A Feminist Cultural Analysis of the New Female Body in Popular Media*. New York: Peter Lang, 2003.

Hendershot, Heather. "Belaboring Reality." *Flow: A Critical Forum on Television and Media Culture* 1:11 (2005).

Hennessy, Rosemary. *Materialist Feminism and the Politics of Discourse*. New York: Routledge, 1993.

Henry, Astrid. "Feminism's Family Problem." In *Catching a Wave: Reclaiming Feminism for the Twenty-first Century*, ed. Rory Dicker and Alison Peipmeir. Boston: Northeastern University Press, 2003.

———. *Not My Mother's Sister: Generational Conflict and Third-Wave Feminism*. Bloomington: Indiana University Press, 2004.

Hernandez, Daisy, and Bushra Rehman, eds. *Colonize This! Young Women of Color on Today's Feminism*. New York: Seal Press, 2002.

Hewlett, Sylvia Ann, and Carolyn Buck Luce. "Off-Ramps and On-Ramps: Keeping Talented Women on the Road to Success." *Harvard Business Review*, March 2005, 43–54.

Higginbotham, Evelyn Brooks. *Righteous Discontent: The Women's Movement in the Black Baptist Church, 1880–1920*. Cambridge, Mass.: Harvard University Press, 1993.

Highmore, Ben. *Everyday Life and Cultural Theory*. London: Routledge, 2001.

Hill, Sheila Radford. "Keepin' It Real: A Generational Commentary on Kimberly Springer's Third Wave Black Feminism." *Signs: Journal of Women in Culture and Society* 27:4 (2002): 1083–90.

Hinds, Hilary, and Jackie Stacey. "Imagining Feminism, Imagining Femininity: the Bra-Burner, Diana, and the Woman Who Kills." *Feminist Media Studies* 1:2 (2001): 153–77.

Hoberman, J. "Hungry Hearts." *Village Voice*, August 2002.

Hochschild, Arlie. *The Managed Heart: Commercialization and Human Feeling*. Berkeley: University of California Press, 1983.

Hogeland, Lisa. "Against Generational Thinking; or, Some Things That 'Third Wave' Feminism Isn't." *Women's Studies in Communication* 24 (2001): 107.

Hollinger, Karen. *In the Company of Women: Contemporary Female Friendship Films*. Minneapolis: University of Minnesota Press, 1998.

Hollows, Joanne. "Can I Go Home Yet? Feminism, Postfeminism, and Domesticity." In *Feminism in Popular Culture*, ed. Joanne Hollows and Rachel Moseley. London: Berg, 2006.

———. *Feminism, Femininity, and Popular Culture*. Manchester: Manchester University Press, 2000.

Holmes, Su, and Deborah Jermyn, eds. *Understanding Reality Television*. London: Routledge, 2004.

Holmlund, Christine. *Impossible Bodies: Femininity and Masculinity at the Movies*. London: Routledge, 2002.

———. "Wham! Bam! Pam! Pam Grier as Hot Action Babe and Cool Action Mama." *Quarterly Review of Film and Video* 22 (2005): 97–112.

hooks, bell. "Eating the Other." In *Black Looks: Race and Representation*. Boston: South End Press, 1992.

————. "Feminism: A Movement to End Sexist Oppression." In *Feminisms*, ed. S. Kemp and J. Squires. Oxford: Oxford University Press, 1997.

————. *Feminism Is for Everybody: Passionate Politics*. London: Pluto, 2000.

Hughes, Zondra. "How Tyler Perry Rose from Homelessness to a $5 Million Mansion." *Ebony*, January 2004.

Hyman, Peter. *The Reluctant Metrosexual: Dispatches from an Almost-Hip Life*. New York: Random House, 2004.

Illouz, Eva. *Oprah Winfrey and the Glamour of Misery: An Essay on Popular Culture*. New York: Columbia University Press, 2003.

Ingraham, Chrys. *White Weddings: Romancing Heterosexuality in Popular Culture*. New York: Routledge, 1999.

Inness, Sherrie A. *Tough Girls: Women Warriors and Wonder Women in Popular Culture*. Philadelphia: University of Pennsylvania Press, 1999.

————, ed. *Action Chicks: New Images of Tough Women in Popular Culture*. London: Palgrave, 2004.

Jacob, Iris. *My Sisters' Voices: Teenage Girls of Color Speak Out*. New York: Henry Holt, 2002.

Jameson, Fredric. *The Cultural Turn: Selected Writings on the Postmodern, 1983–1998*. London: Verso, 1998.

————. *Postmodernism; or, the Cultural Logic of Late Capitalism*. Durham: Duke University Press, 1991.

Jong, Erica. *Witches*. New York: Abrams, 1981.

Kaplan, E. Ann. "Trauma and Aging: Marlene Dietrich, Melanie Klein, and Marguerite Duras." In *Figuring Age: Women, Bodies, Generations*, ed. Kathleen Woodward. Bloomington: Indiana University Press, 1997.

Karlyn, Kathleen Rowe. "Feminism and Its Discontents: Identity, Politics, and the New Humanism." Plenary paper presented at the conference "Interrogating Postfeminism: Gender and the Politics of Popular Culture," University of East Anglia, April 2004.

————. "*Scream*, Popular Culture, and Feminism's Third Wave: 'I'm Not My Mother.'" *Genders OnLine Journal* 38 (2003), http://www.genders.org/g38/g38_rowe_karlyn.html.

————. "'Too Close for Comfort': *American Beauty* and the Incest Motif." *Cinema Journal* 44:1 (fall 2004): 69–93.

Kat, G. "The Donnas." *Rolling Stone*, 1 February 2001.

Katz, Stephen, and Barbara Marshall. "New Sex for Old: Lifestyle, Consumerism, and the Ethics of Aging Well." *Journal of Aging Studies* 17 (2003): 3–16.

Kearney, Mary Celeste. "Don't Need You: Rethinking Identity Politics and Separatism from a Grrrl Perspective." In *Youth Culture: Identity in a Postmodern World*, ed. S. Epstein. Oxford: Blackwell, 1998.

————. "Girlfriends and Girl Power: Female Adolescence in Contemporary Cinema." In *Sugar, Spice, and Everything Nice: Cinemas of Girlhood*, ed. Frances Gateward and Murray Pomerance. Detroit: Wayne State University Press, 2002.

————. *Girls Make Media*. New York: Routledge, 2006.

Kenny, Lorraine Delia. *Daughters of Suburbia: Growing up White, Middle Class, and Female*. New Brunswick, N.J.: Rutgers University Press, 2000.

Kim, L. S. "Elevating Servants, Elevating American Families." *Flow* 1:12 (2005).

————. "Race and Reality . . . TV." *Flow* 1:4 (2004).

————. "'Sex and the Single Girl' in Postfeminism: The 'F' Word on Television." *Television and New Media* 2:4 (November 2001): 319–34.

Kinder, Marsha. "Violence American Style: The Narrative Orchestration of Violent Attractions." In *Violence and American Cinema*, ed. David J. Slocum. London: Routledge, 2001.

King, Lisa. "Subjectivity as Identity: Gender through the Lens of Foucault." In *Foucault, Cultural Studies, and Governmentality*, ed. Jack Z. Bratich, Jeremy Packer, and Cameron McCarthy. Albany: State University of New York Press, 2003.

King, Samantha. *Pink Ribbons, Inc.: Breast Cancer and the Politics of Philanthropy*. Minneapolis: University of Minnesota Press, 2006.

Kinser, Amber E. "Negotiating Spaces for/through Third-Wave Feminism." *NWSA Journal* 16:3 (2004): 124–53.

Kipnis, Laura. "Adultery." *Critical Inquiry* 24:2 (1998): 307.

Kitch, Carolyn. *The Girl on the Magazine Cover: The Origins of Visual Stereotypes in American Mass Media*. Chapel Hill: University of North Carolina Press, 2001.

Klatzker, S. "riot grrrl." www.music.dartmouth.edu, 1999.

Klein, Naomi. *No Logo: No Space, No Choice, No Jobs*. New York: Picador, 2002.

Koyama, Emi. "On Third Wave Feminisms." www.eminism.org, 2002.

Kruckemeyer, Kate. "Making Room for Teen Voices: Feminist Discourse in Magazines by and for Girls." *Iris* 44 (2002).

Kruse, Holly. "Abandoning the Absolute: Transcendence and Gender in Popular Music Discourse." In *Pop Music and the Press*, ed. S. Jones. Philadelphia: Temple University Press, 2002.

Krzywinska, Tanya. *A Skin for Dancing In: Possession, Witchcraft, and Voodoo in Film*. Wiltshire: Flicks Books, 2000.

Kuhn, Annette. *Women's Pictures: Feminism and Cinema*. London: Verso, 1994.

Lange, Alexandra. "Deal with It." *New York Magazine*, 13 September 1999.

Lehnus, Donald J. *Who's On Time? A Study of TIME's Covers from March 3, 1923, to January 3, 1977*. New York: Oceana, 1980.

Leidner, Robin. *Service Work and the Routinization of Everyday Life*. Berkeley: University of California Press, 1993.

Leland, John. "Everything a Man Can Do, Decapitation Included." *New York Times*, 19 October 2003.

Leonard, Marion. "Paper Planes: Travelling the New Grrrl Geographies." In *Cool Places: Geographies of Youth Cultures*, ed. T. Skelton and G. Valentine. London: Routledge, 1997.

Levine, Elana. "Fractured Fairy Tales and Fragmented Markets: Disney's *Weddings of a Lifetime* and the Cultural Politics of Media Conglomeration." *Television and New Media* 6:1 (2005): 71–88.

Levy, Ariel. *Female Chauvinist Pigs: Women and the Rise of Raunch Culture*. New York: Free Press, 2005.

Lilith, Leah. "Sticks and Stones May Break My Bones." In *A Girl's Guide to Taking over the World: Writings from the Girl Zine Revolution*, ed. Karen Green and Tristan Taormino. New York: Saint Martin's, 1997.

Loth, Reneé. "Women Who Vote and Those That Don't." *International Herald Tribune*, 29 July 2004.

Lotz, Amanda D. "Postfeminist Television Criticism: Rehabilitating Critical Terms and Identifying Postfeminist Attributes." *Feminist Media Studies* 1:1 (2001): 105–21.

Lucia, Cynthia. *Framing Female Lawyers: Women on Trial in Film*. Austin: University of Texas Press, 2005.

Macdonald, Cameron Lynne, and Carmen Sirianni. *Working in the Service Society*. Philadelphia: Temple University Press, 1996.

Marshall, Barbara L. "'Hard Science': Gendered Constructions of Sexual Dysfunction in the 'Viagra Age.'" *Sexualities* 5:2 (2002): 131–58.

Martens, T. "The Donnas Keep Building with Move to Atlantic." *Billboard*, 5 October 2002.

McCabe, Janet, and Kim Akass. *Reading "Sex and the City."* London: I. B. Tauris, 2004.

McCarthy, Anna. "Crab People from the Center of the Earth." *GLQ* 11:1 (2005): 99.

McCaughey, Martha, and Neal King, eds. *Reel Knockouts: Violent Women in the Movies*. Austin: University of Texas Press, 2001.

McPherson, Tara. "Who's Got Next? Gender, Race, and the Mediation of the WNBA." In *Basketball Jones: America Above the Rim*, ed. Todd Boyd and Kenneth L. Shropshire. New York: New York University Press, 2000.

McRobbie, Angela. "Extended Notes" on *What Not to Wear*. In *The Uses of Cultural Studies*. London: Sage, 2005.

———. *Feminism and Youth Culture: From "Jackie" to "Just Seventeen."* Basingstoke: Macmillan, 1991.

———. *Feminism and Youth Culture*. 2d ed. London: Routledge, 2000.

———. "Feminism v. the TV Blondes." Inaugural lecture, Goldsmiths College, 1999.

———. *In the Culture Society: Art, Fashion, and Popular Music*. London: Routledge, 1999.

———. "*More!*: New Sexualities in Girls' and Women's Magazines." In *Back to Reality? Social Experience and Cultural Studies*, ed. Angela McRobbie. Manchester: Manchester University Press, 1997.

———. "Mothers and Fathers, Who Needs Them? A Review Essay of Butler's *Antigone*." *Feminist Review* 73 (autumn 2003): 129–36.

———. "Notes on Postfeminism and Popular Culture: Bridget Jones and the New Gender Regime." In *All about the Girl: Culture, Power, and Identity*, ed. Anita Harris. London: Routledge, 2004.

———. "Notes on *What Not to Wear* and Post-feminist Symbolic Violence." In *Feminism after Bourdieu*, ed. Lisa Adkins and Bev Skeggs. Oxford: Blackwell, 2005.

———. "Post-feminism and Popular Culture." *Feminist Media Studies* 4:3 (2004): 255–64.

———. *Postmodernism and Popular Culture*. London: Routledge, 1994.

Mellencamp, Patricia. "From Anxiety to Equanimity: Crisis and Generational Continuity on TV, at the Movies, in Life, in Death." In *Figuring Age: Women, Bodies, Generations*, ed. Kathleen Woodward. Bloomington: Indiana University Press, 1999.

Merritt, Stephanie. "Yes, Your Bum Looks Big in That . . ." *Observer*, 28 October 2001.

Miller, Toby. "A Metrosexual Eye on *Queer Guy*." *GLQ* 11:1 (2005): 112–17.

———. *The Well-Tempered Self: Citizenship, Culture, and the Postmodern Subject*. Baltimore: Johns Hopkins University Press, 1993.

Mitchell, Dean. *Governmentality: Power and Rule in Modern Society*. London: Sage, 1999.

Mizejewski, Linda. *Hardboiled and High Heeled: The Woman Detective in Popular Culture*. New York: Routledge, 2004.

Modleski, Tania. *Feminism without Women: Culture and Criticism in a 'Postfeminist' Era*. London: Routledge, 1991.

Moen, Phyllis, and Patricia Roehling. *The Career Mystique: Cracks in the American Dream*. Lanham, Md.: Rowman and Littlefield, 2005.

Mohanty, Chandra Talpade. "Under Western Eyes." In *The Post-colonial Studies Reader*, ed. Bill Ashcroft, Gareth Griffiths, and Helen Tiffin. London: Routledge, 1995.

Moon, Troy. "'Queer Eye' Opens Window to Gay Life: Show Wins over Straight Crowd, but Not Everyone Sees Eye to Eye." *Pensacola News-Journal*, 14 August 2003.

Moore, Suzanne. "Here's Looking at You, Kid!" In *The Female Gaze: Women as Viewers of Popular Culture*, ed. Lorraine Gammon and Margaret Marshment. London: Women's Press, 1988.

Morgan, Joan. *When Chickenheads Come Home to Roost: My Life as a HipHop Feminist*. New York: Simon and Schuster, 1999.

Moseley, Rachel. "Glamorous Witchcraft: Gender and Magic in Teen Film and Television." *Screen* 43:4 (winter 2002): 403–22.

———. "Makeover Takeover on British Television." *Screen* 41:3 (2000): 299–314.

Moseley, Rachel, and Jacinda Read. "Having It Ally: Popular Television (Post)Feminism." *Feminist Media Studies* 2:2 (2002): 231–49.

Moynihan, Daniel Patrick. *The Negro Family: The Case for National Action*. Washington, D.C.: U.S. Labor Department, 1965.

Mulvey, Laura. "Visual Pleasure and Narrative Cinema." *Screen* 16:3 (1975): 6–18.

Nam, Vickie, ed. *Yell-Oh Girls! Emerging Voices Explore Culture, Identity, and Growing up Asian American*. New York: Quill, 2001.

Negra, Diane. "Girls Who Go Home: Retreatism, the Chick Flick, and the Female-Centred Television Drama." Paper presented at the "Console-ing Passions International Conference on Feminism, TV, and New Media," New Orleans, April 2004.

———. *Off-White Hollywood: American Culture and Ethnic Female Stardom*. London: Routledge, 2001.

———. "Quality Postfeminism? Sex and the Single Girl on HBO." *Genders OnLine Journal* 39 (2004), http://www.genders.org/g39/g39_negra.html.

———. "Structural Integrity, Historical Reversion, and the Post-9/11 Chick Flick." *Feminist Media Studies* 8:1 (March 2008), forthcoming.

Newitz, Annalee. 2004. "Suck My Left One." *AlterNet.*, www.alternet.org, 16 November 2004.

Newton, Esther. *Mother Camp: Female Impersonators in America*. Chicago: University of Chicago Press, 1979.

Nguyen, Mimi. "Punk Planet 40." www.worsethanqueer.com, November–December 2000.

O'Brien, Lucy. *She Bop II*. London: Continuum, 2002.

Orenstein, Peggy. *Schoolgirls: Young Women, Self-Esteem, and the Confidence Gap*. New York: Anchor, 1994.

Otnes, Cele C., and Elizabeth H. Pleck. *Cinderella Dreams: The Allure of the Lavish Wedding*. Berkeley: University of California Press, 2003.

Ouellette, Laurie. "Nanny TV." *Flow* 1:11 (2005).

———. "'Take Responsibility for Yourself': *Judge Judy* and the Neoliberal Citizen." In *Reality TV: Remaking Television Culture*, ed. Susan Murray and Laurie Ouellette. New York: New York University Press, 2004.

Ouellette, Laurie, and Susan Murray, eds. *Reality TV: Remaking Television Culture*. New York: New York University Press, 2004.

Owen, Susan A. "Vampires, Postmodernity, and Postfeminism: *Buffy the Vampire Slayer*." *Journal of Popular Film and Television* 27:2 (1999): 24–31.

Palmer, Gareth. "*Big Brother*: An Experiment in Governance." *Television and New Media* 3:3 (2002): 295–310.

———. *Discipline and Liberty: Television and Governance*. Manchester: Manchester University Press, 2003.

———. "'The New You': Class and Transformation in Lifestyle Television." In *Understanding Reality Television*, ed. Su Holmes and Deborah Jermyn. London: Routledge, 2004.

Payette, Patricia. "The Feminist Wife?" In *Jane Sexes It Up*, ed. Merri Lisa Johnson. New York: Four Walls, Eight Windows, 2002.

Peixoto Labre, Magdala, and Lisa Duke. "'Nothing Like a Brisk Walk and a Spot of Demon Slaughter to Make a Girl's Night': The Construction of the Female Hero in the Buffy Video Game." *Journal of Communication Inquiry* 28:2 (2004): 138–56.

Petrakis, John. "Wasteland, Texas." *Christian Century*, 11 September 2002.

Petro, Patrice. *Aftershocks of the New: Feminism and Film History*. New Brunswick, N.J.: Rutgers University Press, 2002.

Phillips, Adam. *On Kissing, Tickling, and Being Bored: Psychoanalytic Essays on the Unexamined Life*. Cambridge, Mass.: Harvard University Press, 1993.

Pipher, Mary. *Reviving Ophelia: Saving the Selves of Adolescent Girls*. New York: Ballantine, 1994.

Postrel, Virginia. *The Substance of Style: How the Rise of Aesthetic Value Is Remembering Commerce, Culture, and Consciousness*. New York: Harper Collins, 2003.

Potts, Leanne. "'Queer Eye' Makes over View of Homosexuals." *Alberquerque Journal*, 12 August 2003.

Pozner, Jennifer. "The 'Big Lie': False Feminist Death Syndrome, Profit, and the Media." In *Catching a Wave: Reclaiming Feminism for the Twenty-first Century*, ed. Rory Dicker and Alison Peipmeir. Boston: Northeastern University Press, 2003.

————. "The Unreal World: Why Women on Reality TV Have to Be Hot, Dumb, and Desperate." *Ms.*, fall, 2004.

Press, Joy, and Simon Reynolds. *The Sex Revolts: Gender, Rebellion, and Rock 'n' Roll*. Cambridge, Mass.: Harvard University Press, 1995.

Prince, Stephen, ed. *Screening Violence*. New Brunswick, N.J.: Rutgers University Press, 2000.

Probyn, Elspeth. "Choosing Choice: Images of Sexuality and 'Choiceoisie' in Popular Culture." In *Negotiating at the Margins: The Gendered Discourses of Power and Resistance*, ed. Sue Fisher and Kathy Davis. New Brunswick, N.J.: Rutgers University Press, 1993.

————. "New Traditionalism and Post-feminism: TV Does the Home." In *Feminist Television Criticism*, ed. Charlotte Brunsdon, Julie D'Acci, and Lynn Spigel. Oxford: Clarendon, 1997.

Projansky, Sarah. "Girls Who Act Like Women Who Fly: Jessica Dubroff as Cultural Troublemaker." *Signs: Journal of Women in Culture and Society* 23:3 (1998): 771–807.

————. *Watching Rape: Film and Television in Postfeminist Culture*. New York: New York University Press, 2001.

Projansky, Sarah, and Kent A. Ono. "Strategic Whiteness as Cinematic Racial Politics." In *Whiteness: The Communication of Social Identity*, ed. Thomas K. Nakayama and Judith N. Martin. Thousand Oaks, Calif.: Sage, 1998.

Projansky, Sarah, and Leah R. Vande Berg. "Sabrina, the Teenage . . . ? Girls, Witches, Mortals, and the Limitations of Prime-Time Feminism." In *Fantasy Girls: Gender and the New Universe of Science Fiction and Fantasy Television*, ed. Elyce Rae Helford. Lanham, Md.: Rowman and Littlefield, 2000.

Purkiss, Diane. *The Witch in History: Early Modern and Twentieth-Century Representations*. London: Routledge, 1996.

Quart, Alyssa. *Branded: The Buying and Selling of Teenagers*. New York: Perseus, 2003.

Quinn, Bill. *How Wal-Mart Is Destroying America and the World and What You Can Do about It*. Berkeley: Ten Speed Press, 2000.

Radner, Hilary. "Pretty Is as Pretty Does: Free Enterprise and the Marriage Plot." In *Film Theory Goes to the Movies*, ed. Jim Collins, Hilary Radner, and Ava Preacher Collins. New York: Routledge, 1993.

Ravenwolf, Silver. *Teen Witch: Wicca for a New Generation*. Saint Paul, Minn.: Llewellyn Press, 1998.

Read, Jacinda. *The New Avengers: Feminism, Femininity, and the Rape-Revenge Cycle*. Manchester: Manchester University Press, 2000.

Readings, Bill, and Bennet Schaber. "Introduction: The Question Mark in the Midst of Modernity." In *Postmodernism Across the Ages*, ed. Bill Readings and Bennet Schaber. New York: Syracuse University Press, 1993.

Rich, B. Ruby. *Chick Flicks: Theories and Memories of the Feminist Film Movement*. Durham: Duke University Press, 1998.

Riordan, Ellen. "Commodified Agents and Empowered Girls: Consuming and Producing Feminism." *Journal of Communication Inquiry* 25:3 (2001): 279–97.

Ritzer, George. *The McDonaldization of Society*. Thousand Oaks, Calif.: Pine Forge Press, 1996.

————. *The McDonaldization Thesis*. London: Sage, 1998.

Roberts, Kimberly. "Pleasures and Problems of the 'Angry Girl.'" In *Sugar, Spice, and Everything Nice: Cinemas of Girlhood*, ed. Frances Gateward and Murray Pomerance. Detroit: Wayne State University Press, 2002.

Robertson, Pamela. *Guilty Pleasures: Feminist Camp from Mae West to Madonna*. Durham: Duke University Press, 1996.

Root, Jane. "Distributing *A Question of Silence*: A Cautionary Tale." In *Films for Women*, ed. Charlotte Brunsdon. London: British Film Institute, 1986.

Rose, Jacqueline. "Margaret Thatcher and Ruth Ellis." *New Formations* 6 (winter 1988): 3–30.

————. *On Not Being Able to Sleep: Psychoanalysis and the Modern World*. London: Vintage, 2004.

Rose, Nikolas. "Assembling the Modern Self." In *The History of the Self*, ed. Roy Porter. London: Routledge, 1996.

————. *Governing the Soul: The Shaping of the Private Self*. London: Routledge, 1990.

————. "Neurochemical Selves." *Society* 41:1 (November–December 2003): 46–59.

————. "The Politics of Life Itself." *Theory, Culture and Society* 18:6 (2001): 1–30.

————. *Powers of Freedom: Reframing Political Thought*. Cambridge: Cambridge University Press, 1999.

Ross, Andrew. "Uses of Camp." In *Camp Grounds: Style and Homosexuality*, ed. David Bergman. Amherst: University of Massachusetts Press, [1988] 1993.

Rothenberg, Randall. "Claiborne's Approach to Today's Man." *New York Times*, 18 August 1989.

Ruiz, Vicki L. "The Flapper and the Chaperone: Cultural Constructions of Identity and Heterosexual Politics among Adolescent Mexican American Women, 1920–1950." In *Delinquents and Debutantes: Twentieth-Century American Girls' Cultures*, ed. Sherrie A. Inness. New York: New York University Press, 1998.

Russakoff, Dale. "Lessons of Might and Right: How Segregation and an Indomitable Family Shaped National Security Adviser Condoleezza Rice." *Washington Post Magazine*, 9 September 2001.

Russo, Mary. "Aging and the Scandal of Anachronism." In *Figuring Age: Women, Bodies, Generations*, ed. Kathleen Woodward. Bloomington: Indiana University Press, 1999.

Sanders, Hannah E. "New Generation Witches: The Teenage Witch as Cultural Icon and Lived Identity." PhD thesis, Norwich School of Art and Design, 2004.

Scannell, Herb. "Why Not Diversity?" *Children Now*, summer 2002. Newsletter.

Schaefer, Eric. *"Bold! Daring! Shocking! True!" A History of Exploitation Films, 1919–1959*. Durham: Duke University Press, 1999.

Schilt, Kristen. "'A Little Too Ironic': The Appropriation and Packaging of Riot Grrrl Politics by Mainstream Female Musicians." *Popular Music and Society* 26:1 (2003): 5–16.

Schor, Juliet. *The Overworked American: The Unexpected Decline of Leisure*. New York: Basic Books, 1992.

Schrum, Kelly. "'Teena Means Business': Teenage Girls' Culture and *Seventeen* Magazine, 1944–1950." In *Delinquents and Debutantes: Twentieth-Century American Girls' Cultures*, ed. Sherrie A. Inness. New York: New York University Press, 1998.

Sconce, Jeffrey. "Irony, Nihilism, and the American 'Smart' Film." *Screen* 43:3 (2003): 352.

Seaman, D. "Piercy, Marge." *Booklist*, 1 February 1999.

Seiter, Ellen. *Sold Separately: Parents and Children in Consumer Culture*. New Brunswick, N.J.: Rutgers University Press, 1995.

Shandler, Sara. *Ophelia Speaks: Adolescent Girls Write about Their Search for Self*. New York: Harper Perennial, 1999.

Sharrett, Christopher, ed. *Mythologies of Violence in Postmodern Media*. Detroit: Wayne State University Press, 1999.

Shipler, David. *The Working Poor: Invisible in America*. New York: Knopf, 2004.

Sidler, Michele. "Living in McJobdom: Third Wave Feminism and Class Inequity." In *Third Wave Agenda: Being Feminist, Doing Feminism*, ed. Leslie Heywood and Jennifer Drake. Minneapolis: University of Minnesota Press, 1997.

Simmons, Rachel. *Odd Girl Out: The Hidden Culture of Aggression in Girls*. Orlando: Harcourt, 2002.

———. *Odd Girl Speaks Out: Girls Write about Bullies, Cliques, Popularity, and Jealousy*. Orlando: Harcourt, 2004.

Sims, Melanie. "Angry Black Woman." *Indiana Daily Student News*, 29 January 2004.

Sinker, D., ed. *We Owe You Nothing, Punk Planet: The Collected Interviews*. New York: Akashic Books, 2001.

Slocum, J. David, ed. *Violence and American Cinema*. London: Routledge, 2001.

Smiley, Jane. *The Age of Grief*. New York: Anchor, [1987] 2002.

Smith, Cassandra. "Riot Grrrls: Girl-Pop-Punk Explosion." www.riotgrrrleurope.net, 21 July 2005.

Smith, Christopher Holmes. "'I Don't Like to Dream about Getting Paid': Representations of Social Mobility and the Emergence of the Hip-Hop Mogul." *Social Text* 77 (winter 2003): 69–98.

Smith-Shomade, Beretta E. *Shaded Lives: African-American Women and Television*. New Brunswick, N.J.: Rutgers University Press, 2002.

Sobchack, Vivian. "Scary Women: Cinema, Surgery, and Special Effects." In *Figuring Age: Women, Bodies, Generations*, ed. Kathleen Woodward. Bloomington: Indiana University Press, 1997.

Sommers, Christine Hoff. *Who Stole Feminism? How Women Have Betrayed Women*. New York: Simon and Schuster, 1995.

Sonnie, Amy, ed. *Revolutionary Voices: A Multicultural Queer Youth Anthology*. Los Angeles: Alyson Books, 2000.

Sontag, Susan. "The Double Standard of Aging." In *The Other Within Us: Feminist Explorations of Women and Aging*, ed. Marilyn Pearsall. Boulder: Westview, 1997.

———. "Notes on Camp." In *Camp: Queer Aesthetics and the Performing Subject*, ed. Fabio Cleto. Ann Arbor: University of Michigan Press, [1964] 1999.

Spigel, Lynn. "From Domestic Space to Outer Space: The 1960s Fantastic Family Sit-Com." In *Close Encounters: Film, Feminism, and Science Fiction*, ed. Constance Penley, Elisabeth Lyon, Lynn Spigel, and Janet Bergstrom. Minneapolis: University of Minnesota Press, 1991.

————. *Make Room for TV: Television and the Family Ideal in Postwar America*. Chicago: University of Chicago Press, 1992.

————. "Theorizing the Bachelorette: 'Waves' of Feminist Media Studies." *Signs: Journal of Women in Culture and Society* 30:1 (autumn 2004): 1209–21.

Spivak, Gayatri Chakravorty. *A Critique of Postcolonial Reason*. Cambridge, Mass.: Harvard University Press, 1988.

Springer, Kimberly. "Third Wave Black Feminism?" *Signs: Journal of Women in Culture and Society* 27:4 (2002): 1059–82.

Squier, Susan Merrill. *Liminal Lives: Imagining the Human at the Frontiers of Biomedicine*. Durham: Duke University Press, 2004.

Starhawk. *The Spiral Dance: A Rebirth of the Ancient Religion of the Great Goddess*. San Francisco: Harper and Row, 1979.

————. *Truth or Dare: Encounters with Power, Authority, and Mystery*. San Francisco: Harper and Row, 1987.

Stone, Merlin. *When God Was a Woman*. New York: Barnes and Noble, 1976.

Stuart, Andrea. "Feminism: Dead or Alive?" In *Identity: Community, Culture, Difference*, ed. Jonathan Rutherford. London: Lawrence and Wishart, 1990.

Sturken, Marita. "Masculinity, Courage, and Sacrifice." *Signs: Journal of Women in Culture and Society* 28:1 (autumn 2002): 444–45.

Taft, Jessica K. "Girl Power Politics: Pop-Culture Barriers and Organizational Resistance." In *All about the Girl: Culture, Power, and Identity*, ed. Anita Harris. London: Routledge, 2004.

Tarrier, August. "Victoria's Secrets at the OK Corral: The "Bad Girls" of Postfeminist Nineties." *ALT-X Online Network*, www.altx.com, 1996.

Tasker, Yvonne. *Working Girls: Gender and Sexuality in Popular Cinema*. London: Routledge, 1998.

Tasker, Yvonne, and Diane Negra, eds. "In Focus: Postfeminism and Contemporary Media Studies." *Cinema Journal* 44:2 (winter 2005): 107–110.

Teish, Luisah. *Jambalaya: The Natural Woman's Book of Personal Charms and Practical Rituals*. San Francisco: HarperCollins, 1988.

Thomas, Richard. "The Power of Women." *Observer*, 18 October 1998. Thompson, Stacey. *Punk Productions: Unfinished Business*. Albany: State University of New York Press, 2004.

Tomlin, Annie. "Sex, Dreads, and Rock 'n' Roll." *Bitch*, December 2002.

Torres, Sasha. "Why Can't Johnny Shave?" *GLQ* 11:1 (2005): 96.

Trinh Thi Minh-ha. *Women Native Other*. Bloomington: Indiana University Press, 1989.

Tyrangiel, Josh. "The New Diva-Disease." *Time*, 21 October 2002.

Ulanov, Ann, and Barry Ulanov. *The Witch and the Clown: Two Archetypes of Human Sexuality*. Chicago: Chiron, 1987.

Valdivia, Angharad N., and Rhiannon S. Bettivia. "A Guided Tour through One Adolescent Girl's Culture." In *Growing up Girls: Popular Culture and the Construction of Identity*, ed. Sharon R. Mazzarella and Norma Odom Pecora. New York: Peter Lang, 1999.

Vered, Karen Orr. "White and Black in Black and White: Management of Race and

Sexuality in the Coupling of Child-Star Shirley Temple and Bill Robinson." *Velvet Light Trap* 39 (1997): 52–65.

Wald, Gayle. "'I Want It That Way': Teenybopper Music and the Girling of Boy Bands." *Genders OnLine Journal* 35 (2002), http://www.genders.org/g35/g35_wald.html.

———. "Just a Girl? Rock Music, Feminism, and the Cultural Construction of Female Youth." In *Rock over the Edge: Transformations in Popular Music Culture*, ed. Roger Beebe, Denis Fulbrook, and Ben Saunders. Durham: Duke University Press, 2002.

Walker, Barbara. *Woman's Encyclopaedia of Myths and Secrets*. San Francisco: HarperCollins. 1983.

Walkerdine, Valerie. *Daddy's Girl: Young Girls and Popular Culture*. London: Palgrave, 1997.

Walters, Natasha. *The New Feminism*. London: Palgrave, 2002.

Ward, Janie Victoria, and Beth Cooper. *How Schools Shortchange Girls*. Washington, D.C.: American Association of University Women Education Foundation, 1992.

Ward, Janie Victoria, and Beth Cooper Benjamin. "Women, Girls, and the Unfinished Work of Connections: A Critical Review of American Girls' Studies." In *All about the Girl: Culture, Power, and Identity*, ed. Anita Harris. London: Routledge, 2004.

Watts, Eric, and Mark Orbe. "The Spectacular Consumption of 'True' African American Culture: 'Whassup' with the Budweiser Guys?" *Critical Studies in Media Communication* 19:1 (2002): 1–20.

Weber, Brenda R. "Beauty, Desire, and Anxiety: The Economy of Sameness in ABC's *Extreme Makeover*." *Genders Online Journal* 41 (2005), http://www.genders.org/g41/g41_weber.html.

Whelehan, Imelda. *Modern Feminist Thought: From the Second Wave to 'PostFeminism.'* Edinburgh: Edinburgh University Press, 1995.

———. *Overloaded: Popular Culture and the Future of Feminism*. London: Women's Press, 2000.

Whiteley, Sheila. *Too Much Too Young: Popular Music, Age, and Gender*. London: Routledge, 2005.

Wilde, Oscar. "The Picture of Dorian Gray." In *The Complete Works of Oscar Wilde*. Glasgow: Harper Collins, [1892] 1994.

Williams, Linda. "A Jury of Their Peers: Marlene Gorris' *A Question of Silence*." In *Postmodernism and Its Discontents*, ed. E. Ann Kaplan. London: Verso, 1988.

Williams, Linda Ruth. *The Erotic Thriller in Contemporary Cinema*. Edinburgh: Edinburgh University Press, 2004.

Williamson, Judith. *Decoding Advertisements*. London: Marion Boyars, 1987.

Willis, Sharon. *High Contrast: Race and Gender in Contemporary Hollywood Films*. Durham: Duke University Press, 1998.

Wiltz, Teresa. "The Evil Sista of Reality Television." *Washington Post*, 25 February 2004.

Wiseman, Rosalind. *Queen Bees and Wannabes: Helping Your Daughter Survive Cliques, Gossip, Boyfriends, and Other Realities of Adolescence*. New York: Random House, 2002.

Wolcott, James. "Caution, Women Seething." *Vanity Fair*, June 2005.

Wolf, Naomi. *Fire with Fire: The New Female Power and How to Use It*. New York: Fawcett, 1994.

Woodall, Trinny, and Susannah Constantine. *Ready 2 Dress: How to Have Style without Following Fashion*. London: Weidenfeld and Nicolson, 2000.

———. *What Not to Wear*. London: Weidenfeld and Nicolson, 2002.

———. *What Not to Wear: For Every Occasion*. London: Weidenfeld and Nicolson, 2003.

———. *What Not to Wear: The Rules*. London: Weidenfeld and Nicolson, 2004.

———. *What Your Clothes Say about You: How to Look Different, Act Different, and Feel Different*. London: Weidenfeld and Nicolson, 2005.

———. *What You Wear Can Change Your Life*. London: Weidenfeld and Nicolson, 2004.

Woodward, Kathleen. "Youthfulness as a Masquerade." *Discourse* 11:1 (fall–winter 1988–89): 119–42.

Woolf, Virginia. "The Legacy." In *A Haunted House and Other Stories*. London: Hogarth, 1944.

Wynter, Leon. *American Skin: Pop Culture, Big Business, and the End of White America*. New York: Crown, 2002.

Žižek, Slavoj. *The Art of the Ridiculous Sublime: On David Lynch's* "Lost Highway." Seattle: University of Washington Press, 2000.

SARAH BANET-WEISER is an associate professor at the Annenberg School for Communication, University of Southern California. She is the author of *Kids Rule! Nickelodeon and Consumer Citizenship* (2007), also published by Duke University Press, and *The Most Beautiful Girl in the World: Beauty Pageants and National Identity* (1999).

STEVEN COHAN is a professor of English at Syracuse University, where he teaches courses in film, gender, and cultural studies. His books include *Incongruous Entertainment: Camp, Cultural Value, and the MGM Musical* (2005), also published by Duke University Press, as well as *Telling Stories: A Theoretical Analysis of Narrative* (1988), *Screening the Male: Exploring Masculinities in Hollywood Film* (1993), *The Road Movie Book* (1997), *Masked Men: Masculinity and the Movies in the Fifties* (1997), and *Hollywood Musicals, The Film Reader* (2001).

LISA COULTHARD is an assistant professor of film studies at the University of British Columbia and works in the areas of film theory and violence. She has published articles on John Woo, Abigail Lane, Jenny Holzer, and Kiki Smith and is currently working on a manuscript on postmodern film melodrama and perversion.

ANNA FEIGENBAUM is a Ph.D. candidate in communication studies at McGill University in Montreal, Quebec, where she is also co-coordinator of the Graduate Group for Feminist Scholarship. She has published a paper on gender issues in rock reviews in the journal *Popular Music*. Her dissertation research investigates feminist theorists' and activists' engagements with new technologies from the 1970s to the present.

SUZANNE LEONARD is an assistant professor of English at Simmons College. She recently completed a dissertation on representations of unfaithful wives in contemporary American print fiction and film. Her essays have been published in *Women's Studies Quarterly* (forthcoming) and *Reclaiming the Archive: Feminism and Film History*, edited by Vicki Callahan and Allison McKee (forthcoming). Her literary scholarship has appeared in *MELUS*, *Doris Lessing Studies*, and *The Dictionary of Literary Biography*.

ANGELA MCROBBIE is a professor of communications at Goldsmiths College, University of London. She has written extensively on young women and popular culture. Her books include *British Fashion Design: Rag Trade or Image Industry?* (1998), *In the Culture Society:*

Art, Fashion and Popular Music (1999) and *Feminism and Youth Culture* (2nd ed. 2000). She is currently at work on a book about postfeminism.

DIANE NEGRA is a professor of film and television studies at the University of East Anglia. She is the editor of *The Irish in Us: Irishness, Performativity and Popular Culture* (2006) and a co-editor of *A Feminist Reader in Early Cinema* (2002), both published by Duke University Press, as well as the author of *Off-White Hollywood: American Culture and Ethnic Female Stardom* (2001). She co-edited, with Yvonne Tasker, an *In Focus* section of *Cinema Journal* exploring postfeminism and contemporary media studies. She is the author of *What a Girl Wants?: Fantasizing the Reclamation of Self in Postfeminism* (forthcoming, 2008).

SARAH PROJANSKY is an associate professor of gender and women's studies and of cinema studies at the University of Illinois, Urbana-Champaign. She is a co-editor of *Enterprise Zones: Critical Positions on Star Trek* (1996) and author of *Watching Rape: Film, Television and Postfeminist Culture* (2001). She has published articles in *Cinema Journal*, *Signs*, and various anthologies. She is currently completing a book about the representation of girls in U.S. popular culture.

MARTIN ROBERTS is an assistant professor of media and cultural studies at the New School. His publications include articles on ethnography and surrealism, world music, and the global documentary film *Baraka*. More recent publications focus on the role of media in the formation of national and transnational identities, including chapters for an anthology on cinema and nationalism and a collection on the Danish Dogme 95 group. His current project focuses on globalization and subcultures.

HANNAH E. SANDERS is an adjunct lecturer in cultural studies and media studies at Emerson College. Her doctoral thesis considered contemporary cinematic and televisual representations of teen witches and their reception by teen girls identifying as Witches. She is currently co-editing an anthology titled *New Generation Witches: Adolescents, Agency and Magic* and has articles forthcoming in *Syzygy* and the *Journal for the Academic Study of Magic*.

KIMBERLY SPRINGER is a senior lecturer in American studies at King's College, London. She is the author of *Living for the Revolution: Black Feminist Organisations, 1968–1980* (2005), published by Duke University Press, and the editor of *Still Lifting, Still Climbing: African American Women's Contemporary Activism* (1999). Her current work examines state and community censorship of black women's sexuality in the popular and fine arts.

YVONNE TASKER is a professor of film and television studies at the University of East Anglia. She is the author of various books and articles on gender and popular culture, including *Working Girls: Gender and Sexuality in Popular Cinema* (1998). She has co-edited, with Diane Negra, an *In Focus* section of *Cinema Journal* exploring postfeminism and contemporary media studies, and is currently completing a study of military women in cinema and television since WWII.

SADIE WEARING is a tutorial fellow in the Gender Institute at the London School of Economics, where she teaches media and gender theory. Her research interests include representations of time, memory, age, and national identity in late-nineteenth-century and contemporary culture. She is currently working on a monograph entitled *Aspects of Victorian Memory* and on a project on age and gender in popular culture.

Norma Rae, 115–16, 130 n. 45
nostalgia, 166, 169–70, 223; second-wave
    feminism and, 209–10
Nuns, The (band), 134

One Day at a Time, 209
101 Most Sensational Crimes of Fashion, 233–34
Ono, Yoko, 136
Open Range, 194
Orbe, Mark P., 217

Palmer, Gareth, 228, 233, 234–36, 242, 245
parenthood, 63–64
passing, 285, 288
pastiche, 159, 161, 162
Perry, Tyler, 270, 276 n. 55
Phillips, Adam, 119
Piercy, Marge, 135
Pink, 138
pinups, 3, 34
Pipher, Mary, 41–42, 52, 65–66, 69
Pixie Meat, 137
Playboy, 181
Poison Ivy, 168
political correctness, 33, 213
Poly Styrene, 134
pornography, 12, 34, 133, 182
postfeminism: academia and, 4–6, 12,
    30; Anglo-American culture and,
    13–14; as contradictory/ambivalent,
    68–69; disruption and, 66–67; double
    entanglement of, 1–4, 8, 20–22, 27,
    28–30, 43–44, 204, 206, 216, 223, 250,
    251; femininity and, 9–10, 44, 284;
    generational differences and, 9, 11,
    18, 27–28, 30–31, 82, 135–36, 141, 204,
    207–8, 278–82; post–civil rights period
    and, 250–54, 268, 273–74; race and, 7–
    8; sexuality and, 3, 53, 283; spectatorial
    pleasure and, 21, 77, 38, 161, 291; third-
    wave feminism and, 18–19, 207–10
postfeminist canon, 14–15, 20
posthuman, 290, 299

postmodernism, 6, 21, 154, 211, 242; genre
    and, 168–69; identity and, 231–32; sur-
    face and, 158, 161–62, 168–69, 242–43
postracial, 204–5, 213–15, 223. *See also*
    diversity
Postrel, Virginia, 7
Potter, Andrew, 211
Pozner, Jennifer, 133, 265
Practical Magic, 80
preschool television, 219
Pride and Prejudice, 303
Princess Diaries, The, 18
prison films, 161, 170
Projansky, Sarah, 8, 16, 17, 18, 20, 83, 94,
    104, 214, 292
Project Runway, 243
psychology, 241–43, 266
psychotherapy, 10, 288–89
public service television, 227–28
punk, 132–34, 137–41, 144
Purkiss, Diane, 79

Queer Eye for the Straight Girl, 233
Queer Eye for the Straight Guy, 14, 177–81,
    183–98, 229, 233; cast members on
    Oprah, 178, 193–94, 197–98; on *The
    Tonight Show*, 178, 193, 194–98
queerness: postfeminism and, 19; queer
    subcultures, 280; queer theory, 177
Question of Silence, A, 156–57, 172

race: authenticity and, 269, 272; in Bud-
    weiser ads, 217, 218; as commodity,
    202–5, 251–52, 258, 273; drug use and,
    254; generational differences and,
    204–6, 212–15, 282–83; New Economy
    and, 212–15; Riot Grrrls and, 141–44
Raising Helen, 103
rape revenge film, 161–65, 170, 172
rap music, 265, 282, 283
Read, Jacinda, 17, 153, 162
Readings, Bill, 6
Reagan administration, 212

Yvonne Tasker is a professor of film and television studies at the University of East Anglia. Diane Negra is a professor of film and television studies at the University of East Anglia.

Library of Congress Cataloging-in-Publication Data
Interrogating postfeminism: gender and the politics of popular culture / edited by Yvonne Tasker and Diane Negra.
p. cm. — (Console-ing passions)
Includes bibliographical references and index.
ISBN 978-0-8223-4014-0 (cloth: alk. paper) — ISBN 978-0-8223-4032-4 (pbk.: alk. paper)
1. Feminist theory. 2. Popular culture. 3. Sex role. 4. Mass media and women. I. Tasker, Yvonne, 1964– II. Negra, Diane, 1966–
HQ1190.I58 2007
305.4201—dc22   2007016094